American Homicide

Second Edition

Sara Miller McCune founded SAGE Publishing in 1965 to support the dissemination of usable knowledge and educate a global community. SAGE publishes more than 1000 journals and over 600 new books each year, spanning a wide range of subject areas. Our growing selection of library products includes archives, data, case studies and video. SAGE remains majority owned by our founder and after her lifetime will become owned by a charitable trust that secures the company's continued independence.

Los Angeles | London | New Delhi | Singapore | Washington DC | Melbourne

American Homicide

Second Edition

Richard M. Hough
University of West Florida

Kimberly D. McCorkle
University of West Florida

Los Angeles | London | New Delhi
Singapore | Washington DC | Melbourne

FOR INFORMATION:

SAGE Publications, Inc.
2455 Teller Road
Thousand Oaks, California 91320
E-mail: order@sagepub.com

SAGE Publications Ltd.
1 Oliver's Yard
55 City Road
London, EC1Y 1SP
United Kingdom

SAGE Publications India Pvt. Ltd.
B 1/I 1 Mohan Cooperative Industrial Area
Mathura Road, New Delhi 110 044
India

SAGE Publications Asia-Pacific Pte. Ltd.
18 Cross Street #10-10/11/12
China Square Central
Singapore 048423

Acquisitions Editor: Jessica Miller
Editorial Assistant: Sarah Manheim
Production Editor: Andrew Olson
Copy Editor: Ashley Horne
Typesetter: Hurix Digital
Proofreader: Susan Schon
Indexer: Karen Wiley
Cover Designer: Candice Harman
Marketing Manager: Jillian Ragusa

Printed in Canada

Library of Congress Cataloging-in-Publication Data

Names: Hough, Richard M, author. | McCorkle, Kimberly D, author.

Title: American homicide / Richard M. Hough, University of West Florida, Kimberly D. McCorkle, University of West Florida.

Description: Second edition. | Los Angeles : Sage, [2020] | Includes bibliographical references.

Identifiers: LCCN 2019020463 | ISBN 9781544356037 (paperback)

Subjects: LCSH: Homicide—United States. | Murder—United States.

Classification: LCC HV6529.H69 2020 | DDC 364.1520973—dc23 LC record available at https://lccn.loc.gov/2019020463

This book is printed on acid-free paper.

MIX
Paper from
responsible sources
FSC® C004071

19 20 21 22 23 10 9 8 7 6 5 4 3 2 1

BRIEF CONTENTS

DETAILED CONTENTS

PREFACE

What we are shown through Hollywood and the media is a carnival mirror reflection of reality—distorted and out of proportion. Hollywood dramatizations of criminal homicide may entertain, but they are not intended to inform. The impression one might get is that serial killers are everywhere and that no one is safe from this increasing danger. This is obviously far from accurate, and it often falls to college and university professors to present the balanced picture of homicide, supported by current research, to make sense of what we learn. We are often asked by our students how we explain the rising homicide or violence rates. We endeavor in this book to address this inaccurate perception of increasing homicide rates and other myths about the justice system.

Over many years of teaching courses on homicide, we were never quite satisfied with the few available texts. They did not, in our view, provide either the right balance or emphasis. While there were some early high-quality books devoted to the study of homicide, these were not as useful or relevant to the current student of homicide. We continually found that we had to supplement them with extensive readings. The result was this book, which we believe will be useful to faculty everywhere who take on the task of explaining to students why and how people kill and what society does about it. This book provides any instructor the ability to credibly approach the subject of homicide and present to students something more than a criminology text with limited discussion of practical issues or a book of sensationalized news accounts with the occasional empirical observation thrown in.

The text examines homicides and suspicious deaths in the United States. Several introductory chapters include definitions of homicide, measurement, trends in homicide, and theories of why people commit homicide. The book addresses all types of homicide and gives additional attention to the more prevalent types of homicide in the United States. Therefore, we include full chapters on confrontational homicide, intimate partner homicide, and family homicide. As Daly and Wilson (1988) noted,

"Most killers turn out to be ordinary folks" (p. ix). We also cover extraordinary homicide, which includes more rare and sensational types of homicide. The investigations chapter is a hallmark of the book. Contemporary students are very interested in homicide investigations, even if they do not plan or hope to become investigators. The chapter addresses the structure and function of homicide units and the interactions that investigators have with various other players, including media, medical examiners (MEs), crime scene technicians, prosecutors, and more. We also examine in depth in one full chapter the process of a criminal homicide case through the courts, an area of great interest and importance. The final chapter discusses key contemporary issues about those impacted by homicide and what society can do about those impacts.

We recognize that criminology is the foundation for criminal justice. As such, we are in an era that tries harder than ever to use intelligence-led and evidence-based strategies and research to guide policymakers and practitioners. We provide and comment on suggested interventions that reflect this fact. The increasing role of the social sciences in the construction of policies and programs is key to any comprehensive discussion of violence and murder in society. We did not want to set considerations of policy as a stand-alone chapter, and so, where appropriate, policy impacts are noted. It is our hope that instructors might incorporate some level of discussion at every available opportunity to frame the practical context of theories and known or observed facts. We like to ask students to bring to class current news articles related to homicide crime that might serve as discussion points as we apply the theoretical constructs in the textbook. We hope current users of the book will do this.

Other pedagogical aspects of our approach are to provide the scholarly foundation for the field of homicide examination by including in every chapter references to current literature to provide students the opportunity for additional research. The chapter features reinforce student learning of concepts through examples;

critical-thinking questions; boxed coverage of cases and material under the title of "Why Would They Do It?"; a "Try This" section to suggest further relevant learning activities; and chapter summaries. We suggest that instructors use the "Why Would They Do It" examples to pose critical thinking questions to students about *theories*, *policies*, and *practices* within criminal justice. Student learning objectives (SLOs) are included at the beginning of each chapter.

A pure academic orientation often results in an unbalanced emphasis on only theory. This book provides more of what interests our students, while also requiring them to think critically and apply what they have learned. We also both bring a somewhat unique perspective to the approach of this textbook. While we are currently university faculty, we both come from practitioner backgrounds. Richard was a homicide investigator and a 30-year law enforcement officer. Kimberly was a prosecutor and a criminal defense attorney before joining academe. We both continue to be actively involved in working with the criminal justice system and conducting applied research. We know that our practical experiences have informed the content and the approach of the book, and we hope that students and instructors will find it helpful.

What's New in the Second Edition

In the second edition of the book you will find the following new topics:

- Expanded coverage of the UCR (Chapter 2)

- New trends in violent crime data (Chapter 2)

- Violent crime trends in Chicago (Chapter 3)

- Expanded discussion of traumatic brain injury and connections to violent behaviors (Chapter 4)

- Factors to consider when attempting to predict violence (Chapter 5)

- The connection between intimate partner homicide and strangulation (Chapter 6)

- Intergenerational transmission of violence (Chapter 7)

- Juvenile murderers (Chapter 7)

- The role of school size in school violence (Chapter 8)

- The role of school leaders and staff to prevent violence (Chapter 8)

- New technology in school safety, such as facial recognition technology (Chapter 8)

- Legislative responses to recent school shootings (Chapter 8)

- Indicators of workplace violence (Chapter 9)

- Policy implications of violence in public spaces (Chapter 9)

- Expanded discussion of American Right-Wing and Left-Wing terrorism (Chapter 10)

- Added emphasis on hate-motivated murders (Chapter 10)

- Impact of technology, including the use of social media on solving homicides (Chapter 13)

- Cold case investigations, including the use of DNA and genealogical databases and methods (Chapter 13)

- Expert testimony in homicide cases (Chapter 14)

- Expanded discussion of violence prevention initiatives (Chapter 15)

New "Why Would They Do It" boxes examine recent case studies, such as:

- The Marjory Stoneman Douglas school shooting

- The 2018 shooting at the Borderline Bar and Grill

- Recent terrorist attacks and hate crimes

- The Golden State Killer cold case investigation and apprehension

- Church shootings and security

- Gun access policies

ACKNOWLEDGMENTS

RICHARD M. HOUGH, SR.

My acknowledgments begin where the project began, with my coauthor Kimberly McCorkle. I could not have picked a more collegial and insightful writing partner. She is a dedicated researcher and gifted teacher who continually works to create a learning atmosphere for her students to understand substance and subtlety in the social sciences—and she succeeds. As coauthors and friends, we had a vision for this book and saw it through. I thank my kids, who were encouraging throughout the writing. My dad, who viewed the world and the people in it as fundamentally good, gave me the grounding to lead a successful law enforcement career of helping others. My mother, a librarian for 40 years, would be proud to know I still have the passion for knowledge she imbued me with.

KIMBERLY D. McCORKLE

I would like to acknowledge the love and encouragement of my dear friends and family as we have spent so much time working on this book, while continuing to work our day jobs. To my mother Dianne Muse, I offer special gratitude for her enduring love and support for all of my projects, personal and professional. Finally, to my coauthor and friend Richard Hough, I express my deepest thanks for including me on this journey to explore a topic that he has devoted his professional career to addressing and exploring. He has a rare gift of the practitioner's passion and the academic's mind, and his talents are immeasurable. It was a joy to write this with you.

THE AUTHORS

We gratefully acknowledge the time and expertise of the reviewers of the initial proposal and book content. While a book is ultimately a realization of the vision of the authors, the insights, comments, and suggestions made the final product so much better. While we were not able to incorporate every suggestion, we carefully considered and appreciated them all, and numerous additions, deletions, and organizational issues resulted from the helpful reviews from:

> Thomas S. Alexander, University of MD College Park-Shady Grove
>
> David M. Feldman, Barry University
>
> Krystal R. Hans, Delaware State University
>
> Donald N. Raley, Eastern New Mexico University
>
> Melissa J. Tetzlaff-Bemiller, Augusta University
>
> Mark Winton, University of Central Florida

We want to acknowledge all of our students over the years who have shared our interest in homicide and violence and recognized the need to know more about these important topics and do something about them. For early research help with the manuscript, we thank Charla Ngatcha, and for research assistance to the second edition, our thanks to Amelia Lane. We appreciate the encouragement and support of Dr. Glenn Rohrer, our department chair when we first began our journey. We also thank him for his thoughtful contributions on capital sentence mitigation. We appreciate the many members of the Homicide Research Working Group (HRWG)—colleagues who share our interest in the field of homicide research and the implementation of policies and programs to address it. Special thanks to HRWG member, criminologist, and Executive Director of the Homicide Research Center, Dallas Drake, for specific help with LGBT homicide information. We thank the editorial staff at SAGE, for their cheerful, timely, and competent guidance and help. We appreciated so much the sage, warm, and ever-supportive wisdom of publisher Jerry Westby, during the development and writing of the first edition. We have so enjoyed the support and always caring guidance of Jessica Miller, acquisitions editor at SAGE in shepherding this second edition of *American Homicide*.

Richard M. Hough Sr. has taught criminal justice and criminology courses in the college and university setting for 30 years, and he has taught investigative methods and other law enforcement and corrections topics in the academy and in-service law enforcement settings for 35 years. This is in addition to the author's extensive professional experience, including investigating homicide. Dr. Hough has held increasingly responsible positions in law enforcement and has served as director of law enforcement and corrections in sheriff's offices as well as superintendent of detention centers for the Florida Department of Juvenile Justice. Dr. Hough has served as both a law enforcement and corrections academy director. He is currently a faculty member in the Department of Criminology and Criminal Justice at the University of West Florida.

Dr. Richard Hough has conducted more than 100 training seminars, conference presentations, and international briefings on criminal justice issues, and he is the primary instructor for contemporary policing practices and gangs and hate groups at the regional law enforcement academy in Pensacola, Florida. Dr. Hough is a member of the Homicide Research Working Group (HRWG), the Police Executive Research Forum (PERF), the International Homicide Investigators Association (IHIA), the International Association of Chiefs of Police (IACP), the Southern Criminal Justice Association (SCJA), and the Academy of Criminal Justice Sciences (ACJS). In 2018, Dr. Hough was named an International Ambassador of the British Society of Criminology (BSC). Dr. Hough has been interviewed by local, regional, and national news media and has appeared on radio and television speaking on criminal justice issues. Dr. Hough is the author of the books *The Use of Force in Criminal Justice* and *Criminal Investigations Today: The Essentials*. He has published journal articles and book chapters. Dr. Hough actively consults as an expert witness on police and correctional practices and the use of force.

Kimberly D. McCorkle is a former state prosecutor and currently serves as Vice Provost and Professor at the University of West Florida, where she has been on the faculty since 2002. As a prosecutor, she worked as a specialized domestic violence (DV) prosecutor and conducted over 50 misdemeanor and felony jury trials as lead counsel. In that position, she also trained law enforcement officers on the legal aspects of investigating domestic violence crime. Over the last 20 years, she has been interviewed numerous times by local and national media as an expert on domestic violence crime.

Her primary research focus is intimate partner and family violence and homicide. Dr. McCorkle has published numerous articles and has presented and trained on DV and DV homicide. She is a member of the Florida Bar, the Homicide Research Working Group (HRWG), the Southern Criminal Justice Association (SCJA), and the Academy of Criminal Justice Sciences (ACJS).

Both authors have presented together on domestic violence homicide to national and international groups. Both have also served as members of fatality review teams and have presented at regional and national criminal justice conferences on this topic.

1

INTRODUCING YOU TO HOMICIDE

"There will be killing till the score is paid."

—Homer, *The Odyssey*

"Nobody owns life, but anyone who can pick
up a frying pan owns death."

—William S. Burroughs

CHAPTER OUTLINE

INTRODUCTION

Murder continues to fascinate. The average person is drawn like a moth to a flame when a headline, CNN ticker, news anchor, or web browser announces, "Three shot at factory," "Father murders family," or "Elementary school student accidentally gunned down in gang drive-by." There is no shortage of attention by the entertainment industry as television series and movies thrill us and scare us with often exaggerated versions of killing. The news and the entertainment media offer information that might seem to provide preventive knowledge or caution—don't go to this part of town; don't be out late at night. Much like the haunted house we pay to walk through at Halloween, the public also seems to like a good scare. Horror movies also speak to how we like to be scared. Murder mysteries are not entirely the same. Do we want to be seen as the hero of the story? Be the killer vicariously experiencing the thrill?

In this chapter, we open as most textbooks do with a bit of overview to set context as well as expectations. Violence in the world comes in a number of forms and has been with us throughout history. In this book, we will examine the prevalence of violence in contemporary U.S. society that results specifically in homicide. While violence is implicated in the study of homicide, we will not spend a great deal of time discussing violence widely. Our focus is homicide generally and criminal homicide specifically.

Societies have codified rules to forbid different acts. If a forbidden act is attempted or committed, the society imposes a sanction upon the offending person or entity. This is generally the province of criminal justice studies and the criminal justice system. We necessarily concern ourselves with laws that proscribe violence since it is precisely criminal violence that we study as opposed to all violence in a general way. *Why* people commit such criminalized acts is the focus of criminology.

HOMICIDE: WHAT MOST PEOPLE THINK THEY KNOW

We have all grown up watching crime dramas on television and going to the movies to see our favorite Hollywood stars pursuing and catching the killers (our other favorite actors). While we may have different preferences on which shows we enjoy the most or which ones we feel are most *realistic*, we *do* watch them. In most of the fictionalized plots where the bad guy is caught and is headed to court, we listen to the police or prosecutor state what the charge will be against the defendant. Often, the charge is *first-degree murder* because of its brutal or premeditated nature. If the state cannot make a solid case, the charge of first degree may be reduced or initially entered as a lesser charge, including manslaughter. The differing charges hold the potential for various levels of punishment that in some cases include the death penalty.

Homicide is not a common event. Homicide does not even make the top-fifteen list of causes of death in the United States. While many people find it hard to believe, the trend in homicide has been one of decline over the last two decades, with a recent uptick in some cities and areas of the United States. Even with this increase, the homicide rate today is significantly lower than 25 years ago. The criminal homicide clearance rate is not as high as many would expect, with the latest available data showing only about 61.6% of all homicide cases resulting in clearance (FBI, 2018). Even with technology advances, such as the use of DNA in forensic identification, clearance rates for criminal homicides have dipped (Schroeder, 2007).

People also believe that the more they understand a thing, the more control they may have over it or the emotions it engenders. This is not an unreasonable hope or expectation. The more we learn about many things in our environment, the better we may be able to control circumstances, including not becoming a victim. An unintended consequence of such an approach, however, is that it has partly led to the phenomenon known as the CSI effect. Unending television, movie, and fiction novel offerings of stories of murder lead to an awareness of modern forensic technology and investigative method but exaggerate the efficacy of both. The viewer (and potential juror) believes he has received a thorough education on forensics and crime investigation through his vicarious experience. The impact of this fallacy is felt in court proceedings as jurors (and some judges) may consider police work incomplete or incompetent because the investigators did not use 3-D imaging, DNA analysis, alternate light source (ALS) technologies, and other techniques and equipment that may have been quite unnecessary to an investigation.

The representations in drama and the disproportionate coverage by the media of extraordinary homicides such as mass and serial killings are notable. The general public is fascinated, horrified, or curious about such homicides, for various reasons. The problem is that such attention to rare forms of criminal homicide seems to impede people's understanding of the most numerous and intractable forms:

confrontational homicides arising out of arguments or so-called slights of honor and intimate partner homicide (IPH). It is important for researchers and practitioners from public health, social work, education, psychology, the criminal justice system, and others to inform the public and policymakers about the dynamics and possible strategies to use against these most common but deadly situations. Experts can provide the context often missing when someone conducts a web search and holds out the one second response as complete *knowledge* of a subject. And that context provided by relevant experts can change or inform the perspective of the citizen, practitioner, or policymaking legislator.

ORGANIZATION OF THE BOOK

One of the things that we learned in our years of studying criminal homicide and the investigation of death is that while each of us has a concern about homicide, our personal orientation to the topic will influence what parts we focus on or emphasize when we think about or comment on homicide. Various authors have written textbooks, true-crime books, and novels that inform, entertain, but often exaggerate certain types of murder over others. Our aim in this book is to provide broad coverage of criminal homicide encountered in society but to spend what we believe to be important time examining the most common types of murder in America—argument-based or confrontational homicide and intimate partner homicide—and societal responses to such acts.

Any textbook represents a conscious selection of what to include and what to exclude. This book is no different in that regard. Our aim was to include topics of general consensus that are of interest to researchers, practitioners, policymakers, and you, the student, in your various disciplines. While much is included in this broad coverage of the topic of homicide generally and criminal homicide more specifically, we have surely not covered every aspect of every form of the crime or act. Textbooks are also by their nature a repository of information first

about a main topic and then varying amounts of information about subtopics. Each chapter of the book attempts to address significant aspects or categories of homicide. Due to the nature of such coverage, a single thread or theme does not always bind the subtopics covered in the chapter. This early notification will help you absorb the material and make some of the connections among the topics in your own way, in addition to the connections that we have tried to point out.

Chapter 2 provides students and readers with the foundation of *why* we measure various aspects of lethal violence as well as *what* specific things are measured. The chapter discusses fatal violence, of course, but also provides some information about nonfatal violence. In this chapter, we provide general comments about the degrees of various crimes associated with one person killing another but also note that there is some variation among and between jurisdictions. The chapter examines the major programs in place to collect data about death by criminal, natural, and unknown causes. We also provide some general commentary about how cases are resolved, or *cleared*, by agencies that investigate such matters. The chapter addresses the need for and practice of studying homicide *situations*. This helps keep the reader's mind open and focused broadly on all of the factors that impact a lethal event. Some authors narrowly study or comment on victims or perpetrators rather than examining the context of the event as well as precipitating acts and contributing factors. Throughout the book, we try to highlight various factors and urge readers to consider the role these various factors and perspectives (e.g., laws, neighborhoods, victims, offenders, citizens, media, and justice system actors) play in violent encounters and deadly incidents.

Other factors first mentioned in Chapter 2, and explored later, include the use and abuse of alcohol and drugs and the presence of an audience and how these affect the escalation or de-escalation of a tense and possibly violent encounter. Considering the homicide situation and various domains, as opposed to narrowly examining individual factors, has been emphasized by Miethe and Regoeczi (2004) and Hawk and Dabney (2019). Their work looked at the *structure* and *process* underlying homicide situations, and comprehensive models, respectively. The authors logically discuss how the elements of victim, offender, offense, and even the investigator are situated in a place and at a time and show that the combination of all of these are important to understanding the homicide event, as well as trying to solve the crime after it occurs.

Chapter 3 provides statistical information about various aspects of homicide. The expected recounting of demographic factors about victims and offenders is present, but we also provide information about other aspects of homicide situations. The location where a deadly assault occurs is critical to an understanding of why the event took place but also how related future events might be prevented. The same is true regarding the availability and choice of weapons used by one person against another. Under a section we title "Other Circumstances," we include some initial thoughts about the role arguments play in many, if not a majority, of criminal homicide events. The significance of interpersonal conflict to understanding and hopefully mitigating violence cannot be overstated. The complexity of human behavior is not given to simple explanations. It is important to remember this as you learn about homicide given that most people have a low tolerance for lengthy or nuanced explanations.

Chapter 3 also looks at trends and patterns in homicide. Known to researchers and law enforcement officials alike is the fact that in many criminal homicide situations, the victim and the perpetrator share similarities; often they know one another. The overlaps between the two are examined in this chapter. While homicide in the United States has generally declined over the last 20 years to a rate half of that in the mid-1990s, we note that assaults and murders among youth remain a great concern and key area for researchers, policymakers, and practitioners to devote their focus and energies to. We also provide some commentary about international homicide statistics to provide further context to what happens here in the United States as well as to understand possible broader patterns of violence in the world.

Chapter 4 introduces readers to a broad but not exhaustive treatment of criminological theories implicated in much of the study of homicide today. The chapter contains summaries of various theoretical approaches to the study of violence and homicide. As people grapple with the idea of individuals killing other individuals, we offer avenues of research that have provided information about this important question. Criminology examines individual behavior as well as larger social movements as befits its sociological heritage. Theory can help us understand somewhat why people do what they do and also aid us in addressing the challenges of homicide in American society. Our approach in the book directs you to thinking about what information regarding homicide is of greatest importance and what as a society we can do about the information that research provides us.

Chapter 5, on confrontational homicide, and Chapter 6, which addresses intimate partner homicide (IPH), take up the two types of crime responsible for the largest number of murders in our society. While many textbooks provide equal chapter coverage to even rare types of murder, we try to make clear that even in a general text on homicide intended to comment broadly, these two areas are of special significance. We also believe that given what is known about confrontational homicide, strategies can be developed to encourage individuals to reduce the behavior and reactions that can escalate to a lethal event. Similarly, through research, we understand that intimate partner *homicide* is virtually never the first act of violence in a relationship on a trajectory of intimate partner *violence*. It is not only critical but quite probably productive to examine the points in the system where intervention might be used more forcefully or strategically to interrupt the cycle of violence often resulting in intimate partner homicide. Some of this is accomplished through tools such as lethality assessments and fatality review teams.

In Chapter 7, we look at forms of homicide within the family structure aside from intimate partner homicide. Familicide as a form of multiple murder is also known by the term *family annihilation*. A member of the family, often the father, kills his spouse or significant other and one or more of their children, or he kills only the children to *punish* his spouse. We discuss the general findings about such incidents and examine less common forms of familicide in which one of the children, perhaps as an adult, carries out similar killings by first murdering one parent and then perhaps others in the family. The troubling nature of family homicide, already within the difficult area of all homicides, also involves parents who kill their children and children who kill others. Less well known are other forms of family killing, such as so-called honor killings, more prevalent in several other cultures around the world.

Multiple murders (commonly known as multicide) are addressed in Chapters 8 and 9. Chapter 8 addresses school killings, and while these incidents are less frequent than media coverage would have lay citizens believe, they remain of intense interest because the school population, composed mainly of our children, is seen as the most precious and often most vulnerable group in our society. The chapter examines at some length not merely those students who act against fellow students and adults but policy responses by schools, law enforcement, and legislators. The chapter necessarily focuses on the facts of these incidents and general responses. In the limited space of the text, it is not possible to examine the many psychosocial and other factors that marked the journey of an individual to his or her choice to murder others.

In Chapter 9, we turn to workplace and other public mass killings. Here we describe many of the characteristics found frequently among those who have killed in the workplace or in locations such as religious or public event venues. While not receiving the same level of media attention, we also note that nonemployees and individuals committing other crimes, such as robbery, are also responsible for deaths in the workplace not related to the stereotypical disgruntled employee or former employee. The mass killings that occur in places of worship and in public venues distinguish them from the workplace, where the killer will typically have greater knowledge of his victims.

In Chapter 10, we address two major topics and the relative balance between those topics. Gangs and cults are not asserted to be equivalent either in their involvement with homicide or the overall intention of their social grouping. Gang killings, much like organized crime killings of an earlier era, reflect some of the more challenging murders for law enforcement investigative efforts. With few witnesses or reluctant witnesses, these types of killings are seen to account for much of the diminishing clearance rates for homicide investigations in the last several decades. Some gangs, as with some organized crime organizations, have a hierarchy and structure that allows some success through investigating the process and flow of orders and information within the gang organization. Some gang structure is more akin to some terrorist organizational structures that model the cell organization that compartmentalizes knowledge of leaders and methods so that if one clique or group is successfully prosecuted, it may limit the threat to other members of the criminal organization. We provide what we hope is a thoughtful and thorough coverage of new religious movements (NRM), some of which are known as or considered by many people to be cults, and we point out that the vast majority of these groups have no interest in or involvement with violence of any kind. In considering cults that are dangerous, gangs who commit violent crimes, and terrorist organizations, we often observe disenfranchised or otherwise aimless followers who are attracted to the notion of a strong or charismatic leader or philosophy to follow blindly.

Chapter 11 takes up homicide as a tool of terror. The attention of the public is often focused on the Middle East and Islamic extremism when contemplating terrorism. ISIS, Boko Haram, and other now well-known groups represent only one part of a much larger and much older practice of terrorizing civilians in the hopes of influencing government policy in a country. The use of murder in an age of social media and the 24/7/365 news cycle can instantly spread the hateful and violent messages of a group. Terrorists, whether domestic or international, also utilize the Internet and other media for recruitment purposes as well as training, meetings, and other aspects of communication for their group. While the 9/11 attacks on the United States remain the largest such attack, representing the greatest loss of life and property, there are other examples, such as the Boston Marathon bombing, the Las Vegas shooting where a lone wolf gunman killed 58 and wounded hundreds, and the attack on four police officers by a machete-wielding individual as well as the attack on the offices of Charlie Hebdo in Paris, that remind us such actions are ongoing.

While consideration of terrorist actions is a dynamic area of research, we should remember that domestic acts of terrorism by different groups and individuals are a far more frequent occurrence than a terrorist attack emanating from outside of the United States. There is also overlap among several types of public or mass shootings. Consider for example Major Nidal Hasan's attack on fellow soldiers as both a terrorist act as well as a workplace mass shooting. This chapter also describes and explores hate-based homicides in contemporary America. While not frequent, this category of violence is important to research and seek interventions as we grapple with the biases and hatred that underlie such acts and that undermine social progress for the country as a whole.

Chapter 12 turns to serial killing and some examples among the infamous and not-so-famous ranks of serial killers. Characteristics of serial killers are covered in the chapter, leaning on the work of Eric Hickey and others in this fascinating subfield of multiple homicide. The major types of serial killers are touched upon for this dramatic though statistically small segment of murders. While there has been disagreement among researchers and experts over the years as to the number of former or active serial killers, a rarely known but increasingly considered typology is the health care serial killer often found to have been responsible for scores if not hundreds of murders over a lengthy period of time. This is often the nurse or medical doctor who silently kills his or her victims in a setting where death is not unexpected and thus evades detection. The increasingly thorough and sophisticated medical surveillance methods in the American health care system are both a boon to discovering and discouraging health care serial killers but also perhaps make homicide in a health care setting appear more prevalent compared to other countries based on those other countries' less robust monitoring practices.

Chapter 13 offers an important look at how law enforcement agencies go about solving criminal homicide. Thorough or appropriate treatment of this topic is important to a full examination of homicide. How and when an individual instructor or class takes up consideration of the investigation of the crime of homicide is somewhat arbitrary. What is important is that academics and practitioners alike understand the importance of policy and research informing criminal justice, education, social work, and health care practices and vice versa. The fact of criminal homicide or murder in society is well established. There is no realistic end in sight to instances of homicide, though we believe they may be reduced. Given this, communities look to their law enforcement agencies to be effective in the retroactive investigation of such acts. We discuss current agency practices investigating homicide, including cold cases, to include the ubiquity of social media, the proliferation of video, as well as the use of other technologies. We provide a realistic description of how officers engage a crime scene and the interaction among law enforcement, medical examiner or coroner, and prosecution personnel. It is important to recognize that all of these actors play important roles in solving homicides and pursuing justice for victims.

As we have mentioned previously, the CSI effect has led to many misunderstandings about actual police procedures relative to homicide and other investigations. The importance of following the very specific protocols and procedures of crime scene and investigative work are emphasized along with the necessity to work in accordance with the Fourth and Fifth Amendments to the Constitution and the various court rulings over the years that expand or contract and certainly clarify police limits as well as responsibilities.

Chapter 14 covers the introduction of a homicide case into the court system and the steps that follow. The physical arrest of a suspect by law enforcement personnel triggers the speedy trial clock for when a defendant must be brought into court and often hastens a defendant's invocation of his Fifth Amendment right against self-incrimination. These procedural aspects of the U.S. system have very real consequences for the investigation of the murder. The early involvement of the prosecutor in a case, even in an advisory role, is important to the eventual successful outcome of a murder case. There are many moving parts within a homicide case, and the coordination between the prosecutor and other actors in the justice system is crucial to seeing that justice is done according to the rules of the American system of jurisprudence. Ethical issues in the conduct of attorneys involved in homicide cases are discussed in this chapter. The factors involved in sentencing those convicted of homicide and typical outcomes are also examined.

Chapter 15 is titled "Victims, Society, and the Future." The role and goal of most summary chapters is to leave the readers with key thoughts to consider. We feel strongly that consideration of victimology and the impacts on individual victims, their families, society, or the community as a whole—and even the offender—is important. The impact of homicide is not isolated. It is not simply made up of the micro-event of one person killing another. The criminal justice system or process deals with the crime of homicide and the victims, both primary and secondary; the offender; and the community effects in various ways, based sometimes on who the victim is and who the suspected perpetrator may be.

There are several perspectives that have value for the consideration of homicide, and we examine public health as a lens by which to view homicide. We also look at legislation intended to impact violent crime as well as other societal issues. We conclude with some observations about predicting violence and the use of risk assessment as ways to continue to better understand violence leading to homicide and how perhaps to reduce both.

HISTORIC AND CONTEMPORARY

Violence in America is sadly nothing new. Violence the world over, in virtually all cultures and throughout recorded history, has been all too common. We are encouraged by the general decline in violence around the globe. Steven Pinker (2011) and others have chronicled the actual, if counterintuitive, reality of the low point in violence we currently see in the world. We say that this is counterintuitive because there is not a day that we cannot turn on the news, read a newspaper, or find at our favorite Internet sites information about killings and brutality in many countries and regions. In an age of the unending news cycle, it is important to remember that the images and stories we read and see do not proportionately represent murder and violence on Earth.

The United States, born in war as it was, has certainly gained great experience in violence over its relatively short life. Each generation of the American experience has seen aspects of homicide. Some places and times have seen more than their expected share of killing. We can point to the experiences and interactions of early European colonists with indigenous people on the North American continent as one example. The push westward by pioneers and entrepreneurs carried with it the challenges and dangers of organizing communities, while the civilizing processes and community entities of order often had to catch up to the wagon trains and trails that outpaced them.

As our country moved forward in time, it continued to struggle with social issues and evolving realities. A clear example of the still-evolving reality of equal opportunity and treatment of minority citizens is the history of oppression, denial of rights, and frequent brutalization of both individuals and entire groups of minority community members and immigrants at the hands of the majority who felt the American dream belonged only to them. This mindset as well as the threat to their earning power presented by freed slaves and industrious immigrants from other countries led to the well-chronicled lynching and other physical, economic, and political mistreatment of so many over the generations. Close examination of available data indicates disparity as well in the rate at which homicides of minority citizens are solved.

WHAT THIS BOOK IS NOT

While the topic of homicide is inextricably bound with the concept of violence, we do not attempt to tackle the entire spectrum of violent behavior in society. Other authors, for example Alvarez and Bachman (2017), Riedel and Welsh (2011), and Ferguson (2010) in his edited book on violent crime, have all addressed the many aspects of violence in its various forms. Alvarez and Bachman (2016) refer to violence in their text as American as apple pie. We agree that it would be difficult for an objective observer to look at the breadth and depth of the American experience and think otherwise.

We continue to assert, however, that violence is not the beginning and ending of the American experience, nor does it define who we are as people or as a culture. Improving our society in regard to violence is up to the readers of this book and all of the professionals who work to study violence and homicide, establish policy to address its causative factors, and work to diminish its impact. This also means holding those who commit the act accountable.

While this book is a criminology text, it is not a theory text intended to replace the ones used in a criminological-theory course. Again, this work, by its nature, incorporates historic and contemporary threads of what we believe we know to be many of the causes and circumstances of homicide. The theoretical traditions of sociology and criminology are critical to understanding murder and homicide in its different forms. In fact, we believe the multidisciplinary approach is the one best suited to dealing with what some might view as a narrow issue—homicide. Biological, psychological, sociological, and less common theoretical tools and traditions in examining the intentional killing of others are all important to a well-rounded understanding, critical to developing policy, law, and practice. Our treatment is necessarily broad as we try to equip students with a general knowledge of how homicide is studied by the academic world and dealt with by the policy and practitioner world. Human behavior is complex. This behavior has been productively studied through a lens of societal variables, including age, gender, economic standing, neighborhood, and race and ethnicity, that are sociological. The behavior has also been examined from a psychological perspective of the mental processes of individuals. Biological influences on human behavior have received a renewed surge of research activity that contributes further pieces to the vast puzzle of criminal human behavior. These and other theoretical frameworks provide structure to the work of researchers. The scientific approach of the past several hundred years is one of systematically observing and measuring various phenomena. This also involves experimentation based on the hypotheses of those conducting research.

There are a number of topics that could easily occupy their own textbook. While readers will not find encyclopedic coverage of every circumstance of unlawful killing within society, they will come away with much to think about in regard to homicide. In a general book addressing homicide, there will necessarily be topics of great importance and great interest to some that are excluded. In-depth aspects of the contemporary biological perspective are researched and written about with great clarity by (for example) Adrian Raine. The psychosocial approach to criminal behavior has long been studied and persuasively documented by Bartol and Bartol. They have also made great strides in explaining criminal profiling. We hope to bring attention to the different topics and point readers in some of the right directions to gain more in-depth knowledge about each.

POLICY IMPLICATIONS

We consider policy implications to be an important component of this book and our examination of homicide. As we have already noted, this is not a pure theory text, and as such, it perhaps offers some of its greatest benefit by asking you the reader to not only consider homicide from many perspectives but also to ask what can be done about lethal violence. How researchers approach the larger or smaller components of violence generally and homicide specifically has ramifications for what information is available to policymakers and others. Law enforcement administrators, social-work agencies, the health care industry, and others are all stakeholders in responding proactively as well as retroactively to violence and homicide.

Policymakers, just as average citizens, can fall into a reactionary mindset based on a misperception of actual crime or crime risk factors. This may be driven by the zealous advocacy of a particular viewpoint or through the common over-coverage of certain crimes by the media. When the field of public policy analysis began to gain voice several decades ago, many astute policymakers paused to listen. While elected officials and appointed administrators are not bound to enact policy options that appear objectively to hold the greatest potential, many at least spend more time and energy researching and examining alternatives for policy implementation. Some of the issues in contemporary homicide research that draw a lot of attention include homicide rates, clearance rates, the role of firearms, public concern about mass killings, and gang killings. This list is not exhaustive and these topics certainly overlap. The current trend in criminal justice is to use evidence-based methods and intelligence-led strategies. As you read, think of how the concepts and facts might shape policies and practices.

DISCUSSION QUESTIONS

1. Why is the study of homicide interesting and relevant to students and researchers?
2. What do most people think they know about homicide? How might these perceptions differ from what the data show?
3. How should researchers better inform the public perception about crime in general and homicide specifically?
4. What are the most compelling questions in the contemporary study of homicide? How should these questions be addressed by the criminal justice system, the health care system, and policymakers?

TRY THIS

Go to the FBI's most recent Uniform Crime Reporting (UCR) website and read the section on murder. What is the UCR definition of murder? What is included in this data and what is not included? Look at the most recent data on rates. How many people were killed in the United States in the most recent data reported there?

There has been a lot of focus in recent years on efforts by law enforcement in large cities where the homicide rate has been above the national average. Go to the NPR story on New Orleans and its murder rate at https://www.npr.org/2017/02/23/516669151/new-orleans-and-the-hard-work-of-pushing-down-the-murder-rate

What efforts did the city of New Orleans embark upon to address their homicide rate? What were the results? What can be learned from this example?

2

WHO'S KILLING WHOM AND HOW MUCH

"It is forbidden to kill; therefore all murderers are punished unless they kill in large numbers and to the sound of trumpets."

—Voltaire

"Homicide is the crime of choice for measures of violence because regardless of how the people of a distant culture conceptualize crime, a dead body is hard to define away, and it always arouses curiosity about who or what produced it."

—Steven Pinker, *The Better Angels of Our Nature: Why Violence Has Declined*

Student Learning Outcomes

Students will be able to:

- explain the difference between homicide charges and degrees.

- describe factors involved in measuring homicide situations.

- discuss the circumstances of homicide events.

- identify the sources of homicide data.

- analyze the challenges and limitations of data in homicide research.

CHAPTER OUTLINE

INTRODUCTION

Why We Measure

We opened in Chapter 1 with discussion about why we are fascinated by the subject of **murder**. In addition to the interest homicide in its various forms holds for the general public, there are practical implications for the study of homicide as well. Greater understanding of killing is helpful to researchers as they investigate the causes and motivations of people harming one another. Insights into motivations and patterns of behavior can aid criminal investigators as they seek evidence to offer the courts about who is accountable for taking a human life. Research and data can be a tremendous aid to legislators and other policymakers as they attempt to craft legislation and programs to prevent violence in society. Citizens have their own reasons for watching news programs and entertainment shows that focus on murder. Sometimes studying a topic can better prepare us to deal with such matters or lower our risk of becoming a victim. We also mentioned that it seems part of the human psyche to want to experience fear, even if vicariously.

But fear of victimization and the desire for a good scare are not the only reasons we measure and study murder (or violence). In creating laws and policies or in devising specific tactics to deal with an issue, we rely on data. The decision-maker needs accurate and comprehensive information to construct sound policies. These policies may include those that attempt to reduce crime or those that seek to punish offenders appropriately to achieve societal goals. The researcher must have data to form hypotheses and theories. And so we measure incidence rates, demographics, and many different factors we believe to be connected in some way with violence and homicide. The offender and his personal history are retroactively scrutinized for early signs that could have been recognized. The victim and his movements and actions are studied to glean what he could have done to avoid his untimely demise. The physical environment and circumstances surrounding a homicide event are examined along with economic conditions of an area in hopes of understanding influences on people's predisposition to violence.

Some of these questions and lines of inquiry are presented to the public through mediums that rarely match the objective approach of a social scientist or the well-intentioned search for preventive strategies of a policymaker. Are the images and plotlines of TV and movies accurate? Perhaps not as much as depicted. Do horrific crimes and tragic deaths occur? Every day, several times a day.

WHAT WE MEASURE

Measurement in criminology and criminal justice covers many things. While ostensibly a significant focus is counting homicide cases and perhaps the solving of crimes or **clearances**, the complexity of violence demands that researchers study many obvious and not so obvious aspects of individuals, places, communities, and society. Data collection in criminology allows for analysis and understanding of what we know and how we know it. As for violent acts, homicide is not the only one of interest to homicide researchers. Both nonfatal and fatal violence are of interest to researchers, policymakers, and the criminal justice system. Over time, the focus for some researchers has been examining the offender. What was the killer's background? What was known about his mental capacity or intelligence? Was his childhood troubled and possibly influenced by violence or trauma? Other research has looked at the behavior and habits of victims to assess what impact such factors had on the path to their becoming victims. Still other efforts look at the aspects of a setting: physical, temporal, inside or outside, populated or not, and so forth.

We want simple explanations. A touchstone of scientific inquiry is to develop succinct explanations for phenomena. Members of the public similarly want simple solutions to perceived problems, such as crimes of violence. Policymakers add that they would prefer a solution that is inexpensive and could take effect before they next face reelection. The media has a role to play in educating the public through the dissemination of information it obtains or editorial views it puts forward through the way the stories are presented. Each perspective is understandable, yet the causes of violence and crime, including criminal homicide, are not always simple or amenable to a single and elegant response.

Fatal and Nonfatal

Measuring nonfatal violence is every bit as important as measuring fatal violence. There is a particular importance in tracking the nonfatal crime of aggravated assault. The Model Penal Code, developed in 1962 by the American Law Institute, defines aggravated assault and states that a person is guilty if he

a. attempts to cause serious bodily injury to another, or causes such injury purposely, knowingly or recklessly under circumstances manifesting extreme indifference to the value of human life; or

b. attempts to cause or purposely or knowingly causes bodily injury to another with a deadly weapon.

The important point here is that many, if not most, aggravated assaults (separated in some states by assault or battery) could cause a death if not for one of several intervening variables. The availability of 9-1-1 systems to quickly summon aid; the advances in medicine such as penicillin and other drugs that dramatically decreased mortality after infections or complications from trauma; the training of emergency first responders, including law enforcement, ambulance, and fire crews; and the evolution of emergency medicine as a distinct specialization within the practice of medicine and the corresponding improvement in emergency care at virtually all hospital emergency rooms have all had tremendous effect on the likelihood of surviving trauma, including criminal assault. The degree to which medical and other advances have reduced mortality following assault is not, however, a settled issue (Eckberg, 2015). And so, simply tabulating who *dies* from criminal violence is not an entirely accurate gauge of serious societal violence.

Crimes are classified in various ways, which also has an impact on what we measure. The FBI's **Uniform Crime Report** (UCR), which will be discussed later, gathers limited data on a number of more and less serious crimes. The measurement of these crimes reflects the legal definitions that compose one type of crime definition. From the English common law roots and tradition of the legal system in the United States, most adults are aware of a second type of definition or categorization: felonies and misdemeanors. A third manner of categorizing criminal acts distinguishes among crimes against persons, crimes against property, and crimes against public order. This framework is also used by various criminal justice agencies in assigning duties to members such as detectives or prosecutors.

Degrees and Definitions

The study of homicide appropriately begins with definitions of relevant terms and commentary about the scope of the issues involved. In the text, we address death cases examined by law enforcement agencies in the United States. This examination is not always about criminal homicide (murder). In addition to murder and **manslaughter**, agencies are also tasked with investigating suicides and suspicious deaths in their jurisdictions. Sometimes cases begin in one category and end up in another.

Degrees and definitions of homicide vary somewhat from state to state. Simply put, homicide is the killing of one person by another and may be criminal, justifiable, or even accidental. If this at first seems odd, think about the sanctioned killing of soldiers during a time of war, the execution of an inmate under sentence of death, or perhaps the justified use of deadly force by a criminal justice officer in the performance of duty. Even the category of excusable homicide in self-defense may not be categorized as murder as it lacks the amount of *intent* considered necessary to be charged as criminal homicide. The focus of the book will be on acts of criminal homicide: killings that violate the law or deaths that result from unjustified acts or failures to act.

Murder is the criminal killing of one human by another. First-degree murder is most frequently charged when the act is premeditated. To be considered first-degree murder, the killing also requires malice or the intent to do harm. The amount of time that a person thinks about the act beforehand can be brief, perhaps even seconds. In a number of jurisdictions, charging first-degree murder may also result from extremely brutal or cruel acts that lead to the death. Second-degree murder charges may arise from acts that could foreseeably lead to death or great bodily harm but were not necessarily

intended to do so. Second-degree cases are often a catchall for cases that are not clearly first degree. So the impulsive or spur-of-the moment killing may be charged as second-degree murder. The offender's indifference to human life may also bring about a second-degree murder charge. A homicide charged as manslaughter typically reflects the judgment of the prosecutor that the offender lacked malice or premeditation.

The Uniform Crime Report (UCR) program of the FBI collects statistics on offenses, which excludes, therefore, various non-criminal homicides. The definition of criminal homicide is:

> **Criminal homicide**—a.) Murder and nonnegligent manslaughter: the willful (nonnegligent) killing of one human being by another. Deaths caused by negligence, attempts to kill, assaults to kill, suicides, and accidental deaths are excluded. The program classifies justifiable homicides separately and limits the definition to: (1) the killing of a felon by a law enforcement officer in the line of duty; or (2) the killing of a felon, during the commission of a felony, by a private citizen. b.) Manslaughter by negligence: the killing of another person through gross negligence. Deaths of persons due to their own negligence, accidental deaths not resulting from gross negligence, and traffic fatalities are not included in the category Manslaughter by Negligence. (FBI, 2018)

As already noted, the aim of this book is to equip readers with an understanding of criminal homicide specifically. **Justifiable** or **excusable homicides** such as the killing of a felon by police in the line of duty, government-sanctioned executions, and cases ruled self-defense by a prosecutor are therefore not examined here.

HOW WE MEASURE

There are various types of deaths that are investigated by different governmental entities. While murder grabs the headlines, deaths from accidents, natural events, self-defense, and suicide are also examined after the fact to determine the circumstances leading to someone dying. The examination of homicides is done in various ways. Deaths and murders are measured geographically by state, region, or city. Homicides are also looked at according to demographic factors such as age, race, sex, and economic strata of the victim or offender. Researchers are interested in where such crimes occur and what processes underlie the event.

The initial report to law enforcement that triggers most homicide cases may initially be reported as a murder and later be found to be a death not attributable to crime. Likewise, a death first reported as accidental, natural, suicide, or perhaps as a result of self-defense may turn out to actually be the result of criminal homicide. Once a determination is made of the manner of death, usually by the medical examiner or coroner, law enforcement will include the incident within the reporting forwarded to the state's reporting agency. The information is subsequently collected by the Uniform Crime Reporting Program.

Uniform Crime Report

Gathering the data that determine the number and rate of crime is challenging. The effort to compile and tabulate crime statistics in the United States was begun in the late 1920s by the International Association of Chiefs of Police (IACP). The IACP is the world's largest and most influential organization of law enforcement administrators. By 1930, the IACP had worked successfully to have Congress enact legislation designating the FBI as the agency to gather crime data from U.S. police agencies. While the FBI's Uniform Crime Report enjoys nearly 95% participation from nearly 18,000 law enforcement agencies nationwide, the instrument receives information on only some crimes. The reported incidents are compiled for two categories of crimes: Part I and Part II. Part I crimes are murder and non-negligent manslaughter, forcible rape, robbery, aggravated assault, burglary, larceny, arson, and motor

vehicle theft. Some 21 other reported lesser crimes are considered Part II. Law enforcement agencies also report the age, race, and gender of arrested persons.

The volume and the rate of the reported crimes are tabulated and presented in the Uniform Crime Report. The volume describes the frequency of crimes known to police. While the volume of crimes reported in a particular jurisdiction or region is instructive, it is desirable to have the ability to compare areas. To accomplish such comparisons of crimes across different cities, counties, states, or nations, see the example from the UCR's data tool document "Crime Statistics for Decision-Making" for an example.

You can try this yourself by obtaining a population estimate from the FactFinder tool of the U.S. Census Bureau and the homicide number from the FBI's *Crime in the United States* for the year of interest. The use of different estimates of the population or semantic differences in the definition of murder and non-negligent manslaughter can influence the final estimated rate for the crime.

Agencies also report the number of crimes they have *cleared* on a monthly basis. A crime is designated as cleared if 1) a person is arrested, formally charged, or turned over to the courts for prosecution; or 2) by exceptional clearance. Exceptional clearance is when something prevents law enforcement from physically arresting someone. This includes circumstances such as the death of a suspect, the suspect leaving U.S. jurisdiction, a homicide-suicide, and a homicide ruled self-defense. While just over 20% of crime is cleared each year, violent crimes generally have a higher clearance rate. Frequently in violent crimes, there are witnesses, or the investigation reveals who had a relationship with the victim. Physical evidence may be more likely at the scene of a violent crime. There are quality and completeness issues with such data gathering, especially given the voluntary nature of the process. While *reported* crimes necessarily misses crimes *not* reported, homicide typically has a near 100% reporting rate given the presence of a victim's body. Of course, this does not account for persons murdered but not reported missing by anyone.

UCR Offense Definitions

The UCR Program collects statistics on the number of offenses known to law enforcement. In the traditional Summary Reporting System (SRS), there are eight crimes, or Part I offenses, (murder and nonnegligent homicide, rape (legacy & revised), robbery, aggravated assault, burglary, motor vehicle theft, larceny-theft, and arson) to be reported to the UCR Program. These offenses were chosen because they are serious crimes, they occur with regularity in all areas of the country, and they are likely to be reported to police. The Part I offenses are defined in Table 2.1.

Offense and Arrest Rates

Crime rates are indicators of reported crime activity standardized by population. They are more refined indicators for comparative purposes than are volume figures. The UCR Program provides three types of crime rates: offense rates, arrest rates, and clearance rates.

An offense rate, or crime rate, defined as the number of offenses per 100,000 people, is derived by first dividing a jurisdiction's population by 100,000 and then dividing the number of offenses by the resulting figure. Crime or arrest rates are derived from law enforcement agencies for which 12 months of complete offense or arrest data have been submitted.

Example:

a. Population for jurisdiction: 75,000

b. Number of known burglaries for jurisdiction for a year: 215

Divide 75,000 by 100,000 = 0.75

Divide 215 by 0.75 = 286.7

The burglary rate is 286.7 per 100,000 inhabitants.

Table 2.1   Uniform Crime Reporting Offense Definitions—Part I Crimes

Part I Offenses	Definition
Criminal homicide	a.) Murder and nonnegligent manslaughter: the willful (nonnegligent) killing of one human being by another. Deaths caused by negligence, attempts to kill, assaults to kill, suicides, and accidental deaths are excluded. The program classifies justifiable homicides separately and limits the definition to: (1) the killing of a felon by a law enforcement officer in the line of duty; or (2) the killing of a felon, during the commission of a felony, by a private citizen. b.) Manslaughter by negligence: the killing of another person through gross negligence. Deaths of persons due to their own negligence, accidental deaths not resulting from gross negligence, and traffic fatalities are not included in the category Manslaughter by Negligence.
Forcible Rape/ Legacy Rape*	The carnal knowledge of a female forcibly and against her will. Rapes by force and attempts or assaults to rape, regardless of the age of the victim, are included. Statutory offenses (no force used—victim under age of consent) are excluded.
Revised Rape	Penetration, no matter how slight, of the vagina or anus with any body part or object, or oral penetration by a sex organ of another person, without the consent of the victim. Attempts or assaults to commit rape are also included; however, statutory rape and incest are excluded. In December 2011, the UCR program changed its definition of SRS rape to this revised definition. This change can be seen in the UCR data starting in 2013. Any data reported under the older definition of rape will be called "legacy rape."

Robbery	The taking or attempting to take anything of value from the care, custody, or control of a person or persons by force or threat of force or violence and/or by putting the victim in fear.
Aggravated assault	An unlawful attack by one person upon another for the purpose of inflicting severe or aggravated bodily injury. This type of assault usually is accompanied by the use of a weapon or by means likely to produce death or great bodily harm. Simple assaults are excluded.
Burglary (breaking or entering)	The unlawful entry of a structure to commit a felony or a theft. Attempted forcible entry is included.
Larceny-theft (except motor vehicle theft)	The unlawful taking, carrying, leading, or riding away of property from the possession or constructive possession of another. Examples are thefts of bicycles, motor vehicle parts and accessories, shoplifting, pocket picking, or the stealing of any property or article that is not taken by force and violence or by fraud. Attempted larcenies are included. Embezzlement, confidence games, forgery, check fraud, etc., are excluded.
Motor vehicle theft	The theft or attempted theft of a motor vehicle. A motor vehicle is self-propelled and runs on land surface and not on rails. Motorboats, construction equipment, airplanes, and farming equipment are specifically excluded from this category.
Arson	Any willful or malicious burning or attempt to burn, with or without intent to defraud, a dwelling house, public building, motor vehicle or aircraft, personal property of another, etc. Arson statistics are not included in this table-building tool.

*Note: In December 2011, the UCR Program changed its SRS definition of rape: "Penetration, no matter how slight, of the vagina or anus with any body part or object, or oral penetration by a sex organ of another person, without the consent of the victim." Starting in 2013, rape data may be reported under either the historical definition, known as "legacy rape" or the updated definition, referred to as "revised". For more information, see the FBI's New Rape Definition Frequently Asked Questions: https://ucr.fbi.gov/recent-program-updates/new-rape-definition-frequently-asked-questions

Source: United States Department of Justice, Federal Bureau of Investigation. *Uniform Crime Reporting Statistics, 2017.*

The number 0.75 can now be divided into the totals of any offense category to produce a crime rate for that offense. The same procedure may be used to obtain arrest rates per 100,000 inhabitants.

Analysis of cleared incidents finds differences in the rates at which cases of differing circumstances are cleared, "but many questions regarding the correlates of homicide clearance remain unanswered" (Rydberg & Pizarro, 2014, p. 343). For example, cases with female or younger victims are more likely to be cleared (Roberts, 2007). Also, homicides with victims involved in drug and gang-related activities were more likely to be cleared. However, the significant impact of victim characteristics disappeared after controlling for situational variables related to physical evidence, information, and witnesses. Situational characteristics such as under-the-influence offenders, nonstranger offenders, weapons, and related serious offenses significantly increased the odds of homicide clearance (Roberts, 2007).

Clearance Rates

A clearance rate differs conceptually from a crime or arrest rate in that both the numerator and denominator constitute the same unit of count (i.e., crimes). Unlike a crime or arrest rate, a clearance rate represents percentage data. A clearance rate is, therefore, equivalent to the percentage of crime cleared.

The percentage of crimes cleared by arrest and exceptional means (i.e., clearance rate) is obtained first by dividing the number of offenses cleared by the number of offenses known and then multiplying the resulting figure by 100.

Example:

a. Number of clearances in robbery: 38

b. Number of total robberies: 72

Divide 38 by 72 = 0.528

Multiply 0.528 by 100 = 52.8%

The clearance rate for robbery is 52.8%.

While police investigative methods are addressed elsewhere in the book, it is important to note that police actions can lead to higher clearance rates (Braga & Dusseault, 2018). The factors leading to clearance have been categorized as those within police control and those outside of their control. From the same UCR "Crime Statistics for Decision-Making" document, see the explanation for how clearance rates are calculated.

The Congressional Research Service (James, 2018) analyzed data regarding violent crime in the United States since 1960. Some of the items noted, focusing on changes from 2014 to 2016, were:

- At the national level, violent crime and homicide rates increased from 2014 to 2015 and again from 2015 to 2016, but both rates remain near historical lows.

- Violent crime and homicide rates for the 48 largest cities in the United States with available data generally followed national-level trends, with some exceptions. For example, violent crime rates in cities of 500,000–999,999 people and 250,000–499,999 people decreased from 2014 to 2015, and the homicide rate in small cities of 50,000–99,999 people decreased from 2015 to 2016.

- Some of the largest cities in the United States saw increases in violent crime

rates, homicide rates, or both from 2014 to 2015 and/or 2015 to 2016. For some of these cities, violent crime or homicide rates were the highest they have been in the past 20 years.

- Recent increases in violent crime and homicide in large cities have received a great deal of attention, but in smaller communities, violent crime and homicide rates also increased from 2014 to 2015 and again from 2015 to 2016, although not as much as in the largest cities.

The Uniform Crime Report showed the following overview in regard to violent crime in 2017:

- In 2017, an estimated 1,247,321 violent crimes occurred nationwide, a decrease of 0.2 percent from the 2016 estimate.

- When considering 5- and 10-year trends, the 2017 estimated violent crime total was 6.8 percent above the 2013 level but 10.6 percent below the 2008 level.

- There were an estimated 382.9 violent crimes per 100,000 inhabitants in 2017, a rate that fell 0.9 percent when compared with the 2016 estimated violent crime rate and dropped 16.5 percent from the 2008 estimate.

- Aggravated assaults accounted for 65.0 percent of violent crimes reported to law enforcement in 2017. Robbery offenses accounted for 25.6 percent of violent crime offenses; rape (legacy definition) accounted for 8.0 percent; and murder accounted for 1.4 percent.

- Information collected regarding types of weapons used in violent crime showed that firearms were used in 72.6 percent of the nation's murders, 40.6 percent of robberies, and 26.3 percent of aggravated assaults. (Weapons data are not collected for rape.) (FBI, 2018, n.p.)

In addition, the 2018 *Crime in the United States* report showed:

- The South, the most populous region of the nation, accounted for 40.8 percent of all violent crimes in 2017. Lesser volumes of violent crime were recorded in the West at 25.5 percent, the Midwest at 20.2 percent, and the Northeast at 13.4 percent.

- In 2017, 45.9 percent of the nation's estimated total number of murders occurred in the South. The Midwest had 22.6 percent of murders, followed by the West with 20.2 percent and the Northeast with 11.3 percent.

- During 2017, 41.9 percent of the estimated number of property crimes were recorded in the South. The West was next highest with 27.0 percent, followed by the Midwest with 19.6 percent, and the Northeast with 11.4 percent. (FBI, 2018)

In homicide cases, there are secondary sources of data that provide additional information. These include the **Supplemental Homicide Report (SHR)** of the FBI, the **National Incident-Based Reporting System (NIBRS)**, the **National Violent Death Reporting System (NVDRS)**, and the **National Center for Health Statistics (NCHS)** of the Centers for Disease Control and Prevention (CDC). The UCR reports that are generated are aggregations of 12-month data submitted by the various states.

Supplemental Homicide Report

In addition to the UCR reporting done by law enforcement, supplemental reporting is called for in homicide situations. The SHR is part of the UCR and provides information about individual cases. The Supplemental Homicide Report, requested from each agency that reports a criminal homicide, gathers additional detail on homicides, including data about the agency, the

incident, the victim, and the offender, if known. For example, any known relationship between the victim and offender, weapons used in the incident, and other circumstances should be included. A challenge with the SHR is that many agencies fail to submit the supplementary report after they have cleared their immediate case. As a voluntary submission, it may be forgotten by the time the case is finally closed.

Data limitations are expected in the gathering of data. "Despite their [the SHR's] widespread use by researchers and policymakers alike, these data are not completely without their limitations, the most important of which involves missing or incomplete incident reports" (Fox & Swatt, 2009, p. 51). In their article, Fox and Swatt (2009) talk about how the use of supplemental homicide reports by the FBI have been a valuable source of information regarding certain trends and patterns in homicide. There are concerns with the reliability of these data due to incompleteness and the lack of mandatory reporting. If information in reports is missing, cases may not be completely resolved, and they may be incorrectly categorized.

A study by Pampel and Williams (2000), addressed the SHR data problems that often result from "the failure to file, inconsistent filing of reports to the FBI by local police agencies, or incomplete records . . . even when reports are filed" (p. 661). They noted that, "Madison, Columbus, and Syracuse identified the perpetrator for all homicides, although these cities experienced only a combined total of 38 reported incidents" (p. 664). The authors go on to discuss larger cities, such as Washington, D.C., Boston, and New York, that do not or cannot fully report relationship information regarding the perpetrator and victim. Lacking such relationship information on a large percentage of reported incidents is problematic. Without knowing the relationship between a victim and perpetrator, it is harder to investigate many murders. Knowledge of the relationship is useful in resolving and clearing the case as well as correctly placing it by category.

We note that all data sources suffer from one challenge or another to reliability. According to Wadsworth and Roberts (2008), SHR challenges include missing information about offenders. Both the UCR and NIBRS similarly suffer from incomplete and missing information. Incomplete data often lead researchers to exclude records. This may inadvertently do away with partial information that nonetheless could have valuable explanatory power on various aspects of homicide events. Many supplemental homicide reports place cases as unknown, and that leaves the question of patterns and trends often unclear. Unknown cases may reflect the lack of an apparent motive in the killing. This has implications for data, but it may also mean that not knowing motive may make it more difficult to identify a suspect in a homicide case. And so again, solving and clearing a case is more difficult.

National Incident-Based Reporting System

As more is usually better when it comes to data, the FBI has been working for many years to implement a more thorough information-gathering method called the National Incident-Based Reporting System. While many agencies have transitioned to the more labor-intensive system, adoption has not been as rapid as anyone would like. There are certainly current limitations of NIBRS. One significant limitation is that not all states have this system in place. The FBI says that 43% of the nation's 17,429 law enforcement agencies are participating and reporting as of 2019. Further, not all of the law enforcement agencies in those states participate in the system. Without having this system in place universally, it is hard to measure the clearance rates that need to be determined (Chilton & Jarvis, 1999). Many states and agencies do not have resources to implement NIBRS. The NIBRS can collect and provide more specifics and context to far more data than the outdated summary reporting system (SRS) of the UCR.

Centers for Disease Control and Prevention

The Centers for Disease Control and Prevention provides a great deal of information useful to researchers, citizens, policymakers, and the media. The interactive online database available to all users is called WISQARS, the Web-based Injury Statistics Query and Reporting System. The WISQARS website (https://www.cdc.gov/injury/wisqars/index.html) notes that

> Researchers, the media, public health professionals, and the public can use WISQARS™ data to learn more about the public health and economic burden associated with unintentional and violence-related injury in the United States.

- Intent of injury (unintentional injury, violence-related, homicide/assault, legal intervention, suicide/intentional self-harm)

- Mechanism (cause) of injury (e.g., fall, fire, firearm, motor vehicle crash, poisoning, suffocation)

- Body region (e.g., traumatic brain injury, spinal cord, torso, upper and lower extremities)

- Nature (type) of injury (e.g., fracture, dislocation, internal injury, open wound, amputation, and burn)

- Geographic location (national, regional, state)

- Sex, race/ethnicity, and age of the injured person

National Vital Statistics System of the National Center for Health Statistics

The National Vital Statistics System (NVSS) is a component of the CDC and is maintained by the National Center for Health Statistics (NCHS). According to the Bureau of Justice Statistics (BJS),

> The National Vital Statistics System is the oldest and most successful example of inter-governmental data sharing in Public Health and the shared relationships, standards, and procedures form the mechanism by which NCHS collects and disseminates the Nation's

official vital statistics. These data are provided through contracts between NCHS and vital registration systems operated in the various jurisdictions (https://www.cdc.gov/stltpublichealth/sitesgovernance/index.html) legally responsible for the registration of vital events—births, deaths, marriages, divorces, and fetal deaths. Vital Statistics data are also available online. In the United States, legal authority for the registration of these events resides individually with the 50 States, 2 cities (Washington, DC, and New York City), and 5 territories (Puerto Rico, the Virgin Islands, Guam, American Samoa, and the Commonwealth of the Northern Mariana Islands). These jurisdictions are responsible for maintaining registries of vital events and for issuing copies of birth, marriage, divorce, and death certificates. (CDC/National Center for Health Statistics, 2016)

There is consistency to the manner in which death certificates have been standardized throughout the United States. This consistency is notable and important in tracking data trends in homicide. While the NVSS has consistently shown a higher number and rate of homicides compared to the SHR, the Bureau of Justice Statistics assumes this reflects the voluntary versus mandatory data collection of the two methods.

National Violent Death Reporting System

Each year the NVDRS compiles, in summary fashion, data on violent deaths and those for which the manner is undetermined in the United States. "Results are reported by sex, age group, race/ethnicity, marital status, location of injury, method of injury, circumstances of injury, and other selected characteristics" (Karch, Logan, McDaniel, Parks, & Patel, 2012, p. 1). The NVDRS began in 2002 with a handful of states. The data are gleaned from several sources: death certificates, coroner and medical examiner reports, and law enforcement reports. The state-based surveillance systems collect data from the previously mentioned sources and compile them into a consolidated report. In 2018, the CDC reported that the NVDRS had expanded to every state as well as the District of Columbia and Puerto Rico. The NVDRS Fact Sheet notes that, "To help find answers to prevent violent deaths, we need to know the facts. CDC's NVDRS links information about the 'who, when, where, and how' from data on violent deaths and provides insights about 'why' they occurred." (CDC, 2019)

The initial report that the NVDRS issues is preliminary, and there remains the opportunity and hope that states will submit additional information on cases. This is one representation of the incomplete nature of much data. The efforts and information also illustrate the need for data in developing policy from legal or public-health perspectives. Timely and thorough information is essential to sound policymaking. Policy related to violent death is no exception.

The report by Karch et al. (2012) lists the goals of the NVDRS as follows:

- collect and analyze timely, high-quality data that monitor the magnitude and characteristics of violent death at the national, state, and local levels;

- ensure that data are disseminated routinely and expeditiously to public health officials, law enforcement officials, policymakers, and the public;

- ensure that data are used to develop, implement, and evaluate programs and strategies that are intended to reduce and prevent violent deaths and injuries at the national, state, and local levels; and

- build and strengthen partnerships among organizations and communities at the national, state, and local levels to ensure that data are collected and used to reduce and prevent violent deaths and injuries. (p. 2)

Since the NVDRS has expanded to all fifty states and the districts, the findings are even more important, and it is hoped that policymakers and others will benefit from the data.

Self-Reports, Surveys, and the National Crime Victimization Survey

In the social sciences research, there is a long tradition of using self-report surveys. Such surveys ask the individuals of interest for information about themselves and their experiences. The National Crime Victimization Survey (NCVS) is a self-report study administered by the Bureau of Justice Statistics twice each year. Respondents are asked about whether they have been the victim of a crime. The NCVS then asks the individuals for further aspects of the crimes reported. The NCVS samples approximately 50,000 to 75,000 households during each interview period. The NCVS does not address homicide, for obvious reasons, but it provides information on other unreported crimes of violence.

In other self-report surveys, the respondents are asked whether they have *committed* crimes in a given time period. The sample of people selected is often termed a *convenience sample* because the group can be readily surveyed. The group may be high school or college students, inmate populations in juvenile or adult facilities, or other places or organizations where a researcher can gain access. It may occur to you that sample groups who are demographically similar but for being incarcerated provide a good opportunity to study and understand deviance and criminal acts. There have been notable examples of *longitudinal* studies, such as the NCVS that re-interviews or examines the criminal records of people periodically over time. When respondents are interviewed at only one time, the sample is referred to as *cross-sectional*.

As with all other methods of data gathering, self-report studies have potential weaknesses. Averdijk (2014) differentiated the respondent cohorts of the NCVS by age to determine if one or multiple victimization curves became evident. Part of Averdijk's analyses revealed that "for every age cohort studied, self-reported victimization decreases over consecutive measurements. Explanations offered for this decrease include selective panel attrition, the American crime drop, and panel-respondent fatigue" (p. 265). The finding was that the separate age cohorts do not share a single victimization curve.

In addition to these challenges to self-report data, respondents can lie about their criminal or delinquent involvement by saying they committed less or more than what they actually have. The individuals may also forget acts committed even a few weeks or months previously. In addition, it is believed that people who do respond to such survey methods may be more forthcoming regarding relatively minor crimes and not serious or violent ones.

Clearing Homicide Cases

Citizens generally may hear the term *clearance* as *solved* and assume that someone was arrested. Cases may be classified as cleared with no one actually being in custody. The clearance rate of an agency is the ratio of solved cases to reported cases in some period of time. If the Hometown Police Department has investigated four reported homicides for the year and they have solved two of them, the agency's clearance rate is two out of four, or 50%. The homicides need not have been criminal homicides.

Historically, homicide saw higher clearance rates than almost any other crime. Suspects were generally easy to identify based on the fact that most offenders and victims were known to each other. While acquaintance murder is still cleared at high rates, clearance of stranger homicide has decreased. With this, solved cases have declined over the last several decades. Homicide clearance rates have dropped nearly 30% since the early 1960s, from 91% to 61% in 2007. At year-end 2017, the clearance rate for murder offenses in the United States was 61.6% (FBI, 2018). Without a readily discerned suspect, willing witnesses, or significant physical evidence, clearance rates as a segment of the whole have dropped. Gang killings as well as drug-involved killings and those perpetrated by youth with firearms are, in part, responsible for this change in the numbers. While clearance rates have declined nationally, some agencies have maintained relatively high case closures.

The general public is often surprised to learn of *low* clearance rates for homicide. Given the advance of technologies such as DNA evidence

The *New York Times* reported that a survey of retired officers of the NYPD shows a long-time culture of downgrading serious crimes to minor ones and discouraging the filing of complaints by victims in the first place. In an article from June 2012, the newspaper quotes Professor Eli Silverman of John Jay College of Criminal Justice in New York saying of his coauthored survey, "This really demonstrates a rotten barrel." Dr. Silverman's comment refers to the concept of whether an inappropriate act by someone in an organization represents an isolated *bad apple* or whether the entire organization or barrel is involved.

There has been debate over UCR crime reporting by the NYPD. The report also notes research by Professor Frank Zimring of the Berkley Law School that supports the assertion of crime reduction in New York.

Whether agencies have achieved reductions as a result of crime control strategies, community involvement, or drops in crime likely occurring as a result of these and external factors not attributable to law enforcement or criminal justice actions, gauging what is effective and to what extent is complicated if statistics are manipulated, resulting in a skewed picture of crime.

Source: Ruderman (2012).

and Automated Fingerprint Identification Systems (AFIS) and increasingly sensitive methods of collecting and identifying trace evidence, it is the thought of many people that most (or all) murders should be solved. Television and movies certainly portray that the vast majority of homicides are solved and solved quickly. Homicides are not frequent, and their investigation makes up a very small portion of the activities of an agency. Nonetheless, members of a community often judge an agency's effectiveness based on its ability to solve the crime of murder. Given that murder is considered the most serious crime in society and given that law enforcement learns of almost all murders, citizens have high expectations for their law enforcement officers to solve such crimes. This is true even if the average citizen of a community has an incredibly low statistical chance of being a victim of a murder.

The Uniform Crime Reporting Program provides for *closing* crimes via two main categories: arrest and exceptional means. Arrest may be an actual physical arrest based on probable cause, charging someone with the crime, or turning the case over to the prosecutor's office. Clearance by exceptional means acknowledges that law enforcement agencies may not always be able to charge the offender. According to the UCR guidelines, for agencies to clear offenses exceptionally, they must have done the following:

- Identified the offender.

- Gathered enough evidence to support an arrest, make a charge, and turn over the offender to the court for prosecution.

- Identified the offender's exact location so that the suspect could be taken into custody immediately.

- Encountered a circumstance outside the control of law enforcement that prohibits the agency from arresting, charging, and prosecuting the offender. (FBI, 2018, p. 2)

Success in clearing cases is based on a number of factors. In a study by Wellford and Cronin (2000), the researchers examined 798 homicides in four cities. They found 589 (74%) of these cases were solved, with half being solved in one week and 93% of those solved cases being solved in one year. As you might assume, various victim and situational characteristics in different homicide cases impact the clearance rates of these cases. Additional circumstances surrounding homicide cases are noted, such as perpetrators acting under the influence of drugs or alcohol or when the perpetrator is someone the victim knows. Wellford and Cronin note two categories of factors affecting homicide case clearances:

1. police practices and procedures, over which the police have complete control, such as the actions of the first officer on the scene and the number of detectives assigned to the case, and

2. case characteristics, over which the police have no control, such as type of weapon used and involvement of drugs. (p. 3)

These factors are notable as they suggest clearances might be amenable to some boost in rate by improved procedures on the part of law enforcement agencies or broader public policy issues, such as gun regulation or drug usage. We deal later with policies and practices related to homicide prevention and investigation.

We note at this point that the general decline in homicide does not signal a decline in all types. Data examined by Buzawa, Buzawa, and Stark (2012) "suggest the rates of domestic homicides have resumed increasing" (p. 25). Each year more than one-third of female murder victims for whom the relationship to their attacker is known were killed by their husbands or boyfriends. It is our view that **intimate partner homicides** (IPH) are not as intractable as other categories of criminal homicide, and there may be some policy prevention efforts that can have some effect. We address this more fully in a separate chapter. The variation in types of homicides and causes underscores the importance of examining not just the aggregate figures on murder rates and administrative clearance. Prevention remains an important public policy goal. We will discuss policies more fully in later chapters as well.

STUDYING HOMICIDE SITUATIONS

The examination of quantitative data has the benefit of numerical clarity. The insights needed to understand violent crime and how to craft public policy to address such crime may not flow easily from such numerical summations of complex and emotional events. Qualitative research uses case studies and interviews with offenders, criminal justice personnel, witnesses, and others to fill in crucial details not captured by a percentage or number. Such approaches can address some data concerns. The dynamics of a conflict situation may involve the ongoing relationship issues of the participants, the setting and time of day, the use or influence of drugs or alcohol or both, the presence and subsequent threat or use of weapons, and the *audience* presence or interaction.

Mixed methods that combine aspects of quantitative and qualitative research have also yielded useful information to both describe homicide and other violent crime and to help

The *Los Angeles Times* reported serious errors in UCR crime reporting by the Los Angeles County Sheriff's Office as well as the LAPD. The report resulted from independent investigations of the agencies conducted after the newspaper discovered that the LAPD had misclassified 1,200 violent crimes as minor crimes in 2013 and reported that the city had experienced an 11% overall decrease in violent crime. LAPD Police Chief Charlie Beck acknowledged the errors and explained that the agency realized its mistake "in coding the most difficult crime category under the FBI's system."

Both agencies explain that they use this type of crime data to examine trends and to allocate resources in their patrol. They also hold officers accountable when crime rates rise in their districts. Many experts assert that this type of pressure on commanders has led to numerous problems with data reporting in agencies across the country.

Source: Poston & Rubin (2014).

suggest methods to address such crime. While most studies examine the effect of variables individually, attention has turned to examination of the interactive effects of significant elements of homicide events. This may take the form of examining offense pathways in homicide offenders (Crabbe, Decoene, & Vertommen, 2008). This view joins psychological concepts underlying the offense and characteristics of the homicide offender in casting the homicide as a process that develops over time.

Miethe and Regoeczi (2004) examined homicide situations using qualitative comparative analysis (QCA) to assess the structural context of homicide events. Using a significant sample in several major cities, they also investigated the process features in homicides. This approach is beneficial and further bridges the gap between the succinct yet limited summary provided by quantitative counting of correlates to homicide and the sometimes anecdotal case study of individual events. Relatively large samples with complex variable interactions can be modeled using QCA, which permits a qualitatively better understanding of the event.

DATA CHALLENGES

Evidence-based policies and practices obviously must rely on data—the evidence. How reliable is the information on violence and homicide in the United States? We feel confident that the majority of homicides get counted in American society. Murder is taken quite seriously. People notice when someone is missing. Media coverage of such incidents has the ability to keep focus on an unresolved investigation or case.

At the same time, we know that, for example, some child murders may not be accurately counted due to lack of evidence resulting in misclassification. This can be true with so-called medical murder cases as well. So too, many vulnerable victims may disappear (such as prostitutes or illegal immigrants) or may be miscategorized, such as elderly victims of homicide thought to have died of natural causes. Such missing or incomplete data are problematic (Riedel & Regoeczi, 2004).

The UCR, SHR, and NIBRS all suffer some level of inaccuracy. While the gathered data are comprehensive, they suffer from several limitations. First, the data represent only crimes reported to law enforcement. Many crimes are never reported to officials, for various reasons. Some people fear retribution, some want to handle the matter themselves, some do not want to trouble police with seemingly trivial crimes, or they believe the police will not do anything about their report. Second, of those crimes reported, the FBI currently uses what is known as the hierarchy rule for UCR reported crime. This means that only the most serious offense within an incident reported to local law enforcement will be tabulated in the UCR. Therefore, if during the course of a murder, the offender stole a car, broke into a home, kidnapped the eventual victim of the homicide, and also raped her, the UCR will only count the murder. However, if the subject is caught, he will likely be charged with all the various crimes, and these will be tabulated in the UCR as cases cleared by arrest. A third problem is the UCR providing only crime data by certain groupings and not by individual community. The use of such aggregate reports in policy formulation is currently necessary but must be used with a cautionary note.

The National Center for Health Statistics of the Centers for Disease Control and Prevention compiles information submitted by medical examiners and gleaned from death certificates. This is a great source of information for researchers regarding victim information, but the NCHS data offer no information about offenders or circumstances of the homicide. Some level of confidence in the information comes from a general convergence of the data from these official sources.

Newspaper accounts of incidents are also used to examine the circumstances of and participants in homicides. Content analysis of law enforcement agency reports and court records are used in this way, too. The lack of uniform procedures among thousands of jurisdictions, agencies, and news outlets is another reminder of the weakness of the available data. The challenges noted in this section are magnified in many cross-national comparisons of homicide and other crimes in countries without a robust data collection structure.

Another serious challenge to the confidence in official data is the occasional instances of intentional misrepresentation of crime statistics. An agency may feel the pressure to show effectiveness through numbers. In one year, an agency administrator may point to declining crime numbers and claim the department is responsible. In a year when the numbers are not favorable, the same administrator may direct the public's attention to the economy, immigration, or some other false or misleading issue as the culprit behind a crime increase. The fact is that many factors are involved in the frequency of any crime. In the same vein, many factors are involved in arrest clearance, and quite a few are beyond the control of police (Roberts, 2015). Given these facts, the simplistic assessment of an agency's effectiveness based on the clearance rate is problematic at best.

SUMMARY

The National Crime Victimization Survey (United States Department of Justice, 2017) showed an increase in violent crime experienced by those 12 or older from 2.7 million in 2015 to 2.9 million in 2016. The report goes on to note however,

> There was no statistically significant change in the rate of overall violent crime from 2015 (18.6 victimizations per 1,000 persons age 12 or older) to 2016 (19.7 per 1,000). There was also no statistically significant difference in the rate of serious violence, which excludes simple assault, from 2015 (6.8 per 1,000) to 2016 (6.6 per 1,000). (p. 2)

Crime had been in a 20-year decline in the United States. The results mark a two-year increase in such crimes. Whether this ends the trend of reduction, signals persistent increases, or shows a *new normal* is yet to be seen. Many metropolitan areas have experienced the increases where others have not. Determining the dynamics of why one community experiences more violent crime than another is challenging. Our response to homicide becomes more effective due to the improving ability to detect homicides and accurately measure and report the circumstances surrounding such events and the elements involved.

The clearance of homicide cases has declined as a percentage over the last 40 to 50 years. Some see this as counterintuitive given the apparent increased reliance on technology and forensic improvements. A significant portion of unsolved cases involve stranger homicide. When hearing *stranger homicide*, a number of people immediately conjure thoughts of lurking serial killers. In fact, most of the stranger killings are cases resulting from confrontational violence or are gang-related. These are at least partly attributed to gang violence where participants do not know one another but believe they have opposing gang affiliations.

Sources of information on homicide range from narrative accounts of participants, newspaper stories, police reports, and the more focused official reports compiled by the FBI, the CDC, and other agencies. Each source provides important information to help us understand homicide, investigate the criminal incidents of homicide, and formulate policies and programs to address the

causes. Throughout the book, we will note the results of various studies and ongoing measurement activities to help illustrate the concepts and support insights or theories.

Concerns exist about missing or inaccurate data. Some inaccurate classification of deaths occur based on lack of evidence to support identifying a death as a criminal homicide. In a significant percentage of murder cases, the offender is unknown, and this leaves police and researchers without important information. Improvements in data gathering include developing strategies to encourage states and individual agencies to contribute information to the Supplemental Homicide Report.

KEY TERMS

Murder 12
Clearances 13
Uniform Crime Report
  (UCR) 13
Manslaughter 14
Excusable homicide 14

Justifiable homicide 14
Supplemental Homicide
  Report (SHR) 19
National Incident-Based
  Reporting System
  (NIBRS) 19

National Violent Death
  Reporting System
  (NVDRS) 19
National Center for Health
  Statistics (NCHS) 19
Intimate partner homicide 24

DISCUSSION QUESTIONS

1. What are the sources of homicide information?
2. Can unofficial sources of information be helpful to researchers?
3. What are the limitations of the various national crime data sources?
4. Describe and discuss the effects that homicide and violence data have on forming public policy.

5. What role does research have in understanding and reducing crime and homicide?
6. What does it mean to have a UCR clearance in a homicide case?
7. What improvements are needed in data collection to improve the accuracy and completeness of the data?

TRY THIS

Locate web sources that provide statistics on violent death in the United States. As a researcher, think about how you would use the information you find to support a public policy to address homicide prevention.

Visit the homicides page of Our World in Data at https://ourworldindata.org/homicides. Scroll through the website and examine contemporary and historical data visualization of homicide information. Discuss the nature of the sources of data.

3

MURDER BY THE NUMBERS

"A single death is a tragedy; a million deaths is a statistic."

—Attributed to Joseph Stalin or a French diplomat

"Facts are stubborn things, but statistics are pliable."

—Mark Twain

CHAPTER OUTLINE

Student Learning Outcomes

Students will be able to:

- discuss different factors measured in homicide situations.

- explain the benefits of knowing homicide statistics.

- analyze the limitations of statistics and their application.

- evaluate the influence of statistics in law and policy development.

- list challenges in comparing homicide data to other countries.

INTRODUCTION

It is not overstating to say that crime is tremendously important in this or any society. Whether or not you are directly affected by being a victim (or perpetrator) of crime, you are impacted in some way. Your quality of life may be lessened if the area where you live or work is beset by ongoing crime. The value of your home and your insurance rates may be impacted. If you have children, the choice of schools and the afterschool options may be less than desirable.

To know what to do about social issues and problems, we must first know what we know. Academic research helps us in this regard. The design of law or programs should proceed from empirical observations, though this is not always the case. Examining homicide may be done from many angles with different purposes in mind. For example, we may examine victim-offender dynamics and relations; demographic and societal criteria, such as age, race, ethnicity, gender, and economic or social status; and factors such as motives or weapons employed. The demographics of homicides have remained relatively constant for some time. In this chapter, we provide several examples of recent statistics as well as **trends** over time from the Bureau of Justice Statistics and various sources.

Access to data is obviously important. Researchers, policymakers, writers, and students of the social sciences all have a clear need for current information, properly developed or gathered. But it is also the case that data should be actively *provided*. The movement to disseminate crime statistics and analysis has been under way for some time through government publications and academic journals and conference proceedings. The effort found a boon through the Internet and the ubiquitous presence of information portals in our daily lives.

Police departments use agency webpages as well as neighborhood watch groups, reports, and efforts through the media to provide information to the public. Criminal justice agencies increasingly have websites and other forms of social media that perform the functions of education, recruitment, asking the public for information, and providing statistics to the public. Many agency sites also possess interactive crime mapping in real time. News organizations have aggregated stories and information from official sources to provide timelines and big-picture information to the public who may see only local impact rather than the context of broader issues in society.

The relevance of data regarding all murders and aggravated assaults may give an overall big-picture sense of violence (see Figures 3.1, 3.2, and 3.3 later in the chapter). The same data must be disaggregated to be helpful as we consider different types of murder. Knowing that most murderers are male is informative. Knowing the age groupings, ethnicity and race breakdowns, and the settings where homicides occur provides critical information to begin a discussion of crime reduction strategies as well as possible insights for investigators conducting the retroactive investigation of a murder.

The statistics compiled by the FBI indicate the following:

- In 2017, the estimated number of murders in the nation was 17,284. This was a .2 percent decrease from the 2016 estimate of 17,413, an increase from the 2015 figure of 15,883, and a raw number increase from 2014, when the estimate was 14,164.

- There were 5.3 murders per 100,000 people in 2017. The murder rate fell from 5.4 percent in 2016, compared with the 2017 rate. The murder rate was down from the rates in 2007 (5.7) and 1998 (6.3).

- Of the 2017 estimated number of murders in the United States, 45.9 percent were reported in the South, 22.6 percent were reported in the Midwest, 20.2 percent were reported in the West, and 11.3 percent were reported in the Northeast. (Federal Bureau of Investigation, 2018)

Notably, the projected drop in homicides for 2018 appeared likely to become official. While the FBI numbers will not be published until after this edition of the book goes to print, their report of 2017 homicide dropping is poised to be followed by a second year of reductions, according to a report from the Brennan Center for Justice (Grawert & Kimble, 2018). The public policy think tank received figures from America's 30 largest cities, which indicated a nearly 6 percent drop. Lower homicide numbers were large in cities such as Chicago and San Francisco—even Baltimore.

VICTIMS—WHO DIES

No one can or should contend that homicide **rates** in the United States should be of little concern. While the rate is roughly half of what

it was 20 years ago, it remains a crime that takes many victims and impacts many more in society. The young, the old, and the middle aged may all be the victims of murder. But are they all equally at risk of violent assault or death? The answer to this is a qualified *no*. The numbers that represent the **demographic characteristics of victims** reflect some of the dimensions noted previously. But the relationships between the victim and offender, the day-to-day habits of both, the location and time of day, and other people in the area may all be part of the confluence of factors that culminate in a lethal event.

The personal and economic cost to individual victims and society from crime in the United States is significant. The National Institute of

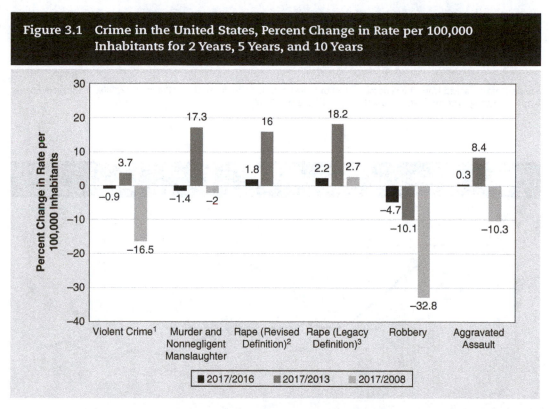

Figure 3.1   Crime in the United States, Percent Change in Rate per 100,000 Inhabitants for 2 Years, 5 Years, and 10 Years

[1] The violent crime figures include the offenses of murder, rape (legacy definition), robbery, and aggravated assault.

[2] The figures shown for the offense of rape (revised definition) were estimated using the revised Uniform Crime Reporting Program's (UCR) definition of rape. See data declaration for further explanation.

[3] The figures shown for the offense of rape (legacy definition) were estimated using the legacy UCR definition of rape. See data declaration for further explanation.

Source: Federal Bureau of Investigation, United States Department of Justice, *Crime in the United States, 2017.* Retrieved from: https://ucr.fbi.gov/crime-in-the-u.s/2017/crime-in-the-u.s.-2017

Figure 3.2   Aggravated Assault Rate, 1998–2017

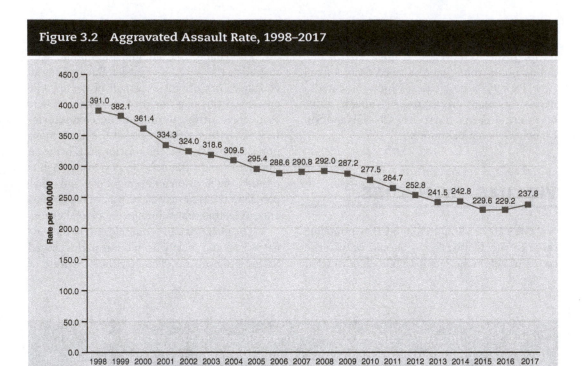

Source: Data obtained from the Federal Bureau of Investigation. *Crime in the United States, 2017, Table 1.* Retrieved from: https://ucr.fbi.gov/crime-in-the-u.s/2017/crime-in-the-u.s.-2017

Figure 3.3   Homicide Rate, 1990–2018 (est.)

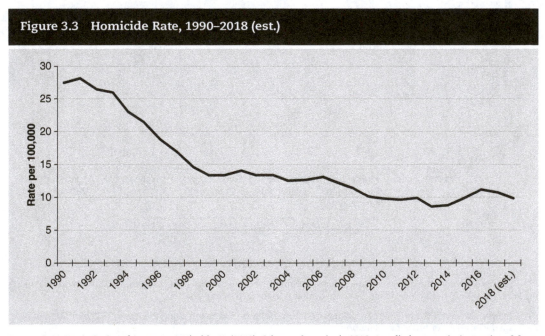

Source: Grawert, A. C., Onyekwere, A., & Kimble, K. (2018). *Crime and murder in 2018: A preliminary analysis.* Retrieved from https://www.brennancenter.org/analysis/crime-murder-2018

Justice, among others, has published studies detailing these annual and ongoing costs from crime. Injuries result in medical and health care costs that can last a lifetime for a victim. These costs may also be borne by society as a whole through taxpayer support of indigent victims. The criminal justice system, as well, expends much of its resources on the attempt to prevent crime in addition to the costs through personnel and other resources to quell ongoing criminal activity and investigate and bring to justice criminal offenders. Understanding the role of the victim in a criminal event is the province of a field of study known as victimology.

While victim impact knowledge has been developing for decades, we continue to see the benefits of carefully considering the social and structural aspects of crime, including costs to society as well as effects on offenders. Several of the theories taken up in the chapter on theoretical understanding of homicide address some of the direct concerns considered in victimology. Two of these are routine activities theory and lifestyle theory. Routine activities theory sees many predatory crimes as stemming from a confluence of a *suitable target*, an absence of *capable guardians*, and the attention of a *motivated offender*. Lifestyle theory highlights the high-risk lifestyle of associates, alcohol and drugs, and criminal activity as ways to put oneself at greater risk of harm including homicide. The two approaches guide some of our understanding about the actions of people who would be victims.

Demographic and Relationship Information

Sex

Homicide victims are overwhelmingly male, and this probably surprises few if any people. Table 3.1 provides a look at victims and offenders by race, sex, and ethnicity. In violent crime, with the exception of rape, both victims and offenders are mostly male. Media coverage has traditionally been more intense when a woman is murdered at the hands of a man. Even with the ever-present dynamic of media outlets focusing on the sensational, the statistical fact is that murder is largely a man's game. What statistics also tell us, however, is that there has been an incremental increase in crimes committed *by* girls and women. In 2017, 12.5% of those arrested for murder and non-negligent manslaughter were women, and 23.3% of those arrested for aggravated assault were women (FBI, 2018). In 2002, females arrested for murder constituted 7% of known offenders, 17.7% for aggravated assault (FBI, 2003). This includes crimes of violence and murders perpetrated by females in American society.

Twenty-five years ago, Baker, Gartner, and Pampel (1990) talked about the numerical fact that

> in most societies, the highest rates of violent victimization are suffered by those with low status, little power, and few economic resources. Females' probabilities of being murdered are a notable exception to this pattern: despite women's deficiencies in social and economic power, their chances of homicide victimization are almost invariably lower than men's risks. (p. 593)

While dated, this statement holds true regarding the differences between the potential for men and women to be the victim of a criminal homicide in the United States. The question is what explains a woman being less likely to be murdered than a man? Being the *weaker sex* is countered by women's changing roles in societies in many parts of the world. Women have made gains in social and economic domains vis-à-vis men. Some patriarchal effect may still result in fewer women being killed by criminal homicide than men. Women are victims of violent crimes, though research continues to show that a woman in our changing world is still less likely to be a victim of murder than a man. But it is important to note that in the category of intimate partner homicide, discussed later in the textbook, women are far more likely to be killed by their partners than men.

In 2017, there were 11,862 male victims of homicide reported in the Uniform Crime Report (UCR), and 3,222 female victims. In 2016, those numbers were 11,821 and 3,208 respectively.

Table 3.1 Race, Sex, and Ethnicity of Victim by Race, Sex, and Ethnicity of Offender, 2017

Race of victim	Race of offender					Sex of offender			Ethnicity of offender		
	Total	White	Black or African American	Other[1]	Unknown	Male	Female	Unknown	Hispanic or Latino	Not Hispanic or Latino	Unknown
White	3,567	2,861	576	59	71	3,144	352	71	758	1,600	1,209
Black or African American	2,970	264	2,627	17	62	2,598	310	62	104	1,767	1,099
Other race[1]	257	72	35	144	6	226	25	6	23	160	74
Unknown race	108	55	25	3	25	78	5	25	4	25	79

Sex of victim	Race of offender					Sex of offender			Ethnicity of offender		
	Total	White	Black or African American	Other[1]	Unknown	Male	Female	Unknown	Hispanic or Latino	Not Hispanic or Latino	Unknown
Male	4,862	2,074	2,523	153	112	4,235	515	112	607	2,567	1,688
Female	1,932	1,123	715	67	27	1,733	172	27	279	960	693
Unknown sex	108	55	25	3	25	78	5	25	3	25	80

Ethnicity of victim	Race of offender					Sex of offender			Ethnicity of offender		
	Total	White	Black or African American	Other[1]	Unknown	Male	Female	Unknown	Hispanic or Latino	Not Hispanic or Latino	Unknown
Hispanic or Latino	824	668	126	10	20	748	56	20	583	211	30
Not Hispanic or Latino	2,886	1,103	1,626	118	39	2,560	287	39	211	2,594	81
Unknown	3,192	1,481	1,511	95	105	2,738	349	105	95	747	2,350

[1] Includes American Indian or Alaska Native, Asian, and Native Hawaiian or Other Pacific Islander.

Note: This table is based on incidents where some information about the offender is known by law enforcement; therefore, when the offender age, sex, race, and ethnicity are all reported as unknown, these data are excluded from the table.

Source: Federal Bureau of Investigation. *Crime in the United States, 2017, Table 1.* Retrieved from: https://ucr.fbi.gov/crime-in-the-u.s/2017/crime-in-the-u.s.-2017

Race/Ethnic Origins

The majority of murders are intraracial. That is, both the victim and the offender are of the same race. This is not apparent in either the news media coverage decided on by news outlets or in the fictional crime dramas of television and movies. An African American, for example, is disproportionately more likely to be the victim of a homicide. An African American is also more likely to be the victim of a violent assault.

Hispanics as a demographic segment of the population have grown and are projected to do so for the foreseeable future. Solving and clearing homicide cases involving minority citizens was accorded less attention than those involving Caucasians. Roberts (2011) commented on how effective an arrest can be in bringing a sense of justice for both the victim's family and the larger community. An important consideration in the investigation and solving of homicide in minority communities or of minority citizens is the potential for improved levels of trust between law enforcement and the community members.

The immigrant experience is shared in the family histories of the majority of people living in America. The initial period of arrival within the country is filled with many challenges. Sadly, one of the challenges is being more vulnerable to victimization, including homicide. Often immigrants are victimized by people outside their ethnic or racial background. Some aspects of an immigrant's background and his or her cultural beliefs may make him or her more likely to be a target. Being a minority or immigrant does not mean that an individual will be a victim, but there is historic evidence to point to increased likelihood or vulnerability.

In explaining why whites are less likely to be victims of homicide than blacks, many researchers identify the ability of whites to live in "better" neighborhoods, away from crime. Whites can be segregated from blacks by seeking out these living situations. The *concentrated advantage* and, conversely, the *group disadvantage* may result from the continuous segregation of blacks and whites in U.S. society as well as the separation of those in differing socioeconomic classes.

Age

A common misperception about victimization is that the elderly are victimized at a higher rate than other age groups. Some people may see this as natural or logical since we assume people are more vulnerable to physical attack as they get older. This notion of vulnerability to violent victimization is appealing but does not account for the realistic intrusion of the general habits (routine activities) of various demographic groups. Older Americans are not out at public locations during many of the hours when, for example, robberies occur. As illustrated by Figure 3.4, more young people are involved in homicide as both victim and offender than relatively older Americans.

Crimes such as theft often occur when a criminal knows the behavior and schedule of a homeowner, for instance. The thief strikes when the person is unaware or absent (routine activities theory). Another example would be when the elderly isolate themselves, it increases the chance for them to be victimized. If older persons live with their family, they are less likely to be victims of crimes such as theft and homicide (except perhaps at the hands of family members). Of course, this is true for people of any age, not only the elderly. One reason for this is that most offenders do not want to risk confronting multiple people at once.

Socioeconomic Category

The state of current large-scale statistics gathering on the socioeconomic status of victims and offenders of homicide provide us some, if not complete, insight to who dies by homicide. Economic data for the United States as well as regionally and locally may provide insight regarding some crimes or criminogenic settings or conditions. Similarly, data regarding residential and business starts give a sense of the robustness of a local economy. Some researchers view poverty as a leading factor in homicide (Pridemore, 2011). We must remember that economic deprivation is one of a constellation of factors that increases a person's potential of being a homicide victim.

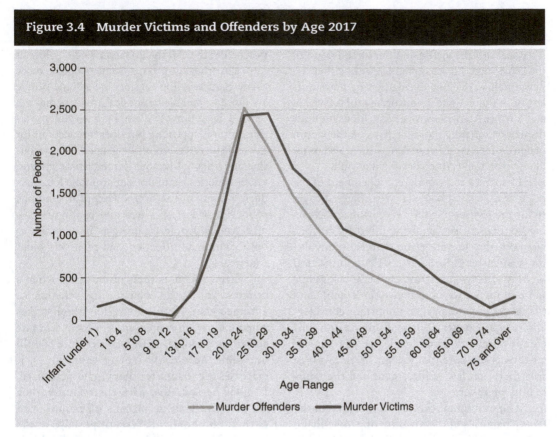

Figure 3.4 Murder Victims and Offenders by Age 2017

Source: Federal Bureau of Investigation. *Crime in the United States, 2017, Table 1.* Retrieved from: https://ucr.fbi.gov/crime-in-the-u.s/2017/crime-in-the-u.s.-2017

Victim–Offender Situations

As previously mentioned, most homicides involve people known to each other, even if only briefly. A much smaller portion of pure stranger homicides occur. Of those murders categorized in statistics as stranger homicide, many are labeled this way because the offender is not known. In other words, the killer and victim *may* have known each other, but in the absence of a charged suspect, official reporting cannot reflect the assumption of a relationship or acquaintance. Figure 3.5 is a chart depicting **homicide circumstances** organized by known victim-and-offender relationship, and Table 3.2 shows murder circumstances by relationship.

Medical Advances and Technology

Advances in medical knowledge, technology, and training account for the survival of many intended victims of homicide and harm. While this may well have occurred to you, the magnitude of the number of lives saved through increasingly sophisticated interventions is notable. The arrival of penicillin in 1928 began to almost immediately save lives. The quality and volume of the intense training that paramedics, emergency medical technicians (EMTs), firefighters, and police officers have received over the last 30 years has resulted in countless lives being saved. Nine-one-one telephone systems provide fast access to summoning professional medical assistance, and the ubiquitous presence of cellular telephones makes that all but assured except in the most remote locations. The lives saved are not specifically documented as such. We must intuit that the trends in aggravated assault and aggravated battery are indicative of a number of potential murders that did not come to pass. This said, the relationship is not linear. Many aggravated assaults or

Figure 3.5 Victim/Offender Situations, 2017

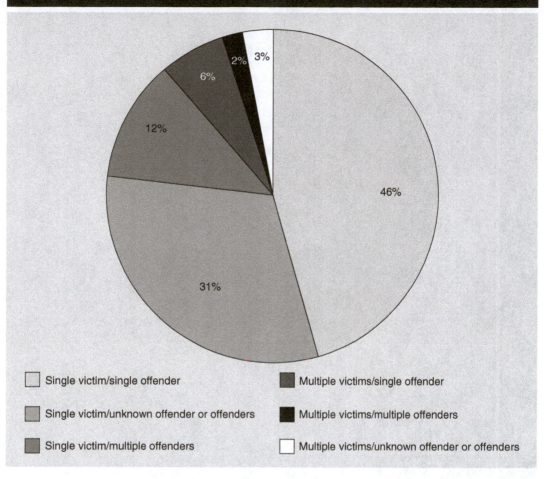

Single victim/single offender

Multiple victims/single offender

Single victim/unknown offender or offenders

Multiple victims/multiple offenders

Single victim/multiple offenders

Multiple victims/unknown offender or offenders

Source: Federal Bureau of Investigation. *Crime in the United States, 2017, Table 10.* Retrieved from: https://ucr.fbi.gov/crime-in-the-u.s/2017/crime-in-the-u.s.-2017

batteries were not intended to be homicides. Also, some research questions to what extent medical advances and training have saved lives given that many shootings are virtually immediately lethal, which precludes the ability of such training and technology to come into play (Eckberg, 2015).

OFFENDERS— CATEGORIES AND DEMOGRAPHICS

Who are they? Comparing the rates of homicide, we find significant variation in the **demographic characteristics of offenders**. The majority of

homicide offenders are male. This **pattern** has been stable over time in official records. This is true from country to country as well.

As mentioned, blacks are overrepresented as both victims and perpetrators of homicide. Juveniles and young persons are also overrepresented as homicide offenders. We remind you that this correlation is not the same as causation. Being male, young, or black does not mean someone will kill or be killed in a criminal homicide event.

We have also noted that girls and women have increased as a percentage of those committing homicide and other violent crimes. The rate of arrested female offenders, including juveniles, has increased in the last few decades. Females have always been seen as the *gentler sex*, and

Table 3.2 Murder Circumstances by Relationship[1], 2017

Circumstances	Total murder victims	Husband	Wife	Mother	Father	Son	Daughter	Brother	Sister	Other family	Acquaintance	Friend	Boyfriend	Girlfriend	Neighbor	Employee	Employer	Stranger	Unknown
Total	15,129	110	549	169	186	253	179	98	27	296	2,999	431	181	488	114	17	6	1,469	7,557
Felony type total:	2,236	8	38	15	8	28	19	4	4	43	561	72	10	30	21	1	2	378	994
Rape	18	0	1	0	0	0	2	0	0	0	3	2	0	0	1	0	0	9	0
Robbery	680	0	1	1	0	0	0	0	1	4	154	16	1	0	7	0	0	175	320
Burglary	90	0	2	1	0	0	0	0	0	1	23	5	1	0	3	0	0	24	30
Larceny-theft	20	0	1	1	0	0	0	0	0	2	1	3	0	1	1	0	0	5	5
Motor vehicle theft	31	0	0	0	0	0	0	0	0	0	8	0	0	2	1	0	0	5	14
Arson	31	1	1	0	0	1	0	0	0	2	10	2	1	1	1	0	0	0	11
Prostitution and commercialized vice	15	0	0	0	0	0	0	0	0	1	6	1	0	1	0	0	0	3	3
Other sex offenses	8	0	0	1	0	0	2	0	0	0	2	0	0	0	0	0	0	2	2
Narcotic drug laws	533	0	0	0	0	3	1	0	0	3	201	28	0	1	1	0	0	44	249
Gambling	10	0	0	0	0	0	0	0	0	0	5	0	1	0	0	0	0	1	2
Other-not specified	800	7	32	11	8	24	14	3	3	28	148	15	6	24	6	1	2	110	358
Suspected felony type	153	0	4	3	1	3	2	1	0	1	23	2	1	5	0	0	0	13	94

Offense	Total																	
Other than felony type total:	6,663	75	378	99	136	154	112	70	17	192	1,755	277	148	347	71	13	4	638	2,177
Romantic triangle	107	2	7	0	0	1	0	0	0	1	70	0	7	7	1	0	0	7	4
Child killed by babysitter	32	0	0	0	0	0	1	0	0	3	27	0	0	0	0	0	0	0	1
Brawl due to influence of alcohol	118	1	7	1	3	4	1	2	0	5	33	18	5	7	1	0	0	16	14
Brawl due to influence of narcotics	129	1	4	3	1	7	3	1	2	1	47	9	0	0	0	0	0	10	40
Argument over money or property	199	0	2	4	10	0	0	6	0	12	106	18	0	3	10	0	0	12	16
Other arguments	3,224	52	255	57	94	44	20	47	8	116	946	155	114	269	46	11	3	294	693
Gangland killings	369	0	0	0	0	0	0	0	0	0	43	7	0	0	0	0	0	30	289
Juvenile gang killings	381	0	0	0	0	0	0	0	0	0	55	1	0	0	0	0	0	27	298
Institutional killings	14	0	0	0	0	0	0	0	0	0	10	0	0	0	0	0	0	2	2
Sniper attack	2	0	0	0	0	0	0	0	0	0	0	0	0	1	1	0	0	1	0
Other-not specified	2,088	19	103	34	28	98	87	14	7	54	418	69	61	61	12	2	1	239	820
Unknown	6,077	27	129	52	41	68	46	23	6	60	660	80	106	106	22	3	0	440	4,292

[1] Relationship is that of victim to offender.

Note: The relationship categories of husband and wife include both common-law and ex-spouses. The categories of mother, father, sister, brother, son, and daughter include step-parents, stepchildren, and stepsiblings. The category of acquaintance includes homosexual relationships and the composite category of other known to victim.

Source: Federal Bureau of Investigation. Crime in the United States, 2017, Table 10. Retrieved from: https://ucr.fbi.gov/crime-in-the-u.s/2017/crime-in-the-u.s.-2017

this may have resulted frequently in getting off lightly in arrests, charging, convictions, and sentencing (Cauffman, 2008). This patriarchal effect no longer stems the rising female offender rates. Popular culture and the rise of feminism are also components considered by various researchers. Female prison populations have risen as a proportion, so it calls into question whether judges overall are still being lenient on female offenders.

Through dramatic and extensive media coverage, we see celebrity cases of wealthy or well-known people, such as star athletes O. J. Simpson and Aaron Hernandez and Drew Peterson, who was a police sergeant, involved in murder cases. The majority of those accused of homicide, however, are neither famous nor wealthy. Violent crime is not confined to the lower socioeconomic classes, but its presence there is more frequently felt.

LOCATION, LOCATION, LOCATION

Most crime statistics identify homicide and other crime locations as having occurred either inside or outside. Not surprisingly, we find that most intimate partner and other domestic violence homicides occur indoors, in the home. Most confrontational homicides erupt in a setting such as a bar or outdoors, perhaps at a gathering of some sort. Numbers of homicides also differ by community size—urban, suburban, or rural, larger rather than smaller cities. As with many lists, we are fascinated by the top cities where the rate of actual homicides is highest. Remember that rate accounts for the population of a city or metropolitan area.

The more densely populated cities and areas have long been observed as having the highest crime rates. Significant crime increases can be traced back to the shift in America from an agrarian economy, with a majority of residents living in rural settings, to the industrial revolution, when large numbers of people moved in a relatively short period of time into cities. Cities grew at a rapid pace and were unprepared for the challenges of improving infrastructure, public-health services, and notably here, adequate responses to the crime surge that came with many people living in close proximity and in difficult physical circumstances.

The statistics on murder, particularly in cities, are at times hard to unravel. Jurisdictions overlap, statistical-reporting sources do not always agree on numbers, and the demographics of race and poverty can confound the contextual analysis of homicide offending. What Figure 3.6, prepared by the Pew Research Center, illustrates is that, as a rate, smaller cities can be ranked higher on a list of jurisdictions with the top homicide numbers. Based on homicide numbers reported to the FBI's UCR Program for cities with a population of at least 100,000, the highest homicide rate per 100,000 population in 2017 were Baton Rouge (38.3 per 100,000); New Orleans (39.5 per 100,000); Detroit (39.8 per 100,000); Baltimore (55.8 per 100,000); and at number one—St. Louis, with 66.1 murders per 100,000 people. The cities noted in Figure 3.6 are familiar to most people and may evoke an image of impoverished areas of urban crowding. This does not accurately depict the entire areas of these communities, but it does tie into several of the theories you will be introduced to in the chapter insets "Why Would They Do It?" For each of these, a chronic history of economic disadvantage for a significant portion of the populace is important to understanding limited options and poor choices made by people who may commit violent acts.

Murder and other crime rates are also gathered by state and by region of the country. FBI figures of numbers and rates for states and regional differences in crime for 2017 show the following:

- The South, the most populous region of the nation, accounted for 40.8 percent of all violent crimes in 2017. Lesser volumes of violent crime were recorded in the West at 25.5 percent, the Midwest at 20.2 percent, and the Northeast at 13.4 percent.

- In 2017, 45.9 percent of the nation's estimated total number of murders occurred in the South. The Midwest had 22.6 percent of murders, followed by the West with 20.2 percent and the Northeast with 11.3 percent.

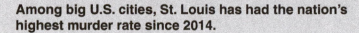

Figure 3.6   City with the Highest Number of Murders per 100,000 People

Among big U.S. cities, St. Louis has had the nation's highest murder rate since 2014.

*City with the **highest** number of murders per 100,000 people*

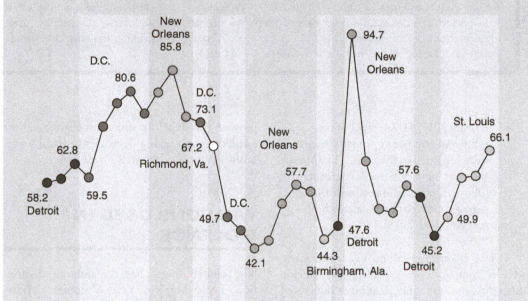

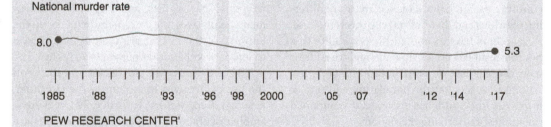

PEW RESEARCH CENTER'

Note: Excludes cities with fewer than 100,000 residents. Includes homicide and non-negligent manslaughter.

Source: Despite recent violence, Chicago is far from the U.S. 'murder capital,' Pew Research Center Fact Tank, Washington, DC (November, 2018), http://www.pewresearch.org/fact-tank/2018/11/13/despite-recent-violence-chicago-far-from-u-s-murder-capital/

The city of Chicago has long been recognized as one that has experienced relatively high homicide rates. Many researchers have focused on the city as a case study for the underlying causes of homicide. The Chicago Tribune has recently embarked on a project to detail all homicides in Chicago over a 60 year period. The newspaper filed a Freedom of Information Act request to the Chicago Police Department for homicide reports from 1958 through 2015. They used this data to analyze homicide trends in the city over several decades. They continue to track and cover the homicides as they occur through their "Crime in Chicagoland Homicide Tracker" which replaced the former "RedEye Tracker" in 2015. The Tribune has been cited by numerous politicians, researchers, and policymakers who study the homicide trends in Chicago.

- During 2017, 41.9 percent of the estimated number of property crimes were recorded in the South. The West was next highest with 27.0 percent, followed by the Midwest with 19.6 percent, and the Northeast with 11.4 percent. (FBI, 2018)

Crime is more common in larger cities, and it has long been observed that the homicide rate in the South is higher than other regions of the country. A common comparison within the United States is to examine crime rates regionally. As to the Southern penchant for settling conflict through lethal violence, there are differing opinions and theories on why this is the case. Researchers have examined the possibility of a Southern subculture of violence, and we address it in the chapter on confrontational violence. Taking into account the population and rate of homicide, the South has historically maintained the highest rate among the regions.

Our attention is often drawn to top-ten lists. This certainly includes top ten cities for crime and murder, top ten best places to live, top ten best beaches, and pretty much anything else we can think of. When it comes to crime and murder, the figures may impact a decision whether to move our family or a business to a particular community or city. On the other hand, we have to be cautious with whether crime numbers represent an anomaly in a given year of data collection or represent one particular area within a larger city with average crime rates. Rates and trends as quantitative measures do not always provide the depth of qualitative information needed when making decisions on family and business moves or the creation of policy.

WEAPONS USED IN VIOLENCE

The United States has the dubious distinction of high homicide rates. Whether a criminal homicide is committed using a firearm or another weapon, the rate of criminal homicide is high. Firearms, cutting weapons, the personal weapons—hands, fists, and feet—blunt instruments, explosives, poison, and more make up the universe of things that are used by one person to injure or kill another person (see Table 3.3).

While there are not exact numbers on the use of firearms in violent crime (Leshner, Altevogt, Lee, McCoy, & Kelley, 2013), there is ample documented evidence that firearms are used in the overwhelming number of murders (Table 3.3) and are represented significantly in suicides and accidental death and injury circumstances. Law enforcement–generated reports of crime that are submitted to the UCR Program confirm the number of incidents police are aware of (FBI, 2018). The National Crime Victimization Survey (NCVS) (as discussed in the previous chapter) provides additional confirmation of the presence of firearms in unreported acts of violence as well.

Offenders use guns to intimidate or overpower their victims in robberies, sexual assaults,

Table 3.3 Number of Murder Victims by Weapon, 2013–2017

Weapons	2013	2014	2015	2016	2017
Total	12,253	12,270	13,750	15,296	15,129
Total firearms:	8,454	8,312	9,778	11,138	10,982
Handguns	5,782	5,673	6,569	7,204	7,032
Rifles	285	258	258	378	403
Shotguns	308	264	272	261	264
Other guns	123	93	177	187	187
Firearms, type not stated	1,956	2,024	2,502	3,108	3,096
Knives or cutting instruments	1,490	1,595	1,589	1,632	1,591
Blunt objects (clubs, hammers, etc.)	428	446	450	479	467
Personal weapons (hands, fists, feet, etc.)[1]	687	682	659	669	696
Poison	11	10	8	13	13
Explosives	2	7	1	1	0
Fire	94	71	84	114	103
Narcotics	53	70	75	122	97
Drowning	4	14	14	9	8
Strangulation	85	89	99	99	88
Asphyxiation	95	102	120	93	105
Other weapons or weapons not stated	850	872	873	927	979

[1] Pushed is included in personal weapons.

Source: Federal Bureau of Investigation, United States Department of Justice, *Crime in the United States, 2018.*

and aggravated assaults and batteries. In committing homicide, it is clear that a killer armed with several firearms or a single automatic or high-capacity firearm can inflict more damage (kill more humans) than a similarly motivated offender with a knife or blunt instrument. In the tragic and now notorious example from October 2017, a man armed with 24 firearms, including more than a dozen assault-style rifles altered to fire near-automatic, fired more than 1,000 bullets at people below his 32nd-floor room at a music venue. He killed 58, and caused injuries to more than 800. The incident occurred at around 10 p.m., while the victims were enjoying the Route 91 Harvest country music festival nearby, never imagining they would be targets.

In the last several years, these are the numbers of cases where a weapon was used to commit murder:

- 2009: 13,752
- 2010: 13,164

- 2011: 12,795

- 2012: 12,765

- 2013: 12,253

- 2014: 12,270

- 2015: 13,750

- 2016: 15,296

- 2017: 15,129

(FBI, 2013, 2018)

Interestingly, the use of handguns decreased in 2010, but then increased in the years 2011 and 2012. In 2009, 6,501 handguns were used, and in 2010, it decreased to 6,115. But in 2011, the use of handguns increased to 6,251, and it increased again in 2012 to 6,371. By 2016 and 2017, the numbers of handguns used was 7,204 and 7,032 respectively (FBI, 2018).

The use of the weapons rifles, shotguns, blunt objects, body parts (feet, hands, etc.), poison, explosives, fire, narcotics, and strangulation vary from year to year but account for far fewer deaths than firearms, even taken all together. Handguns have continued to be used most often as a murder weapon. Poison and explosives were the least used in the years 2008 through 2012 (FBI, 2013). The range of methods or items used by one person to kill another is almost limitless. In a case from 2008, Murat St. Hilaire was found dead in his New York City apartment as a result of being stabbed in the side of his head with a corkscrew. He was found lying face up in his bedroom. While the police located the corkscrew at the scene of the crime, they were unable to find his killer. The weapon, apparently one of convenience, can be helpful by determining who may have been allowed into a victim's residence.

Discussions about firearms in American society frequently go quickly from an objective recitation of numbers of firearms and the potential consequences of widespread availability of guns to emotional rhetoric regarding views on the right to own and use firearms in various settings. We note at this point that there are more firearms than there are adults in the United States and that guns may be obtained rather easily through legal or illegal means. Academic research has arrived at what are sometimes contradictory conclusions. Some research may suggest that the availability of firearms to law-abiding citizens reduces crime, while other studies show the ready access to guns increases violent or lethal responses to conflict situations. Still, other research seems to support the contention that firearms neither increase nor decrease crime, including murder. Various groups utilize statistics to support a position or attempt to educate or persuade the public, such as in comparing gun-related deaths and auto fatalities.

Hogan and Kleck (1999) examined the instances of gun owners becoming offenders. The authors found a correlation between gun ownership and the use of a gun to commit homicide. The debate over such a correlation is not a settled one. Some quickly conclude that if one does not possess a gun, one cannot use it to kill others. Hogan and Kleck also contemplated how owning a weapon might make a person more prone to use one. Gun possession certainly allows a person the option of escalating to or simply choosing first to use this lethal device in a conflict situation. The authors in this study go on to comment on weapons as "sources of power" and their use instrumentally. Firearms are noted to provide a certain quality of being *impersonal* and *emotionally remote*. The shooting of a person is seen, in this way, as less distasteful than stabbing or bludgeoning that individual. In contemplating death by firearm, suicide and unintentional deaths are of note as well. According to the Center for Disease Control (CDC), for the year 2013, firearm deaths by homicide, suicide, and unintentional totaled 33,636. By 2017, that number had climbed to 39,773 (CDC, 2015). As a comparison, motor vehicle deaths for the year 2017 was 37,133 (National Center for Statistics and Analysis, 2018). Motor vehicle safety has gotten ever safer due largely to vehicle equipment improvements since the inception of the automobile. The ubiquitous presence of firearms gives rise to their use for either planned or spur-of-the-moment actions.

OTHER CIRCUMSTANCES

Official reports of homicide typically include the known circumstances surrounding the event. We have already mentioned that police do not always know whether a relationship existed between some victims and offenders if no offender is identified or charged. So too, not all circumstances of a homicide are known and therefore chronicled for analysis later. The public may think of robberies gone bad, intimate partner homicide, and serial killers as familiar homicide events. To be sure, these are important. However, we actually know that the single largest category of known circumstances is some type of argument. While the category of confrontational homicide is taken up in a later chapter, we draw your attention here to the magnitude of killings arising from interpersonal conflict. We also turn later to intimate partner violence and homicide as well as other interpersonal conflict that gives rise to confrontational homicide. It is important to recognize that these two categories account for the greatest number of known homicide events, far more than the unknown stranger who breaks into someone's home and commits an act of homicide.

Alcohol, drugs, and the use, abuse, and business of furnishing intoxicating substances are among the factors noted in many homicide situations. Alcohol is discussed further in the chapter on confrontational homicide, but the statistics are clear and significant in the correlation of alcohol with violent assault and murder. Alcohol is also contemplated by legislators in creating sentencing guidelines and laws and by prosecutors in making charging decisions. While a defendant may be convicted through plea agreement, bench trial, or jury trial, the charge may be mitigated somewhat in certain states by the assertion of the defendant's intoxication by some substance. When the information is available regarding drug or alcohol use, it is coded in the Supplemental Homicide Reports of the FBI. While a direct causal link may not be claimed, the involvement of alcohol and drugs in crimes and other instances of poor decision-making has been well documented.

A circumstance present in certain types of violent encounters and homicides is the presence of others, an *audience*. While we address confrontational homicide more completely in a subsequent chapter, recognize that people can be affected by others nearby when a conflict begins. The stereotypical scene of school children urging on two school yard combatants with screams of "Fight! Fight!" is familiar to everyone. This childhood dynamic is often present at parties, bars, neighborhood gatherings, sporting events, and similar settings. A group of either involved or initially disinterested people can calm a situation or restrain people poised to fight, or that same group of people can inflame the situation. Additionally, even if the audience is passive and simply there, this can affect the thought process of two potential fighters if one or both believe they need to save face in front of onlookers.

TRENDS AND PATTERNS

Trends or patterns in settings are discussed in various ways in most books or articles about homicide. Homicide rates had gone down steadily over the past 20 years in the United States, but 2016 saw an increase of 8.6% compared to the previous year. In 2017, the crimes of murder and nonnegligent manslaughter decreased from 2016 by 0.7 percent (FBI, 2018). The overall trend is promising, though the increases of recent years must be monitored to see if there is an actual trend. Much remains to be done in the effort to reduce the use of lethal violence even further. Overall violent and property crimes continue to trend downward (see Figure 3.7). There continues to be a need to build empirically grounded interventions. This makes the continued gathering of data and the improvement of data-gathering methods and techniques of analysis quite important. The following chapter will introduce you to a number of the theories often used to explain aspects of the homicide event. With that expanded discussion coming soon, it is still appropriate to say here that as far as patterns go, murder is quite often the result of an interaction between two people who are known to each other.

A pattern long known to many local-level law enforcement agencies, and now receiving increased research attention, is that victims and offenders in the homicide dyad often share a number of similarities. Deadman and MacDonald (2004) discussed the correlation between criminal behavior and being a victim. Crime victims can become murderers. Deadman and MacDonald spent time examining how some individuals became murderers after they had been victimized. This includes the possible justifications of the victim turned murderer, at least in their view. Rape victims, for example, may feel justified in murdering their rapist, or robbery victims may kill the robber. This can also reflect a view of exacting *justice* for themselves when they believe the criminal justice system has failed. More commonly examined regarding the victim–offender musical chairs is the view that the two groups are not distinct (Reid & Sullivan, 2012).

As we step back and look at the pattern of overlap between victims and offenders, it is academically interesting and practically vital that we grasp the various aspects of such comparisons.

There are unavoidable overlaps in the individuals who are victims and offenders (Zavala & Spohn, 2013). Offenders do not deserve to be victims. They rightfully deserve to be held accountable through the criminal justice system for any crimes committed but not to be a homicide victim on the street. Victims, for their part, should not become perpetrators as a result of their experiences. These are blurred lines that can dissolve a conversation quickly from its focus on the dynamics of the role switching and what can be done about it.

Something inherent in the act of committing crime or experiencing victimization critically changes the individual and their life circumstances to such a degree that it alters their likelihood of future involvement in crime either as a victim or as an offender. (Reid & Sullivan, 2012, p. 330)

There are unique risk markers: Low self-control, propensity for risk-taking, and

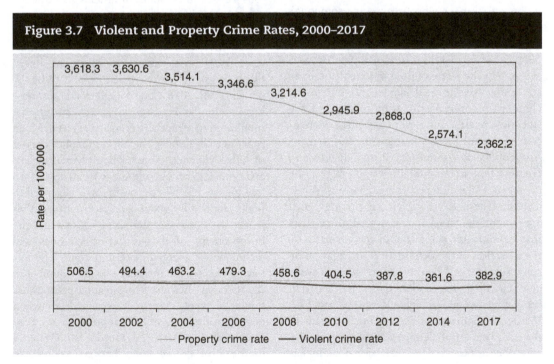

Figure 3.7   Violent and Property Crime Rates, 2000–2017

Source: Compiled from FBI UCR statistics, 1990–2012, Federal Bureau of Investigation, United States Department of Justice.

Figure 3.8 Trends in School-Associated Violent Deaths, 1992–2015

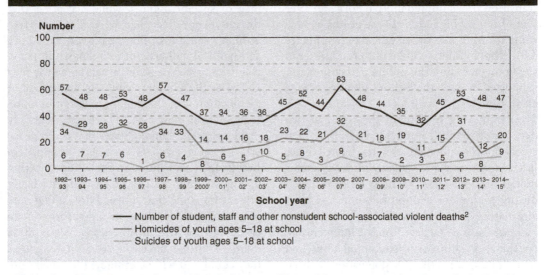

[1]The data from 1999–2000 onward are subject to change until law enforcement reports have been obtained and interviews with school and law enforcement officials have been completed. The details learned during the interviews can occasionally change the classification of a case. For more information on this survey, please see appendix A.

[2]A school-associated violent death is defined as "a homicide, suicide, or legal intervention death (involving a law enforcement officer), in which the fatal injury occurred on the campus of a functioning elementary or secondary school in the United States," while the victim was on the way to or from regular sessions at school, or while the victim was attending or traveling to or from an official school-sponsored event. Victims include students, staff members, and others who are not students or staff members, from July 1, 1992, through June 30, 2015.

Note: "At school" includes on the property of a functioning primary or secondary school, on the way to or from regular sessions at school, and while attending or traveling to or from a school-sponsored event. In this indicator, the term "at school" is comparable in meaning to the term "school-associated."

Source: Centers for Disease Control and Prevention (CDC), 1992–2015 School-Associated Violent Death Surveillance System (SAVD-SS).

insufficient parental supervision are consistently identified for both victimization and offending. Living in disadvantaged neighborhoods and affiliating with delinquent peers has provided some predictive power for offending and some victimization (Reid & Sullivan, 2012; Smith & Ecob, 2007).

Homicides in the United States have fluctuated over time in volume and locale. Most crimes have seen upswings and downturns. The UCR showed crime rise in the 1960s and 1970s and again in the late 1980s. Crimes in general in the United States began a decline in the early to mid 1990s, which continues through today, with a few slight rises in some crimes in only a few years.

In considering patterns and trends of homicide in the United States, it is appropriate to consider a differential risk analysis of homicide. Who is more likely to be a victim of homicide and to what degree? Who might be more likely to be involved in a violent or lethal event as a perpetrator? Along with the general downward trend in violent crime and murder in the United States, we can point to specific types of criminal killing. Workplace violence in general and workplace homicide specifically have decreased. We address expanded aspects of other mass and workplace violence and murder in Chapter 9. According to the National Center for Injury Prevention and Control, Division of Violence Prevention

(2017), most school-associated violent deaths during the years 1992–2015, happen during transition times immediately before and after school and during lunch. These deaths include students, staff, and other nonstudents (Figure 3.8). School killings will be explored further in the book including the public perception, not supported by data, that school shootings are at an all-time high.

Attempting to explain the trend of two decades of reduced homicide and crime (and recent upticks in homicide) in the United States has covered quite a bit of ground. Many criminologists admit puzzlement as crime dropped during periods of economic boom and bust, alternating political parties in Washington, increased use of targeted police intervention, continued swelling of prison populations, and more. The aging of the U.S. population has been pointed to both with the idea of offenders aging out of criminal behavior and having a greater number of older people engaged in monitoring the young. Policing and punishment are social-control mechanisms that are part of the reduction. But so too are other societal factors, such as access and lack of access to economic opportunity and the feeling of relative deprivation compared to others. The U.S. homicide rate is better by far than 30 years ago. Nonetheless, the United States lags behind many other Western democracies.

HOMICIDE INTERNATIONALLY

Citizens, policymakers, and students of criminal justice are quite naturally interested in U.S. crime standings compared to other Western countries and globally. To put global violent and property crime into context, it is helpful to understand how other countries have fared in the last several years. To be sure, different countries have different amounts and rates of different crimes. Cultural and political conditions are thought to have an impact on crime rates as well as societal responses to crime around the globe. Given our earlier discussion of the

challenges associated with data gathering, we should be cautious about accepting the accuracy of specific figures, while accepting that the numbers reflect that the U.S. murder rate is high regardless. The resources, protocols, and political will are not fully known in many countries, which calls for caveats about the reliability of the numbers cited. As mentioned at the beginning of the book, we do not examine sociopolitical homicide. There are definitely incidents in the United States that could properly be categorized as such. For example, in June 2015, a man entered a Bible study meeting in Charleston, South Carolina, and after being present for some time, opened fire, killing nine of those in attendance in an apparent hate crime against African Americans. While these murders will be tallied in 2015 UCR figures, they could and will be examined for their hate crime characteristics.

Postcommunist Eastern Europe, as an example, has concerns with crime and homicide, but there is little in the way of solid data sources upon which to conduct analyses. Stamatel (2009) cautions about the difficulties of cross-national comparisons of homicide. But in looking at Western nations, she found that progressive reforms toward democratic governance and globalization of economic ties have historically decreased homicide rates. The Americas and the Caribbean have many of the top homicide rates in the world, according to the United Nations Office on Drugs and Crime. The United States, by comparison, has a much lower rate than many countries. Table 3.4 provides a sampling of these rates along with a handful of other countries for comparison. An important fact to recall is that reliable statistics are simply not available for many countries.

Cross-national comparisons of homicide have been addressed for many years (Gartner, 1990). There are various circumstances, including political, cultural, economic, to explain the victimization of people in different countries or regions of the world. Comparing the United States' victimization rates with other countries is beneficial not only for perspective but to learn of methods and approaches to addressing violence everywhere. Gartner's work also

Table 3.4   Intentional Homicide Rate per 100,000, Select Countries

Country	Rate by year			
	2000	2005	2010	2016
Japan	0.5	0.5	0.4	0.3
United Kingdom (England and Wales)	1.5	1.3	1.1	1.2
France	1.8	1.6	1.3	1.4
United States of America	5.5	5.7	4.8	5.4
Costa Rica	6.3	7.9	11.6	11.9
Mexico	10.6	9.1	22.0	19.3
Colombia	65.7	41.8	33.7	25.5
Guatemala	24.9	40.8	40.7	27.3
Bahamas	24.8	15.8	26.1	28.4
Brazil	23.7	23.3	22.0	29.5
Belize	16.6	28.6	40.1	37.6
Jamaica	33.4	61.0	51.4	47.0
Venezuela (Bolivarian Republic of)	32.8	37.2	45.1	56.3
Honduras	48.7	43.6	76.1	56.5
El Salvador	60.5	64.4	64.7	82.8

Source: Compiled from UN Office on Drugs and Crime Statistics (2018). Retrieved from https://dataunodc .un.org/crime

points out that the opportunity model for homicide is seen around the world, and it is typically associated with a felony crime, such as robbery. Many U.S. homicides are away from home and involve two men. In some other developed nations, the victim is often a family member. U.S. homicide victimization rates reflect more instances of murder and more examples of stranger homicides than in many developed nations. The comparison of numbers in the United States to other countries shocks many citizens. This is because other countries have much higher rates of homicide than the current U.S. numbers. And while

intimate partner homicide (IPH) remains a crime of significance in the United States, as a percentage of overall homicides, Asia, Europe, and several African nations had higher rates in 2017, according to the **United Nations Office on Drugs and Crime** (UNODC, 2018). Table 3.4 and Figure 3.9 give a graphic representation of relative homicide rates in 2016 (Our World in Data). It is important to consider that some research shows that *crime rates* in various countries vary independently with the *homicide rate*. In other words, if the crime rate is high or low, it does not necessarily follow that the homicide rate is high or low.

Figure 3.9 Homicide Rates Globally, 2016

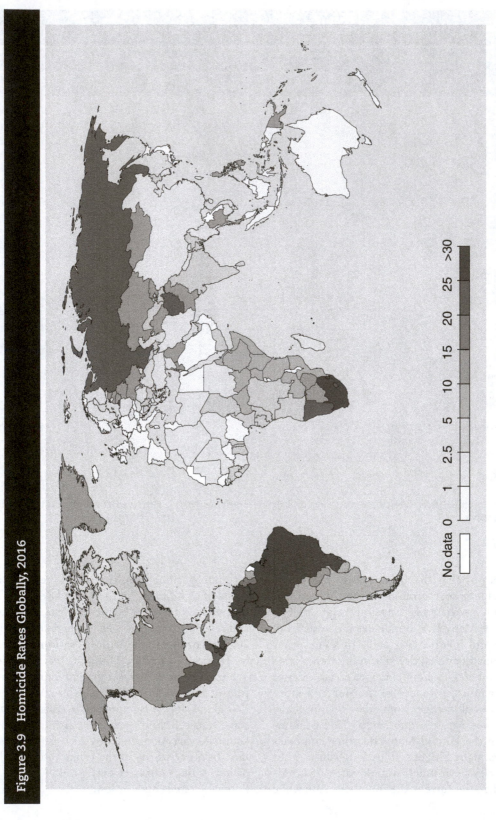

Source: Global Burden of Disease Collaborative Network. Global Burden of Disease Study 2016 (GBD 2016) Results. Seattle, United States: Institute for Health Metrics and Evaluation (IHME), 2017. Visualization provided by Our World in Data, licensed under Creative Commons BY 4.0, https://ourworldindata.org/about/how-to-use-our-world-in-data

SUMMARY

To know what we know about homicide and violent crime, it is vitally important that we gather statistics on all aspects of murder and violent offending. Researchers use the information to describe homicide factors and situations as well as to develop hypotheses and theories on the causes of such behavior. Legislators increasingly utilize research in formulating laws and sentencing guidelines and to develop and implement public programs. Law enforcement and other agencies follow intelligence-led and evidence-based practices to use the best available information to design tactical and program responses to violence in the communities they protect. Comparison to international and historic rates of criminal homicide provides context for examining contemporary rates in the United States.

For many crimes, the arrest data present in the UCR may, in some part, reflect the actions taken by law enforcement, which is different than being representative of those who committed crimes but were not arrested. Some homicides have quickly identifiable suspects, and agency statistics will typically reflect them. Other homicides face the difficulty of being more of a whodunit, such as gang-related drive-by shootings where there may be a strong suspicion of a rival gang's involvement but no witness to the crime and little or no physical evidence. The impact for the clearance rate is obvious: an unsolved crime. The lower agency clearance rate may lead the general public to believe they are less safe when, in fact, this specific category of unsolved crime may not create a less safe existence for the average non-gangbanger citizen. Lower socioeconomic status young males are heavily represented in arrest statistics, but most measures of crime and specifically violent crime indicate this offender profile is also most common in unreported and unsolved crimes.

There have been instances in which police have intentionally misrepresented crime numbers, artificially placing numbers into made-up categories that are not aligned with the UCR or statutes, or they have inflated arrest statistics. While the hard work of most criminal justice professionals and the accountability mechanism built into contemporary governance preclude most such behavior, the need to be attentive to data-gathering practices is always present. The NCVS partly mitigates this concern but not in homicide cases, since murder is not an area of questions in the survey.

Many local police agencies as well as state and federal law enforcement and criminal justice agencies make more information and research available via the Internet than ever before. This facilitates public education about crime and its decline. What has caused the steady drop? Both political parties will claim some ownership of the drop in violent and nonviolent crime since the mid-1990s. Social scientists explore an aging demographic in the United States, economic ups and downs, and sentencing priorities, among others, to try to explain the drops. Criminologists have some confidence in the validity of the identified reductions in crime in part because the UCR, National Incident-Based Reporting System, and the NCVS generally trend together. This raises the question of the use of **open-source data** in the study of homicide. Parkin and Gruenewald (2017) compared official and open-source data in one jurisdiction covering a one-year period and found that for every variable that they measured, the open-sources captured the same data and more. The proliferation of news-aggregation by journalists, non-profits, and scholars underscores value in the volume and variety of information available—and the caution to ensure data integrity and context. Whether law enforcement programs and priorities, retuning of punishment strategies, economics, or an evolving sensitivity to violence are to credit—or all of these—social scientists continue to piece together the mosaic of increases and declines in crime. We do not know if we are at a plateau in the homicide rate or whether recent localized increases in some violent crime and homicide signal that trends may change.

For policymakers, practitioners, and citizens, the question can also be, What data do *you* think you need?

DISCUSSION QUESTIONS

1. Which demographic group by age and race is most represented as homicide victims and offenders?
2. What weapon is most used to commit murder in the United States? Why?
3. What has happened to the involvement of girls and women in violent crime, including murder, in the last 20 years? What does this mean for society?
4. While the United States does not have the world's highest homicide rate, it ranks top among Western nations. What are some of the countries with higher rates of homicide?
5. How might data on victims and offenders of homicide inform agency policies?

TRY THIS

Visit the home page of the FBI's Uniform Crime Reports at http://www.fbi.gov/about-us/cjis/ucr/ucr. Navigate to the preliminary crime stats and look at whether murder and other violent crimes have increased or decreased from the last reporting year.

Visit the home page of Homicide Monitor and view the animation at https://homicide.igarape .org.br/. Compare and consider the listing, in order, of homicide rates of various countries. Were you surprised?

Visit the National Violent Death Reporting System (NVDRS) webpage at https://wisqars.cdc .gov:8443/nvdrs/nvdrsDisplay.jsp and try assembling your own report from the interactive options available.

4

WHY WE DO IT
Theories of Homicide

> "Poverty is the parent of revolution and crime."
>
> —Aristotle

> "Human nature is complex. Even if we do have inclinations toward violence, we also have inclination to empathy, to cooperation, to self-control."
>
> —Steven Pinker

Student Learning Outcomes

Students will be able to:

- differentiate among the major theories used in the study of violence and homicide.

- name and discuss examples of biological explanations of crime.

- describe the similarities between sociopaths and psychopaths.

- explain the role of theories and research in policy formulation.

CHAPTER OUTLINE

INTRODUCTION: SOCIOLOGICAL AND CRIMINOLOGICAL PERSPECTIVES

The question vexes us: Why do people kill each other? We may have some level of understanding or acceptance when killing happens in war, in defense of self or others, or even in state-sanctioned executions. The murder of a person by one or more others may happen during the commission of a crime, in the *heat of passion*, in the quick escalation of a fight, as a result of an ongoing cycle of abuse, or in many other circumstances. *Circumstances* such as these provide some context to the killing that we interpret through common knowledge or the vicarious experience of TV and movies. The *reason* is perhaps more difficult to comprehend.

Criminology is broadly defined as the scientific study of crime. This broad brushstroke places elements such as the definition of crime, the causes of crime, the people who commit crime, responses to crime, the consequences of crime, and the punishment of offenders onto a large canvas indeed. The study of crime so defined is not one intended for pure reflection but as an applied science that draws upon many disciplines to seek answers that may be formed into laws, policies, and strategies to prevent, reduce, or solve crimes. As such, the efforts of criminologists are examined not just by fellow researchers but by legislators, courts, and agency administrators within criminal justice, health, social work, education, and other domains.

Criminology, on the one hand, looks narrowly at an individual's behavior and various attributes but also at larger observations of all behavior by groups of people. Criminologists study homicide in micro and macro ways, including the examination of the individual offender, examination of the area or society in which offender and victim live, and analysis of the various factors involved in individual cases. As we pursue one general line of inquiry or another, we must remember that violent behavior—all behavior—is complex and not to be categorized simplistically.

Criminological **theory** is also situated in the current times. We build upon the efforts of past observers and recognize that future researchers will do the same to our work. How we think about crime **causation** influences how we believe we should proceed in controlling crime. How we currently view the state of the American family may influence how some people (and policymakers) believe crime control methods should be fashioned. To what extent others see the economy affecting the choices made by people to commit crime is another example. Again, social context has a significant impact on *what we do* about crime. Comparative studies that look at multiple cultures or periods of time are also instructive and afford the view of a global criminology (Gottfredson, 2018).

Many people may not understand scientific theory and the process followed for testing theory. A theory tries to explain how concepts are related. The scientist must look beyond mere opinions to form conclusions. A theory in science must be testable, and this certainly sets it apart from mere opinion, conjecture, and the like. To be testable, there must be a viable and ethical way to gather data and measure it. The research gathered must be examined to see if it supports the theory. If not, the theory is not correct. Another aspect of scientific theories, especially perhaps in the social sciences, is that findings from one study or research effort to another on the same question may be inconsistent. Some studies may support a theory while others do not fully support the theory or show no support whatsoever. This leads to many people assessing the weight of the existing evidence. You are already aware that much, if not most, research concludes with a call for further research on the matter to confirm initial findings. A theory that has utility in explaining serial murder, for example, may offer little to an understanding of gang killings.

Theories require that an issue be carefully broken down into its component parts so that it may be described accurately in furtherance of measuring a phenomenon and describing the known interactions and interrelationships as well as the outcomes of any measurements. A picture should emerge that impresses upon you the thoroughness sought in examining and testing a theory. Given the impact that criminological studies have on the formulations of policies and laws, it is hard to overstate the importance of considering all available information on a matter. Social science research is complex and requires careful and continual examination (Alvarez & Bachman, 2003).

Theory and research can be thought of through the experiential learning cycle lens of *What? So what?* and *Now what?* Selection of a topic or phenomenon to study is in response to some issue appearing on someone's agenda. The parameters of what is to be studied are established as the *what*. Recognition by others or agreement on the relevance or value of studying the topic or issue satisfies the *So what?* question. The connection of theory and research to policies and practices is when criminologists, criminal justice specialists, and policymakers address *Now what?* Policy analysis and evaluation research offers the additional step (among others) of determining whether an intervention achieved some level of effectiveness. Ideally, modifications will then be made as needed and a new iteration will begin.

We do not attempt an exhaustive coverage of criminological theories used to examine homicide or even violent behavior. This chapter is likewise not a comprehensive coverage of the history of the field of criminology. That is for a theory text in a theory course. We will discuss several theories that have been utilized to examine violent crime generally and criminal

homicide specifically. In the sections that follow, we look at theories that examine the offender, the victim, the setting, and the situational variables of violent crime and murder.

Criminology developed out of sociology. Sociology is generally defined as the study of groups of people and how they interact. The importance of social context orients the sociologist to examine societal variables as the unit of analysis, instead of the individual. This includes factors such as inequality, economic conditions, availability of guns, and so forth—again, things outside the individual. Changing structural parts of any society is a mighty task and undeniably complex. Cost and political will are variables that must also be considered, and these too reside outside of the being and cognition of the individual. From birth onward, individuals live in homes, interact with other people, exist in their neighborhood, go to school and perhaps work, and consider and make choices about how to exist in society. Patterns may be revealed through sociological examinations that subsequently suggest actions to change the dynamic of what contributes to bad decisions by many people. Understanding the difference in the unit of analysis, societal or individual, is important. Knowing that strain, learning or social-control theories are more of the sociological tradition, as distinct from psychological, biological, and even critical-theory approaches. Different theoretical disciplines have certain attributes or philosophical underpinnings. There is no one answer to crime. A multidisciplinary approach holds great opportunity for expanding our understanding of homicide and *doing something about it*.

INDIVIDUAL EXPLANATIONS

Classical Perspective and Rational Choice Theory

It was not too far in the past that many societies around the world believed that human behavior was subject to the influence of deities, natural spirits, and demonic possession. This supernatural view gave way from the 1500s to the mid-18th century to the notion of *free will*, which is the belief that people choose the actions they take. The main thrust of what was termed the classical school of thought was that people make choices about their behavior and are therefore responsible for their actions. The **classical theory's** first and most notable proponent was Cesare Beccaria (1738–1794). Beccaria maintained that people are rational and that, as a result of that fact, they make decisions that are beneficial to what they value. Beccaria, in other words, believed that an individual will conduct the mental evaluation of pros and cons before acting.

This view of man as an individual weighing the pros and cons of some action has appeal. We can relate to the idea. But how well does this **rational choice theory** fit with the crime of murder? If we envision a calculated and premeditated murder, we may see this applying. If we think of many heat-of-the-moment and confrontational homicides, the view may change. A key assumption then, along with the weighing of pros and cons, is that such a calculation is made in an instant before firing the gun or striking the blow. The utilitarian tradition of considering human acts as rational choices is a clear basis for deterrence theory and the decisions of many policy adherents who have crafted legislation and programs to create and implement sanctions believed effective in making people choose not to commit certain acts. Researchers have long debated what does and does not deter crime. Deterrence has certain conditions and is questionable or complicated at best. How quickly is a deterrent reaction imposed? How consistently is the reaction imposed? Is the deterrent reaction (sanction) proportional to the act? And underlying all of this is the individual with his past experiences, current circumstances, including age, and choice of options.

While the classical approach and its reconceptualized descendant, rational choice theory, emphasize the central role of an individual choosing to commit a wrongful act, the view did not allow that additional factors may affect or influence behavior. This view evolved through time, accounting for other factors that influence wrong choices.

Positivism

Positivism, or the positive school, emerged in the late 1800s with the belief that multiple external factors determined criminal behavior. Three Italian scholars—Lombroso, Ferri, and Garofalo—took the direction of finding the causes of crime and reducing the conditions that gave rise to these causes. This view of factors outside the individual's control gave rise to the idea of *determinism*. Biological, psychological, sociological, and economic factors represent positivistic approaches to explain individual crime. The positivist approach relied on measuring individual behavior and social conditions along with a claim to scientific neutrality and careful attempts to test hypotheses. With these theories shifting the criminological focus to science came a shift in addressing crime through a treatment model instead of a punishment model.

The reality that few offenders specialize in violent crime limits the ability to develop narrow theories of violent offending. Most research has tended toward explanations of offending in general. As mentioned, this book is not a criminology textbook. We leave comprehensive explanation of crime theories to the several solid texts available today. We have chosen to highlight a number of theories most often discussed in research on violence. These theories arose with and after the scientific movement that required a theory be testable. We can examine the assumptions and outcomes, and we can test the observations collected. We believe these theories have important connections to policy formulation.

All serious researchers make a practice of challenging their own assumptions and inviting others to comment on any apparent bias or *agenda* in the researcher's work. How politicians, the media, or advocacy groups use information gleaned through research should always be scrutinized. Social scientists can fall victim to adopting a perspective other than what empirically arrived at facts support. This is, of course, true of everyone. The difficulty here is that when *research says* that a certain idea is supported or not supported, we want to have confidence that this assertion is credible. The history of science, including social science, provides many historical examples of beliefs and assertions that, in contemporary science, look nearly ludicrous. So let us think about how we view the actions of people as influenced or driven by our biological makeup.

Biological

Early criminologists were medical doctors trying to understand criminal behavior based on the physiological makeup of a known criminal. For some time, researchers thought of criminal traits as being inherited. People view homicide and violent crime and comment about how different the criminal must be from them, how alien. We want to be assured that the violent criminal is an anomaly, that *there is something wrong* with that person. Biological research since the mid-18th century has tried to determine if there are links between violence and physical, genetic, neurological, and biochemical factors. The early work, from the mid-1700s to the mid-1800s, tried to show links between biological characteristics, such as body features, and behavior. The studies of facial features, known as **physiognomy**, and the study of the bumps on a person's head, known as **phrenology**, were two examples of the early efforts at *scientific* measurement of body features in the attempt to predict criminal behavior or identify those prone to criminality.

Early scientific research included that done by Cesare **Lombroso** (1825–1909). In Lombroso's book *The Criminal Man*, he expressed a belief that some people are born criminals; they are **atavisms**, similar to primitive peoples or lower form animals. Lombroso also proposed two additional categories of criminal. Those he classified as *insane criminals* and *criminaloids*. The insane, he said, had low intelligence and committed violent crime. The criminaloids were not seen as medically ill but were capable of committing crimes of passion. Lombroso felt that biological and physical forms and structures indicated corresponding behaviors, aptitudes, and proclivities.

Among the criticisms of Lombroso's work was his reliance on autopsies performed exclusively on deceased criminals. This is a clear example of a biased sample because Lombroso did not use control groups. Every school student learns by probably the eighth grade that a proper science experiment must include a control group that does not receive the treatment that a second group does so that the latter can be compared in a

---

Buck v. Bell, 274 U.S. 200 (1927)

In this landmark decision by the U.S. Supreme Court, Justice Oliver Wendell Holmes delivered the majority opinion for the Court and held that state statutes that permitted involuntary sterilization of people deemed unfit or intellectually disabled did not violate the 14th Amendment of the U.S. Constitution. The case involved a Virginia law that allowed compulsory sterilization of those like Carrie Buck, an 18-year-old patient at the Virginia State Colony for Epileptics and Feebleminded. She had the mental age of a 9-year-old child and was considered by doctors to be *feebleminded*, which was a broad term used at the time that included those who had mental disability or exhibited immoral behavior. Carrie had gotten pregnant and given birth to an *illegitimate* child. The law at issue in this case, known as a type of eugenics law, existed widely across many states at the time of this ruling and was supported by the theory that it was in the best interest of society to use sterilization to prevent the transfer of genes that might cause criminality, promiscuity, or mental disability. Justice Holmes's opinion in the case has been widely cited, especially where he writes, "It is better for all the world, if instead of waiting to execute degenerate offspring for crime, or to let them starve for their imbecility, society can prevent those who are manifestly unfit from continuing their kind." In support of the majority opinion, he also wrote, "Three generations of imbeciles are enough." While eugenics laws have now been abandoned and widely criticized by researchers, policymakers, and human rights advocates, they were used by states until the early 1960s in this country.

WHY WOULD THEY DO IT?

Source: Plate 41 from Alphonse Bertillon, "Identification Anthropométrique," 1893.

meaningful way to the former. William Sheldon (1898–1977) introduced a classification of three body types, called somatotypes. Although also largely disproven, Sheldon formed his theory based on observations and measurements. Other scientists of the day followed Lombroso's work or undertook other avenues of inquiry, but the use of ever-increasing scientific rigor had begun.

As use of the scientific method and scientific discoveries increased at an ever-quickening pace coming into the 20th century, **biological theories** of crime fell out of favor, to say the least. Some scientists still included observations regarding physical structure and biometrics as they conducted research of a multidisciplinary nature.

Sheldon and Eleanor Glueck are notable in this regard as they sought out differences between delinquent and nondelinquent juveniles. Overall, sociological theories and methods supplanted biological ones and came into vogue from mid-century on, until science and technology became more sophisticated and turned to increasingly minute examinations of the processes of the human body. One avenue of thought about our biological makeup had to do with our heritage, who we came from.

Evolutionary or hereditary as well as genetic explanations of behavior remain an active area of research. This becomes more productive with advances in our understanding of genetics and large-scale endeavors such as the Human Genome Project. This genetic blueprint of the human body continues to benefit biomedical studies that contribute to improved health and medical treatments. In the past, some limited studies examined criminal behavior in single families to try to make the heredity link before the sophisticated tools of genomic research existed. The studies have often been criticized for failing to take into full account the *circumstances* of the family members under study, such as family environment, nurturing, and economic stability.

Twin studies have also been conducted as a way to compare and contrast heredity and environment. Whether *monozygotic* (identical) twins or *dizygotic* (fraternal) twins share similar traits and to what percentage is referred to as a *concordance rate*. Environment as influence would be supported if both types of twins had similar concordance rates. If identical twins had higher rates of concordance compared to fraternal twins, genetics would be a more likely explanation. While there has been some support for behavior based on genetics, there has been even greater support for environmental influences (Rhee & Waldman, 2002, 2011). The reminder here is to continue recognizing the multiple factors that influence a specific person in a specific circumstance.

Similar in logic to twin studies have been adoption studies. In these research endeavors, the criminal records of those adopted are examined along with the criminal records of the adoptee's biological and adoptive parents. The expectation for a genetic connection would have the adopted person's criminal record be more similar to his or her biological parent. Environment or nurture would project a greater similarity to the criminal record of an adoptive parent. Results are mixed, and more research is needed. Complicating factors include whether the adopted individual had contact with the biological parents, whether he or she was *labeled* by the adoptive parents based on the biological parents' criminal conduct, and more.

The chromosomes that carry our genetic identity have also come under study for a link with criminality. Research in the 1960s revealed that a higher percentage of institutionalized men compared to the general population carried an extra Y chromosome. Current research does not show a connection between the XYY individual and violent offending and murder.

Biochemical topics of research include the various neurotransmitters and hormones. Neurotransmitters take part in passing information from one nerve to the next. Unusually high or low levels of some neurotransmitters have been linked with aggression and violence. Genetic and environmental factors both affect neurotransmitter levels. Serotonin, dopamine, and norepinephrine (adrenaline), among others, have been linked to various aggressive and antisocial behaviors and outcomes (Beaver, 2010). Serotonin in proper amounts, for example, can reduce aggressive behavior, impulsivity, and lack of self-control. Dopamine and norepinephrine have been linked to aggressiveness, and in the case of norepinephrine, impulsivity. Achieving a balance among such chemicals in our systems provides us the ability to avoid certain actions linked or leading to crime.

Hormones are messengers within the body secreted and then released into the bloodstream or stored in various glands. Hormones have important functions in regulating processes within our bodies. While there are many hormones produced in the body, irregular levels of testosterone and cortisol have been implicated in antisocial and violent behavior. While testosterone is present in higher levels in males, women also have the hormone. Studies have consistently linked higher hormone levels to violence, even in women. This link is not fully understood, and we note that violence is influenced by many other factors and not one biological factor in isolation.

Cortisol is a hormone secreted in response to stressful stimuli in our environment. Cortisol interacts with adrenaline when entering the bloodstream of a person, leading to greater arousal. Low cortisol levels have been linked to antisocial behavior and have been shown in some studies to be connected to violence. Underscoring the complexity of examining any potential contributors to aggressive or violent behavior, it is also noted that *high* cortisol levels are implicated in health issues such as weight, cholesterol, heart disease, and more. Both cortisol and testosterone have been examined to determine what effect, if any, these hormones have on psychopathy (Glenn, Raine, Schug, Gao, & Granger, 2011), which is discussed in the next section.

Adrian Raine, a noted criminologist at the University of Pennsylvania and author of *The Anatomy of Violence: The Biological Roots of Crime* (2013), has spent his career studying the brains of violent criminals and murderers and asserts that while environmental factors clearly influence crime, biology also plays a role. Within the biological perspective are examinations of brain injuries or developmental issues involving different areas of the human brain. Owing to the work of Raine and others, the relatively new subfield of **neurobiology** has emerged bringing a contemporary scientific view back to complement social and environmental explanations of violence. The study of brain activity and structure remains a promising and fascinating endeavor (Caldwell, Calhoun, & Kiehl, 2014). One issue studied is minimum brain dysfunction or MBD. This condition can be the result of a brain injury, or it can be inherited. Attention deficit/hyperactivity disorder (ADHD) and the behavioral challenges associated with it are related to neurological issues. Magnetic resonance imaging (MRI), functional MRI (fMRI), and diffusion tensor imaging (DTI) all offer methods to examine brain images, often while the subject performs a task to determine what functions are controlled by which areas of the brain. MR spectroscopy is another imaging method with application as is the magnetoencephalography (MEG) method to measure the brain's electrical activity. Cope et al. (2014) have studied the volume of gray matter in the brains of incarcerated youth offenders of homicide and compared it to various comparison and control groups. This has implications for possible biomarker identification of high-risk youth as well as pharmaceutical or therapeutic interventions to treat or reduce violence.

Allergic reactions to foods can also affect behavior, as can environmental pollutants such as lead and inorganic gases. High and low blood sugar levels have also been shown to affect behavior, attention span, and test taking. For instance, diet and nutrition continue to be researched as factors that influence behavior but not in isolation. Lack of chemicals and minerals can result in behavior disorders and learning blockages.

Contemporary views on biology and behavior favor an interaction effect between biological characteristics and the social surroundings of an individual. Such views incorporate some of the previously discussed biological factors with social conditions to result in *biosocial* theories. Movement in the direction of incorporating these two perspectives is notable. Early efforts in biological examination of crime and the dominant sociological views of the last century have excluded consideration of biological causes or influences. The ever-increasing pace of medical and scientific discovery opens new possibilities for identification of causative factors and the treatment of physiological factors related to violent behavior.

Psychological

Human behavior is complex, and it does not seem reasonable to point at a single cause or explanation, though many have done just that. This concept should be repeated at the introduction of each successive theory or avenue of inquiry related to theories of why people commit crimes. Social psychological researchers examine human interactions and how these are formed and influenced by social context. Our family structure matters in the formation of our behaviors and responses. Our peers matter. School, work, and other social dynamics matter. While the sociological view has dominated, there is

room and cause for considering additional factors, such as the biological considerations just discussed and psychological influences. Other examples of the *determinism* of outside factors are **psychological** and **psychiatric theories**. These theories explain (criminal) behavior in terms of someone's personality traits, **psychopathy**, and their behaviors, **sociopathy**. The contemporary term **antisocial personality disorder** (ASPD) now includes both psychopathy and sociopathy.

Studies indicate that many of the executive functions of the brain, such as planning, decision-making, behavior selection, abstract reasoning, and more, are handled in the frontal lobe, in an area called the prefrontal cortex. The neuropsychological study of how the functioning of this and other parts of the human brain affect cognitive functioning and behavior will only increase. Some relatively recent considerations of **traumatic brain injury (TBI)** in returning veterans has placed some attention on potential negative consequences arising from damage to this area of the brain. Concussions are an example of TBI, which can vary in severity. Additionally, long-term consequences of athletes who may suffer blows to this area of the head, protected or unprotected, highlight important health concerns over the long term. Even falls, car crashes, and being struck by someone or something puts people young or old at some risk of TBI. When brain trauma is experienced by someone repeatedly, the condition may be progressive and degenerative leading to neurological disease such as **chronic traumatic encephalopathy (CTE)** (Lucke-Wold, Turner, Logsdon, Bailes, Huber, & Rosen, 2014). As with so much of what we discuss in research on murder and murderers, we cannot point to head injury or trauma alone as causing someone to kill.

Most college and university students—and most Americans—have heard the terms sociopath and psychopath. Expert opinion regarding the similarity, contrast, or overlap between these two concepts is quite mixed. As of 2013, both terms are listed in the *Diagnostic and Statistical Manual of Mental Disorders* (**DSM-5**) under the heading antisocial personality disorder. Acting without regard to laws or rules and feeling no guilt about such transgressions are considered to be similar traits between sociopaths and

The Rise and Fall of a Football Star

Aaron Hernandez followed the path of many pro athletes, beginning playing football when he was eight years old. The sport is known for the risk of concussion and head trauma resulting from tackling and being tackled. Hernandez achieved prominence as a college football standout before playing in the National Football League for three seasons. Since his college playing days, Hernandez had documented instances of acting violently. In 2013, Hernandez was arrested for the murder of Odin Lloyd. The NFL team he played for immediately released him from the team. He had two diagnosed concussions, and after his death by suicide while incarcerated for life after being convicted of murder, examination of his brain revealed that he suffered from chronic traumatic encephalopathy (CTE), a degenerative brain condition resulting from repeated head trauma. Yet, the athlete had also suffered sexual and physical abuse as a child and was known to use drugs. Whether and to what extent the blows to the head taken in a life of football, and the subsequent diagnosis of CTE, contributed to violent behavior, and possibly his suicide, cannot be definitely known. However the continued scientific scrutiny of behavioral issues possibly linked to head trauma is clearly warranted. With a condition such as CTE, which cannot be diagnosed in a live patient, we should consider the possible effect of head trauma on violent behavior or crime.

psychopaths. A key distinction is that sociopaths are viewed as being able to form some bonds of attachment to individuals or groups whereas psychopaths are not. So the rubric of antisocial behavior seems fitting for both, yet research seems to indicate that the sociopath is formed by environmental factors more than the psychopath, who is seen as more a product of hereditary or genetic influences. The impulsivity of a psychopath lends to the potential for sudden violence and in extreme cases murder. The sociopath, lacking the impulsive nature of the psychopath, may take the time to plan an act, including murder. Which may be harder to catch? Psychologist Robert Hare (2003) developed a psychopathy checklist (**PCL-R**) that assists professionals in assessing an individual's placement on a continuum of psychopathy based on traits such as superficial charm, lack of remorse, and poor behavior control. Seeking immediate gratification, risky behavior, and other traits show a need to consider psychopathy over the life course of individuals (Fox, Jennings, & Farrington, 2015).

Identifying and treating some ASPD-diagnosed persons can be aided by the technological advances that enable brain scans and careful monitoring of activation of various centers in the brain. The traumatic brain injuries mentioned earlier may result from adult trauma or childhood abuse or injury. These injuries may in turn lead to a diagnosis of ASPD.

Sociobiology is yet another theory in the search for the causes of different types of homicide. This theoretical approach considers that we are less likely to kill those related to us because we want, at a biological level perhaps, to ensure the survival of our genes in persons related to us (Daly & Wilson, 1988). An immediate thought might be that we have a greater ability, through time and physical proximity, to kill family members. Sociobiological theory asserts that we are stayed from murder by evolutionary dictates. Of course, we may care more for family than strangers, and that may stay the murderous act. As we will explore in coming chapters, sadly and all too often, family members do not hesitate to kill their *loved ones*.

SOCIAL STRUCTURAL

We move now from individual-level explanations to a broader frame of reference—society. Research from the discipline of sociology has looked for aggregate-level explanations of homicide. Social conditions examined are issues of economic deprivation and the so-called social disorganization of neighborhoods and communities. **Social structural theories**, for example, point to males in their late teens to late twenties who live in poor neighborhoods, exhibit low attachment to the community and others and high disorganization, and are disproportionately represented as both victims and perpetrators of homicide. It is also important to note, as is commonly done by laypeople, policymakers, and researchers, that a person's socioeconomic status does not commit murder, but it is the person himself who does. *At-risk* is not synonymous with either *victim* or *perpetrator*.

Different cultures around the world must be examined in context, and direct comparisons, while sometimes instructive, must be made cautiously and with the aid of theoretical frameworks such as **cultural criminology** (Young, 2003). The structures of society are not the same in Russia, Haiti, and Australia. While many of the building blocks are similar, there are differences that arise from the history and traditions of a country or region (Prieur, 2018). Political systems and the interplay of religion with governing institutions may impact how a culture approaches societal issues and challenges, such as crime. Crime rates, including those for criminal homicide, will vary based on a number of factors in different parts of the world.

Social Learning Theory

Social learning theory, while not familiar to many people by name, has a foundation that posits that people learn by observing others and imitating them. This broad conceptualization was developed by Albert Bandura in the 1960s and 1970s. Other learning theories incorporate the classical conditioning well known through the example of Pavlov's pairing of a neutral stimulus with a consistent second stimulus that elicits a response. The condition eventually elicits a response without the second stimulus. Bandura asserted that learning does not only come through the rewards and punishment of classical conditioning but through vicariously observing a stimulus response in someone else, especially someone of significance to the observer. Others

have considered the impact of violent and other media in this same imitation model. Media includes television and movies, video games, social media, and music.

Early behaviorists, such as Pavlov, Watson, and Skinner, contributed to understanding how learning influenced behavior. A logical progression was that behavior could also be changed through learning principles. This approach held great promise for those working with delinquent youth and adult criminal offenders. Experimentation and observations over time have done much to present a balance of the factors internal to the individual and his perceptions of that which is external in his environment and how both affect behavior. Where Bandura focused on the modeling aspects of how a person observes and learns from others, Rotter and others examined how expectations of behavioral outcomes or consequences influence learning.

Differential Association Theory

Differential association theory, first developed and explored by Sutherland in the 1940s, was one of the first to view deviance and criminal behavior as learned from others. The view suggests that we may arrive at a balance of how we view different acts as acceptable or unacceptable based on the existing or emerging views of family, friends, and others whom we look to. Gangs are the common example of this social control theory. The idea, loosely, is that you somewhat become who you associate with. If you see peers or those you look up to performing criminal acts or violent acts, you may come to accept doing the same things as normal or OK, even if the larger society does not believe so.

Social Control Theory

Social control theories take the view that without some form of constraints, people would commit acts we consider to be crimes. Murder is a foreign concept to most people. We realize, though, that some areas of the modern world have so little central governance or control that the scenario could be partly accurate in those

An ongoing debate in the United States and elsewhere is the connection between violent media and aggressive behavior, mainly in adolescents.

Alvarez and Bachman (2017) point to a great deal of research when they assert, "The evidence connecting media images of violence and actual violent behavior is by now beyond doubt" (p. 59). This view is not uncontested. Fox, Levin, and Quinet (2012) point to research as well but conclude,

> There has been much hype and irresponsibility regarding the claims of the influence of violent media on violent behavior. Given the recent dramatic declines in violence, including youth violence, we certainly have not seen a reduction in violent media consumption. Experts suggest that we should not spend money and time researching media violence as a "cause of crime" when evidence that this is the case simply does not exist in the scientific literature. (p. 36)

In point of fact, there is evidence in the scientific literature regarding the impact and implications of violent media on violent behavior, but the degree of influence and in combination with what other factors are certainly debated. Social learning acknowledges factors such as parental and adult involvement with young people, proportion of time spent viewing or using media, and others as important context for how a particular individual will process media images and experiences. In addition to violent images and scenarios in media is the presence of pornography and what impact it may have on various offenders.

Research on the effects of violent media has been ongoing since the 1970s, including a report of the surgeon general in 2001 titled *Youth Violence*.

countries considered failed states. This would be the case, too, if we think of different cultures through history that lacked a central governing body or laws along with the mechanisms to implement those laws.

Social control theories attempt to explain why individuals do not offend. Citizens conform to most of the rules of society because of internal states or external constraints on action that the individual obeys. When the internal restraint developed through childhood and adolescence is weak, the individual may choose to commit a delinquent or criminal act. Likewise, the external constraints may be ineffective for a variety of reasons. Control theories often look at the attachment we have to prosocial or delinquent others as affecting our adherence to norms.

Anomie Theory

Anomie theory encompasses the work of, among others, Émile Durkheim and later Robert K. Merton. Durkheim initially spoke of the loss of cohesiveness in the social fabric of communities that moved rapidly from a rural to an urban existence. With the complexity that increased industrialization and expanding city populations bring, Durkheim observed that the ties we have to family and to our identifiable community would be weakened. With this weakening of what binds us to one another and to our sense of being part of the collective community, we may be more apt to violate norms and laws. Merton took up much of Durkheim's views and expanded them, with a focus on how Americans particularly value economic gains and success. This view is not that the pursuit of success in itself is wrong but that an overfocus on material acquisition may result in deviant behavior to achieve the desired end state.

Strain Theory

Strain theories assert that when we are blocked from obtaining something we need or want we become frustrated and may resort to illegitimate means to obtain those things. This certainly has implications for the violent crimes of robbery and rape. And these crimes of violence may ultimately involve murder. Some violence in crime is described as *instrumental* as that violence is used as an instrument to further some other goal, such as during a robbery. Some violence is viewed as *expressive* by being the point of the act itself, as in many angry assaults. Even if an individual has legitimate means (e.g., employment) to earn money to pay for some things, he may supplement his activities with criminal pursuits to acquire even more money or other goods and services. The fact is that not everyone has access at the same levels in society. Access to goods and services, access to social capital, or access to the mobility to move to another community with greater opportunity is out of the reach of many.

The stressors in a person's life may lead him to act in many ways considered deviant or criminal. Someone without a job may steal. Someone who feels slighted may harm another person. It is important to remember that most people do not turn to crime as a way of dealing with the stressors they face. In 1992, Robert Agnew published his general strain theory (GST). Agnew's work followed the development of a number of others but focused attention on the individual actor's emotional reactions to his personal social environment. Agnew explained a number of dimensions of strain-related circumstances that may intensify or mediate that event for a specific individual.

Cultural Deviance and Subcultural Theories

Cultural deviance theories and **subcultural theories** are discussed as one group of related views. The norms and values people are taught as they grow up explain their reactions to their environments. Wolfgang and Ferracuti (1967) observed that low socioeconomic classes held views that were not always consistent with the larger society. As a result of adhering to their own set of norms, members of the lower classes committed crimes deemed acceptable by this subculture of the larger American culture. As an example of this, Papachristos (2009) talks about gang homicide in relation to how gang hierarchies are structured. Papachristos expresses gang mentality this way:

> Gang members do not kill because they are poor, black, or young or live in a socially disadvantaged neighborhood. They kill because they live in a structured set of social relations in which violence works its way through a series of connected individuals. (p. 82)

A majority of gang activity involves youth members. Subcultural theory has a focus on juvenile delinquency because understanding the effects of subculture on a young person may lead to interventions prior to or even after delinquent or criminal behavior has occurred. The behavior of a youthful offender is not seen as entirely stable or fixed. Matza (1964) described a state of *drift* where youth (in particular) rationalize their delinquent behavior. Matza recognized that most juveniles "age out" of crime and that they continue to develop and exercise their abilities to make choices. These views lead to the concept of the juvenile drifting between socially acceptable behavior and delinquent behavior.

Most people intuitively grasp that our attitudes and behaviors can be affected by those we associate with most frequently. What is not immediately apparent to the casual observer is the role our very neighborhoods may play as an actor in the day-to-day lives we lead. Anderson (1994) called the set of informal rules for public behavior in the neighborhood the "code of the street," and this code acts as a lens through which many residents, especially young males, see and experience their own and others' actions. Anderson and many others have commented on the role that *respect* plays for how people interact with one another and the potential for violence when the respect demanded by the code of the street is not offered or is perceived to have been violated. Stewart and Simons (2010) examined the street code and the impact the subsequent neighborhood culture has on violent juvenile offending. The authors found that the street culture does interact with the individual-level code or values related to violence. The context of the neighborhood is not on the periphery but is front and center, affecting individual-level responses as we understand the application of subcultural theory.

Social Disorganization Theory

Social disorganization theory describes the conditions in communities that degrade their cohesiveness. It has long been observed that disorder and visible signs of physical decline in neighborhoods create an environment where even more decline and crime can occur. The individual choosing to commit a crime is influenced by the environment where he finds himself along with any other predispositions he brought with him. Physical attributes of a neighborhood or community are not the only aspects that may reflect disorganization. We will begin, though, with some thoughts about the physical surroundings of where we live. We have all grown up or lived in a specific residential setting. For many Americans, this is an urban or suburban neighborhood. For others, the setting may have been distinctively rural. Even if you did not grow up in a neighborhood, you have visited in many and travelled through many more. Some have a decidedly less safe feel than others and might be viewed as more high-risk (Hewitt, Beauregard, Andresen, & Brantingham, 2018). Sometimes, we may mistake the appearance of a neighborhood unfairly as less safe. Often, we have not made a mistake. Why the difference?

Neighborhood characteristics have been identified as relevant to the rate of violent and other crimes since the early work of the University of Chicago researchers. The neighborhood structure, residents, and attachment features have been studied, with a focus on the relationship between characteristics in neighborhoods. Dense urban areas were more crime prone than suburbs. Two notable researchers, Shaw and McKay (1942), identified a *transitional zone* in Chicago where crime and delinquency were higher than more stable areas. They also found that the racial or ethnic makeup of the zone was not important as a variable that explained crime.

In the neighborhood, researchers have examined characteristics of the people and their demographics, the status of how cohesive the neighborhood is, and the physical condition of the area. Nieuwbeerta, McCall, Elffers, and Wittebrood (2008) considered socioeconomic disadvantage, social cohesion, and residents' confidence in the police. Social disorganization theory as well as strain/deprivation theory was considered in this examination of Dutch homicides from the late 1990s to 2003. The study results, unsurprisingly, showed that neighborhood social cohesion and socioeconomic disadvantage did affect the homicide rate in the Netherlands. What is interesting and may have greater import for policymakers in many Western countries is that the *confidence in the police* did *not* have an effect on homicide. While citizens may want to feel that their police impact serious crime, such as murder, various evaluative research efforts from the 1970s to today have failed to consistently show such an effect.

Disorganization is not just the physical condition of a neighborhood. Researchers such as Sutherland (1947) have pointed to conflict within neighborhoods as a signal of a lack of organization. The mobility of residents has also been identified as affecting organization within communities. Residents have had the increasing physical ability, if not always the economic means, to relocate. When people relocate, they may take away with them bits of the stability of the community they leave. If the residents were shopkeepers, long-time residents, and generally engaged in the area, their exodus was seen to destabilize it. The economic means that may limit mobility are another aspect of how the neighborhood residents may or may not be able to contribute to various dimensions of the life of a community. Racial and ethnic heterogeneity has also been observed to affect disorganization. Perhaps the lack of mutual feelings of identity and *sameness* is a barrier of sorts to residents feeling a part of the same neighborhood even if they live next door to one another. Informal social controls may thus be weakened or absent altogether. The loss or weakening of social ties through these mechanisms partly explains the variation of crime rates among communities (Sampson & Groves, 1989). Many factors then appear able to have a hand in moving a community along a continuum from organized to disorganized.

Pairing of Theories

Messner and Rosenfeld (2013) have cogently and succinctly explained the logic by which certain microlevel, social-psychological-based theories align with the traditionally sociological and macrolevel views. Their summation of the major criminological perspectives today links social learning theories with cultural deviance theory, while noting they are not equivalent. Messner and Rosenfeld associate social control theory with social disorganization theory, and finally, they note that strain theory is often linked with anomie and the move away from socially normed behavior to achieve goals that seem otherwise unobtainable.

As you have seen yourself, the micro- and macro-level theories are not mutually exclusive, either between the two levels or among the various perspectives. Individual action and reaction to personal circumstances and environmental conditions do not fit neatly within clearly drawn lines. This state of reality gives rise to the suggestion by Messner and Rosenfeld to consider hybrid theories made up of the pairings they note: cultural-social learning, disorganization-control, and anomie-strain. These complementary theoretical views share important aspects that support the approach and clarify the relationship of individual and external world. These theory pairings are not universally accepted, and criminologists certainly do not think as one about the causes or contributors of homicide or any crime. We again point out that we are providing what we believe are some useful perspectives for you to begin your examination of homicide.

Implicated in many theories, in addition to routine lifestyle, is the fact of whether people live in poverty. Pridemore (2002, 2008) has commented that poverty, even more than inequality, is the leading factor in homicide. Pridemore's results reveal a positive and significant association between a nation's level of poverty and its homicide rate. His work also notes that while this poverty–homicide connection is positive and significant in the United States, that the same **correlation** is "disconcerting" in being absent in many crossnational comparisons to the United States. Poverty as a structural component of the environment in which many people live has long been observed as a correlated factor. As we turn to a discussion of the effect of our daily routine, we are reminded that in these empirical realities lie the seeds of public policies.

LIFE COURSE, LIFESTYLE, AND ROUTINE ACTIVITIES THEORY

Not everyone holds the same *chance* of being the victim of homicide (or any crime). The very young and the relatively old are perhaps more vulnerable to a physical assault by an offender's hands, fists, and feet. Everyone may be harmed by a person with a sharp object, a blunt object, or a firearm. Yet, the relative likelihood of being in a place at a time when an offender is wielding a weapon or is bent on assault varies significantly among age groups as well as along other demographics and lifestyle activities. According to **lifestyle and routine activities theory**, our everyday activities determine whether crime will *happen* to us. Some people engage in more risky behaviors than others by going to bars that are not socially controlled or considered upscale establishments with largely civil behavior among patrons. This concern regarding drinking places is, of course, an issue in many countries. Young people may hang out in areas not supervised well by adults and business owners or law enforcement. And you may well be thinking about the more impulsive behavior of many young people. Conversely, older people are not out and about at the hours and in the locations where disorder is the rule or at least where frequency and risk of victimization is clearly higher than being at home or at the movies. Older people tend to more frequently go out or travel with a companion. Choice of where to go will vary across age groups, but it is clear that some locations are more prone to disorder, including violence, than other places.

The **developmental and life-course criminology (DLC)** perspective sees individuals beginning behaviors early in life and then changing their behaviors as they grow up, or when older, and become exposed to typical experiences along the life course. Psychologist Terrie Moffitt (1993) categorizes the majority of youthful offenders as either *adolescent limited* or *life course persisters*. The adolescent-limited group represents those who may encounter authorities, including juvenile justice and law enforcement, but engage in relatively minor or passing problems or delinquent acts. The smaller group of life course persisters begin committing delinquent acts early in life and continue well into adulthood.

Loeber (1996) also addressed the idea of multiple pathways to delinquent or criminal careers. Sampson and Laub (1993) constructed an age-graded theory of criminal behavior with important observations regarding what may cause people to desist from crime at different points on the life trajectory. Research continues and applicability to specific crimes, such as homicide, is not direct in considering the course, pathways, and style of our living. The map of how someone navigates or is seemingly carried along through life can provide important information on how someone begins crime and perhaps how to help people stop committing crime.

Researchers and experienced police officers both know that *hot spots* exist in most jurisdictions. These are locations or areas of a community where crime is frequent. This reality led to various police intervention activities, such as directed patrols that concentrate on hot spots and the various efforts arising from the *broken windows* concept of George L. Kelling and James Q. Wilson (1982), mentioned earlier in connection with social disorganization. Consideration of social disorganization theory and broken windows can provide a persuasive illustration or picture of how frequenting an area that lacks order can place one in a position of being the victim of crime. There are critics of the explanatory power or logic of public disorder being the—or even *a*—significant signal condition for increased crime. Sampson and Raudenbush (1999), among others, argue that the cohesiveness of the residents of an area and the manner in which the residents interact in and with the public spaces of a neighborhood are quite important.

SUMMARY

As we mentioned at the beginning of the chapter, this discussion was not intended as an exhaustive one about theories of criminality. Nor did we attempt to mention all of the theories suggested as being relevant to the study of homicides. What we hoped to accomplish was to familiarize you with a number of the theories and concepts frequently discussed in connection with violent crime and a bit of how these theoretical perspectives have changed over the relatively short time they have been studied.

Each theory selected for brief review in this chapter holds implications for policy formation. Being able to explain a certain crime has the practical value of helping determine how to respond to that crime. As already mentioned, understanding the causes of one type of crime does not entirely transfer (if at all) to understanding a different crime, even within the broader category of violent crime or the narrower one of homicide. There are many variables related to serious violence. These succinct descriptions should give readers a number of avenues to explore further. In subsequent chapters, we revisit many of these theories with more specific examples of how they may apply.

The discussion of homicide can benefit from considering not only the differences and similarities of homicide events but changing the theory lens back and forth like an optometrist to continually check which view is clearer. Social scientists continue to develop and test theories to explain who will commit homicide and other crimes and why. This academic conceptualization of criminology is important. Law enforcement is interested in practical aspects of what criminals do and why. Preventing crime and effective retroactive investigation of crime should not be abstract concepts to researchers. The nexus of theory and practice remains not just a worthy goal but a critical one.

Criminology 54

Theory 54

Causation 54

Classical theory 56

Rational choice theory 56

Positivism 56

Physiognomy 57

Phrenology 57

Lombroso 57

Atavisms 57

Biological theories 58

Twin studies 58

Neurobiology 59

Psychological and psychiatric
  theories 60

Psychopathy 60

Sociopathy 60

Antisocial personality disorder
  (ASPD) 60

Traumatic brain injury
  (TBI) 60

Chronic traumatic
  encephalopathy (CTE) 60

DSM-5 60

PCL-R 61

Sociobiology 61

Social structural theories 62

Cultural criminology 62

Social learning theory 62

Differential association
  theory 62

Social control theories 62

Anomie theory 63

Strain theories 63

Cultural deviance theories and
  subcultural theories 64

Social disorganization
  theory 65

Correlation 66

Lifestyle and routine activities
  theory 66

Developmental and life-course
  criminology (DLC) 66

DISCUSSION QUESTIONS

1. How should criminologists approach the causation of homicide?
2. If an undergraduate student wants to examine the cause(s) of homicide, how should she proceed?
3. What standards must a theory meet in order to be usable by researchers and policymakers?
4. Describe and discuss the effects criminological theory has on court proceedings.
5. What are some factors of various criminology theories that may help prevent homicides? What are the policy implications of these theories?
6. If there are both biological and environmental factors that influence the commission of crime, what implications does this have for sentencing offenders?

TRY THIS

The U.S. National Library of Medicine of the National Institutes of Health maintains a great deal of research on factors related to homicide. Go to http://www.ncbi.nlm.nih.gov/pmc/?term=homicide and examine several different articles on various homicide-related topics.

NPR recently interviewed noted criminologist Dr. Adrian Raine, the first researcher to study the brains of murderers. Go here to watch the interview:

https://www.npr.org/books/authors/180094551/adrian-raine

5

CONFRONTATIONAL HOMICIDE

"To fight is a radical instinct; if men have nothing else to fight over they will fight over words, fancies, or women, or they will fight because they dislike each other's looks, or because they have met walking in opposite directions."

—George Santayana, Spanish-born American philosopher, poet, and humanist, 1863–1952

"Young man, young man, your arm's too short to box with God."

—James Wheldon Johnson

CHAPTER OUTLINE

Introduction
Victim Precipitation
Honor Contests
Road Rage
Audience
Alcohol
Physiology
Girls, Women, and Confrontational Homicide
Investigative Considerations

Student Learning Outcomes

Students will be able to:

- discuss factors observed in confrontational homicide situations.

- describe the higher rate of confrontational homicide compared to other types of homicide.

- evaluate the hypothesized dynamic of honor contests.

- debate the influence of audience in confrontational violence.

- explain the role of alcohol in violent encounters.

INTRODUCTION

The largest category of murder is that involving a conflict or confrontation between non-intimates. Almost half of all homicides are preceded by a fight or argument. Male-on-male homicides arising from such friction are the most common homicide situation. The lethal event may result from a brief, albeit emotionally charged, encounter or be a culmination of long-standing animosities. While not exclusively the province of men, **confrontational homicide** is overwhelmingly synonymous with men reacting to perceived slights, threats to honor, or encroachment on something that one or both view as theirs. The so-called contest of honor results in innumerous fights and significant numbers of homicides in the United States and in cultures around the world. This has been true throughout history. Consider the news reports of an argument erupting into a violent confrontation at a party or the theater shooting in Tampa where a former police officer shot another moviegoer over texting. A disagreement over the last beer results in a friend shooting another friend.

Kenneth Polk is credited with applying the term confrontational homicide to these types of argument-related killings. The FBI does not categorize confrontational homicide as such. We are left to make reasoned deductions as to the percentage of homicides this type of killing represents. We know that for *known* circumstances, killings resulting from arguments top the list. The circumstances surrounding 2017 murders were known in 59.8 percent of cases and "of those, 44 percent of victims were murdered during arguments, and romantic triangles, and other no-felony-specific circumstances" (FBI, 2018, n.p.). This was followed by felony-related murders at 14.8%. Evidence would also suggest that many of the unknown-cause homicides resulted from circumstances that could be characterized as exhibiting confrontational dynamics. It is also likely that a number of the gang killing homicides would fit under the rubric of confrontational homicide.

Polk (1994) examined murders in Victoria, Australia, between the years 1985 and 1989, and while the rate then and now is well under that of the United States, he found similar dynamics in murders involving men. The perceived slight, the public location, and the frequent involvement of alcohol mix for a rapidly escalating violent situation that may end in homicide. Polk's observations also support the approach that the victim–offender relationship and dynamics resulting in a death should be examined as a social interaction affected by a number of factors that we examine in this chapter.

Schwartz (2010) notes,

Nearly half of all homicides committed by men or women were preceded by some sort of argument or fight, such as conflict over money or property, anger over one partner cheating on another, severe punishment of a child or abuse of a partner, retaliation for an earlier dispute, or a drunken fight over an insult or other affront. (p. 283)

Felony-related homicides follow in frequency for men, then "other," and finally gang related as motives. For women, "other" follows fight, then felony-related, and finally gang related.

We have noted elsewhere in the text that aggravated assaults and aggravated batteries are often indistinguishable from homicide save for one element—someone dies. An offender may have intended his target to die, but through poor aim, intoxication, or dumb luck, the victim escapes death. Again, note that we do not address the ultimate charge that any given prosecutor might level, just the violent assault against another person.

VICTIM PRECIPITATION

A touchstone of homicide research is Marvin Wolfgang's 1958 study of homicides in Philadelphia between 1948 and 1952. Wolfgang's resulting book, *Patterns in Criminal Homicide*, contains a chapter on victim-precipitated homicide. In a murder so labeled, the victim contributes in some significant way to his eventual death. Perhaps this is starting the initial argument or confrontation that, though not intended, leads inexorably to a lethal act. Wolfgang saw this element as the victim using the first physical violence. In his study, Wolfgang found that 26% of the 588 homicides he studied were victim-precipitated. Wolfgang also found that victims had previous arrest records in 62% of the victim-precipitated cases compared with 42% in cases he classified as non-victim precipitated. Also notable was that the offenders in victim-precipitated cases were less likely to have previous arrests compared to non-victim precipitated. A portion of Wolfgang's observations about this category of homicide concerned the public's general sympathy toward a victim and fear of the offender. He points out

that, given the study results, these feelings are perhaps often misplaced.

Given the importance of provocation in determining charge level, Wolfgang's homicide study and others that followed are important and have practical implications for investigators as they work to comprehensively describe a lethal event and for prosecutors as they consider the appropriate charge and sentence recommendation if a conviction results. While Wolfgang's study did not recognize words alone as sufficiently provocative to classify a homicide as victim precipitated, other studies have.

It is important *not* to read **victim precipitation** as *victim blaming*, which occurs at times in the criminal justice system and its response. Provocation is generally considered, in the legal sense, to involve a measure of culpability. Victim precipitation is a social science observation related to the cause of a violent interaction. This fact is further complicated from a research standpoint as well as an investigative one because we may not be able to accurately know the victim's words, actions, or mind-set. The offender may assert that he feared for his life, and a homicide may be placed into a category of self-defense, which may effectively remove it from later research consideration as a criminal homicide. The offender's assertion may certainly be false and intended as manipulation by a psychopath (Porter & Woodworth, 2007) or someone else trying to avoid jail, though the psychopath

Confrontation in Movie Theater Leads to Homicide

An afternoon movie matinee in a Florida theater unexpectedly turned deadly when an argument between two men resulted in a shooting. According to police reports, Chad Oulson, a 43-year-old father, and his wife Nicole were seated and watching movie previews while Chad was texting with their daughter. Another movie patron, Curtis Reeves, a 71-year-old retired police captain, complained about the texting to Oulson and left the theater to alert employees. When Reeves returned to

his seat, Oulson turned around in his seat to ask whether Reeves had reported him to the manager, and the confrontation continued and escalated. During the argument, Reeves shot Oulson and his wife. Oulson died from his injuries, while his wife received a non-life-threatening injury to her hand from the same bullet that killed her husband. Reeves, who had no prior criminal record, was charged with second-degree homicide and aggravated battery, and the case was set for a jury trial. Reeves asserted that he acted in self-defense. The prosecution decided to seek a life sentence.

WHY WOULD THEY DO IT?

tends toward an instrumental use of violence. For homicide investigators and researchers it is important to note that contradictory or no witness accounts for the former, and insufficient case file detail for the latter (Polk, 1997) can make it difficult or impossible to determine degree or presence of victim precipitation.

Past violent behavior can be a predictor of future violent behavior, to an extent (Farrington, 1989). This assertion fits with the finding of a significant number of victims having a previous criminal record. Notable would be a record of violent offenses as it is logical to assume that the actions taken that preceded the lethal assault likely affect someone *primed* for violence more so than someone less inclined to respond violently to provocation. A criminal record is not always present in a homicide victim or offender. The use of a criminal past as a proxy for homicidal capability is suspect.

Victim precipitation may have a further practical value in underscoring the efficacy of providing conflict resolution training to young people to help them learn to **de-escalate**, batterer intervention courses for offenders in intimate partner violence situations, and anger management therapy for persons identified through multiple arrests for violent crimes. We believe that school-based social-awareness training for young people regarding the dynamics of confrontational violence holds promise for averting or diffusing some escalating confrontations. Much as Glasser's "reality therapy" (1965) focused on the immediate behavior and what to do differently, we propose that such a training for adolescents and teens be based on brief, concrete steps they can take to move away from what could become a violent interaction. This is challenging given the rapid escalation so many such instances take and the lack of self-control by many young people. Nonetheless, if there is an awareness created in the mind of a young person that an incident can always go quickly out of control, some percentage may have enough presence of mind to summon a response that takes them away from the dynamic.

HONOR CONTESTS

Male–male homicides by juveniles or adults are often triggered by seemingly insignificant events. The affront may be a minor physical encounter, perhaps a bump or shove, or it may not be physical at all, perhaps just a look or *mean mugging*. These events likely take place around people or in public, such as a party or at a bar where other young men are present. The public humiliation can lead to what Daly and Wilson (1988) called "an escalated showing-off contest" (p. 176).

The role of an audience of other young men seems to have an amplifying effect on the emotions and feelings of the individual(s), such that there is a need to respond with a show of *manhood*. Polk (1994) views this situation as one in which the individuals mutually agree to the forthcoming aggression. Whether the slight was intended or accidental, the audience causes one or both participants to feel a pressure to posture. The interaction escalates through words and gestures to a physical

---

WHY WOULD THEY DO IT?

Shooting Outside Strip Club Leaves Man Dead

In Portland, Oregon, an argument inside a strip club among several bar patrons spilled into the parking lot, where one man was killed and a woman was injured. Witnesses reported that two men were involved in a dispute inside the bar that involved one man's girlfriend. The men did not know each other. After leaving the bar and going to the parking lot, the gunman, 30-year-old Bradley O'Rourke, shot the victim, 33-year-old Anton Hill, one time in the head and shot his girlfriend in the arm. The defendant then fled the scene on foot. He was arrested days later and charged with murder with a firearm, attempted murder, and first-degree assault. Police did not believe the incident was gang related and were investigating whether the confrontation resulted from a fight over a woman.

altercation that may incorporate weapons if they are available. While neither person may have had the initial intention to kill anyone, the dynamic of the situation carries the *context* to a lethal conclusion. Males may act out their concept of masculinity by an aggressive response to establish or reestablish reputation or save face in different settings, such as the street, school, or a social event, which vary the influence of others who are present.

David Luckenbill (1977) examined a group of homicides in his notable effort to explain why murders happen. Luckenbill's analysis of the male *character contest* of Goffman's (1967) earlier description involved six distinct stages that two individuals progress through in a dance to maintain or save face. Luckenbill asserted that these contests involved "a consensus among participants that violence was a suitable if not required means for settling the contest" (p. 177). He termed this progression a **situated transaction.**

The first stage is one in which an offense (to face or honor) is committed. To move to stage two, the other party must interpret the offense as such. This may be self-evident based on past interactions between the two (rehearsals) or by asking nearby friends or persons in the setting (audience). The third stage finds the aggrieved responding in kind to save face. Stage four results if the pair comes to a "working agreement" that the contest will escalate. Note that one or the other may misinterpret the challenge, counter-challenge, or accept the "implicit agreement to violence." The audience may play a significant role in each stage but perhaps especially here, when there is an important opportunity to de-escalate the conflict or egg on one or both participants. Stage five is the physical altercation itself. Stage six finds the now offender remaining, fleeing, or being held by members of the audience.

At each stage of Luckenbill's model, either or both of the participants could, of course, disengage. There can be an apology, a clarification of what was meant, an appeal to audience members to mediate, or perhaps a decision to

Figure 5.1 Luckenbill's Situated Transaction

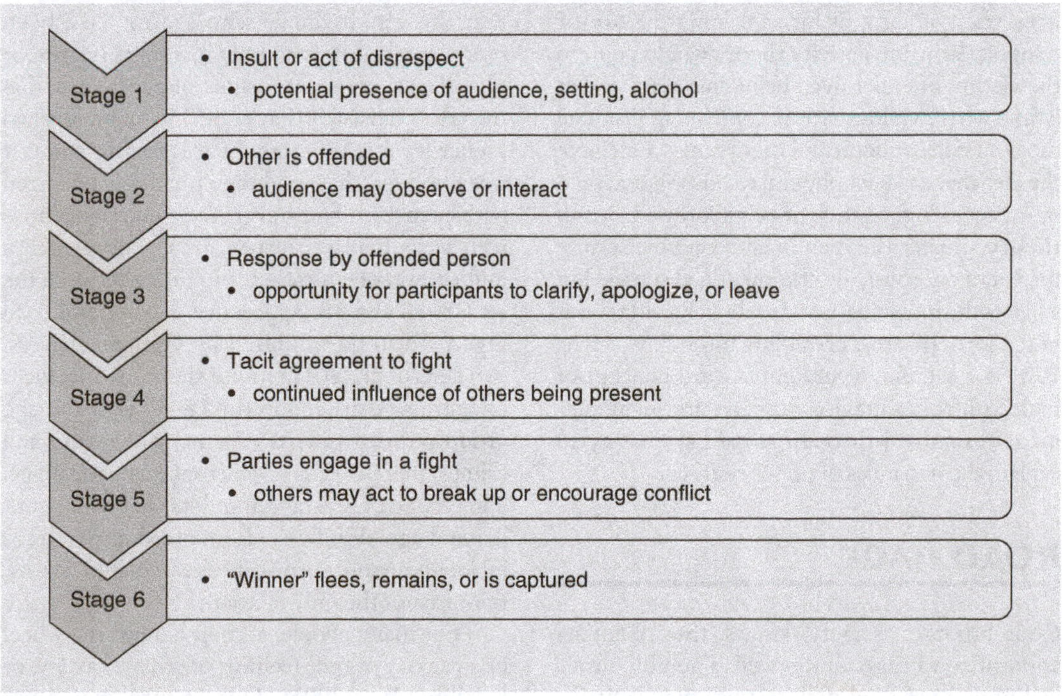

Stage 1
- Insult or act of disrespect
- potential presence of audience, setting, alcohol

Stage 2
- Other is offended
- audience may observe or interact

Stage 3
- Response by offended person
- opportunity for participants to clarify, apologize, or leave

Stage 4
- Tacit agreement to fight
- continued influence of others being present

Stage 5
- Parties engage in a fight
- others may act to break up or encourage conflict

Stage 6
- "Winner" flees, remains, or is captured

Source: Adapted from David F. Luckenbill, "Criminal Homicide as a Situated Transaction," *Social Problems*, Volume 25, Issue 2, 1 December 1977, pp. 176–186.

simply leave the location. On many occasions, a participant who leaves is merely going to get a weapon. Alternatively, after leaving, the participant becomes more convinced that he has lost face and that to remain with this status is intolerable. He then travels back to reengage the contest, or this *rehearsal* becomes a template for a future event that may end in lethal violence.

A number of researchers point out that the six-stage model is not a description of all such argument-based homicides. Brookman and Maguire (2004) contrast the confrontational homicide, for example, with the revenge homicide, which may have also begun as a conflict between two men but took on more advance planning. And while Luckenbill did not purport that it be a comprehensive analysis, the model is important in illustrating that many homicides of this nature are frequently mutual affairs in which each person has (albeit perhaps very brief) opportunities to de-escalate or absent himself. We prefer to envision the stages three-dimensionally and with the addition of branching decision points where the various actors in the event make choices that can alter the many potential outcomes of the affront event.

A number of criminological theories have been tried out as a fit for explaining the **honor contest**. **Routine activity theory** would point to the victim–offender dyad being in a place and at a time where various factors combine to facilitate the homicide. **Subcultural theory** may contribute the idea that a violent physical response is accepted or expected in the group or neighborhood. **Strain theory** situates the men in an economic setting that rules out societally acknowledged success but still lets the individual save face by achieving status in the form of street credibility through violence. Within a seemingly straightforward concept of male confrontational aggression are many elements examined through social psychology to explain the dynamics of honor contests.

ROAD RAGE

Contemporary society knows the phenomenon of **road rage** all too well. The ubiquitous cell phone use (and now texting) may contribute a significant dynamic in the frequency of such events. While research shows males predominate as perpetrators of road rage, victims may be more evenly distributed gender-wise (Asbridge, Smart, & Mann, 2003; Wickens, Mann, Stoduto, Ialomiteanu, & Smart, 2011). Age was also found to have wide variation, with the exception of few elderly drivers. As with many psychological phenomena, it is important to draw a distinction between acts of frustration and anger that consist of hand gestures, honking horns, or shouting and acting physically, such as braking aggressively, unsignaled and aggressive lane changing, steering at another vehicle, or instigating a physical confrontation. Some incidents involving unintended or careless acts behind the wheel may escalate into confrontation and unnecessary violence, most often between men. The U.S. Department of Transportation (USDOT), the American Automobile Association (AAA), and others have conducted studies about aggressive driving and traffic accidents. These groups have consistently shown the link between such behavior and the outcomes of accidents, injuries, and fatalities.

There has been some examination between psychiatric distress and road rage incidents. Smart, Asbridge, Mann, and Adlaf (2003) found that those individuals who are or have been more involved in road rage incidents (victim or offender) show greater signs of psychiatric distress than those who have not. The offenders had higher levels of distress. In at least this study, it was observed that road rage incidents occurred with men who had never been married, those who were living in urban areas, those with a higher level of education, and those between the ages of 30 and 39. Aggressive driving and road rage tend to be exhibited by younger drivers. Wickens et al. (2011) found the most instances of aggressive driving in the 18–34 year-old age group in their study. As with many behaviors and crimes, there is lesser occurrence as people age. This is one of several reminders that while gender and age of individuals involved in road rage incidents are not surprising as associated factors, they are not the only factors.

For many people, getting behind the wheel of a car can trigger feelings of stress, anxiety, or hostility (Ayar, 2006). This, in turn, may cause drivers to use their vehicles in an aggressive

Four Shot and a Boy Dead

According to a *Washington Post* article in June of 2018, a 23-year-old man in Westminster, Colorado, followed a family to a parking lot and argued with a woman before shooting at her, her children, and a bystander. The shots struck the woman, two of her children, and the man standing nearby in the parking lot of a dental office. One of the children died as a result of his wounds. Police later said the shooter did not know any of his victims. Police said the incident stemmed from apparent road rage.

Critical Question: How many such incidents of violence or death occur each year in the United States?

Road Rage Incident Ends in Stabbing Death

Two truck drivers from Wisconsin engaged in a heated confrontation over their CB radios. The incident escalated with the truckers trying to cut each other off on the highway. They pulled over to the side of the road and began a physical altercation that lead to trucker David Seddon, a 49-year-old man, pulling out a knife and repeatedly stabbing Alan Lauritzen, 40 years old, in his chest. Seddon drove off and left the unconscious man bleeding on the side of the road, but the incident had been witnessed by other drivers. Seddon was charged with and convicted of first-degree murder for the incident. The judge sentenced him to 25 years in state prison.

manner. There is little doubt about the millions of accidents and likely thousands of deaths traceable to road rage over the years. This is also not a phenomenon unique to the United States. Road rage also rivals alcohol as a significant factor in traffic fatalities. The amount of time spent driving as well as the driving environment have an impact on some drivers' stress levels. A person's individual factors are also related to the emotions experienced and actions taken when behind the wheel. Techniques in stress reduction and time management can ameliorate driver aggression. These techniques are clearly appropriate for driver education courses.

Roberts and Indermaur (2008) distinguished two types of road rage incidents, criminal and noncriminal. Criminal road rage includes assaults and vehicle damage; noncriminal road rage includes verbal abuse, obscene gestures, flashing lights, horn honking, and tailgating or aggressive braking. Road rage and many honor contest homicides exhibit the concept of homogamy, the tendency of victims and offenders to share behavioral and demographic characteristics. Roberts and Indermaur analyzed demographics, experience driving, and aggressive road tendencies to determine the prevalence of homogamy. With these factors in mind, the researchers found in their research that the odds of criminal road rage repetition were almost 6.5 times greater for males than females. The study identified young males of lower socioeconomic status as being more likely to perpetrate road rage behavior. This correlated with low temper control and being prepared to use violence when they were provoked. It was also noted that individuals who said they had been victims of road rage were quite likely to be road rage offenders themselves.

AUDIENCE

As mentioned earlier, an important aspect of confrontational violence often present is that of an audience. Whether there are casual bar patrons, family members at a BBQ, or peers on the playground at school, the actions to encourage or discourage an incident from escalating have been found to be significant (Hughes & Short, 2005). Polk (1997) observes, "Understanding the nature of the interactions that link victims, offenders, and bystanders in unfolding homicide scenarios may prove theoretically richer than focusing on what may be the unanswerable question of 'who started it?'" (p. 141). The "chorus" can have a strong influence on the direction an interaction takes (Toch, 1969).

To this list of victims, offenders, and bystanders, we add location as another important factor in confrontations. Miethe and Regoeczi (2004) have done much to further our understanding of the situational factors found in a homicide event. An argument at work over a questionable call in yesterday's sports event is tangibly different from being bumped into or insulted in a bar. Social constraints present in some public settings are not present in casual settings. The internal restraints may also be weakened by the use of alcohol, the presence of peers or intimates, and the tone of a crowd.

Conflict can also take the form of a group confrontation. This introduces additional dynamics. Notable is the degree of anonymity that individual group members may feel within the larger group or mass of people. Verma (2007) discusses ways to prevent violent situations, such as riots, mobs, violent protests, and confrontational religious celebrations. Complications are added in the application of rational choice when taking confrontation from the individual to a larger scale. While the group may be destructive and irrational, each person within the group is a rational person who is guided by his or her own self-interest. Understood in this way, there may be techniques for preventing or mitigating large-scale disturbances. Appeals to individual rationality or calm may be effective. Pointing out individual accountability or culpability may influence how many assess remaining in a group intending to be disruptive.

Riots and mobs can, in some ways, be seen through the lens of confrontational homicide. Group behavior due to some type of confrontation can also be an example of behavior that gets taken too far. Calm, rational heads would prevail, but the situation is not conducive to that. If those individuals involved were thinking rationally, then the situation most likely would not escalate to violence. The confrontational violence takes some smaller scale issue and magnifies it and leads to unnecessary and irrational behaviors. Mob actions usually add the quality of shared responsibility, which may psychologically equate to no responsibility.

In many instances, gang violence is directed toward a rival gang or gang member who has threatened or shown disrespect to the *honor* of the gang that assaults someone. When a person joins a gang, he often identifies so strongly with the gang that it becomes the primary aspect of his persona. That person's world and reality is about representing the gang through acts of allegiance, including acting tough or becoming violent (Watkins & Melde, 2018). This can maintain or elevate his status in the gang as well as show the expected allegiance. Gang confrontations, perhaps even more than bar fights and other interactions, can be explained in terms of Luckenbill's (1977) situated transactions.

An audience, such as one at a sporting event, can be quite boisterous. European soccer match crowds have been excited to the point of lethal violence in contemporary settings. Lynch mobs remain a clear example of the rationalization mentality that groups bent on avenging a perceived or real crime or affront to a community member or value may have. Frontier justice may not have been stopped very often by the iconic movie image of the western sheriff standing firm in front of the mob intent on hanging the jail's inmate, especially if the townspeople had just left the saloon.

ALCOHOL

The link between alcohol and aggressive behavior is well established. The involvement of alcohol in crime generally is noted by various monitoring programs, such as the Drug Use Forecasting (DUF). As a public policy matter, the use of alcohol by young people, including minors, continues to merit significant attention. There continue to be studies regarding the impact of alcohol or drug use on both behavior, generally, and criminal behavior, specifically. Reduced inhibitions, increased aggressiveness, and dulled sensitivity to the immediate physical effects of violence clearly results in many bad outcomes. Drug use has not been documented in as many homicide events as alcohol. The relative prevalence of alcohol may, in part, be an artifact of other behaviors and lifestyle issues correlated with alcohol abuse.

While it may not be possible to exactly state the degree of causal relationship between alcohol and violence, we note the high incidence of alcohol involvement in homicide and other crimes (Markowitz, 2001). Problem-oriented policing relies on an examination of underlying causes of crime to construct strategies and programs to address more than the symptoms of those crimes (Goldstein, 1977). If law enforcement and others note a high incidence of crimes such as DUI, vandalism, and disorderly intoxication arrests all in close proximity to one or more bars, further examination would be warranted. If, upon further examination, a temporal linkage to peak patronage and subsequent closing time created a clear link between the bar business and crimes, law enforcement organizations would adopt several tactics to address the apparent underlying problem. This might include contacting the business directly to request that more bouncers be used, a taxi program for intoxicated patrons, or even a warning about the risk to the bar owner's liquor license. Later analysis to determine whether the various crimes and signs of disorder had lessened would be a satisfactory outcome assessment with direct application to a real-world problem.

Drinking alcohol affects the behaviors or vulnerability of victims, which may put them at a greater risk to be victimized. Alcohol-related violence is a public health problem in many countries. The longtime acceptance of alcohol use impedes certain strategies to address the violence associated with use. This difficulty was long evident in the efforts to address driving under the influence of alcohol in the United States. While society's acquiescence or ambivalence to drunk driving has finally waned, the perhaps less apparent problem of *drunk fighting* is not clearly considered a major public health issue. What has been established in the literature, though, is an association between the geographic density of businesses that serve alcohol and violence rates (Grubesic & Pridemore, 2011). Spatial analytic techniques can refine less specific charting of assaultive crimes around alcohol establishments. Grubesic and Pridemore (2011) point to several studies that "suggest that the environmental characteristics in and around bars, including staff organization, intoxication of patrons and people

remaining around bars after closing can influence levels of violence onsite or nearby" (p. 10). They go on to comment on the "propensity for patrons to hang out . . . after closing" and say that "social control mechanisms are weakened" (p. 10). Their work notes that the association of alcohol outlets and violence holds even when controlling for other factors.

In an opinion article on the prevalence of male violence in Australia following the death of a sports figure, Flood (2004) examined violence at bars and pubs in Sydney between 1998 and 2000. According to the article, which references its data from the New South Wales Bureau of Crime Statistics and Research, there were 1,100 assaults reported at licensed premises in Sydney during those years. The article indicated that violent assaults outside of pubs in Australia are a regular weekend occurrence. Most of the noted violence involved a male offender and a male victim, and drinking was typically involved as a factor. Flood, a research fellow with the Australia Institute, found that violence was more likely to occur in those places that had a higher proportion of males, especially strangers. The piece suggests some steps to reduce some violence, such as enforcing liquor laws that address serving intoxicated people and training security staff.

PHYSIOLOGY

As you read the chapter, you may be waiting to hear something about testosterone. Aren't men simply more aggressive and violent because of those chemicals in their system? Aggression can be verbal or physical, and it can take the form of socially acceptable competition, violent assault, or even the "covert manipulation" of passive-aggressive behavior (Bernhardt, 1997). Aggression and violence are not the same, and aggression need not progress to violence. This same observation has been made about the relationship among frustration, stress, and aggressive reactions.

Testosterone and low serotonin levels have been linked to aggressive behavior in various species. Steroid use has been blamed for aggressive action as well (Bernhardt, 1997). In addition to chemical influences on behavior, the overall development of the brain is implicated as well. The prefrontal cortex is identified as the area of the human brain that regulates social behavior. Risky behavior may not be accurately identified as such until after the maturation of this part of our brains. This development may not occur until age 25. The U.S. Department of Health and Human Services notes that this timetable of development may explain why some adolescents act the way they do. The executive functions of the human prefrontal cortex include things such as our ability to pay attention, gauge the consequences of behavior, control impulses, deal with emotions, and other issues of self-control. These aspects of cognition seem to be clearly implicated in risk-taking behavior, such as confrontations.

Most crime is, in fact, committed by men. While there are many factors that contribute to this fact, the neurochemistry of the male has remained implicated as one factor (George, 1997). Chemicals occurring naturally or introduced artificially as well as brain development may be some of the catalysts when considering confrontational homicide and incidents involving male honor, pride, or protective behavior.

GIRLS, WOMEN, AND CONFRONTATIONAL HOMICIDE

While there is no lack of contemporary research about criminality by women and girls, the focus on violent crime remains of keen interest (Franzese, Covey, & Menard, 2016; Kruttschnitt, Gartner, & Hussemann, 2008). There has been reported, in recent years, an increase in violence used by girls and women in the commission of crimes against others, both male and female. The accuracy of this assertion is debated, with some finding little change in overall rates of violent crime while acknowledging some nuanced differences (Kruttschnitt et al., 2008). Whether this trend is an artifact of more violence in society, the predictable fallout of the women's rights movement (Adler, 1975), or various other factors remains under study and

debated. Perhaps the erosion of the protective patriarchal effect in U.S. society simply leads to an increased willingness to arrest, prosecute, and incarcerate girls and women.

Two decades ago, Carter (1999) talked about girls in gangs and concluded that girls are "stepping to the forefront, selling their own drugs, making their own decisions, and avenging their own wrongs" (p. 22). Some of this interest is manufactured by the media approach to sensational stories. Sensational, in this case, are the criminal acts seen as breaking from traditionally accepted female behavior. Given the 24/7 news cycle and the traditional predilection of the media to cover female-committed crime, it is understandable that many in the public view the purported demise of women as nonviolent with alarm. Women commit acts of violence for various reasons (Kruttschnitt & Carbone-Lopez, 2006). As with most issues in criminology, the explanation of violent offending by females is not a simple one.

History is replete with examples of violent acts by women. We see incidents in which many girls and women turn to resolving disputes in violent ways, similar to what we have come to expect from males. Conclusions from crime data are in disagreement as to whether female behavior is more violent or societal expectations have shifted to allow for less *lady-like* actions. Kruttschnitt et al. (2008) assessed data about female offenders at a California women's prison. Relative to a study from 40 years prior that also examined violent offending by women, the authors explained,

> Fewer women are acting alone in the commission of a violent crime (particularly in the case of assaults), gun use has increased in homicides and more women report that a need for money or drugs, or both, motivated their crime. (p. 31)

While availability of longitudinal data calls into question whether we have seen a trend of increasing female involvement in crime generally, incarceration statistics do show an increase in the proportion of female inmates. While males are in no danger of being eclipsed in the commission of crime, the use of violence, or the volume of incarceration, the trends for females are disturbing and need the close attention of policymakers as well as researchers.

Girls and women do participate in confrontational homicide. While women make up a relatively small percentage of homicide offenders and even fewer confrontational homicide offenders, their participation in such crimes deserves research. Some researchers maintain that the gender gap in violent offending is narrowing based on relatively larger decreases in male offending, as opposed to an actual significant increase in female violent offending (Lauritsen, Heimer, & Lynch, 2009). Looking into the factors and possible policy actions to reduce this violence is important. Later in the book, we examine intimate partner violence and the impact on women and their involvement as victims and occasionally offenders.

INVESTIGATIVE CONSIDERATIONS

Given the number and percentage of homicides arising from arguments or fights, investigators should note some factors often present that may help in solving cases. Douglas, Burgess, Burgess, and Ressler (2013) list several factors in their well-known *Crime Classification Manual*. The victimology includes "a high incidence of young-adult, blue-collar or unemployed, male victims with a lower education level. The offender is known to the victim. The victim commonly has a history of assaultive behavior and of using violence to resolve his problems" (p. 183).

Crime scene indicators frequently noted include a scene that is "spread out, demonstrating signs of offender and victim movement as well as signs of struggle. It is random and sloppy" (Douglas et al., 2013, p. 185). Their research also found that the weapon used in the assault was often brought to the scene by the ultimate offender. He brought the weapon because of his "predisposition to assaultive behavior" (p. 185). This makes the weapon one of opportunity, even if the offender leaves briefly to acquire his weapon and return. The method or cause of death often relies on this availability, with weapons such as firearms, sharp objects, and blunt objects being the most common. Often, the victim is unarmed, his body is left at the scene, and the offender makes no attempt to conceal his victim.

Douglas et al. (2013) also say that the precipitating argument or conflict is the "cause of the dispute" (p. 184). They state that "the killing can be a spontaneous or delayed reaction" (p. 184) to the dispute. It is often found that both offender and victim have a history of violence. Because the assault is frequently spontaneous, there may be witnesses, and they may know important information about the offender.

Two Women Found Guilty of Manslaughter in Beating Death of Another Woman

In January 2014, 23-year-old recent college graduate Kim Pham was fatally beaten by two other women outside a nightclub in Huntington Beach, California. Witnesses testified that Candace Brito, 27, and Vanesa Zavala, 26, repeatedly kicked Pham in the head while she was on the ground outside of the club. The witness testimony indicated that Pham threw the first punch in the altercation after a verbal confrontation began because a friend of Brito and Zavala bumped into someone from Pham's group of friends inside the bar. During the trial testimony, Brito testified that the fight scene was a chaotic one, with many men around the scene who appeared to be helping Pham but who did not seem to be trying to stop the fight. Brito asserted that she acted in self-defense, but the jury convicted both defendants of manslaughter. After the verdict, the prosecutor in the case urged people to heed the lesson of the sad case and to walk away from these types of confrontations.

WHY WOULD THEY DO IT?

SUMMARY

Confrontational homicides are understood, generally, as arising from a seemingly trivial matter, occurring in a public place, often with an audience, between younger males, and involving alcohol (Brookman, 2003). Many gang-related killings may fall under the category of confrontational homicide. Completely understanding such events is challenging given the absence of the victim's account. Did either person try to de-escalate the argument before it turned deadly?

Instances of confrontational homicide are with us in everyday life. When we consider the ample opportunities for frustration that can lead to aggression, it is possible for everyone to envision confrontations. There are a number of factors implicated in confrontational situations and ultimately confrontational homicide. Luckenbill's situated transaction is formed on the basis of mutually agreed-upon *contests*. There may have been the rehearsals of previous friction between the two parties, or victim precipitation may play a role. Both victim and offender may have backgrounds that include assaults and criminal charges. Aggravating factors may be present, including alcohol or an audience. While police and investigators are not always interested in the antecedents of a fight, investigation of homicide always involves an interest in motive. Investigating based on the theoretical construct of the confrontational homicide can yield evidence of motive and identification of potential suspects. Combining the investigative approach utilizing multiple investigators to quickly canvass a homicide scene with the insight that witnesses would have been aware of a rapidly escalating minor altercation can yield beneficial results.

Some offenders, overcome with the reality of a killing, remain at the scene. Some call 9-1-1 themselves to report the incident. Some offenders leave the scene in a panic or after the result of the outcome they intended. Some are held by bystanders until law enforcement arrives.

Education programs in the K–12 setting can take the form of both social awareness and driver education training. Recent collaborations led by the Department of Justice, Office of Juvenile Justice and Delinquency Prevention (OJJDP) have focused on youth violence prevention strategies including conflict resolution and de-escalation to try and reduce the rate of violence and homicide. Such training can sensitize young people not only to the dynamics of confrontational violence but the quick and sometimes deadly consequences of reacting to trivial friction, especially when alcohol is involved.

Death comes as a surprise to many. Among the most frequently surprised are those who become embroiled in the confrontational dynamics leading to what is known as confrontational homicide. If people could foresee what was to come, wouldn't they avoid it? Entering into the agreement for confrontation is not necessarily agreeing to the potentially lethal outcome.

From a theoretical perspective, subcultural violence and differential association theory can partly explain violent responses. The expectations of peers and saving face in front of an audience often have a multiplier effect on the emotions driving the behavior of the combatants. Educational approaches focused on immediately diffusing an honor contest, audience mitigation of such contests, the impact of alcohol on behavior, and early driver awareness of dangerous practices may yield a reduction of confrontational violence and homicide.

KEY TERMS

Confrontational homicide 70
Victim precipitation 71
De-escalate 72

Situated transaction 72
Honor contest 74
Routine activity theory 74

Subcultural theory 74
Strain theory 74
Road rage 74

DISCUSSION QUESTIONS

1. How should researchers consider the factors in a homicide situation so that they can determine if the killing was confrontational?
2. How can we reduce the potential for homicide and violence attributed to confrontational situations? What are the policy implications?
3. Why is it said that confrontational homicide is a man's crime?
4. Describe and discuss the effects audience can have on violent confrontations.
5. What role does alcohol play in violence?
6. Discuss the most prevalent criminological theories that help to explain confrontational homicide.

TRY THIS

The Centers for Disease Control and Prevention has examined violence and homicide among youth and determined it to be a significant public health issue. Examine their website here: https://www.cdc .gov/healthcommunication/toolstemplates/entertainmented/tips/ViolenceYouth.html. Analyze and summarize what the data show on the scope of the problem and some prevention strategies.

Examine homicides in your local jurisdiction for the last year. Try to determine which homicides you might classify as confrontational if you were a researcher. List and discuss the factors that led you to classify the homicides in this way.

6

"Home can be the most dangerous place for a woman. It is particularly heartbreaking when those who should be protecting their loved ones are the very people responsible for their murder."

—Jean-Luc Lemahieu, *Director for Policy Analysis and Public Affairs, United Nations Office on Drugs and Crime*

". . . those serpents! There's no pleasing them!"

—Lewis Carroll, *Alice's Adventures in Wonderland*

"Often things are as bad as they seem."

—Sheldon Kopp, *author of All God's Children Are Lost but Only a Few Can Play the Piano: Finding a Life That Is Truly Your Own*

CHAPTER OUTLINE

Student Learning Outcomes

Students will be able to:

- define and explain the rates of intimate partner homicide.

- explain the dynamics of domestic violence.

- describe the circumstances and risk factors that sometimes lead to intimate partner homicide.

- identify the primary theories used to explain intimate partner homicide.

- explain the tools used for lethality assessment in intimate partner violence cases and the limitations and uses of such tools.

- discuss the process of fatality review in intimate partner homicide and its impact on the development of public policy.

- describe some of the challenges faced by prosecutors who handle cases of intimate partner violence and homicide.

INTRODUCTION

In this textbook, we will use the terms **intimate partner violence (IPV)** and **intimate partner homicide (IPH)** instead of **domestic violence (DV)** as these terms are more descriptive of the relationship and the dynamics between the offender and victim. Intimate partner homicides are those that are perpetrated by current or former spouses or partners who share or have shared an intimate relationship. Intimate partner violence and the potential IPH include same-sex and never-married couples as well help with an inclusive definition. While research is less available on lesbian, gay, bisexual, and transgender (LGBT) relationship violence, some suggest that intimate partner homicide is similar regardless of sexual orientation (Mize & Shackelford, 2008). Domestic-violence homicide is a broader category of homicide and includes homicides committed by any family member. We will cover those types of homicides more fully in the next chapter. And to be sure, there are deaths of non-intimates that come about from an incident of intimate partner homicide (Smith, Fowler, & Niolon, 2014). In this chapter, we will first address the rates of intimate partner homicide, both in the United States as well as across the world. Then, we will address some of the dynamics of intimate partner violence and examine various prevailing theories about why IPH occurs. The chapter will also introduce you to some of the current work around lethality assessment and fatality

reviews in the area of intimate partner violence. Finally, we will examine some of the issues that arise when IPH cases are prosecuted and will address recommendations by researchers for ways to reduce intimate partner homicide.

Intimate partner homicide is the most extreme result of intimate partner violence, which is sometimes also referred to as domestic violence in the literature. Clearly, not all intimate partner violence leads to a murder, but unresolved and ongoing abuse can escalate, and the abuser may kill his victim as a culminating act of power and control. "Intimate partner violence is defined as physical violence, sexual violence, stalking, or psychological aggression (including coercive tactics) by a current or former intimate partner" (Smith et al., 2014, p. 461). A major risk factor for IPH, whether the offender is male or female, is prior intimate partner violence (Campbell, Glass, Sharps, Laughon, & Bloom, 2007). Not only has intimate partner homicide typically been preceded by intimate partner violence, but at least some of the prior violence has also usually been reported to authorities. The other risk factors identified by researchers include prior threats of violence or death, the presence of firearms, and whether the victim is pregnant.

The careful study of intimate partner homicide is essential for any student examining homicide. Intimate partner homicide is one of the most prevalent types of homicide in the United States. According to the Bureau of Justice Statistics, between 1980 and 2008, the relationship of the victim and offender was known

Dallas Drake, criminologist and cofounder of the Center for Homicide Research has conducted extensive research on homicide, including LGBT individuals, and provides the following research update:

Homicide among lesbian, gay, bisexual and transgender (LGBT) people is unique in its demographics and behavioral character. The majority of killings within this group are of gay or bisexual men, and the majority of offenders are also homosexual. Victims often die within the context of a sexual encounter, and therefore are often found murdered in a bedroom of a home. Due to the class status of victims, that home is often an apartment, rather than an owned home. Only 15.8% of LGBT homicide victims died in hate-crime homicides (Drake, 2015). Intimate partner homicides occur in roughly the same proportion in gay homicides as in heterosexual homicides (Drake, 2004, 2015).

Transgender homicide characteristics typically mirror heterosexual patterns of homicide because, in most cases, transsexual individuals are heterosexual. Transgender homicide victimization often occurs due to marginalization by known offenders with whom they sometimes are in intimate relations. Society's marginalization of transgendered people further delegitimizes their lives, making homicide a more acceptable behavior when violence does erupt. It appears that the violence within these attacks is more severe than in other kinds of homicides and may be of intrapsychic origin as offenders respond to violations of gender boundaries.

Lesbian victims of homicide are rare. This is because (1) women are seldom victims of homicidal violence and (2) more gay men exist than do lesbian women by a ratio of 2:1. When lesbian women are murdered, they tend to be singled out due to public displays of affection. This also means there are a higher number of lesbian double homicides (Drake, 2004, 2015).

in approximately 63% of all homicide cases. Of those cases where the victim–offender relationship was known, 10% of those were killed by a spouse. Another 6.3% were killed by a boyfriend or girlfriend (Cooper & Smith, 2011). In 2012, the UCR data show that female murder victims were killed by their intimate partners in 35% of cases where the relationship between the victim and offender was known. In 2017, the CDC working from a combination of data sources, asserted that more than half of the homicides of women were IPV-related (Petrosky et al., 2017). We point out again that data suffers from definitional challenges, source, and the ever-present problem of underreporting. We do know that a shocking number of women are murdered by the person who they have shared their life with.

Historically, in this country, intimate partner violence was not treated seriously by law enforcement or by policymakers. As with the broad social movement to reduce drunk driving, so too have many groups and components of the country's social structure mobilized to address intimate partner violence. Campbell, Webster, and Glass (2009) note that this response includes not only criminal justice agencies but social services, health care systems, and the general public. Some came to the IPV movement from a pragmatic orientation. Intimate partner violence costs money. Lost work hours and wages, diminished productivity, medical costs—all have significant dollar amounts attached and impact many parts of society. Visits to hospital emergency rooms by women have been estimated to involve intimate partner violence perhaps one third of the time (Campbell, 2002). Children observe the dynamics between their parents or a parent and her partner. Long-term outcomes associated with intimate partner violence include "increased odds of poor physical health and physical disability, psychological distress and mental illness, and heightened recreational and non-recreational substance use" (Carbone-Lopez, Kruttschnitt, & Macmillan, 2006, p. 382).

States finally began to move (and slowly for many) in the 1970s to create or strengthen laws regarding harming family members, specifically spouses. The move to criminalize domestic

In March 2017, a prominent Houston transplant surgeon, Dr. Sherilyn Gordon-Burroughs, was killed by her husband Daniel Burroughs at their home. When police responded to the scene to conduct a welfare check at the request of the family, after a five hour stand-off as the SWAT team entered the home, the husband killed himself with a shotgun. The coworkers of Dr. Burroughs were shocked by the news and reported that they did not know of any ongoing problems in her marriage. The crime generated a renewed focus by some in the media to address the disproportionate rates, and lack of media coverage, of intimate partner homicide of Black women.

violence was not met with universal enthusiasm, to say the least. Abuse of one's spouse or children was not viewed by many people *as* abuse, and these were generally considered private family matters that police should not meddle in. Feminists, social workers, victim advocacy groups, and victims brought the concerns related to domestic violence to the public agenda and worked tirelessly to educate both the public and government agencies, including legislators and police. Funding eventually came in the 1980s for programming for victims, shelters for battered spouses, and treatment for abusers. As Buzawa, Buzawa, and Stark (2015) note in their informative book *Responding to Domestic Violence: The Integration of Criminal Justice and Human Services*, the confluence of these factors greatly influenced the massive reform efforts related to domestic violence crime. In 1994, Congress passed the Violence Against Women Act (VAWA) and started the federal Office on Violence Against Women (OVW). VAWA gave more funds for shelters and rape crisis services and provided training and support to increase the consistency of laws, enhance sentencing for offenders, and improve law enforcement investigations and prosecutions across the country. The OVW (2019) mission statement is as follows:

> The mission of the Office on Violence Against Women (OVW), a component of the U.S. Department of Justice, is to provide federal leadership in developing the national capacity to reduce violence against women and administer justice for and strengthen services to victims of domestic violence, dating violence, sexual assault, and stalking. (n.p.)

After the first passage of the Violence Against Women Act in 1994, states began to pass a flood of legislation targeting the criminal act of domestic violence and the required law enforcement response to the act. These laws included mandatory arrest for domestic violence crime; the ability for law enforcement officers to make warrantless arrests, even in misdemeanor cases; strict bond conditions for offenders after arrest; mandatory sentencing provisions; mandatory counseling for offenders as part of sentencing; provisions for protective orders; restrictions on gun possession for offenders; and victim notification processes.

RATES

Intimate partner homicide is a gendered crime, both in the United States as well as around the world. This means that the vast majority of victims of IPH are women. We know that men can also be and are victims of IPV and IPH, but when women perpetrate the crime, research shows that the dynamics are usually different than when men are the perpetrators. Neil Websdale (1998), a noted scholar and researcher of IPV, in his ongoing work on studying IPV crime concluded that intimate partner homicide is a sex-specific phenomenon. Nearly one third of all female homicide victims in the United States are killed by an intimate partner, whereas only about 5% of male homicide victims are killed by an intimate. The CDC (Petrosky et al., 2017) recently reported that rates for Black women are the highest at 4.4 per 100,000, followed by American Indian and Alaska Native (4.3). The rates for these women is double the rate for Asian, Hispanic, and White women. Even though women are far more likely to be killed by an intimate partner than by anyone else, it is still an infrequent occurrence, even in at-risk populations (Campbell et al., 2007; Eke, Hilton, Harris, Rice, & Houghton, 2011).

Intimate partner homicide continues to be a major area of concern internationally as well. According to a recent study by the United Nations Office on Drugs and Crime, 437,000 people were killed by intentional homicide across the world in 2012. Almost 15% of all homicides and 35% of the murders of women worldwide stem from domestic violence (UNODC, 2014). The U.N. report found that women account for the majority of deaths in domestic-violence homicides. An international comparison of 66 countries found that, overall, 13.5% of homicides were committed by intimate partners, and the proportion of female homicides to male homicides was 6:1 (Stöckl et al., 2013, p. 860).

The figures for intimate partner homicide carry the same cautionary note as other crimes classified as against persons, which is that we do not have complete knowledge of the relationship between victim and offender. "From 1993 to 2010, the relationship between the victim and offender was not known or missing in 24% to 32% of homicide incidents involving female victims and 40% to 51% of homicide incidents involving male victims" (Catalano, 2013, p. 3). Nonlethal violence between partners is also common and frequently fraught with the data errors brought about by nonreporting. Eriksson and Mazerolle (2013) report that surveys of international victimization estimate lifetime prevalence rates of between 20% and 70%. But with only a small proportion of these incidents resulting in homicide, a lethal outcome is not a frequent outcome of the larger number of violent acts. "Although not unheard of, it is extremely rare for a woman to kill her partner as an end to a long cycle of violence that she has perpetrated against her partner" (Davies, 2008, p. 126).

DYNAMICS OF INTIMATE PARTNER HOMICIDE

Researchers have spent a great deal of time focusing on the dynamics of intimate partner violence, in the last several decades in particular. Either a man or a woman can be the victim of intimate partner homicide, and the crime is virtually always one with a single perpetrator and a single victim. Statistically, since the victim is most frequently a woman, some people erroneously believe that this is a women's issue. In fact, because the abusers are almost always men, this is clearly a men's issue. Although either men or women can act aggressively toward their partners, the relative physical strength and ability of men presents a greater risk of injury to their female partners. In homicide, one person chooses an attack or a weapon that allows him to kill the other, and a man is already well suited for such a lethal assault. The controlling behavior exhibited by men in intimate partner violence situations may escalate incrementally over time and possibly follow a cyclical pattern.

This cycle description, although recent researchers have relied on other models, is initially credited to Lenore Walker (1977) and posits that the abusive relationship moves repeatedly through the three stages of tension building, acute battering, and remorsefulness, or the honeymoon stage. Violence or threats of violence may be minor in the tension-building stage, but it gives way to the acute-battering stage where the abuser exhibits significant violence. This is often followed by apologies and promises of changed behavior as well as rationalizations about why the abuser harmed his victim. Predictably, this stage transitions back to tension building, and the violence continues. While this cycle of violence provides a convenient graphic, researchers now recognize that movements between these stages may not be as cyclical or predictable as described by Walker. Violence expert Gavin de Becker poignantly describes in his book, *The Gift of Fear* (1997), how he learned to recognize this familiar dance of danger in his own household as a child. His perception and resilience helped him survive and go on to help countless other victims of

In August 2018, in Frederick, Colorado, 33 year-old Chris Watts murdered his pregnant wife and his two young daughters at their home. He then disposed of their bodies at a nearby oil field facility where he had worked, burying his wife in a shallow grave and putting his daughters in oil tanks. He initially claimed that he had no idea what had happened to his family and that he was hoping for their safe return. The investigation soon revealed that he had been having an affair with a coworker and told her that he was in the process of obtaining a divorce. His wife had also told friends before the murder that Watts had revealed to her that he was unhappy that they were expecting another child. A neighbor's home camera captured him putting several objects into his car and later leaving his home in the middle of the night at the time his family went missing. He initially claimed that his wife had killed the girls and that he killed her in a rage after that happened. He entered a plea several months later to all of the murders and was sentenced to five consecutive life sentences with no chance for parole.

domestic violence as well as contribute significantly to the science of threat assessment covered later in the chapter.

Situational Factors

There are many factors that may be present in a relationship where intimate partner violence occurs. One example is a significant difference in the age of the partners. This has been shown to have a connection in cases where homicide results (Breitman, Shackleford, & Block, 2004). In the study by Breitman et al., it was found that if a man is at least 16 years older than his female partner, the risk is greater; it is also greater if the female is at least 10 years older than the man. The researchers also found in their sample of intimate partner homicide cases other factors that may affect risk, including race; socioeconomic status; marital status and the length of a relationship; substance use or abuse, including alcohol; and, unsurprisingly, the availability of weapons. In some cases of intimate partner homicide, the act is followed by the suicide of the perpetrator, though it has been found that this is more common among older individuals than those under 40 (Lund & Smorodinsky, 2001). The excessive use of alcohol and recreational drugs has been observed as a risk factor in IPV. Relationship problems, jealousy, and a lack of social support have also been noted (O'Leary, Smith-Slep, & O'Leary, 2007).

Weizmann-Henelius et al. (2012) reported that drinking and arguing as well as unemployment are factors often found in cases considered IPH. None of the factors in isolation directly or simply explain the occurrence of IPV. Our frequent caution in the text is mentioned here again: A correlation of factors or demographics does not amount to causation or a successful checklist approach to violence or homicide risk.

Intimate partner *violence* that may lead to intimate partner *homicide* has also been found to be more prevalent when it involves a man who has a history of violence toward women, threats of death to his partner or children in the relationship, or using a weapon (Guggisberg, 2012). An additional predictor of increased homicide risk, found in the Guggisberg study and several others, is when the perpetrator strangles or attempts to strangle his victim. Researchers and medical professionals have focused increased efforts on the study of **strangulation** because of the potential for serious injury of death that can result from blocking one's breathing. Numerous studies have found that if there has been a prior strangulation, which some people inaccurately call *choking*, an increased risk for fatality may exist. As result of these finding, 23 states and the federal government have elevated strangulation crimes to felonies to recognize the serious threat this crime carries. Motivations also differ between men and women who kill an intimate partner (Eriksson & Mazerolle, 2013). Research has indicated that increased danger for both IPV

In South Africa on Valentine's Day in 2013, Olympic hero Oscar Pistorius, known as the Blade Runner, fatally shot his girlfriend, Reva Steenkamp, in his home. Pistorius was well known to the world as a double amputee who overcame great physical barriers to become a world-class runner. He was known as a risk taker and a driven athlete.

Pistorius claimed to have awoken from sleep in fear that there was an intruder in the room and fired a gun through the bathroom door, fatally wounding Steenkamp by striking her four times. After the killing of his girlfriend, it became known that he had previously shot his firearm in public places on several occasions and had also been arrested for a prior domestic violence charge against another partner. After a long trial in which Mr. Pistorius' defense team claimed that he shot Reeva mistakenly in the middle of the night believing that a burglar was in the bathroom, Pistorius was convicted of the lesser included offense of culpable homicide by the trial court judge in the South African courtroom. She asserted that the state had failed to prove murder in the case. Pistorius was sentenced to just five years in prison and served only one year before being released to house arrest. An appellate court later reviewed the case and changed his conviction from manslaughter to murder and increased the sentence to 13 years and five months. The victim's family called the decision "justice for Reeva." Critics claimed that the trial court judge failed to weigh the evidence properly and did not consider the implausibility of his story. Many alleged that Pistorius's celebrity status and the history of the acceptance of male violence against women, particularly in South Africa, led to the initial surprising verdict.

and IPH exists when the victim is pregnant. In fact, IPH is a leading cause of death of pregnant women. This danger extends to the unborn child (McMahon & Armstrong, 2012). Some researchers have theorized that increased danger during pregnancy relates to the offender's concerns about losing control and about his belief that the pregnancy was a mistake that he needs to address.

Some cases of intimate partner homicide claim noninvolved victims as well as the intimate or former intimate partner. Called corollary homicide, according to Smith et al. (2014), this is "the murder of other people that occurs in the context of a domestic violence incident (such as new intimate partners, intervening friends, family or strangers, or responding law enforcement officers)" (p. 462). Their study also separated victims into the categories of "family, other intimate partner involvement, friend/acquaintance, stranger, and law enforcement officer" (p. 462). Family members were killed at the highest rate.

The weapon most used in the United States in IPH is the firearm. Men most often use a firearm to kill their intimate partners. The rate is nearly two thirds of all IPH incidents, and this is higher than in any other industrialized nation (Adams, 2007). "More than half of the victims (54.1%) were killed with a firearm, followed by sharp instrument (25%); hanging, strangulation, or suffocation (8.4%); blunt instrument (5.3%); personal weapons (e.g., fists, 3.2%) and other weapons (4%)" (Smith et al., 2014, p. 463). This also holds true for the corollary victims in IPH as well. "Approximately 70% of corollary victims were killed with a firearm, followed by a sharp instrument (12.4), and other weapons (17.3%)" (Smith et al., 2014, p. 463).

The dynamics in intimate partner homicide situations differ for men and women. Often, "men who kill their partners report experiences of losing control, suspecting infidelity, involuntary separation, jealousy, and rage" (Eriksson & Mazerolle, 2013, p. 463). "Women who kill their partners report feelings of fear and desperation resulting from exposure to domestic violence and social isolation" (Eriksson & Mazerolle, 2013, p. 463). While women kill spouses in some cases of self-defense after years of suffering violence, research shows that women commit intimate partner violence for other reasons (Dutton, Nicholls, & Spidel, 2005). We turn now to some theoretical reasons to help explain why IPH may occur.

THEORIES TO EXPLAIN INTIMATE PARTNER HOMICIDE

Theory examining intimate partner homicide has mainly extended from the lengthier tradition of explaining intimate partner violence. The comparatively smaller number of lethal incidents out of the significant number of abusive but nonlethal behaviors against intimate partners is the cause for less theoretical literature. Much of IPV tends to be discussed in terms of risk factors for victims and batterers. Sometimes passing as a theory is the **battered woman syndrome**, described by Walker (1979) as various behaviors that seemed similar among victims of IPV. Subsequent research has moved away from this approach and has pointed out that victims are a heterogeneous group and so are their behaviors (Bartol & Bartol, 2011). There is not consensus on the syndrome as causal or consistent or on its utility to either therapeutic or legal professionals.

Long a prominent theoretical approach in intimate partner violence is **feminist theory** (Taylor & Jasinski, 2011). Most cultures have been or are patriarchal, and as such, societies accept or at least recognize some of the historically or religiously designated roles and behaviors of men and women. Inequality of the sexes has resulted in power imbalance in opposite-sex relationships and explains part of the domineering treatment of women by men. The physiological weakness of women vis-à-vis men introduces consideration of a **biological** connection for theoretical examination. Literature too numerous to review informs us about the acceptance, approval, and encouragement of male aggressiveness in society. This biological and psychological state of affairs is a backdrop to the abuse of women, even where there are a small percentage of cases where a woman is the physical abuser of her partner. Same-sex partner abuse and cases of female-perpetrated violence show the limitations of feminist theory.

Dobash and Dobash (1978) identified male privilege as a social-structural contributor to the abuse of women. Sociological theories have contributed a view that cultural factors not under the control of victims set the stage for abuse through societal acceptance or cues. **Social learning theory** explains acts (including violent ones) as role modeling the behavior of significant individuals. A study by Adams (2009) examined a relatively small sample of IPH offenders and those who attempted IPH and found high rates of child abuse and observation of spouse abuse in the childhood environments of both sets of offenders. Social learning sees individuals as rationally acting in their own interests, including controlling family members. The theory is also used to explain intergenerational transmission of such behaviors to children, who observe and adopt the practices of abusive and abused parents. Some connection has also been found to IPV for some males who had witnessed or been subjected to physical or sexual abuse in childhood (Eriksson & Mazerolle, 2015; Weizmann-Henelius et al., 2012).

In addition to learning theories, other psychological theories, such as **labeling**, look at whether the seemingly intractable cycle of abuse and a victim remaining in a relationship may be in part the result of accepting her role as a victim. The victim, situated as she is within her home setting and family dynamics, may also be partly understood or studied via a theory such as **nested ecological**.

Fiske and Rai introduced the **virtuous violence theory** in their 2015 book *Virtuous Violence*. This theory sees most violence as perpetrators acting in ways they believe are morally right. Far from an apologist view, Fiske and Rai explore important and fertile territory on the motivations of those people, down through history, who have committed acts of violence, including intimate partner homicide. Fiske and Rai draw from their examination of cultures around the world and conclude that violence has been enmeshed in the regulation of intimate relations. In *Virtuous Violence*, the authors describe how partners develop a joint "moral" framework for the relationship and both may "more or less" agree that a beating was deserved. Fiske and Rai emphasize how completely morally wrong physical abuse is but that many perpetrators of intimate partner violence view themselves as morally "entitled, even obligated, to do violence to redress wrongs that they perceive themselves to have suffered, and to sustain what seems to them to be the right

Drew Peterson, a former Illinois police officer, was convicted in 2012 of the killing of his third wife, Kathleen Savio. This death was not immediately pursued as homicide, and only when Peterson's fourth wife, Stacy Ann Cales, disappeared in 2007 was a second autopsy performed on Savio, revealing evidence of a struggle. Savio's body had been found in a dry bathtub in her home in 2003, and her hair was covered in blood, but Peterson had never been charged as the death was initially ruled an accidental drowning. At trial, he claimed that Savio had fallen, hit her head, and then drowned.

Several witnesses at trial testified that, before her death, Savio had told them that Peterson threatened to kill her on numerous occasions and told her that he could make it look like an accident. A jury convicted Peterson of Savio's death in 2012, and in 2013, he began serving a 38-year sentence. Stacy Ann Cales's body has never been found, but her family reports that Cales was trying to leave the abusive relationship with Peterson when she disappeared. After his murder conviction, Peterson was charged with trying to hire a hit man to kill the prosecutor who helped to convict him.

kind of relationship" (p. 167). The empirical work and direction of the research suggests possibilities for prevention, treatment, and interventions in dealing with social relationships and the intrinsic violence present in many of them.

Economic deprivation, as represented within **strain theory**, has been studied and found as a factor correlated with IPV and IPH. Diem and Pizarro (2010) showed that when economic deprivation increased, so did family homicides as a whole. The authors rightly caution that family homicide is infrequent and economic deprivation but one factor. This theory has been used to explain why homicide rates may be higher among minority groups who experience higher rates of poverty. Yet the suggestion remains that legislators and policymakers should consider the effects of economic deprivation on the family and the contribution to violence.

The loss of initially perceived control by a man over his partner can generate a stress that brings us to a final theory used to explain some intimate partner homicide: **general strain theory** (GST). GST (Agnew, 1992) might hold that homicide is used to keep the wife under her husband's control. Disputes over custody can be a source of strain suffered by both. And perceived infidelity, while a clear stressor, has also been examined by adherents of evolutionary psychology (Daly & Wilson, 1994). Relationship separation can trigger the strain response of violence. The separation that occurs when a woman is

leaving a relationship has long been seen as perhaps the most potentially lethal time. The man may view this as truly losing the control he has exercised over someone and strike out, believing he is justified in doing so. Called abandonment rage, incidents of this nature may also have multiple victims, including children or family pets. GST has been used to examine different reactions to strain experienced by men and women. Eriksson and Mazerolle (2013) posit that men and women experience similar levels of strain but differ in their response. They explain that this is caused by differing concerns, with women focused on interpersonal relationships and men on financial status. A threat to a man's perception of a fair outcome may bring anger and jealousy and result in a moral outrage (Eriksson & Mazerolle, 2013; Fiske & Rai, 2015).

According to Eriksson and Mazerolle (2013), some of the stressors women are more frequently exposed to, compared with men, are physical, sexual, and emotional abuse. Strain comes, as well, from feelings of fear and desperation at being abused and often isolated through the offender's actions. Research has also examined the emotional aftereffects of a woman killing her partner. Some of these include posttraumatic stress disorders, anxiety, fear, depression, feelings of powerlessness, and elevated substance abuse. Eriksson and Mazzerolle and other researchers have also noted the strain of vicarious victimization of a woman's children and the feeling of losing one's identity. Many women who kill their intimate partners may reexperience abuse in prison.

Serran and Firestone (2004) assert that there appears to be a difference in motivations between when men and women in an intimate relationship kill one another. A man's proprietary feelings of *owning* a woman is explanatory in many instances, whereas the self-defense concept may be the basis for many incidents of a woman killing her intimate partner. The male view also includes jealousy, entitlement, and adultery. The proposed self-defense concept with females includes when another is threatened, usually their child. The use of such theories to help understand the dynamics of intimate partner violence and homicide may provide insights to help reduce these acts. The general idea of man's proprietary nature in IPV has been further split into more specific subtypes with a hope to better target therapy (Pornari, Dixon, & Humphreys, 2013).

LETHALITY ASSESSMENT

Many researchers and practitioners in recent years have focused on the practice of **lethality** or **risk assessment** in various crimes. In the areas of intimate partner violence and intimate partner homicide, there have been some helpful tools developed and evaluated that show promise in predicting which domestic violence cases may become lethal. As we have cautioned throughout the textbook, lethality assessment is certainly not a perfect tool and cannot always be used to predict or prevent violence. But in the area of intimate partner crime specifically, these tools have been used with results.

While there has been some emerging research in the area of lethality assessment for intimate partner homicide, perhaps the largest concern is that, since the event is relatively rare, there are not enough cases to inform a scientifically predictive model. One of the leading scholars in the field of assessing lethality in intimate partner violence cases is Dr. Jacquelyn Campbell, a faculty member at the Johns Hopkins School of Nursing. She has worked for decades in refining and developing a tool for researchers,

policymakers, and practitioners to use to help victims assess their own risk for lethal violence. The tool is intended to be used by a trained advocate to help victims take steps to protect themselves and is based on a growing body of research that indicates the factors most associated with lethal violence in domestic violence situations.

As mentioned at the beginning of the chapter, intimate partner violence sometimes results in intimate partner homicide. In an attempt to better gauge the level of risk or danger a person faces at the hands of her current or former intimate partner, the Danger Assessment (Campbell, 2004) was developed. Campbell et al. (2009) explain that "the danger assessment is an instrument designed to assess the likelihood of lethality or near lethality occurring in a case of intimate partner violence" (p. 654). The United States currently has the highest rate of intimate partner homicide out of all industrialized nations (Campbell et al., 2009). The 20-question Danger Assessment (Campbell, 2004) includes questions about prior individual behavior as well as factors in the relationship. Even though the research and tools to assess IPV have progressed quite a bit, their use is often to help prevent repeat violence as opposed to identifying risk of initial violence or abuse. Because revictimization occurs at a higher rate, it is easier to predict. Initially, a 15-item danger assessment was developed to help previously battered women assess their danger of being murdered by an intimate or ex-intimate partner (Campbell et al., 2009), but the tool has been updated to include more questions. Dr. Campbell and her team have also been conducting evaluation research funded by the National Institute of Justice across the country to test the validity of another lethality tool, the Lethality Screen, which is an evidence-based assessment tool used by law enforcement and that includes a process for referral to trained victim advocates for high-risk victims. The results of these assessments can also assist law enforcement and prosecutors as they investigate the case and make charging decisions.

In his best-selling book, *The Gift of Fear*, noted violence expert Gavin de Becker (1997) listed 30 signals that battered women experience that an intimate partner may kill them. De

EXHIBIT 6.1

DANGER ASSESSMENT

Jacquelyn C. Campbell, Ph.D., R.N.
Copyright, 2003; www.dangerassessment.com

Several risk factors have been associated with increased risk of homicides (murders) of women and men in violent relationships. We cannot predict what will happen in your case, but we would like you to be aware of the danger of homicide in situations of abuse and for you to see how many of the risk factors apply to your situation.

Using the calendar, please mark the approximate dates during the past year when you were abused by your partner or ex partner. Write on that date how bad the incident was according to the following scale:

1. Slapping, pushing; no injuries and/or lasting pain
2. Punching, kicking; bruises, cuts, and/or continuing pain
3. "Beating up"; severe contusions, burns, broken bones
4. Threat to use weapon; head injury, internal injury, permanent injury
5. Use of weapon; wounds from weapon

(If **any** of the descriptions for the higher number apply, use the higher number.)

Mark **Yes** or **No** for each of the following. ("He" refers to your husband, partner, ex-husband, ex-partner, or whoever is currently physically hurting you.)

____ 1. Has the physical violence increased in severity or frequency over the past year?
____ 2. Does he own a gun?
____ 3. Have you left him after living together during the past year?
       3a. (If have *never* lived with him, check here___)
____ 4. Is he unemployed?
____ 5. Has he ever used a weapon against you or threatened you with a lethal weapon?
                              (If yes, was the weapon a gun?____)
____ 6. Does he threaten to kill you?
____ 7. Has he avoided being arrested for domestic violence?
____ 8. Do you have a child that is not his?
____ 9. Has he ever forced you to have sex when you did not wish to do so?
____ 10. Does he ever try to choke you?
____ 11. Does he use illegal drugs? By drugs, I mean "uppers" or amphetamines, "meth", speed, angel dust, cocaine, "crack", street drugs or mixtures.
____ 12. Is he an alcoholic or problem drinker?
____ 13. Does he control most or all of your daily activities? For instance: does he tell you who you can be friends with, when you can see your family, how much money you can use, or when you can take the car? (If he tries, but you do not let him, check here: ___)
____ 14. Is he violently and constantly jealous of you? (For instance, does he say "If I can't have you, no one can.")
____ 15. Have you ever been beaten by him while you were pregnant? (If you have never been pregnant by him, check here: ___)
____ 16. Has he ever threatened or tried to commit suicide?
____ 17. Does he threaten to harm your children?
____ 18. Do you believe he is capable of killing you?
____ 19. Does he follow or spy on you, leave threatening notes or messages, destroy your property, or call you when you don't want him to?
____ 20. Have you ever threatened or tried to commit suicide?
____   Total "Yes" Answers

Thank you. Please talk to your nurse, advocate, or counselor about what the Danger Assessment means in terms of your situation.

Sources: Campbell, J. C. (2004). Danger assessment. Retrieved May 28, 2008, from http://www .dangerassessment.org; Campbell, J. C., Webster, D. W., Glass, N. (2009). The danger assessment: validation of a lethality risk assessment instrument for intimate partner femicide. *Journal of Interpersonal Violence*, 24(4): 653–74.

Becker and others continue to refine the methods of assessment and train professionals in its application. The sharing of valid risk assessment data can be helpful, and one of the mechanisms to accomplish this sharing is fatality review teams (Eke et al., 2011).

FATALITY REVIEW TEAMS

Given that intimate partner homicide is often the culmination of ongoing and persistent abuse and violence, the use of an engaged and active **fatality review team** has the ability to impact developing situations where a lethal outcome is more than a mere possibility. The first domestic violence fatality review team (DVFRT) was developed in San Francisco nearly 25 years ago (Wilson & Websdale, 2006). The ability for such teams to identify and then act on common risk factors has eluded many if not most such teams who work conscientiously after the fact of a murder to point back at where opportunities or miscommunications existed. The hope is to alter policies and procedures to incorporate actions that may have caught the missed opportunity to intervene before it resulted in death. Many of the recommendations from these reviews address education and awareness efforts for victims as well as perpetrators.

Today, nearly 80% of states have one or more active teams, but most are regional or countywide only. This means that even though some parts of a state are served by a DVFRT, large portions of a state may not be. Many teams are focused on helping spread information on best practices in fatality review in addition to the actual review of individual cases. The recommendations offered by teams are intended to improve policies, practices, and overall response without blaming. An important point made by Wilson and Websdale (2006) is that "an underlying assumption of any domestic violence fatality review is that the perpetrator is the one responsible for the homicide" (p. 539). This repeated assertion helps remind teams that everyone wants the same thing—to reduce fatalities and intimate partner violence. The information gathered by these teams helps local communities design systemic changes or approaches that will help keep victims safe.

Jaffe, Dawson, and Campbell (2013), in discussing the Canadian status of domestic violence death review teams, noted a need to develop a national database, such as that used in the United States, the National Domestic Violence Fatality Review Initiative (www.ndvfri.org). The Canadian review study also addressed the need for review teams to share information and address any privacy concerns about information held by criminal justice agencies. Also, the theme of accepting accountability by partner agencies without finger pointing is critical to a successful undertaking to cooperate and coordinate. The balance or complexity of role identification is challenging as groups struggle with advocacy, monitoring, policy recommendations, and education as themes to guide their work. There is no agreed-upon structure that works best in all jurisdictions. Running parallel to the question of which methods or structures are best is the issue of effectiveness. While it is always challenging to gauge what has *not* happened, it may be especially tricky to tie reductions in homicides (which have occurred steadily in the United States for 20 years) to the activities of the various and relatively unexamined DVFRTs. Some support does appear for helping move agencies away from past practices in assessing and intervening in IPV and toward more contemporary research through the vehicle of active fatality teams who meet to examine and discuss dynamics and agency responses.

PROSECUTION OF INTIMATE PARTNER HOMICIDE

Later in the text, we will devote an entire chapter to the court process for intimate partner and other homicide crimes, including the role of the prosecutor. In this chapter, we wanted to highlight some common issues prosecutors encounter in the prosecution of IPH cases. We are a nation with still-subtle and not-so-subtle manifestations of inequality. This reality is noted in the criminal justice system, as it is in other social spheres of our country. While the role of gender and race have lessened in the criminal justice system, it can still be noted in how some cases, such as intimate partner violence, are investigated, selected for prosecution, and followed through to conviction and punishment. In our legal system, prosecutors have great discretion in deciding which cases to prosecute and which charges to pursue.

Over the last several decades, researchers have spent a great deal of time examining prosecution practices in IPV and IPH cases specifically in order to determine best practices in handling these cases. Efforts by the National District Attorneys Association (NDAA) and others have been aimed at giving specific guidelines to prosecutors who handle these cases in recognition that the dynamics present in IPV cases differ from other types of cases. These dynamics greatly impact the prosecutorial approach. Most students are aware that IPV cases can be difficult to prosecute, given the reality that many victims may not support the prosecution of the offender, for various reasons. The challenge for prosecutors has been to focus on building evidence-based cases with the sometimes-competing goals of victim safety and offender accountability at play. Organizations, like the NDAA, and researchers alike have recommended specialized training for prosecutors (and others in the criminal justice system) who are assigned to handle IPV and IPH cases. Given that prior intimate partner violence is an indicator of future lethality, many have advocated for prosecutors to focus on prosecuting lower level IPV cases as a way to prevent these situations from escalating to lethal outcomes for victims. But there has been some debate in the research about whether aggressive prosecution of IPV does deter future and more lethal offending by perpetrators of IPV.

Since intimate partner violence and homicide are leading causes of injury and death for women in the United States, local officials and prosecutors must carefully consider these cases and prioritize them. In spite of similar facts, cases processed by humans may be handled differently and arrive at different outcomes. For example, Ramsey (2010) notes that "heat-of-passion claims have become the new 'abuse excuse' for men" (p. 33), allowing at times for a reduced charge or conviction for manslaughter. In IPH cases specifically, prosecutors face the challenge early in the case to decide appropriate charges for offenders. As we discuss later in the book, there are a number of factors to consider in the charging decision, but the most important is the consideration about what the prosecutor believes the evidence can support. If there has been a history of violence, including a history of the victim seeking protective orders, prosecutors will need to make sure they can have this history introduced at trial under the rules of evidence. Additionally, prosecutors will need to determine whether the victim ever told others about her fear of the offender and whether he ever made threats of violence. Did the victim keep a journal or write letters to friends or family members about these fears? Did she take photographs of prior injuries? These forms of evidence can generally be introduced as long as the prosecutor can lay proper foundation and demonstrate that they qualify as exceptions to the hearsay rule. Some of you may recall that in the criminal prosecution of O. J. Simpson for the death of his ex-wife Nicole, prosecutors were able to play prior 9-1-1 tapes with Nicole reporting violence. Prosecutors may also need to consider the use of expert witnesses during the trial to help jurors understand the dynamics in IPV cases. Finally, most prosecutors' offices utilize victim advocates in homicide cases who can assist in working with the family as the case progresses through the court process.

Castle Doctrine and Stand-Your-Ground Laws

There are a few legal doctrines related to self-defense that have had implications for the prosecution of intimate partner homicide. The first of these is known as the **Castle Doctrine**, colloquially known in the history of Western civilization as

"A MAN'S HOME is his castle," or so runs the old adage. The notion that our homes are our sanctuaries and that we can defend against an invader within them is hardly new. In fact, the right to protect ourselves or others in our homes, with deadly force if necessary, dates back through civilized society at least as far as early English common law. (Jansen & Nugent-Borakove, 2007, p. 3)

The Castle Doctrine has been used in cases where a person using deadly force was in imminent fear for his life while in his home. While the doctrine is not an actual law, the legal concept has been recognized in various ways in the statutes of many states. The burden of proof when employing the concept of the Castle Doctrine would be less than that employed in a claim of justifiable homicide since the latter typically involves an element of being in fear. Most state statutes contain verbiage requiring the person who uses such force be in fear and have a *reasonable belief* that he is in danger of being seriously injured or killed. Most such statutes contain language requiring that an individual retreat from a threat where possible and when *not* in his home. More recently, there has been some focus on a new category of self-defense laws known as stand-your-ground laws. These laws allow a person to use deadly force, even outside of the home, without the requirement to retreat from someone who he perceives as a threat. Florida was the first state to expand the Castle Doctrine to include not just the home but also any place where a person has a right to be, including public places like sidewalks. There has been criticism of these laws by domestic violence advocates, which, in some cases, has to do with the wording of specific state statutes and a labeling of all self-defense-type laws as "stand your ground." A victim of intimate partner violence is not prohibited from asserting self-defense and would likely point to her fear of imminent harm. The other concern with these laws voiced by advocates and researchers has to do with offenders who assert these defenses by claiming that they shot the victim because they were in fear.

With the expansion of Castle Doctrine laws comes a need to continue research regarding any asserted benefits to removing restrictions on using deadly force. The National District Attorneys Association noted in their paper "Expansion to the Castle Doctrine" that "the judicial system's failure to adequately protect victims of domestic violence may be one of the reasons for expanding the Castle Doctrine" (Jansen & Nugent-Borakove, 2007, p. 14). What remains unclear and in dispute among researchers and advocates is whether such laws help or not.

SUMMARY

While the rate of intimate partner homicide has declined, intimate partner violence and intimate partner homicide remain challenges for the United States and for countries the world over. The spreading of gender equality holds hope of reducing some such violence as we consider feminist theory and a general view that when women live a reality of being equal to men, there may be improved dynamics to resist abuse or control by men. Assessment of danger and risk continues to improve. Factors implicated in the dynamics of IPH are varied. Staffing levels and specific activities of police agencies, statutes to prevent IPV abusers from possessing firearms (Zeoli & Webster, 2010), and programs and laws to address economic deprivation (Adams, 2007) are but several pathways to reductions in intimate partner violence and homicide. Medical professionals also hold an important position as people who may first see a victim of IPV. The health care provider is uniquely positioned to offer guidance (Feder, Wathen, & MacMillan, 2013).

Part of the improved process of assessing risk to potential victims and the risk of violence by potential perpetrators comes from the multidisciplinary approaches seen in lethality assessment and fatality review teams and the efforts of researchers (Eke et al., 2011). The increase in programs and resources, such as victim assistance programs, shelters, and hotlines available to battered women, has shown evidence of helping to reduce the risk of intimate partner homicide (Dugan, Nagin, &

Rosenfeld, 2003). If a victim hopes to remove herself and her children from an abusive environment, she must be aware of and have assistance in gaining the resources to do so.

It is important for advocates, law enforcement, prosecutors, and others to remain vigilant and aware that the point at which an intimate partner violence victim finally leaves a relationship is often the most lethal. The perpetrator, in a final act of control, may declare verbally and through killing that if he cannot have and control his victim, then no one can. "Although intimate partner homicide has decreased during the past 15 to 20 years, it remains a disturbing possibility for people experiencing abusive relationships" (Smith et al., 2014, p. 461).

KEY TERMS

Intimate partner violence (IPV) 84
Intimate partner homicide (IPH) 84
Domestic violence (DV) 84
Strangulation 88
Battered woman syndrome 90

Feminist theory 90
Biological 90
Social learning theory 90
Labeling 90
Nested ecological 90
Virtuous violence theory 90
Economic deprivation 91

Strain theory 91
General strain theory 91
Lethality assessment 92
Risk assessment 92
Fatality review team 94
Castle Doctrine 95

DISCUSSION QUESTIONS

1. How have the rates of intimate partner homicide changed in the last 25 years and why?
2. List and discuss several risk factors that appear to contribute to intimate partner homicide.
3. How does feminist theory contribute to our understanding of intimate partner homicide?
4. In what ways does social learning theory connect to intergenerational transmission of violent behavior?
5. How can agencies utilize lethality assessment to improve outcomes for battered persons?
6. What agencies and groups should be part of a fatality review team or process? Why?

TRY THIS

Visit the website of the National Domestic Violence Fatality Review Initiative (NDVFRI) at http://www.ndvfri.org and examine various team reports archived there to get a better idea of how coalitions and teams provide input to help prevent intimate partner homicide.

Go to the report *Global and Regional Estimates of Violence Against Women: Prevalence and Health Effects of Intimate Partner Violence and Non-partner Sexual Violence* issued by the World Health Organization at http://apps.who.int/iris/bitstream/10665/85239/1/9789241564625_eng.pdf

Which regions of the world report the highest and lowest IPH rates?

Visit the website of the National District Attorneys Association, and look through various parts of the special topic series publication "Introducing Expert Testimony to Explain Victim Behavior in Sexual and Domestic Violence Prosecutions" at https://ndaa.org/publications/#prosecution-of-violence-against-women

What are some of the myths about the dynamics of domestic violence, and what is the potential impact on juries?

7

ALL IN THE FAMILY

No peace in the world without peace in the nations

No peace in the nations without peace in the town

No peace in the town without peace in the home

No peace in the home without peace in the heart

—Tao Te Ching

"There's been an awful lot of silence in male culture about this ongoing tragedy of men's violence against women and children . . . we need to break that silence, and we need more men to do that."

—Jackson Katz

Student Learning Outcomes

Students will be able to:

- explain the dynamics of familicide.

- describe the cycle of violence.

- list and describe instances when parents kill their children.

- discuss the motivations for children to kill their parents.

- identify honor killings and cultural dynamics that lead to such homicides.

CHAPTER OUTLINE

Introduction
  Juveniles Who Kill
Familicide

INTRODUCTION

It is a tragic reality that family members sometimes kill one another. Parents kill their children, and children sometimes kill one or both parents. Siblings die at the hands of their brother or sister. Extended family members can fall victim to homicide by their relatives. The most common of family-involved murders are the **intimate partner homicides** (IPH) addressed in the previous chapter. In this chapter, we take up the killing of family by family in situations other than IPH.

Violence within the family setting includes physical acts, such as sexual abuse and battery, as well as psychological violence, including emotional abuse, financial abuse, and other actions by one family member against another. Because of the number of intimate partner homicides, we devote an entire chapter to considering its causes, effects, and interventions. It is important to comment here that many of the acts of physical and emotional violence may be predecessors in a trajectory that leads to murder, including intimate partner homicide. In 2017, UCR figures show that for homicides for which the relationship between victim and offender was known, 12.3%, or 1,867 victims, were killed by a family member (FBI, 2018).

As with cases of intimate partner violence (IPV), other forms of family violence are often explained (in part at least) by what is called the cycle of violence and the intergenerational transmission of violence. The cycle of violence describes a pattern of abuse. The pattern progresses through phases of tension building, acting out, reconciliation, and calm. As discussed in the chapter on intimate partner homicide, the acting-out phase can signal the most dangerous time for lethal violence. Family members, such as children, exposed repeatedly to the cycle of abuse or violence cannot help but be affected. The intergenerational transmission of violence concept explains that behaviors, including violent behavior, are passed from one generation to the next as the accepted or expected norms of a family. The abuse or harsh treatment of children in a family does not create a certainty of future abusive behavior toward others, yet it is a risk factor. The abuse–violence association has been noted in the case histories of murderers, notably ones who killed their parents.

Our discussion earlier in the book of **social learning theory** provides the foundation for such observations. Aside from challenges to studying individuals and families for historical evidence of violence is the fact that most children who experience violence personally or vicariously do not become abusers themselves, nor do they murder their parents. Given the close proximity and amount of time family members spend together, some researchers have used **routine activities theory** as one possible explanation of some family violence. Other theoretical approaches have looked at psychological and social dimensions of family violence that result in death (Stroud & Pritchard, 2001). Some researchers have found mental disorders

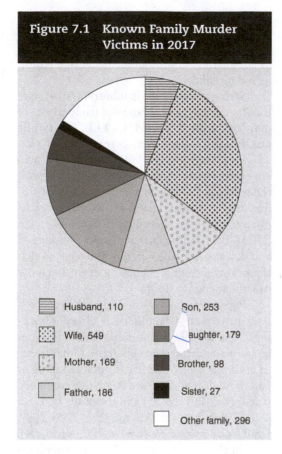

Figure 7.1   Known Family Murder Victims in 2017

Husband, 110
Wife, 549
Mother, 169
Father, 186
Son, 253
Daughter, 179
Brother, 98
Sister, 27
Other family, 296

Source: Federal Bureau of Investigation, United States Department of Justice, "Crime in the United States, 2017."

diagnosed in many of the mothers who kill their children. Each of these theoretical orientations contributes to understanding the pathway to familicide. There is no single overarching theory of cause.

Other factors appearing as correlates of violence in the home include poverty and substance abuse. We repeat here our important caution about confusing correlation with causation or conflating factors in a formula that attempts to predict certain types of violence. Being abused or witnessing abuse does not mean an individual will become an abuser, though this is a heightened risk factor. Living in poverty or being exposed to or using drugs or alcohol does not inexorably lead to violent behavior. Two secondary components of being exposed to high levels of violence for an extended period of time can be a varied degree of desensitization to violence or exhibiting symptoms of post-traumatic stress disorder (PTSD).

Juveniles Who Kill

While we discussed school shootings at length in a separate chapter, in this chapter, we delve a bit more deeply into homicides committed by young people within the family unit. Many killings perpetrated by individuals under the age of 18 are in the context of confrontational homicide or gang killings. We address confrontational homicide, one of the largest categories of murder, in its own chapter, and gang killings we deal with in the chapter joined with cult killings.

Some juveniles begin on a path of violence early in their lives. This may stem from **intergenerational transmission of violence** (IGT), with juveniles modeling their behavior based on the adults they are exposed to or abuse they have suffered at the hands of others. The juvenile, in turn, will find someone more vulnerable than even himself to exact revenge upon. Still others take up violent behavior and violent crime as a way to prove themselves as they attempt to earn acceptance by other peers or older role models they seek to impress, including gang members. In this chapter on violence within the family, we focus on those youth who kill family members as opposed to those who kill in organized settings, such as school or a gang.

Research has provided us with a good deal of information regarding both risk factors and protective factors for juveniles, especially those considered to be at risk. Many of the risk factors for being a perpetrator of violence sound like a familiar listing of the challenges of disaffected youth: feelings of alienation, predominantly male, absent parents or capable adult guardians, abuse at the hands of those who are the juvenile's guardian, associating with other delinquent youth, and the list goes on (Meehan & Kerig, 2010). Within the family, other risk factors appear in the form of inconsistent or absent guidance or discipline, poverty, divorce, high level of parent-child conflict and more (Office of the Surgeon General, 2001). The school experience may similarly be disappointing or disaffecting, with poor academic performance, hanging out with the wrong crowd, and seeking negative attention. While a checklist approach is never certain for the prediction of violent behavior, concerted efforts to mitigate these types of risk factors for any child can go a long way to improving long-term positive outcomes in all aspects of a person's life.

Meehan and Kerig (2010) also talk about protective factors that tend to prevent a juvenile from becoming a perpetrator in their article about violence among school-aged youth. The authors discuss a general intolerance toward violence; relatively high intelligence, presumably compared to delinquent peers; and expectations of consequences for antisocial actions taken. We experience an overlap here in the circumstances involved in young people violently acting out in killing someone, whether it is in the home setting, the school, or within the context of a gang or other peer environment. There are risk factors and red flags potentially signaling violence by or against others in the family, including the elderly. We turn first to a discussion of what is the most shocking event in family violence: family annihilation.

FAMILICIDE

Familicide "refers to the killing of multiple family members, most commonly the homicide of an intimate partner and at least one child" (Liem, Levin, Holland, & Fox, 2013, p. 351). The authors point to two major motivations for familicide. The first is a response of anger and revenge for a partner leaving or threatening to leave. The second motivation finds the male believing he is *saving* family members from a future of disappointment and destitution following, typically, a setback or series of setbacks he has encountered. Thus, he kills them and himself. These multiple murders often involve the suicide of the killer after he has murdered family members (Alder & Polk, 2001; Wilson, Daly, & Daniele, 1995). This has been referred to as intimate partner homicide–suicide (IPHS) (Sillito & Salari, 2011).

A somewhat inevitable semantic debate may occur over whether familicides are to be considered a mass killing, based on whether three or more victims exist. Because the familicide would involve killing at least two other family members, sometimes the incident will be considered

a **mass murder**. Familicide is a statistically rare event but one that clearly garners a great deal of media attention as a result of the dramatic nature of eliminating most or all members of a family, including children.

Sachmann and Harris Johnson (2014) state that "familicide incorporates the triple taboos of murder, suicide, and child" (p. 130). The **family annihilator** is the common term for the person who murders his whole family or all who are available to him at the time he acts. As with the workplace killer, the family annihilator frequently has a relationship and work record of disappointments. According to Fox and Levin (2015), the "lifelong accumulation of upheaval and defeat places the killer on the edge so that the occurrence of a triggering event becomes overwhelming" (p. 187).

Rare as it may be—and in part because it is so infrequent—familicide is always shocking. "The most common form is the killing of an intimate partner and child(ren). Other forms of multiple-family homicides, such as killing of parents and/or siblings are much less common" (Liem et al., 2013, p. 351). In this study by Liem et al. (2013) that looked at the years 2000–2009, familicide occurred approximately 23 times each year in the United States. The 207 incidents of familicide represented situations where one intimate partner and at least one child were killed. This combination of victims revealed a frequency greater than that of workplace or school mass killings. Less well known is that in four to five of those annual killings, financial motives were identified. Financial reasons are not as often contemplated as say mental illness, yet economic stress or the perception of extreme loss is a recurring theme in such homicides.

Liem and Reichelmann (2014) also predicted that as the economy softened and unemployment rates increased, there would be more instances of familicide. Sillito and Salari (2011) also suggested that economic strife may increase the potential for familicide. There has not been sufficient time in the current economic era to determine whether this will prove to be the case, though some small sample research has supported economic loss as a motivation for **homicide-suicide** in families (Cheung, Hatters Friedman, & Sundram,

On January 19, 2019, a 42 year-old Oregon man named Mark Gago killed four of his family members, including his mother, stepfather, girlfriend, and their 9 month-old child, and attempted to kill the 8 year-old child of his girlfriend as well as another adult in the home outside of Portland. They all resided in the rural home. Police reported that when they arrived Gago was attempting to kill the 8 year-old child and they shot and killed him, and the child survived. They described a horrific scene where Gago used an ax to kill the family, and they noted the presence of numerous other weapons at the home. Gago had a prior arrest for unlawful weapons possession just months before the killings.

2015). Liem and Reichelmann (2014) also divided familicides into subgroups based on "the perpetrator's age, relationship between perpetrator and victims, and perpetrator's suicide" (p. 44). The clusters developed from the preceding factors consisted of two that have been examined by various researchers and two more offered by Liem and Reichelmann for future research. The clusters respectively are *despondent fathers*, *spousal revenge*, *extended parricide*, and *diffuse conflict*. The clusters offer important focal points to help broaden our understanding of familicide, including the impact on and inclusion of secondary victims.

The study by Liem et al. (2013) is notable for its size as well as for addressing the relatively unexplored area about familicide and the financial difficulties suffered by the perpetrator (and presumably his family). Examples the authors provided included sudden unemployment, debt, or foreclosure. The study found that firearms were used in 42% of all instances of familicide. In suicides that followed the homicide, a firearm was used in 82% of the cases. The researchers found 64% of the perpetrators committed suicide after they completed the familicide. Most of the adult victims in familicide were women. Based on other theoretical work, it was not surprising but notable that 20% of the killings involved stepchildren (Daly & Wilson, 1988). In the Liem et al. (2013) study, the authors noted that more of the perpetrators had a criminal record or history of family violence than what they had believed would be the case, though less frequently than men who committed intimate partner violence. A number of the perpetrators

examined in the study had prior involvement with law enforcement as the result of intimate partner violence incidents. The report authors also note that while a perpetrator of familicide might be motivated by financial problems, this was not related to overall periods of economic downturn in the country. Rather, the financial issues were personal. Most of the cases examined involved a murder committed by a man, with an age range of perpetrators from 18 years old to 90 years old.

Uniform Crime Report (UCR) data and the Supplemental Homicide Report (SHR) are the primary means of measuring the volume, rate, and trends in the instances of parents murdering their children. Studies cited in the article by Liem et al. (2013) show that a majority of perpetrators who kill their children and spouse are white males in their 30s or 40s. The two types of motives generally associated with family annihilators are murder by proxy and suicide by proxy. In murder by proxy, the perpetrator seeks revenge for his spouse leaving him (Liem et al., 2013). The killer's sense of being betrayed brings on his rage, and by killing their children, he strikes at his former partner. The killer sees his children's absence as an extension of the act of his partner leaving him (Sachmann & Harris Johnson, 2014).

Even with the rare occurrence of child-perpetrated familicide, Fegadel and Heide (2017) isolated a sampling of 14 cases between 1991 and 2010 using the NIBRS database in which a child within the family killed at least three family members, including one parent. These instances of offspring-perpetrated familicide had an age range of offenders between 12 to 43 years. The mean age was 25. In half of the cases, the perpetrator killed both parents, with siblings and other family members as other victims in the familicide. Firearms were most often used (nine times) in the killings, with three individuals using knives or other cutting instrument. Fathers were more likely to have been killed using a firearm. Such a small sample of cases makes it impossible to draw conclusions, but white males in their mid-20s were the most common offender.

In suicide by proxy, the individual sees himself as *protecting* his family (Liem et al., 2013). This view may come from the parent losing his job and method of caring for his family. This inability to support his family may lead a man to feelings of hopelessness and emasculation. Suicidal thoughts may come out of the depression the parent experiences. Killing the other members of his family comes before his own suicide as he believes he is keeping the family members from an intolerable situation. The man's belief may be that his family cannot go on without him, and so he must kill the entire family (Liem et al., 2013).

Sachmann and Harris Johnson (2014) examined offender motivation in cases of suicide by proxy. While harming a child may be retaliation for the wife leaving a relationship, there has been relatively little exploration of why some individuals experience this separation in a way that leads them to kill their own children. While it is accurate to say that killing the children will harm the surviving parent, this does not completely capture the depth and complexity of taking the lives of one's own offspring. Hurting one's child may be intended to inflict pain on the other parent or further control that former intimate partner (Sillito & Salari, 2011). Even if the children do not suffer physical harm from the offending parent, they become secondary victims, often psychologically damaged and at risk of further complications in their later life. Such an action often leads to the perpetrator's suicide.

While we have seen instances of familicide committed by women, the significant majority of family annihilators remain male (Scott & Fleming, 2014). Scott and Fleming (2014) examined a sample of female family annihilators, comparing these offenders to an overall and essentially male profile of the family annihilator.

The authors note that many criminologists have explained female offending based on adolescent and adult *male* criminal behavior. They explain the *shock value* is in keeping with the general patriarchal view that women have rarely been involved in crime, let alone violent crime. The authors point to the relative dearth of research literature until the last 30 years. Some of the authors' cited research shows women committing violent crimes in domestic relationships after being abused. These homicides committed by women occurred far more often than the killing of their children.

Women kill their children for a variety of reasons. Scott and Fleming (2014), in their exploratory study, compared their small sample of female family annihilators against a profile of male familicide perpetrators. They summarized their conclusions as follows:

> This family annihilator profile assumes that offenders are older, heterosexual, married, more mature males, who are the sole or primary income earners for their households. The murderer suffers from mental illness, in that they are usually depressed and/or paranoid and also may be under the influence of either alcohol and/or drugs. He is often an authoritarian figure, often with a history controlling many aspects of family life before ending the lives of his immediate family. He kills all members of the family that are present including his spouse, often with a gun, and this may include a family pet. The killings are more often motivated by revenge against the spouse, and the children are killed as a proxy to that spouse-directed anger, usually in or near the family home. The family annihilation ends when the father either takes his own life or forces police to kill him. (p. 72)

Their sample of female annihilators showed a number of similarities to the male profile. The woman as head of household was common as was the woman's status as separated, widowed, or divorced. Most of the killings occurred in the

A Male Family Annihilator

A 28-year-old mother of two boys, Susan Cox Powell, disappeared from her Utah home in December 2009. Her husband, Josh Powell, told detectives that he had taken his young sons camping in freezing weather in the middle of the night of her disappearance. Despite the fact that the investigators doubted his implausible story and that they suspected him in her disappearance, they did not find her body, and they asserted that they did not have enough evidence to charge him. Before the disappearance, Susan had placed a handwritten note in a safety deposit box that said, "If I die, it may not be an accident, even if it looks like one." After Susan's disappearance, her parents were granted custody of the two boys after a contested custody battle with Josh, but the court granted visitation rights to Josh. Two years after Susan's disappearance, the boys, ages 5 and 7, showed up at Josh's home in Washington State with a Child Protective Services worker for a scheduled supervised visit. Josh locked the worker outside the home as the boys entered. When the boys got inside the home, Josh brutally attacked them with a hatchet and then set fire to the home. Both boys and Josh died while the social worker watched helplessly from outside. The small police department in Utah recently announced that it was officially closing the Susan Powell investigation and stated that they were confident that Josh Powell had been involved in the disappearance, but they did not have enough evidence to prove it.

A Female Family Annihilator

A female family annihilator of recent memory is Andrea Yates. Yates was a 36-year-old mother of five children who lived in Texas. She was married and in a financially stable relationship. Yates's case is infamous. She waited until her husband Robert had gone to work before drowning all five of their children in the bathtub in their home. The children were ages 6 months old to 7 years old. She told law enforcement that she believed she was possessed by Satan and that she had to kill her children to save their souls. During the first criminal trial, Yates was convicted, but the case was overturned on appeal. During her retrial in 2006, Yates was found not guilty by reason of insanity and committed to a state mental hospital.

During the trial, her defense successfully argued that she suffered from postpartum psychosis (PPP). PPP is a relatively rare but serious condition, with estimates ranging from 1 to 3 cases per 1,000 childbirths. Women who suffer from PPP show increased risk of infanticide and suicide, and psychiatric hospitalization is usually required in these cases to protect mothers and their children. Yates had been a nurse who worked at one of the nation's leading cancer centers but gave up her job after the birth of her first child. It was revealed that she had attempted suicide after the birth of her fourth child and that she had reported having delusional thoughts and hearing voices around that time. Just five months after the birth of her fifth child, her father died. Her husband Russell reported that before she killed the children, Yates had taken numerous drugs for her depression and emotional problems, including the powerful drug Haldol, which is used to treat psychosis, including schizophrenia.

Source: Associated Press (2006, July 27). Woman not guilty in retrial in the deaths of her 5 children. *The New York Times.* Retrieved from http://www.nytimes.com/2006/07/27/us/27yates.html

family home. Depression was noted at or before the killings in all but one case study. In most of the cases, all the family members who had been present were killed. All except one of the women planned or attempted to commit suicide after their murders. Scott and Fleming point out the need for the literature to be more inclusive of women as perpetrators.

Some researchers have found that it is more common for women than men to kill those they have close ties to, such as family members. Messing and Heeren (2004) looked at a decade of cases where women killed more than one person and noted that women more often killed people known to them when compared to male multiple murderers; they less frequently killed strangers, opting instead for people closely related to them. The authors examined the span of years from 1993 to 2001 to locate women who committed two or more murders in a domestic setting. Multiple murders committed by a woman receive not only a great deal of news coverage but the attention of researchers who recognize this type of violent behavior as a break from traditional female role behavior.

Even less common than familicide is the killing of one parent and then a sibling. Killing a parent is known as parricide, and the killing of a brother or sister is known as siblicide. And while parricide is not unknown, this rare murder combination of a parent and a sibling is thought to occur when the individual kills his brother or sister along with the parent because the perpetrator sees the parent and sibling as allied against him (Liem & Reichelmann, 2014). The person may see his parent as smothering his identity and the murder as a way to permanently eliminate the parent's dominance.

The portrayal of familicide in the media belies the extremely rare occurrence of the act. Although few cases occur from a statistical standpoint, media coverage of this type of dramatic mass murder elevates public awareness and leads to the perception of frequency.

PARENTS AND CHILDREN

Parents Who Kill Their Children

When children are killed by one or both of their parents, it is termed **filicide**, which includes neonaticide and infanticide. **Neonaticide** is the killing of a child within the first day after it is born. **Infanticide** is the killing of a child within the first year of life. Filicide typically refers to the killing of a child between 1 and 17 years of age. While familicide perpetrators tend to be men, this is less true of filicide (Liem & Koenraadt, 2008). "On average, over 500 children aged 5 and under are killed annually. The majority . . . by a parent" (Alvarez & Bachman, 2014, p. 131). The state of reporting and statistical tabulation of homicide is such that calculating numbers and percentage of filicide versus infanticide, "the killing of a child by anyone" (Alvarez & Bachman, 2003, p. 105),

WHY WOULD THEY DO IT?

John List killed his wife, children, and mother in November 1971. Like other offenders summarized in the chapter on mass and workplace killings, List had been a white-collar employee (accountant) who had lost his job. List had other financial troubles, including being behind on his home mortgage, and he had been taking money out of his mother's bank account. List came home and shot and killed each member of his family: his wife, Helen, 46; his daughter, Patricia, 16; his sons, John, 15, and Frederick, 13; and his mother, Alma, 85.

Police were called to the home one month later when they discovered the bodies of all of the victims. A teacher of one of the List children had also informed law enforcement that John List's daughter Patricia had not been to class in nearly a month. List left a note at the scene of the murders addressed to his pastor saying that he killed his family to save them from an evil world. John List did not commit suicide. Eighteen years later, List was found in Richmond, Virginia, using the alias Robert Clark.

Source: Stout, D. (2008, March 25). John E. List, 82, killer of 5 family members, dies. *The New York Times.* Retrieved from http://www.nytimes.com/2008/03/25/nyregion/25list1.html?_r=0

is challenging. Alvarez and Bachman go on to point out that a well-known issue in this regard is positively confirming the manner of death in such cases. The challenge for the medical examiner or coroner is often significant when determining the manner of death as either accidental or homicide. Because of the problems in definitively classifying the death of a young child as intentional, there is a subsequent challenge gauging how accurate estimates of such homicides are in the United States.

Research reveals that younger children are killed most often as a result of physical abuse, though in many cultures, filicide was a tacitly accepted form of birth or population control related in many cases to economic strain (Hunnicutt & LaFree, 2008; Spinelli, 2005). The physical abuse cases are often neonaticide or infanticide. Older children, on the other hand, tend to be victims of familicide where a parent kills multiple family members. Individual psychological variables and situational variables in combination have been examined to explain filicide (Léveillée, Marleau, & Dubé, 2007).

Contrary to a somewhat common belief, the killing of children is roughly split between the father and the mother (Léveillée, Marleau, & Dubé, 2007). When the perpetrator is the mother, some of the same motivations as men are discovered. Some factors may appear more gendered. Not uncommon in many cultures are the factors of social isolation of women and the limited resources these women possess to change or better their circumstances. An all-too-familiar theme of lacking self-confidence combined with the stressors women suffer from physical and psychological abuse may result in violence acted out toward family members, notably children. As previously established, while not all killings are the result of mental illness or delusion, the killing of children by a parent may be the result of an extension of an existing delusion. The view by a mother may be altruistic. She may believe that killing her children is part of her self-image as a good mother. These circumstances are supported in research as the actions of someone possibly suffering from psychosis or delusion. The theme again is someone believing she is caring for and protecting her loved ones by ending their lives (Scott & Fleming, 2014).

Sillito and Salari (2011) suggest depression as one motive that can explain a family murder. This may be the homicide of a child followed by the suicide of the parent. This type of incident is referred to as intimate partner homicide–suicide (IPHS), and the authors state that such instances are typically perpetrated by the biological father. The authors go on to cite Japan as a culture where the practice of family suicide was actually to some extent accepted. When a family was experiencing extreme financial difficulties or had suffered a dishonor within society, it was not uncommon for the parent to kill the children and then himself.

Familicide perpetrators may have had a history of intimate partner violence. The controlling behaviors familiar to intimate partner abuse and violence include isolation of one's partner, physical or sexual abuse, and control measures to exhibit power over the person. It was not always the case, however, that the suicidal parent had a previous history of intimate partner abuse (Sillito & Salari, 2011).

The most recent comprehensive Bureau of Justice Statistics (BJS, 2011) report covered the years between 1980 and 2008 and showed the number of children under the age of 5 killed by homicide declined between 1993 and 2006, but then it increased in 2007 and 2008. In 2006, this rate had been 2.1 homicides per 100,000 population, and this rose slightly to 2.3 by 2008. The rate of homicide for black children under the age of 5 has remained substantially higher than the rate of homicide for white children or other groups. The report points out that, "in general, the younger the child, the greater the risk for being the victim of homicide" (p. 6). The total number of murdered children ages 1-4 reported by the FBI (2018) for the year 2017 was 248. The BJS report says that 63% of the children under age 5 who were murdered during this timeframe were killed by a parent. The percentage of the perpetrator relationship was not quite equally split, with 33% of children being killed by their fathers and 30% by their mothers. The report notes 23% of children in this age range were killed by male acquaintances, 5% killed by female acquaintances, 7% by other relatives, and only 3% were killed by strangers. Juveniles killed by family members represented 19% of all of those persons killed by family members.

Münchausen syndrome by proxy (MSBP) is defined by the U.S. National Library of Medicine (n.d.) as "a mental illness and a form of child abuse. The caretaker of a child, usually a mother, either makes up fake symptoms or causes real symptoms to make it look like the child is sick" (n.p.). It goes on to point out that it is not currently known what causes the psychological disorder MSBP, also known as factitious disorder by proxy. What is known is that some perpetrators of this behavior were abused when they were a child or perhaps claim a current fake sickness of their own (Münchausen syndrome). Psychotherapy is recommended to treat someone with the disorder.

According to various authors, the offending mother may believe that the sickness of her child may bring her closer in her relationship with her husband. The woman may be depressed and insecure and manifest these feelings by sickening her child or children.

KidsHealth (2012) lists some of the symptoms faked by the parent, usually the child's mother, including

- failure to thrive,
- allergies,
- asthma,
- vomiting,
- diarrhea,
- seizures, and
- infections. (n.p.)

News coverage of kidnapping-murders can lead people to believe these events are more common than they are or responsible for the deaths of many children. Death at the hands of a caretaker is troubling, and juries are sometimes more willing to believe a fatality resulted from an overreaction by a parent or guardian or discipline that was a bit too rough than to consider the evil intent to actually kill a child (Phipps, 1999). Child abuse, which takes many forms, results in the death of a child at its most extreme. This type of case typifies a story of family tragedy often reported by the media. While the killing of one's child is beyond the comprehension of most people, there are sadly ample examples of just such acts occurring. The death is the final outcome of abuse over a lengthy period of time.

In regard to filicide, a finding noted in one recent study is that a review of cases of a parent killing her child reveals that women who commit these crimes frequently suffer economically prior to the act (Diem & Pizarro, 2010). Hunnicutt (2007) found that a woman's economic status is related to child victimization and homicide rates but is less associated in rural areas compared to urban. They point out that most research on the causes of filicide has focused on female-committed crimes. In fact, they note that women may act out of a sense of helplessness, because of a self-view of failing in the maternal role, and as a result of psychiatric illness, which often attracts media attention. Men, on the other hand, are generally seen as fulfilling a patriarchal model of dominance and control over their families.

Shaken baby syndrome is a cause of death for infants who suffer internal damage to their brains or spinal cords as a result of being struck or shaken, usually by a parent or caregiver. The damage caused by shaking the infant can be short of death but serious and include paralysis and other functional impairments. Also known as abusive head trauma, or AHT, the victims are typically younger than 1 year old. News accounts and research document the scenario that often a parent or babysitter, out of frustration with a child who is crying, will shake or strike the baby until the crying stops, and likely, the brain will be irreparably damaged. While 25% of such cases result in the death of the child, surviving children may also suffer seizures, mental disability, memory and attention difficulties, and cerebral palsy, among other physical and cognitive problems. Most perpetrators of shaken baby syndrome are men, often a boyfriend of the mother and not the child's natural father. This finding has support at least as far back as the work of Daly and Wilson (1988) in their discussion of evolutionary psychology.

Though the killing of children makes for a horrific story on the nightly news or tomorrow's paper, there has not been a marked increase in the rate of such homicides over the past several decades. The vulnerability of children makes societal reaction condemnatory and emotional when a parent murders his child. Filicide, as with other forms of homicide, rarely sees a successful insanity defense mounted by the perpetrator. A parent convicted of murdering her child quite often faces a life of imprisonment.

Children Who Kill Their Parents

Parricide is murder carried out against a mother, father, stepmother, or stepfather by their natural or stepchild. Most parricide comes in the form of **patricide**, killing one's father and is frequently connected to prior abuse from that father or stepfather (Cooke, 2001; Heide, 2013, 2017). Less frequent is **matricide**, killing one's mother. Parricide typically has just one victim. To be sure, there are notable examples of more than one child taking part in the murder of a parent as well as a child or children killing both parents. The killer is often the adult child of his victim (Heide & Petee, 2007). Some patricides are not initially identified as such because a scene may be staged to appear as suicide or a claim of self-defense is made (Campobasso, Laviola, Grattagliano, Strada, & Dell'Erba, 2015).

As with much homicide, the raw numbers of parricide murders committed is low (Heide, 2017). The larger issue and an important point when considering policy and program directions is that parricide is but the extreme end of the continuum of violence directed toward parents. An examination of data from the National Incident-Based Reporting System (NIBRS) between 1995 and 2005 shows an important and significant difference between parricide and what is considered child–parent violence (CPV). Walsh and Krienert (2009) found that parricide offenders and victims were older than either offenders or victims in the examined cases of child–parent violence. They also note that child–parent violence offenders are "more likely to be female, more likely to be African American, and less likely to use a weapon than parricide offenders" (p. 1450). Heide and Petee (2007) point out that

> The data indicate that at least half of parricidal incidents stem from arguments. Efforts aimed at helping individuals, particularly males, to learn how to deal appropriately with strong emotion and to communicate more effectively would seem a promising place to begin. The research suggests that efforts to strengthen family bonds and to increase respect for family relationships should be targeted at both the White and Black communities. (p. 1396)

Hart and Helms (2003) also examined and compared cases of parricide involving adolescent offenders to the adult children of victims. In their research, they noted that the characteristics of adolescent parricide offenders differed from juveniles who killed strangers. Their argument proposes consideration of battered child syndrome as a basis for a legal self-defense claim by juvenile offenders. While this policy consideration would be a state-by-state matter, it continues an important discussion of the differences in maturity and psychosocial development between children and adults. Marleau, Auclair, and Millaud (2006) noted that age differences of offenders seemed to show the adult killer often had a severe mental illness, whereas the adolescent most frequently was trying to stop being victimized. Viñas-Racionero, Schlesinger, Scalora, and Jarvis (2017) reported in their sample of 16 familicides committed by 19 offenders age 14 to 21, that immediately after the attacks "75% of the offenders stole money from their families, and in 50% of the cases they either called their friends to report the murders or to plan leisure activities" (p. 535). While the authors note a number of important research areas to follow up on, this study once again reflects the difference in adolescent offender response to such murders as compared to many older individuals.

The Menendez brothers, Joseph "Lyle" and Erik Galen, were tried and convicted for the 1989 shotgun slaying of their parents, Jose and Kitty Menendez. At ages 21 and 18, Lyle and Erik killed their parents, who sat watching a movie in the family's Beverly Hills home. After shooting their father Jose in the back of the head, they shot their mother multiple times and then shot each in the kneecaps in an attempt to mislead police into believing the killings were related to organized crime.

The two sons established an alibi by going to a local restaurant to eat with friends and then returned home just before midnight and called police to report someone had killed their parents. In the six months following the murders, the brothers spent a great deal of money purchasing many expensive items and traveling abroad.

Erik confessed to his psychologist, who informed law enforcement officials. Both brothers were arrested and jailed separately while awaiting trial. Court TV aired the trial in 1993. After a defense of having been abused by their father, a deadlocked jury for each son was the initial outcome. The state retried the two, and this jury accepted the assertion that they had murdered their parents for the inheritance. Both were sentenced to life without parole.

The murder of a parent is also committed by juvenile children of the victim, though far less frequently. The study conducted by Heide and Petee (2007) examined data from the FBI's Supplemental Homicide Report covering the years 1976 through 1999. And while the authors note the difficulty of using this data set due in part to the UCR hierarchy rule, they were most interested in comparing patterns to work done by Heide (1993) on parricide and the killing of mothers and fathers in incidents of one victim and one offender.

The majority of cases of parricide involved a male child as the offender, though the child was most often age 18 or older (Heide & Petee, 2007). In their study, Heide and Petee (2007) found that in 72% of the cases of patricide, the children were less than 30 years old. They further found that as to age, approximately one fourth of patricide was committed by an offender less than 18 years of age. The researchers, in their multiple time frame analysis, observed that after the time period of 1976 through 1981, the percentage of murders of parents committed by juveniles dropped to roughly 1 in 5. As to the question of comparison between the earlier work and the publication of their 2007 article, it was found that offender and victim characteristics were stable over time. Fegadel and Heide (2015) also looked at a small number of cases in which a person (usually a white male approximately 26 years old) killed his parents and other family members, such as a sibling or grandparent. This is a small number of cases of family killing and has been called *extended parricide* by Liem and Reichelmann (2014). We may be demographically set to see an increase in these currently small numbers with an aging population. The U.S. Census Bureau reports, "In 2050, the population aged 65 and over is projected to be 83.7 million, almost double its estimated population of 43.1 million in 2012" (Ortman, Velkoff, & Hogan, 2014, para. 2). A cross-national comparison of the motivations for such murders was examined by Lennings (2002), who found in a small sample of Australian cases that the influence of prior abuse was absent. It is important to continue research comparing different cultures.

Motivation for killing a parent can be as banal as greed (Heide & McCurdy, 2010). Christopher Porco was convicted of the killing of his father and the attempted murder of his mother. On November 15, 2004, law enforcement officials found the body of Peter Porco inside the door to his home, dead from a brutal attack by someone using a fireman's ax. Joan Porco, Peter's wife and mother of Christopher, was found upstairs severely injured from a similar attack. Joan Porco was presumably left for dead, and in fact, lost an eye and a portion of her skull as a result of the attack. Joan nodded affirmatively that her son Christopher was her attacker. After awakening from a medically induced coma, Joan said she could not remember the event, though she felt sure her son Christopher was not the one who did it. Christopher Porco was a Rochester University student, where he had been experiencing difficulties, including financial ones. He had signed for student loans using his father's name. Christopher also forged his father's name to buy a Jeep. Christopher's father, Peter, told him in an e-mail that any similar behavior would result in his father reporting him. Joan Porco also e-mailed her son about the incident just a few days before the attack on Peter and Joan (Perri, Lichtenwald, & McKenzie, 2008). The type of crime that begins with a family member's fraudulent activity being discovered and ultimately leads to a murder in an attempt to cover the fraud has been referred to as **redcollar crime** (Perri & Lichtenwald, 2007).

OTHER FAMILY KILLINGS

"Honor Killings"

This section of the chapter receives quotation marks around the term due to the debate surrounding its use for what many scholars, advocates, and law enforcement officials deem as nothing more than intimate partner or domestic abuse and homicide (Aujla & Gill, 2014; Doğan, 2013). So-called **honor killings** evoke an image of a religious or ethnic cultural practice that aspires to legitimacy not due to it. The dynamics of the interactions between, typically, a female family member, most likely a daughter, and the patriarch or father of the family, generally, shows the same pattern of controlling dominance exhibited across most cultures when someone is psychologically abused in a relationship.

There are a variety of practices used to control or correct behaviors by female family members that are perceived as an affront to the family's standing or honor. Chesler (2009) lists things such as girls and women refusing to cover their hair, their faces, or their bodies or act as their family's domestic servant; wear makeup or

Western clothing; choose friends from another religion; date; seek to obtain an advanced education; refuse an arranged marriage; seek a divorce from a violent husband; marry against their parents' wishes; or behave in ways that are considered too independent, which might mean anything from driving a car to spending time or living away from home or family (p. 61).

Chesler (2009) goes on to point out a number of the differences seen between so-called ordinary **domestic violence** among Westerners and actions labeled as honor killings. In cases of domestic violence, brothers are not often seen to kill their sisters, and likewise, male cousins are rarely reported to kill female cousins. Western fathers do not, as a rule, kill their teenage daughters, even though they may kill their infant children. The killer of a female family member may also be aided and abetted by a number of family members in an honor killing. Chesler notes this would not be the case typically in an intimate partner homicide event where a man kills his wife or significant other. So the case is made for contextual differences between intimate partner homicide and honor killings.

The cultural practices involved in responding to self-perceived honor and shaming have developed over lengthy periods of time and manifest in different ways based on the particular culture. Nonetheless, the idea of killing a family member based on her choice of dress, affiliation, or other behaviors is repugnant to modern sensibilities. This assertion of unquestioned power and the dramatic, uncivilized action of killing one's child or relative does not logically invite a debate over modernity. Rather, all cultures should view such killings as the murders they are under criminal code and contemporary religious beliefs. Immigrant communities in the United States see instances of this type of homicide typically in first or second-generation immigrants. Hayes, Mills, Freilich, and Chermak (2018) make the observation that, "Honor in the United States, and in Western norms, is considered an individual attribute, whereas honor rests on the family unit in traditional cultures" (p. 72).

A related action is referred to as *honor suicide*. This generally involves female members of a family killing themselves to atone for dishonor

On January 1, 2008, the bodies of sisters Sarah and Amina Said, 17 and 18 years old, who grew up in Texas, were found in a cab in a hotel parking lot in Irving, Texas, with multiple gunshot wounds. Authorities suspected that their father, Yaser Abdel Said, an Egyptian-born cab driver who was a U.S. resident, killed the teenagers for refusing to marry Egyptian men. Just two weeks before the murders, Patricia Said, the mother of the girls, had taken the girls to Oklahoma, apparently fearing what their father might do to them based on escalating threats he made to them. Yaser Said convinced Patricia to return with the girls to Texas just the day before the murders. On the day of the murders, he picked them up in his cab, and that was the last time the girls were seen alive. Yaser had threatened his daughters on numerous occasions for refusing to marry older Egyptian husbands he picked for them and for dating boys they had met in Texas. Friends and family members of the girls reported that both of them had talked of repeated physical abuse, threats of violence, and controlling behaviors by their father before their murders. The murder of Sarah and Amina has become the subject of a documentary on honor killings called *The Price of Honor*. Yaser Said disappeared after the murders and is currently listed on the FBI's Ten Most Wanted Fugitives List for capital murder and unlawful flight to avoid prosecution. Many believe he fled to New York and that he may be driving a cab there.

or embarrassment brought to the family. While the United States has seen few examples of honor suicide, Kremen (2014) also describes this phenomenon by example in Turkey, where many young women commit suicide from the same notion of preserving or regaining a family's honor.

Termen (2010) observes that the use of the term honor killing is a specific form of violence against women but that the term can also be a misleading label that unfairly stereotypes Muslims as being practitioners and proponents of these violent practices. Terman states that while law enforcement needs specific training in regard to honor-based violence, policymakers need to understand the topic so as to respond effectively to this form of violence that stems from longtime cultural practices. Women from various cultures, ethnic backgrounds, and religious practices are rightly proud of their identity and choices. It is important that we not get caught up in unfair and inaccurate stereotyping and risk losing sight of fundamentally abusive practices against girls and women, including murder. Kremen (2014) points out that honor-related violence remains present around the world and continued legal changes are in order. The United Nations cites as many as 5,000 honor killings around the world each year while noting these are just the reported instances. Research in the United States is limited, in part due to the infrequency with which such murders are believed to occur (Hayes, Mills, Freilich, and Chermak, 2018).

Siblicide

The category of **siblicide** is made up of those who kill a brother, known as fratricide, and those who kill a sister, known as **sororicide**. Siblicide is seen frequently in birds as siblings struggle for scarce food. Sadly, humans also engage in the killing of a sibling. In their article on social structure and family homicide, Diem and Pizarro (2010) examined Supplementary Homicide Reports for the years of 2000 and 2007 as well as the Decennial Census to determine effects of economic deprivation and social disorganization. The authors note that studies involving family homicide are somewhat limited, owing at least in part to the relative infrequency of such acts. While their study included consideration of intimate partner homicide, here we discuss only filicide, parricide, and siblicide.

Gebo (2002) examined siblicide in relation to other family murder. Down through history, stories and mythology capture sibling rivalry (particularly male) and its lethal outcome.

Sororicide

In a small town in Florida outside of Jacksonville, a 15-year-old girl shot and killed her 16-year-old brother after retrieving a handgun from a locked bedroom in their home. The girl alleged that she was upset because her brother had beaten her up earlier in the day. Investigators were also shocked to learn that the 11-year-old sister of the two was involved by being on lookout patrol while the older sister broke into the bedroom window of the locked room to retrieve the unloaded handgun after her brother had gone to sleep. The older sister loaded the gun and shot her brother, who was sleeping in the living room. Law enforcement also arrested the parents of the children and charged them with child neglect for leaving the children unsupervised. Reports revealed that there had been a history of abuse and molestation in the home. The 15-year-old's uncle was convicted of molesting her when she was 10 years old, and the mother of the children had also reported to authorities that she had previously found the siblings having sex. After reviewing the family history, the prosecutor decided not to charge the 11-year-old and allowed the 15-year-old to plead to a burglary charge. She will be on probation with the Florida Department of Juvenile Justice until her 19th birthday and will be required to complete counseling.

Fratricide

In June 2018, in an Atlanta suburb, 27 year-old Gavin Henderson killed his 15 year-old sister Keaira Henderson by stabbing her to death. Henderson had recently moved back into the home with his mother and younger siblings after he was released from prison where he had served time for committing several violent crimes. According to the testimony of his 12-year-old sister who witnessed the killing, Henderson was angry that his sister had taken too long in the bathroom. After arguing with his sister, he followed her outside their apartment with a knife and stabbed her 53 times. There had been a recent prior incident where Henderson threatened his siblings with a knife, but no arrest had been made.

While the vast majority of the country's citizens have siblings, and sibling strife and violence is not rare, murder of a sibling is quite uncommon. This, Gebo notes, is the reason the crime has received little research attention. And while other violence *may* be a precursor to lethal violence, that outcome is rare enough to occupy separate attention by researchers. Differences were clearly noted between juvenile-sibling homicide and adult homicides.

In comparing fratricide (killing of a brother) to sororicide (killing of a sister), Peck and Heide (2012) examined Supplementary Homicide Report data from 1976 to 2007 for single-offender and single-victim homicides of this type. A major finding was that siblings who killed a sister were significantly more likely to be female. A second finding was that the sibling killed was younger than the offending sister. Again, we tend to think of siblicide in a gendered way, with a picture of Cain and Abel in our minds. Peck and Heide's findings are interesting to contemplate along with the increases in female-perpetrated violent crime over the last 30 to 40 years.

Gebo (2002) used both routine activities theory and sociobiology as theoretical lenses to consider siblicide. As we have access to our siblings and typically spend a great deal of time in their company, routine activities theory seems a viable candidate to explain sibling violence and perhaps murder. Confounding this, however, is the statistic that most siblicide occurs between adult siblings when time spent together is greatly reduced. Sociobiological theories combine biological attributes and the prerogative of genes with the social context of humans to arrive at a possible explanation for sibling homicide. Support for either position likely will continue to receive less research attention than other more prevalent types of family and nonfamily homicide.

Violence and sometimes killing by and among family members is a tragedy born of circumstances and proximity. Killing a parent, child, sibling, or other family member comes about through a conflation of circumstances. The enduring specter of arguments can result in murder of a family member as well as the seemingly common murder of a stranger. Daly and Wilson (1988) gave us much to think about regarding evolutionary psychology and what they believe were inherent (genetic) protections against killing our kin. Violence may follow a twisted and lengthy path before it results in the death of one person at the hands of a close relative. The numbers and percentage of family murders have gone down over the last several decades, yet the implications of violence within the family unit are many.

Familicide, or family annihilation, is most often committed by the patriarchal figure of a family. The incident may come about from the father's inability to grapple with trying financial conditions coupled with a background of individual factors. He may also kill his children as a way of inflicting pain psychologically on his spouse who may not have died in the event. A man or a woman committing family annihilation may also view him or herself as caring for the family by taking them away from a cruel or disappointing world. Suicide typically follows the family annihilation act by the perpetrator. Though rare, extended parricide, the killing of parents and other family members, typically by a male child, should receive further study. With an aging population (Ortman et al., 2014) and increasing involvement in violent crime, in part due to equalizing factors in society for girls and women, we may see an increase in this segment of family homicide.

Theoretical approaches have been varied, and in this chapter, we touched on only a few. Social learning theory and routine activities theory provide insights on repeat and intergenerational violent behaviors in families, and proximity to potential victims is also an explanatory factor. Multiple researchers have examined the impact of economic stress on both the father and the mother in incidents of family homicide. Diem and Pizarro (2010) suggest as one example "economically based institutions to help those in need before financial strain reaches a point of violence" (p. 521). Policymakers in government and private organizations should consider the nexus of economic strain or deprivation and dysfunctional family dynamics, including violence.

Familicide can be committed by either a man or a woman. While some stressors affect the mother or father similarly, others have been seen as unique based on gender roles. Siblicide, as well, may be committed by either a male or female, and research continues into this type of family murder. The killing of one's children is difficult for most people to comprehend. While family murder excluding intimate partner homicide is rare, media coverage of these dramatic events can influence public perception of their prevalence. Incidents of children who kill their parents are indeed unusual. Of these cases, some have resulted from what is referred to as defense against abuse, where perhaps a father has physically or sexually abused his child or children over a period of time. Other instances of parricide are the result of greed and the potential to gain access to a parent's money.

So-called honor killings, more frequent in many cultures around the world, can occur in immigrant communities or first and second-generation immigrant families in the United States. The generational differences between children born or raised in America and their parents, especially a father rooted in a patriarchal cultural view of proper behavior, can rise to lethal proportions. This dynamic is also reflected in the victimization of women in intimate partner violence and homicide and is a challenging dynamic for law enforcement, social work, and public health professionals trying to serve community members isolated by language and other social structural barriers from assistance.

Intimate partner homicides (IPH) 100
Social learning theory 100
Routine activities theory 100
Intergenerational transmission of violence 101
Familicide 102

Mass murder 102
Family annihilator 102
Homicide-suicide 102
Filicide 106
Neonaticide 106
Infanticide 106
Parricide 109

Patricide 109
Matricide 109
Red-collar crime 111
Honor killings 111
Domestic violence (DV) 111
Siblicide 112
Sororicide 112

DISCUSSION QUESTIONS

1. Discuss the dynamics of familicide.
2. How does the cycle of violence apply to family violence?
3. What are the reasons parents kill their children?

4. Discuss one of the types of parricide.
5. Explain why eliminating honor killings is particularly challenging.

TRY THIS

Visit the National Institute of Justice page for "Murder-Suicide in Families" at https://www.nij.gov/topics/crime/intimate-partner-violence/Pages/murder-suicide.aspx

Read one or more of the sections on risk factors, role of guns, role of shelters, or role of the economy. What are some key impressions or facts you come away with?

8

SCHOOL KILLINGS

"The cure for crime is not the electric chair,
but the high chair."

—J. Edgar Hoover

"What we must do now is enact change
because that is what we do to things that fail:
We change them."

—Lorenzo Prado, *survivor of Parkland
school shooting*

CHAPTER OUTLINE

Student Learning Outcomes

Students will be able to:

- differentiate among the types of violence and homicides involving the school setting.

- explain the criteria used for categorizing school shootings.

- describe the connections between factors and conditions in school murders.

- analyze the role of theories and school violence research in policy formulation.

INTRODUCTION

In this chapter and the next, we look at forms of homicide that have single and multiple victims in the school and work settings, as well as other venues. One form of multiple homicide is the mass murder. Depending on whose definition one uses, **mass murder** is an event where either three or more or four or more persons are murdered at one time. Eric Hickey (2013) offers the definition of mass murders as one "in which several victims are killed within a few moments or hours" (p. 11). The debate over the threshold number of victims for a mass shooting or murder is often viewed as an academic one. This debate may be impacted by the selection of victims. And selection is, in fact, implicated in considering this method of multicide. Victims may or may not be selected based on a particular group membership. Serial murder as a multicide involves killing a number of victims but over months or years, perhaps, and with breaks of time or a *cooling off* period in between the murders. Terror attacks that involve multiple victims and genocide or politicide carried out in various countries are considered separately in a subsequent chapter.

In this chapter, we will first address attacks on multiple victims by a fellow student. Following this, we discuss attacks on students and school personnel by individuals who are not students and who often have no connection to the schools they target. Finally, we will examine individual homicide events in the school setting and some of the known motivations and suspected causes.

The public is generally informed about crime and specifically about single and multiple homicide incidents through the various news media. News organizations have a need to present stories in a manner that holds the potential to increase reader or viewership. This underlying presentation motivation can often misinform and distort the factual attributes of news stories. "When the media focuses a great deal of attention on a rare type of crime, it can seem that the crime is more prevalent" (Hough & Tatum, 2014, p. 72). The media frequently presents a skewed view of violence and many of the crimes that occur in a community. There is a general misperception of the prevalence of **school shootings**

and mass shootings overall, and this is often a result of the disproportionate focus of the media on school crime and a not-altogether-accurate presentation of school rampage shooting violence as random (Madfis, 2016).

News organizations do have ready access to more in-depth factual information regarding homicide overall. Huff-Corzine et al. (2014) conducted a comparison of news media sources to the generally used Supplemental Homicide Reports (SHR) of the Uniform Crime Reports (UCR) as well as the still growing National Incident-Based Reporting System (NIBRS). The authors note that prior to 1976, news stories were far more available and more detailed than the SHR. Media organizations can and sometimes do acquire factual research. It is hoped that access to more complete information, such as that found in the SHR and NIBRS, can lead to presenting a balanced view and proper context of any serious crime, especially ones receiving the level of coverage of school shootings.

MASS SHOOTINGS AND ATTACKS

Incidents of mass murder are not new in the United States or elsewhere, but the study of such crimes was not frequently pursued before the 1980s. Workplace shootings, mass killings at places of worship, and the public assault of multiple victims for a cause or terror group are other examples, and we deal with those elsewhere in the book. The examination of such crimes, school shootings in particular, has received tremendous attention since the 1990s. Since that time, shooters now have access to more and more powerful firearms, increasing the opportunity and likelihood of killing and injuring greater numbers of schoolmates, teachers, and staff.

In the past 20 years, school shootings, both attempted and completed, have become a tragically familiar occurrence in the United States (Agnich, 2015). The incidence of such events coupled with the rise of the 24/7 news cycle in the 1990s has resulted in an ongoing safety concern for children at school, students in college, associated faculty and staff, and the causes and

Figure 8.1   Sample of School Shootings, 1997–2018

October 1, 1997	Student shoots nine people at his school in Pearl, MS
December 1, 1997	Student shoots eight people at his school in West Paducah, KY
December 15, 1997	Student shoots two people at his school in Stamps, AK
March 24, 1998	Two students shoot 15 people at their school in Jonesboro, AK
April 24, 1998	Student shoots four people at his school in Edinboro, PA
May 21, 1998	Student kills parents at home and then shoots 27 people at his school in Springfield, OR
April 20, 1999	Two students shoot 33 people at their school in Littleton, CO
November 19, 1999	Student shoots one classmate at school in Deming, NM
February 29, 2000	Student shoots one classmate at school in Mount Morris Township, MI
May 26, 2000	Student shoots one teacher at school in Lake Worth, FL
March 5, 2001	Student shoots 15 people at school in Santee, CA
September 24, 2003	Student shoots two people at school in Cold Spring, MN
March 21, 2005	Student kills grandfather and his friend and then goes to school and shoots seven people at school at Red Lake Indian Reservation, MN
November 8, 2005	Student shoots three people at school in Jacksboro, TN
August 3, 2006	Former student kills father, then goes to former school and shoots two people in Hillsborough, NC
September 27, 2006	Adult takes six girls hostage and shoots one to death at school in Bailey, CO
October 2, 2006	Adult enters Amish school, kills five people and wounds five others in Lancaster, PA.
April 16, 2007	College student kills two people in a dormitory and then shoots 30 more people in a building on campus in Blacksburg, VA
February 14, 2008	College student shoots 25 people on campus in DeKalb, IL
October 26, 2008	Four individuals shot three people on college campus in Conway, AK
September 28, 2010	College sophomore wearing a ski mask fires shots using an AK-47 inside University of Texas library before killing himself
February 27, 2012	Student shoots six people at school in Chardon, OH
December 24, 2012	Adult kills his mother and then goes to an elementary school and kills 26 in Newtown, CT
June 7, 2013	Adult kills his father and brother, then goes to college campus shooting eight more people on the way and at campus in Santa Monica, CA
October 21, 2013	Student shoots three people at middle school in Sparks, NV
December 13, 2013	Student shoots one person at school in Littleton, CO

(Continued)

Figure 8.1 (Continued)

June 5, 2014	Adult shoots three people on university campus in Seattle, WA
October 24, 2014	Student shoots in school cafeteria in Marysville, WA
April 27, 2015	Student at school fires shots in common area, teacher tackled him before anyone was injured in Lacey, WA
September 30, 2015	Principal shot in the arm by 16-year-old in Harrisburg, SD
February 12, 2016	Murder-suicide of two girls at high school in Glendale, AZ
June 8, 2016	One student is killed and three are wounded when evacuating after a fire alarm at a high school in Dorchester, MA
September 3, 2017	Four students shot by another student wielding an AR-15 and a pistol at a high school in Rockford, WA
December 7, 2017	Former student shot and killed two students, then self at a high school in Aztec, NM
January 23, 2018	A student shot 18 students in high school lobby, killing two and wounding 16 in Marshall, KY
February 14, 2018	Former student shot and killed 17 students, 17 more were injured in Parkland, FL
May 18, 2018	Fire alarm evacuation of high school; shooter killed 10 people and 13 more were injured in Santa Fe, TX
December 13, 2018	Fourteen-year-old planned shooting at school in Richmond, IN; mother warned police who arrived, and student killed himself

responses to this type of violence. Violence in the school setting is of obvious concern because we think of school as a place of security for our children. In specifically considering youth in the kindergarten through 12th grade (K–12) setting, it is frequently noted that kids spend a significant portion of the waking day in the school environment. Ironically, this very fact means that the potential for some of the interpersonal conflict between or among young people and some adults will likely occur here.

It seems that there are some months when school shootings and other mass shootings occupy a great deal of media coverage. Michele Richinick of MSNBC News reported in July 2014 that there had been 110 mass shootings since January 2009 (Richinick, 2014). Using figures from a report released by a group called Everytown for Gun Safety, Richinick wrote about the focus that sometimes exists on

the mental health of the alleged shooter. The researchers in this report found only 11% had exhibited signs of such illness before they opened fire. The report authors used the Federal Bureau of Investigation (FBI) definition of a mass shooting as four or more people murdered.

A report released by the Federal Bureau of Investigation in late September 2014 stated that instances of a gunman opening fire on multiple people have increased in the last several years. The FBI's report looked at 160 such attacks between 2000 and 2013. The average number of shootings increased over the study years from 6.4 to an average of 11.4 per year as of 2013. Our interest in this chapter is primarily acts of lethal violence related to schools. It is important to note that some dynamics of other mass shooting events are similar. The FBI study indicates that mass shootings analyzed in their study occurred in 40 out of 50 states and in the District of Columbia. The settings varied in both public and private locations and in communities large and small, urban and rural. This work followed the efforts more than a decade before of the U.S. Department of Education and the U.S. Secret Service in the Safe School Initiative (Vossekuil, Fein, Reddy, Borum, & Modzeleski, 2002). The two agencies looked comprehensively at nearly 40 incidents of targeted school violence spanning the years 1974 to 2000. The full report issued by the Secret Service can be found online at http://www.secretservice.gov/ntac/ssi_final_report.pdf. These two agencies concluded that there are no simple explanations and no simple solutions to violent attacks inside of the school setting. They do agree however that continued research and efforts can lead to prevention strategies for much school violence.

On December 14, 2012, 20-year-old Adam Lanza went to Sandy Hook Elementary School in Newtown, Connecticut, where he killed 20 children and six adults. Before going to the school, Lanza fatally shot his mother. Lanza committed suicide at the scene of his rampage. Following the Sandy Hook killings, polls revealed a majority of people believed that a school shooting could occur in their own community. Regardless of the ubiquitous media coverage of school shootings and the impact this has on many in the public, it is important to note that such attacks are still rare.

This event occurred in a relatively small community. The public has come to understand that this is not the startling aspect of such mass attacks. Commonly recognized school shooting incidents such as Columbine High School in Littleton, Colorado, brought forward discussion among scholars, the media, and the public at large about the potential for this type of incident happening in any location. In fact, a look at a number of the incidents during the period of years surrounding Columbine gives ample evidence of the frequent setting of such attacks: Pearl, Mississippi; West Paducah, Kentucky; Jonesboro, Arkansas; Edinboro, Pennsylvania; and Springfield, Oregon, to name but several.

Researchers have examined the actions of mass murderers and as a result have developed a number of typologies for these individuals. Noted researcher Park Dietz identified three categories of mass murderers, which he labeled *family annihilators*, *pseudocommandos*, and *set-and-run killers* (Dietz, 1986). In this early work, Dietz noted that no solid typologies yet existed for the examination of mass murder. He viewed the mass murders he had reviewed as fitting into the aforementioned categories, which he defined as follows:

Family annihilators, usually the senior man of the house, who is depressed, paranoid, intoxicated or a combination of these. He kills each member of the family who is present, sometimes including pets. He may commit suicide after killing the others, or may force the police to kill him. *Pseudocommandos*, who are preoccupied by firearms and commit their raids after long deliberation ... *Set-and-run killers*, who employ techniques allowing themselves the possibility of escape before the deaths occur. (p. 482)

We will examine in a separate chapter the family annihilator, who often kills his entire family. This mass murderer will often then kill himself. Pseudocommandos plan their killing, and this is the category where we find most school shooters. The selection of the school is tied to his thought process about his circumstances and who symbolizes or who, in his mind, is to blame for those circumstances. The pseudocommando in the school or other location will often kill himself or manipulate the circumstance so that the police kill him. School massacres and other attacks by the so-called set-and-run killers will employ bombs or perhaps a poison to accomplish their murderous task so that they may leave the immediate area but be able to see what they have done. The categories specified by Dietz do not emphasize whether three, four, or more victims constitute the *mass* but do clarify the type of victim selected: family member, coworker, or whoever may have been present at the chosen location, like a school.

Katherine Newman, in her 2004 book *Rampage: The Social Roots of School Shootings*, provides a sociological view of the causes of school killings by youth. Newman, as others, does not

May 18, 2018, eight students and two teachers were killed by a gunman at Santa Fe High School in Santa Fe, TX. Thirteen others were wounded when a 17-year-old student began walking through the school shooting at people with a revolver and a shotgun. Two police officers assigned to the school engaged the young man and tried to get him to surrender. When the student was injured, after critically wounding one of the officers, he surrendered. He was charged with numerous counts of capital murder and aggravated assault on a peace officer.

assert that any one of the causes she notes is a singular cause. Rather, Newman points to several conditions that, taken together, set the context for a potential rampage event. The following five points underscore the view by researchers that opinions that point to a single cause of such incidents are shortsighted. The conditions are

- the shooter's perception of himself as extremely marginal in the social worlds that matter to him;

- the shooter must suffer from psychosocial problems that magnify the impact of marginality;

- prescriptions for behavior referred to as "cultural scripts" make problem solving through shootings appear acceptable;

- a failure of surveillance systems that are intended to identify troubled teens before their problems become extreme; and

- the ability for the youth to attain unsupervised access to a weapon. (Newman, Fox, Harding, Mehta, & Roth, 2004, p. 230)

Holmes and Holmes (2001) proposed additional categories built on Dietz's typologies of mass murderers: disciples, disgruntled employees, disgruntled citizens, and psychotic people.

The disciple mass murderer is typically a cult member killing to gain the acceptance of the leader. The followers of Jim Jones are examples of disciples as they assisted in carrying out the mass murder and suicide of their entire group of children, women, and men to fulfill Jones's vision. The motivation of this type of mass killer may differ only in degree from some gang initiates who also commit violent acts to gain acceptance or please a charismatic leader. Disgruntled employees and disgruntled citizens are murderers who express their anger by killing. While the disgruntled employee kills his current or former coworkers, the "disgruntled citizen tends to be angry at the world rather than particular individuals" (Davies, 2008, p. 192). Lastly, the psychotic mass murderer described by Holmes and Holmes has had a break with reality and acts based on imagined instructions or threats that do not exist in reality. In several cases identified as committed by a psychotic killer, family members have also been killed prior to or following the mass killing (Lake, 2014).

In addition to Park Dietz and Holmes and Holmes, other researchers have created categories to sort mass killers. Among these, Fox and Levin (2015) developed the categories of power, revenge, loyalty, profit, and terror. The various typologies developed by researchers assist other researchers in approaching the phenomenon of school killing and mass killing. The categories also help the public understand the motivations or genesis of such shooters and killers. While the different classifications help us structure our study of mass killers, each has predictable overlaps between and among the categories, reflecting the mixed motivations different killers may have.

THE KILLERS

The typologies of mass murderers discussed in the preceding section give us general motivation categories. Here we look at some of the so-called **risk factors** for violent behavior as well as some of the attributes that might be considered a profile of sorts. Factors and attributes are perhaps two slightly different ways of observing the background or circumstances of the eventual shooter. As we begin this section, let us caution you that there is no agreed-upon profile of school shooters such that school, social work, or law enforcement authorities could intervene on a consistent basis with accuracy. The commonalities of behaviors among school shooters does not lead quickly to a mechanism for even psychiatrists or other health professionals to accurately perform threat assessment (Haeney, Ash, & Galletly, 2018).

There is no lack of *risk factors* checklists examined or commented on by researchers, educators, law enforcement, politicians, and pundits. We often hear of a killer's alleged issues of mental illness and what efforts were or were not made to address them. Various mental disorders are not infrequent in most countries, though the United States is among the countries with the highest rates. The prevalence of diagnosable mental illness has been estimated by the World Health Organization (WHO), the Substance Abuse and Mental Health Services Administration (SAMHSA), and others, which illustrates the concern for the impact of mental illness worldwide on every society. The U.S. Congressional Research Service (CRS), in its February 2014 *Prevalence of Mental Illness in the United States* report to Congress, cited various surveys and studies by the U.S. Department of Health and Human Services (HHS). In their report, the CRS noted that one of the large-scale studies showed a 12-month prevalence rate of mental illness (excluding substance use disorders) at more than 18% (Bagalman & Napili, 2014). Among adults, the prevalence of mental illness was estimated at more than a quarter of all adults. In the same period, the prevalence of serious mental illness was just over 4%. Among adolescents, one of the surveys used by the CRS showed the prevalence of *any* mental illness in a 12-month period to be just over 40%. Serious mental illness was estimated at 18%.

The figures about the prevalence of mental illness, even serious mental illness, in U.S. society are shocking to many people. This is largely because of the initial visceral reaction to the term mental illness. The negative connotation of mental illness is still the default view by many people. This view is unfortunate for many reasons, but chief among those is that an incredibly small number of people with any type of mental illness act out violently against others or commit a school shooting. To most people's credit, they can move quickly to understanding that the various challenges experienced by many do not signal a debilitating, let alone dangerous, condition. Stuart (2003) posed three useful questions to guide a productive conversation to inform us on our understanding of mental illness and its connection to violence:

- Are the mentally ill violent?

- Are the mentally ill at increased risk of violence?

- Are the public at risk? (p. 121)

The *difference* in behavior that may lead a juvenile to be ostracized can result in bullying of the youth who is labeled as different by his peers. Retaliation may follow the victimization of the youth so branded. Yet most kids who get picked on have not resorted to the extreme measure of acquiring a gun to shoot their classmates. And so the manner in which someone with mental illness is treated may prime that person to eventually or episodically react with violence. While it is difficult, if not impossible, to categorically answer a question such as, "Are the mentally ill at increased risk of violence?" Stuart (2003) notes "a modest association between mental illness and violence" (p. 122). She further notes that the research she relies on controls for the "main risk factors" of being "young, male, single, or of lower socio-economic status" (p. 122). Answering the question of the risk to the public, given the relative infrequence of serious violent acts committed by someone with a serious mental illness, is also problematic. The family and social circumstances a person with serious mental illness finds himself in may tell us more about his pathway to violence than the condition he suffers from. Mental health care is not sought by or affordable for many families. A serious condition, such as delusional schizophrenia, results in reduced productivity at home, school, or work, but untrained parents may not know how to deal with the behaviors they are seeing. Clearly there are many types of disorder, and each brings challenges that may have little or nothing to do with the risk of mass violence.

On April 16, 2007, the deadliest school shooting in U.S. history occurred on the campus of Virginia Polytechnic Institute and State University in Blacksburg, Virginia. On that day, a senior undergraduate student named Seung-Hui Cho murdered 32 students and faculty and wounded 17 others before killing himself. Others were injured trying to escape the building where the attack occurred. Cho had a history of diagnosed mental illness, including severe anxiety and depressive disorders, and he had received treatment for his conditions. He had also been found to be a danger to himself and others and been ordered to receive outpatient assessment and counseling about two years before the rampage. In spite of this history of mental illness, he was allowed to purchase firearms legally. After the shooting, investigators found notes from him that indicated his disdain for his classmates who were *rich kids* and found videos where he mentioned the Columbine school shooters and called them *martyrs*.

Several professional observers believe that Adam Lanza may have possessed traits associated with personality disorder or autism. When Lanza's father spoke to the media following the murders, he said that Adam had been challenged by various anxiety behaviors, making him socially awkward. Lanza was diagnosed with Asperger's Syndrome, which Peter Lanza, his father, believed masked a schizophrenia that may have explained better his behavior over a long period of years. Some researchers believe that mental challenges are at the root of Lanza's murderous acts.

MOTIVATIONS OF THOSE WHO KILL

Revenge for being bullied, ignored, marginalized, or rejected figures prominently in the psychological autopsy conducted following a school shooting (and other mass murders). The young person's identity and self-worth receives attention, sometimes without the caveat that the period of adolescence is preoccupied with identity formation for all juveniles. Some of the bullying already mentioned may interact with an adolescent male's self-view of "failing masculinity" by the emasculating harassment from schoolmates (Farr, 2018). The rage felt by a school shooting perpetrator may not find any other outlet in the eyes of the shooter. The buildup of resentment and rage over time also allows the potential shooter to fantasize about and in that way plan for the eventual attack. Although evidence of extreme anger and a desire for revenge are often present, the shooter still shows sufficient control of his impulses to plan out his attack (Declercq & Audenaert, 2011). Another misperception of the public is the belief that the school shooter *snaps* one day and goes on an impulsive shooting spree. This is not the typical school mass killing or attack scenario.

With the anger the school shooter feels toward a group of peers and perhaps the school as an entity, he may see the attention of the community coming through the killing of classmates. The effects and implications of bullying and undiagnosed serious mental illness of a student can be significant. The reality is that K–12 teachers and guidance counselors do not have the time or resources to adequately identify and reach out to children and their families who have any number of challenges in their lives. As we reflect on this important aspect of adolescent development, we can easily envision that resources devoted to early identification and intervention can be put to great use in building the child into a healthy and productive adult.

Another of the risk factors that may impede that path to healthy adulthood is being abused and being exposed to abuse directed at others. This is most frequently thought of in the home, but the exposure may also occur in the school, the neighborhood, and society in general. Each dimension of the abuse or exposure may have a stronger effect, depending on the balancing factors or resiliency experienced by the individual.

The role modeling discussed as one aspect of social learning theory may come into play as the influence of a parent, an older sibling, or perhaps a feared and respected local gang member establishes a template for how the young person develops his responses to life. This may also be seen in incidents of confrontational homicide discussed earlier in the book.

The age and gender of killers bears comment. The vast majority of mass murders, in general, have been committed by males. Katsavdakis, Meloy, and White (2011) note that "criminal databases suggest that no more than four to six women have ever acted alone to carry out a civilian massacre" (p. 813). School shootings, in particular, have been committed predominantly by teenage males. In mass shootings, most of the assailants have been white. It is a cultural reality that males find violence to be a more acceptable way of resolving conflict than females. Acculturation in most countries leads to males being more likely to act out through violence.

The school shooter is frequently from a middle-class background and attends a rural or suburban-based school. Holmes and Holmes, in their 2001 work on mass murder, add several other commonly seen components of the individual's existence. The student felt disenfranchised and as a result was an outcast or associated with others who were members of an *outgroup*. Violent and other video game play has been identified by many of the shooters, but as we comment elsewhere, the connection is tenuous and debated. Many shooters are secretive just prior to the lethal event, even though many have spoken to someone previously about their general intentions to kill classmates. An interest in firearms and access to them has been noted in many cases.

Access to firearms inevitably enters the debate over the *causes* of violence. Gun violence prevention is considered important by everyone. There is no consensus on how to go about achieving it. School functions may include policies of educating youth about the need to exercise caution around firearms, and most schools have addressed students about precautionary measures in the event of a shooting. An important and effective approach in this regard remains getting children involved with as many school activities as practical to increase the attachment a child has to prosocial groups and behaviors.

Policy efforts aimed at stopping any type of violence rely upon accurate information. School shootings generate policies and laws that attempt to identify potentially harmful individuals, intervene prior to mass attacks, or impede the actions of those on a trajectory to harming students and others. Considerable effort has also been expended to address the tragic and traumatic aftermath of incidents such as the Sandy Hook shooting. The various categories proposed over the last several decades by various researchers and observers speak to the difficulty of designing universal measures given the many factors and conditions that may contribute to the killers' actions. Hickey (2013), on that point, says,

> It would appear that not all mass murderers are motivated by similar circumstances, yet the final outcome is the same. Feelings of rejection, failure, and loss of autonomy create frustrations that inevitably overwhelm them, and they experience a need to strike back. And for many killers the best way to lash out against a cold, forbidding society is to destroy its children. (p. 21)

It is to this continuing point that we caution against the use of checklists for formulating policy or as a single-instrument method of excluding a student from the school environment. Early warning signs are sought in many domains of life and human behavior. These can certainly be valuable as we work to help people and organizations address a potential challenge or problem before it escalates or grows in impact. Bartol and Bartol (2011) provide a discussion of many of the commonalities or warning signs of violence with the same caution against using such lists as definitive. Social rejection surfaces in almost all such conversations of school shooters. Some fellow students are almost always found to have known of their peer's deadly intentions, often not taking them seriously. A fascination with death, an interest in guns or explosives, and psychological problems were additional factors often learned about after a deadly incident. Bartol and Bartol

WHY WOULD THEY DO IT?

In October 2006, a 32-year-old milk truck driver entered a one-room school house in a Pennsylvania Amish community, heavily armed with three guns, 600 rounds of ammunition, a stun gun, zip ties, petroleum jelly, two knives, tape, toilet paper, and other hardware. He was there to carry out his careful plan to attack the children in the school. During the attack, Charles C. Roberts ordered the 11 girls in the room to line up facing the blackboard and allowed the boys and several adults to leave. He killed five girls and wounded six more, who ranged in age from 6 to 13, before killing himself as the police arrived at the scene. The police investigation revealed that while Mr. Roberts was not Amish, he likely selected the school because it appeared to be an easier target than a larger school. In the suicide notes he left for his wife, he mentioned the loss of his first daughter, who died right after being born and his need to get back at god for the loss he suffered. His wife also mentioned that her husband suffered bouts of depression but that she did not believe he would ever commit such horrific acts.

go on to point out that little empirical evidence has supported such checklists and that many students exhibit many of the behaviors with little chance of being a future mass killer.

The threat from school shootings does not always come from within. A number of notorious cases in the recent past illustrate this aspect of mass murders in the school setting. These attacks are even rarer than school shootings by students. Bartol and Bartol (2013) observe that the adult shooter does not make a threat that may provide any type of warning for schools to take action. A rare but notable mass killing at a school is the outside person who selects the venue of a school to carry out his terrible acts.

Our focus in this chapter is largely the type of rampage killings committed by students that claim multiple victims. In addition to shooters who enter a school setting to kill but who are not themselves connected to the school are students who commit violent acts that are not on the scale of a mass murder. Local news stories around the country describe one-on-one instances of a student killing or seriously injuring a fellow student or staff member in a specific assault. These crimes may result from all manner of causes, including an ongoing friction; a troubled relationship; in the course of perpetrating a crime, such as a robbery; and of course, anger and frustration that the individual chooses to take out on one or two people rather than in a planned attack on many. These tragic incidents also deserve attention and efforts to limit their frequency.

INTERNATIONAL INCIDENTS

Mass school killings have also occurred outside of the United States. On April 26, 2002, at a school in Erfurt, Germany, a 19-year-old gunman named Robert Steinhauser shot and killed 16 people, including 13 faculty members, two students, and one police officer who responded to the scene. He then committed suicide. Steinhauser had been expelled from the school months before the shooting and was disqualified from taking university entrance exams. In Osaka, Japan, on June 8, 2001, 37-year-old janitor Mamoru Takuma, who had a history of mental illness, entered an elementary school with a knife and killed eight children and seriously wounded 13 other children and two teachers. It was the second largest mass murder in Japanese history and set off serious public alarm about the treatment of the mentally ill and the safety of schools. In considering Japan's strong gun control laws, it is not surprising that the weapon used for his attack was a knife. This example illustrates a stark contrast from most mass murders in the United States, where firearms are readily accessible.

Akiba, Baker, Goesling, and LeTendre (2002) discussed school violence statistics available from 37 countries. The perspective is beneficial when viewing rates of school violence in the United States. The international perspective is useful regarding overall school violence, and of course, U.S. rates are most relevant in America for making policy decisions. Decisions are aided by longitudinally examining statistics within the United States. While school shootings are rare, citizens worldwide have great concern over the safety of children away from home. The United States joins most countries in having some fear and challenges in regard to school violence. Other nations, such as Japan, fear an increase in school killings (Akiba et al., 2002). Many of the factors implicated in school violence in America, such as student ages, level of social integration, and family economics, are examined in other countries as well.

POLICY RESPONSES

Schools

Incidents of school killings in the United States continue to demand the attention of policymakers. The causes of attacks by students or others on students at K–12 schools and institutions of higher education are varied. The public school system has policies that attempt to identify troubled students and intervene to prevent such shootings. Some feel that shootings and attacks reflect a failing by the information systems in a school about its students (Fox & Harding, 2005). Likewise, colleges, universities, and other institutions utilize crisis teams and protocols to educate and reach out to students. Schildkraut and Hernandez (2014) note,

> While legislation could be useful in deterring or preventing some future acts, the key purpose of these legal responses is to ease the mind of citizens who fear future attacks and to provide assurance that something is being done to address gun violence. (p. 370)

Parents and schools must also deal with the aftermath of a shooting incident. This may be physical reconstruction or renovation of school buildings in addition to rebuilding a sense of safety and confidence in the students, parents, and school staff through a "renewal discourse" that can be very much place-bound (Wombacher, Herovic, Sellnow, & Seeger,

2018). Psychological support must be immediate and continue for some time, with specific plans for individual students and staff (Turunen & Punamäki, 2014).

Chapin (2008) found, in a study conducted with students in a school-based violence prevention session, that many students fail to accurately assess the threats or statements of a peer who says he will bring a gun to school and shoot people. School threat assessment teams became a common response after the shootings of the 1990s. The challenges of discriminating between more and less serious threats or behavior are daunting. Parents and schools face this challenge together in preventing potential school shootings. The responsibilities of school leaders and staff are tremendous, not only in working to prevent violence but during any emergency and in the aftermath (Brown, 2018). A number of experts warn that an overreaction to the statistical danger to children in schools can leave those schools looking like fortified and armed encampments. And at home, some 1.7 million children live with unlocked, loaded guns, according to the Children's Hospital of Philadelphia, Center for Injury Research and Prevention (2019). They point to the body of scientific literature regarding the risk of injury and death in a country with nearly 400 million guns—more than there are people in the United States. The website notes that in 2015, 2,824 children aged 0-19 years old died by gunshot and more than 13,000 were injured.

Least Violent Time in History

The 1990s seemed to bring a significant upswing in school violence: Littleton, Colorado; Pearl, Mississippi; West Paducah, Kentucky; Jonesboro, Arkansas; and Springfield, Oregon. There were many other shootings and certainly other violent incidents that seemed to signal a new era of *super-predators* in society and on campus. While we have learned much about violence and our skills in threat assessment have improved thanks to the efforts of various law enforcement agencies and experts such as Gavin de Becker, we still recognize that often we are reacting to an assault rather than preventing one.

Human aggression expert Lt. Col. Dave Grossman (USA, Ret.) has expanded our thinking and discussion about school shooters to include the socially promoted high schooler, who may now act out his frustration as a workplace killer. For good reason, schools, law enforcement, and politicians all want checklists of demographic and dispositional factors so that they can quickly assess who is a threat and remove them. We know that even though premeditated violence is often predictable and preventable, such a quick assessment is rarely possible. On this, we refer you to more of de Becker's work along with Bob Martin (LAPD, Ret.) and the MOSAIC approach they pioneered. The individual who clearly stands out is quickly dealt with. More common is the person whose violence is situational. That person may well function quietly, under the radar, all the while planning a horrendous attack. Recent events provide no shortage of those examples.

In what some are already calling the Homeland Security era of policing, we work more closely to gather information, develop intelligence, and share with public-safety organizations and other stakeholders. Such cooperation and coordination is a boon to antiterrorism work and in building cases against organized-crime groups and others. The information, however, that might help identify a potential shooter does not reside with law enforcement groups alone. Local law enforcement agencies practice and refine **active shooter** tactics, and school districts, colleges, and universities have developed policies to address crises that occur on campus.

Prominent Harvard University psychologist Steven Pinker (2011) chronicles the ubiquitous nature of violence throughout history and its current low point in his recent book, *The Better Angels of Our Nature: Why Violence Has Declined*. Why do most people find this pronouncement hard to believe? Most would point to the 24/7 news cycle that arose early in the 1990s and gave us the sense that juveniles were spiraling out of control and our culture was helpless to stop them. And while we can be comforted that the world is inching its way toward less viciousness, as public-safety professionals and first responders, we have to deal with what violence does exist.

Active shooter incidents tend, in most peoples' minds, to involve an aggrieved student (or adult worker, in the case of businesses), though active shooters are not unique to the school setting.

Active shooter is a term used by law enforcement to describe a situation in which a shooting is in progress and an aspect of the crime may affect the protocols used in responding to and reacting at the scene of the incident. (Blair & Schweit, 2014, p. 4)

There are examples of shooters who plan an assault at a location where they may have only a tangential connection or no connection at all. Schools have created policies for emergencies such as these and others, and they have made efforts to maintain awareness and training for students and employees. The distinction between K–12 and college or university campuses and students is an important factor in any plans developed. Flexibility in planning is warranted.

Buerger and Buerger (2010) succinctly recapped the active shooter campus playbook with the following direction: hide, lock doors, give 9-1-1 operators information, and wait for help. Many people picture empty hallways with a single shooter profiled and vulnerable. If students and others are fleeing, the shooter has more access to random targets or the chaos needed to escape, in the event he has any intention of fleeing. This last assumption of a shooter intending to leave the scene of his assault is belied by many of the incidents studied over time. Campus shootings and workplace shootings are infrequent. Nonetheless, authorities must do all that they can to prevent them, when possible, or respond to such events.

School Settings and Design

This discussion is not intended as a complete examination of threat assessment of members of the campus community. The art and science of individual threat assessment deserves its own discussion, at a later time, and consideration of the processes and tasks that agencies and individuals must take to screen information and assess intent. Here, our observations run more as to whether and how to **shelter-in-place** or evacuate all or part of a school campus.

Before responding with a blanket assertion of which course to take, there are a number of factors to consider. Certainly, a significant issue that has received much attention is the physi-cal plant and site. You need only to think about the city or county you live in and the variety of school campuses there to grasp the complexity of safety planning in the school environment. While some research has shown that smaller schools may be less likely to experience a mass shooting, the same research adds an interesting factor that a student transitioning from a smaller rural school to a larger, *more anonymous* school, may contribute to mental health challenge of a potential shooter (Baird, Roellke, & Zeifman, 2017). The authors note that school size alone is not necessarily the most important factor, but a lack of adequate support to perhaps assist stu-dents transferring from a more close-knit or psy-chologically manageable environment. If your community or region has a college or university, this adds other dimensions to the policy choice and preparations to be considered. SWAT and emergency response team training often take place physically in school settings. Individual officers also patrol their assigned areas with sce-nario planning in mind, in the same way banks and businesses are assessed for robbery response.

Crime Prevention Through Environmental Design

Law enforcement agencies have conducted commercial and residential crime prevention assessments for a very long time indeed. The early 1970s brought the first articulation of **Crime Prevention Through Environmental Design** (CPTED). CPTED initially included concepts from biology and psychology but later expanded to deter criminal behavior through building design and then grounds and even street layouts. Today, internal environment and the psy-chological cues of layout and design also feature prominently in CPTED applications. Signage, access control, and surveillance enhance building security. *Feng shui* to a security consultant means clear sight lines and a good fit between layout and the awareness and acclimation of employees to potential campus disruptions.

In considering school design, CPTED concepts have suggested that *natural surveil-lance* is desirable. It is important that people or electronic-surveillance devices be able to view activity around a structure or area of the campus. Borrowing from correctional-design concerns, avoiding blind spots is of primary importance. Access control is more achievable during new design and construction. However, some retrofit opportunities exist that are cost-effective. Often, employees unwittingly defeat access control devices by circumventing them for convenience (e.g., the "locked" back door propped open so that an employee can take a cigarette break or receive a shipment). A security specialist who understands facilities management, construc-tion, and security methods is needed for such evaluations. A walkthrough by local law enforce-ment is not sufficient for these purposes.

While design utilizing CPTED principles can increase deterrence through the perception of an offender being caught, individuals who may be intent on an act of mass violence may be unconcerned with escape. Offenders make choices based on various considerations. It is established, however, that many criminals pre-fer secrecy and an opportunity to evade capture when planning a crime. Spontaneous criminal acts or planned acts that do *not* anticipate escape compel agencies to focus their planning more on response efforts. CPTED does not offer a guarantee of prevention or deterrence. CPTED is not a panacea, and any application of its prin-ciples must be in conjunction with policy review, training and awareness, and an ongoing commit-ment to review the components of campus safety.

Most organizations will be looking at planning for existing structures or an existing campus. Following the shooting at Marjory Stoneman Douglas High School in Parkland, FL, the Broward County School District said that it will install facial recognition cameras at 36 of its schools (Hansen, 2019). An assess-ment should involve specific personnel of the organization and the security professional. Law enforcement participation is needed as one of the several inputs. Whether opting for evacu-ation, shelter-in-place, or a hybrid approach, some considerations that a security consultant might evaluate in conjunction with campus personnel include policies, new construction or work on existing facilities, signage, security elec-tronics and locking systems, movement patterns and designated ingress and egress points, budget considerations, and safety awareness and training. This last point is key because even though a site may be designed with natural or enhanced surveillance in mind, personnel may not be oriented to observe and note potentially threatening actions or individuals. In fact, we know that few people are attuned to such behaviors. This suggests the use of more electronic augmentation in the form of cameras for both monitoring and recording. Following any number of events, it may be helpful or critical to review video to determine not only responsible persons but how a sequence of events unfolded.

The acreage, number and dispersion of buildings, including number of floors of various structures, and population density are considerations for planning responses to emergencies. The challenge of knowing who and how many people are present on the property at a given time is generally less in the K–8 setting. As the age and number of students increases, such as on a high school campus, school authorities may have an idea, though the numbers and identities are unlikely to be completely known. Colleges and universities become even more problematic. The less structured schedule, open-flow design, and independent-activity nature of an institution of higher education makes it a practical impossibility to know who is on campus at any given time.

Considerations

Policy issues are always important. Who makes the decision to stay or to evacuate? If a building is on fire, we expect occupants to evacuate. If someone sees or hears some aggressive or violent acts, should they try to isolate or secret themselves? You cannot force employees or students to shelter-in-place (SIP). You can communicate what the concerns are and whether leaving a location may be a greater risk than staying at the location—or vice versa. Hospital complexes, shopping centers, housing developments, and government facilities are also locations where adults with the means to do so may elect to leave the area if they perceive danger.

Planning for any policy requires the inclusion of individuals with disabilities, including asthma, vision impairment, and hearing impairment—not just mobility impairment. The Office of Civil Rights (OCR) and court cases have made this clear. Policies on evacuation or SIP would need to include considerations for these individuals as well as be included in any training conducted.

A fire calls for evacuation. Shelter-in-place has been determined to be better for health outcomes after a nuclear detonation and some chemical or biohazards. Tornado, hail, and other weather-related disasters typically call for shelter-in-place. An active shooter incident may call for both approaches.

Shelter-in-Place: Steps to Consider

Designate which areas or buildings are to be used as shelters. Discuss and reach consensus on what criteria will be used to determine SIP locations. Specify how to secure the buildings and rooms designated for SIP and who is responsible for accomplishing this. Determine who is to secure buildings and rooms if the designated personnel are *not* present. Someone will not be at work that day or will have left for lunch. Identify who gives the all clear or notifies people they can leave and what the criteria are for declaring all clear. Develop the methods to be used to notify employees, students, vendors, and visitors of a dangerous situation or area of campus. Determine how to make people aware of this on an ongoing basis. If there is a central campus location where visitors must check in or where they might go to get a campus map or parking permit, consider issuing emergency procedures pamphlets from this spot. If the alert system incorporates notification via cell phones, test this often. If the buildings or campus has an audible alarm, work to ensure maximum knowledge by campus community members of what everyone should do if they hear it. Is there differentiation between a notification to evacuate and SIP? If this is a potential active shooter(s) event, what procedures will take place in the SIP room or area? What if it is a fire, spill, or other potential health emergency?

On most campuses, there are not sufficient security or law enforcement personnel to handle this quickly or effectively. Law enforcement personnel are responding to where they have information the crisis is located. Some classrooms have telephone capability but not necessarily personnel to contact each room. Again, at a college or university, such two-way communication is impractical or unlikely. While reverse telephone systems can deliver preprogrammed or current messages, the ability to reach all people on campus is obviously not assured by this method. There will be a good bit of cellular telephone traffic that will be a disruption to some aspect of a response. Almost all college students, faculty, and staff have cell phones. There is something of a universal axiom about a procedure with too many moving parts relative to the diversity of people who would be expected to carry out said procedure at a random and unexpected time, if ever.

Law Enforcement

Law enforcement agencies work in conjunction with one another through interlocal agreements or the authority of state law during a crisis or when summoned by an agency from their jurisdiction. Proximity to surrounding jurisdiction agencies is relevant for planning and response. If the physical site is campus style and has multiple buildings, your resources may be quickly overtaxed with multiple responsibilities arising from an emergency. For college and university police, it is important to frankly and accurately assess internal capabilities. The number of officers on duty during various times of the day on a campus will impact contingency or branching approaches in a response plan. Just as urban areas decrease in population significantly at the end of a workday, so too does the campus population drop. Of course, this might be a time selected for an assault event or simply be when it happens.

Campus administration, police, security, and others must plan for how to reach all persons on campus. The transient campus population has to be contacted as well; these are people such as vendors, parents, and visitors. Some application of telephone trees can be of assistance, but remember, turnover of personnel, students, and commuter population will complicate this. The ability to reach people can involve decisions and follow-through on whether and where to shelter-in-place or move. In part for this reason, SIP may be more suitable to office buildings and single-structure schools compared to shopping centers. The school campus or office building has a relatively more stable population that can be familiarized with emergency plans.

From a law enforcement perspective, we always caution that an initial emergency, perhaps a fire alarm, can be a distraction to draw secondary targets to an assembly or roll call area if there is a shooter involved. In the evacuation of schools or other facilities, such a potential assault should always be a consideration. Children are conditioned to follow the direction of teachers during emergency drills. In addition, most adults will defer to figures that appear to be authorities during emergencies.

On January 22, 2013, gunshots disrupted the campus of Lone Star College, just north of Houston. An initial lockdown became an evacuation within about 30 min. Many students made the decision on their own to leave campus when they realized that gunshots had been fired. Employees or adult students cannot be compelled to remain on campus or in a building. This fact must be part of planning for response to real or perceived crises on campus. The Department of Homeland Security (DHS), in their booklet *Active Shooter: How to Respond*, advises people to evacuate if there is an accessible path when there is an active shooter in the vicinity.

On October 1, 2015, at Umpqua Community College near Roseburg, Oregon, a 26-year-old white male student, Christopher Harper-Mercer, shot and killed nine people and injured nine others. After exchanging gunfire with the police officers who arrived at the campus within minutes of the shooting, the suspect fatally shot himself. Harper-Mercer first shot an English professor teaching the writing class he was attending. He had arrived on campus with a number of handguns, a rifle, ammunition, and a bullet-resistant jacket. In selecting his victims, the shooter is reported to have instructed students to state their religion. Several victims and students acted dead as they saw and listened to classmates being shot around them. The victims were between the ages of 18 and 67.

Law enforcement recovered 14 firearms either in the possession of the shooter or connected to him and located at his home. Harper-Mercer's father, who lives in California, said that he was unaware that his adult son owned firearms. Harper-Mercer lived with his mother, and she was reported to be well aware of his interest in firearms and stated that she herself not only kept firearms in their home but also was knowledgeable about them. His mother's social media accounts also alleged that her son had been diagnosed with Asperger's. All of the guns recovered had been obtained legally by members of his family or by the shooter himself. He was described as a loner and frustrated with organized religion. Harper-Mercer had been dismissed from Army basic training years earlier, and his social media postings indicated he had knowledge of mass shootings and admiration for other mass shooters. Much of the immediate and intense national discussion following the shootings focused on access to firearms by individuals challenged by mental illness.

When students, faculty, and staff begin to leave campus, recognize that, depending on the time of day, there will likely be traffic congestion on the egress routes. Students, employees, and transient visitors with cars will be leaving, whether planned, directed, or otherwise. Law enforcement recognizes that a shooter may try to take advantage of this activity to conceal his escape. It is not always possible to immediately identify those involved. Also, there is not always just one participant. Given the need to keep people safe ahead of capturing a suspect, orderly and expeditious evacuation may be the appropriate option.

Training by key campus representatives should be ongoing. If there is a safety committee, the members or units represented should have specific review assignments for policy, procedures, and physical-site assessment and change recommendations. Many school districts use a *crisis guide* to provide guidance to faculty and staff. Such guides can be useful for many reasons if they are updated periodically.

A hybrid-response model addresses the variation in crises faced by the campus community. As noted, weather or chemical and radiation events typically call for shelter-in-place. Fire calls for evacuation of a structure. Active shooter situations may demand a combined strategy that has people in clearly imminent jeopardy sheltering but has others being evacuated from surrounding areas. Law enforcement is actually quite familiar with this concept as they move people away from a building where a barricaded subject may fire indiscriminately and strike unintended victims.

Parents and the Public

Parents and the general public expect that children will go to a safe place of learning. This belief is largely supported from a statistical standpoint. An airplane crash generates great attention and concern, in part due to the number of people who may die all at once in this event. We realize, intellectually, that the number of traffic accident victims eclipses the death toll from air disasters. Similarly, school killings are shocking based on the numbers of students and others killed at once and our view of the victims as young, innocent, and precious to society beyond all other members. Schools work to monitor every aspect of a student's experience for many reasons, including whether that student is in danger or may present a danger. Understandably, school personnel are most likely to notice the aggressive or boisterous discipline problem student. This student may not be the one with the greatest potential to become a school shooter. What do we want our schools to focus on? The debate continues about how many dimensions of the social reality of children should be the concern of schools (Schildkraut & Hernandez, 2014).

The challenges of youth violence and youth homicide are not new. Some of the challenges arise out of the developmental trajectory of a young person as he works through creating an identity and interacting with peers and others. Parents and other adults play an important role in the shaping of the young individual. There are many examples where we see parents who recognize their child struggling with the dynamics of growing up and not yet being able to cope in an effective or healthy way with these challenges. Sometimes these parents or school officials will refer the child or young adult to counseling or therapy. There may be prescribed medications involved, and the young person who otherwise might make a choice that involves some type of violence is saved that pain and the pain it could cause others. Sadly, we also know of many instances in which parents and adults either are unaware of or do not notice for what they are the difficulties faced by their children or family members. This includes circumstances in which adequate parental involvement is missing altogether or is impaired by the dynamics of the family and their day-to-day lives.

Inevitably, when serious violence or homicide occurs in the school setting, law enforcement becomes involved as well as additional school personnel. Parents look to the school personnel as well as law enforcement to explain what has happened and often also seek answers from these officials, which they are simply unable to provide, regarding what path led their child either to commit violence or be in the pathway of violence. As we noted, schools work very hard at ensuring the safety of their charges, our children. But schools, like law enforcement, have a limited perspective on the overall juvenile and his or her inner thoughts and emotions. While ongoing communication within the school setting and between school personnel and parents is important, it is not a panacea. We admire the work done in communities all across America to help young people as they grow, mature, and learn to deal with all aspects of life.

Law

As with virtually every incident of school shootings, there was an immediate and passionate discussion of gun control measures after the shooting at Sandy Hook Elementary in December 2012, and another significant upsurge in displays of support for gun control measures and school safety improvements following the shooting at Marjory Stoneman Douglas High School in Parkland, Florida, in February 2018. The latter motivated the legislative formation of a commission to identify and address issues of the Parkland shooting (Kennedy, 2019). When the newly-elected governor of Florida took office in January, 2019, he suspended the sheriff of Broward County in an unusual action. The governor said that the elected sheriff "failed to protect Floridians" in an airport shooting in 2017, and "failed . . . to keep our families and children safe" in the 2018 shooting at Marjory Stoneman Douglas High School.

For example, in the Florida case, the Parkland School Shooting Commission recommended a variety of measures, and the Florida legislature provided a one-time appropriation for some of them. Among the commission's recommendations were classroom areas where students and staff can hide, first aid kits designed to aid in bleeding control, active assailant policies in every school, police or armed security on every school campus, real-time monitored surveillance cameras, changes to the law to allow schools to share relevant information with law enforcement, and the most controversial suggestion—arming some school staff and teachers with firearms. The practicality and potential unintended consequences of this last recommendation bear close examination and consideration.

Historical efforts at gun legislation have been mixed. Legislation did pass in 1934 in the form of the National Firearms Act as a response to the use of machine guns by criminals during

Prohibition. And then the Gun Control Act of 1968 passed following the assassinations of President John F. Kennedy and Reverend Martin Luther King Jr. (Schildkraut & Hernandez, 2014). Recent efforts to enact gun control measures have faced greater organized opposition from interest groups and politicians either philosophically opposed to regulations or concerned with the support of those who oppose various control efforts. There has also been proposed legislation to arm teachers in the K–12 system as well as at some colleges and universities. The debate over accessibility to firearms will not end at any time in the foreseeable future. It is generally recognized that when firearms are present, there is at least a statistically increased chance that one will be used and not always responsibly. Similar regulations were suggested to provide firearms to airline pilots.

Laws have also been passed prohibiting firearms on school grounds. Two federal acts passed include the **Gun-Free Schools Act** (GFSA) and the **Gun-Free School Zones Act** (GFSZA). The former addresses possession of guns on school grounds, while the latter is directed at student behavior in bringing weapons to school grounds or functions. The Gun-Free Schools Act was enacted in 1994, at a time when school shootings appeared to be increasing. The re-enaction of GFSA in 2002 called for students who brought a firearm to school to be expelled for a minimum of one year. The 1995 Gun-Free School Zones Act focused more on prohibited areas for individuals to possess a firearm. Statistics support the conclusion that the two acts have helped reduce the targeted behavior.

Following the shooting at Sandy Hook, President Obama took additional federal action by directing the Departments of Justice, Homeland Security, and Education to focus attention on providing resources addressing school safety and mental-health issues. Additional federal training for law enforcement, school officials, and other first responders was provided as part of these initiatives by the White House. The resources also included further emergency management planning guides or assistance in updating such guides by schools. To bolster the number of school resource officers and other officers assigned at schools, the Department of Justice awarded several hundred-million dollars in grants for hiring (Law Center to Prevent Gun Violence, 2013). Following the killings in Parkland, Florida, renewed calls for **red flag laws** and other measures met with some one-time funding from the state legislature. For more than twenty years, a de facto ban on firearm research by federal agencies limits an important source of facts to help craft law and policy. And while a March 2018 bill in congress clarified that at least the Centers for Disease Control (CDC) *can* conduct research, there was no money allocated for the effort.

SUMMARY

Incidents of school shooting are quite rare. Nonetheless, the discussion of school shootings is an important one. The shock and tragedy of such cases can cloud or delay the dispassionate examination needed to try to understand the instant case but also glean continued intelligence about why any such killings occur. The United States is not alone in the experience of school and mass shootings. A school killing takes one of a few different forms. We are perhaps most familiar with the mass shootings seen in American society since the 1990s. The study of school homicides includes an individual offender killing an individual victim, as in a revenge act for bullying, a spurned boyfriend, or perhaps a drug crime gone bad. Individuals may kill or attack only one or two victims as the result of the same motivations discussed in the chapter. The interaction may instead result from a confrontational-homicide situation, a drug crime, or some other matter that does not result in the attacker choosing to attack many people.

Campus shootings are rare. Being the victim of a mass shooting is not likely, yet the emotional impact and sense of outrage that accompanies such horrific events compel public safety and school officials to do everything they can to prevent such occurrences and be prepared to respond to such an occasion. Whether the K–12 school, college, university, or other campus-style location uses a predominantly SIP or evacuation response plan or a hybrid is a decision that carries the same responsibility to plan, prepare, practice, and revise as needed. Planning must be school specific. While there are many articles about the topic of active shooters generally, and there have arisen a variety of recommendations over the last several years, the admonition for flexible, situation-based plans and actions is suggested.

Examination of mass killing, and specifically school shootings, is done by many disciplines. A significant portion of the theoretical work on criminal and deviant behavior is implicated. Policy responses in the form of laws, programs, and enforcement strategies are developed, implemented, and refined to help those students and others in need and to protect everyone in or connected to school communities, whether in K–12 schools or institutions of higher education. The school setting has a context all its own. The culture of the students, the culture of the faculty, and the very culture of the school itself all play their parts in the contextual setting for behavior by young people.

Explanations for school shootings often sound like a profile checklist: being bullied or rejected by peers, depression and youthful angst, lack of connection to people and institutions, the influence of violent media, access to firearms, and various aspects of mental illness or the medications used to ameliorate them. This is not, however, a checklist or profile of a student who may commit mass murder. Human behavior is complex, and there has been no single factor (nor is there likely to be) identified as causing such a violent act. Checklists and proposed profiles invariably include far too many people as likely to commit a particular act and just as surely exclude individuals perhaps on a path to a lethal event. Each of these potential factors and others have been taken and examined carefully and at great length in trying to understand motivations and actions to do violence to others.

Adolescent psychosocial development as well as a young person's interaction with peers and his various social environments all hold clues to behavior. There is the potential to view a juvenile who threatens or commits school violence as simply a *perpetrator*, as in the parlance of law enforcement. However, the complexity and ramifications of child development must continually be examined and applied. In fact, we know that through the inattention or lack of resources in the school setting, a juvenile may react to being bullied or resenting others by withdrawing, coping through healthy or unhealthy strategies to deal with stress or mental illness, or tragically, even committing suicide. An incredibly small number of individuals who suffer mental illness act out violently, let alone carry out acts of murder in a school setting.

KEY TERMS

Mass murder 118
School shootings 118
Categories of mass
   murderers 121
Risk factors 122

Active shooter 128
Shelter-in-place 128
Crime Prevention Through
   Environmental Design
   (CPTED) 129

Gun-Free Schools Act
   (GFSA) 134
Gun-Free School Zones Act
   (GFSZA) 134
Red flag laws 134

DISCUSSION QUESTIONS

1. How common are school shootings, and what impacts the public's perception of such events?

2. Describe the average school killer.
3. What are the motivations of those who kill students in a school setting?

4. What have researchers noted as the most common risk factors of those who commit school shootings?
5. Describe and discuss the ways that school and law enforcement have responded to the threat of school shootings. Explain how policy has been impacted as a result.
6. What are ways that parents may help prevent school homicides?
7. How do schools, colleges, universities, or organizations in your area approach the issue of SIP versus evacuate?
8. What potential problems arise in a policy discussion of arming teachers?

TRY THIS

Go to https://www.cnn.com/2018/08/15/health/school-design-era-mass-shootings-trnd/index.html, and read the CNN article on school design and shootings. Is the public adequately and accurately informed about these issues?

Visit the *USA Today* website article at https://www.usatoday.com/story/news/2018/05/31/red-flag-laws-santa-fe-shooting-texas-guns-abbott-trump/658843002/. Consider the logistics of red flag laws. How might such laws impact suicides by firearm?

9

MASS MURDER IN PUBLIC AND THE WORKPLACE

"I hate to advocate drugs, alcohol, violence, or insanity to anyone, but they've always worked for me."

—Hunter S. Thompson

"I object to violence because when it appears to do good, the good is only temporary; the evil it does is permanent."

—Mahatma Gandhi

CHAPTER OUTLINE

Student Learning Outcomes

Students will be able to:

- describe the different types of mass murders.

- differentiate among the types of violence and homicides in the work setting.

- discuss the motivations of workplace murderers.

- explain the role of workplace violence research in policy formulation.

November 7, 2018, a man armed with a .45-caliber Glock semi-automatic pistol and several illegal high-capacity magazines, began an assault by shooting and killing the security guard outside of the Borderline Bar and Grill in Thousand Oaks, CA. Thirteen people including the gunman died and a dozen were injured during the shooting. The killer was identified by police after the shootings as 28-year-old Marine Corps veteran Ian David Long. Long took his own life at the scene after firing approximately 60 rounds and throwing a smoke bomb. Seven of the twelve who died were college students. Long posted messages on Instagram during his shootings in the bar claiming no reason to commit the shootings, just that life was boring.

INTRODUCTION

We have already discussed deviant acts that fall short of crime, crimes that do not involve violence, violence that does not attempt or achieve murder, and attacks that involve multiple murders. In this chapter, we focus first on non-school and non-familial mass murder and then a disturbing form of multicide called **workplace homicide**. As with school shootings, for workplace homicide we will talk first about some different forms of violence and conflict in the work setting before focusing our attention on the shocking acts of murdering numerous employees, coworkers, and former coworkers in the workplace.

We begin with mass killings in venues other than school, home, or work. These have included places of worship and public events as well as other locations. **Mass murder** is generally considered to be either three, four, or more victims killed in one place at one time or over a relatively short period of time. If the killer changes location during the killings, the event may be seen as continuous or "bifurcated" (Hickey, 2013). Hickey's bifurcation distinction is when a killer begins in a public place, stops, and then continues killing in another public or private place. Alternatively, the killer can begin in a private place, and after a pause in his attack, continue in another private place or a public place. Examples would include those who kill on a college campus and move to another area of campus or the killer who first murders family members and then moves on to a larger venue to continue his murderous assault. This description as bifurcated can also be applied to a spree killer, though the semantics can get distracting.

PUBLIC PLACES

A mass shooting, or assault with some other weapon, can occur anywhere. This aspect of mass killing incidents bears comment since simply being somewhere at the wrong time is different from being at a specific place for affiliation through religion, work, school, or some particular reason. Whereas workplace killers most frequently act based on a perceived slight or adverse job action, other mass killers target victims based on a group characteristic such as race or ethnicity. In some instances, such as the 2017 Las Vegas shooting at the Route 91 Harvest music festival, the motive remains unknown—but the consequences of the killer's action are abundantly clear. The white, 64-year-old, former businessman and gambler brought a stockpile of weapons into a casino hotel overlooking the venue. From his 32nd floor vantage point, the man fired more than 1,100 rounds of ammunition in the music festival killing 58 people and causing injuries to more than 800.

The ever-present question of why looms over the mass killing of people. Why go to the extreme of not only killing, but killing or injuring many? Mass killing researchers Grant Duwe and Michael Rocque, in a 2018 op-ed in the *Los Angeles Times*, assert that the statistics of this rare form of murder does reveal "a relatively high rate of mental illness." In research they conducted of 185 public mass shootings between 1900 and 2017, they identified 59% had been carried out by individuals diagnosed with or demonstrating signs of a **serious mental illness** before they committed their killings. Duwe and Rocque point out, as almost all researchers do, that it is important not to conflate the variety of mental disorders among the public that are not *severe* and that the majority of people with mental illness do not commit violent acts. The final points they put forward are that policymakers should focus on promising gun violence reduction, media should not glorify violence, and research must continue.

Mass murder is perpetrated using firearms in the majority of recorded incidents and this has come to be known as a **rampage**. But the crime is also perpetrated using other methods including bombs, airplanes, and fire. Mass shootings are more prevalent and continue to grab the public's attention and the concerns of law enforcement, policymakers, and others. The term **active shooter** was coined and an entire law enforcement training program quickly grew around the need to prepare for these types of incidents.

The National Threat Assessment Center (NTAC) of the Department of Homeland Security, United States Secret Service in their 2018 report on 2017 mass attacks in public spaces documented 28 such incidents in calendar year 2017. The NTAC identified the following themes among these attacks across work, home, school, or other location:

- Nearly half were motivated by a *personal grievance* related to a workplace, domestic, or other issue.

- Over half had histories of *criminal charges*, *mental health symptoms*, and/or *illicit substance use or abuse*.

- All had at least one *significant stressor* within the last five years, and over half had indications of *financial instability* in that time frame.

- Over three-quarters made *concerning communications and/or elicited concern* from others prior to carrying out their attacks. On average, those who did elicit concern caused more harm than those who did not. (Department of Homeland Security, 2018)

In this same report of 2017 incidents, the NTAC notes a number of stressors deemed significant in the lives of the attackers within five years of the assault. Each of them had at least one of the stressors, most often related to:

- Family/romantic relationships, such as spousal estrangements, divorces, romantic breakups, rejected proposals, physical or emotional abuse, or the death of a parent;

- Personal issues, such as unstable living conditions, physical illnesses, or other significant disorders;

- Work or school environments, such as being fired or suspended, filing grievances, being bullied at work or at school, feeling disrespected, or being the subject of real or perceived gossip; and/or

- Contact with law enforcement that did not result in arrests or charges, such as being the subject of domestic disturbance calls or being sought for a crime unrelated to their attack.

The NTAC also noted that more than half had experienced stressors related to financial instability in the five years before their attack. It is also important to consider attacks or shootings in which fewer than the agreed upon number of people are killed. Fridel and Fox (2018, 2019) argue for consideration of two- and three-or-more homicide event examinations to glean unique and similar data to aid both research and criminal investigators. Jamie Fox at Northeastern University in Boston, long an authority on homicide, particularly dramatic and rare forms, has noted that researchers and policymakers must consider the impact of media, definitions, and the use of datasets in considering actual changes in numbers of mass shootings and killings. Considering differences in the level of both cognitive abilities and premeditation between single victim murderers and those who kill multiple victims (Fox, Brook, Stratton, & Hanlon, 2016), there seems every reason to continue focused study of both types and appropriate subtypes.

We discuss the family annihilator, the most frequent mass killer, in a separate chapter, as well as those who kill multiple people in a terror attack. Here we focus on the second most common form of mass killing, the workplace killer, and other mass killings at locations other than school or the workplace. The offender, like most murderers, remains predominantly male. Though while most non-family murderers are young, there is age variation among those who commit mass killings. And in the workplace, about half of killers are at least 35. This reflects, in part, that mass shootings and killings are not the result of a heated confrontation that is the province of young men in quickly developing arguments. Rather, the mass killer may have built up resentments, rationales—and weapons—over a long period of time before deciding on his targets. Some of these attacks are carried out in a seemingly indiscriminate manner, but most killers have selected their victims as people to blame for their own perceived misfortune or failure, or as a proxy for those who aggrieved them.

WORKPLACE VIOLENCE

Workplace violence takes a number of forms and arises from several different motivations. Verbal arguments and offensive behaviors that fall short of exchanging physical blows happen each day in many work settings in the United States and around the world. These actions may, in fact, lead to an escalation and eventual physical violence and in some cases, murder. The National Crime Victimization Survey (NCVS) and the **Census of Fatal Occupational Injuries** (CFOI) define workplace violence as "nonfatal violence (rape/sexual assault, robbery, and aggravated and simple assault) against employed persons age 16 or older that occurred while they were at work or on duty" (Harrell, 2011, p. 2). They define *workplace homicide*, our main focus in this chapter, as "homicide of employed victims age 16 or older who were killed while at work or on duty. Excludes death by accident" (Harrell, 2011, p. 2). Violence in this context can include "threatening behaviors, verbal abuse and physical assault" (Bruce & Nowlin, 2011, p. 294).

It is also important to consider the social context of the workplace. People interact with other workers in an environment of expectations, rules, and supervised work. Most often, workers do not choose who their coworkers are, and there may be overlap in the social contact of employees away from the work setting. When we consider that homicide takes several forms, both at work and not at work, it is clear that social context must be considered along with individual motivation. Rampage-style killings at work are the rarest homicides in that setting and are tangibly different from interpersonal disputes—though both are thought of as *expressive* forms of violence—and the robbery or felony-related typology, which is largely *instrumental* as the killer eliminates obstacles to the valuables he seeks. This social context also differentiates the workplace killing from a mass shooter who enters a place of worship or market intent on killing many people but lacking the acquaintance or relationship with his intended victims.

There has been considerable research on the mass and workplace killer and the rates at which these killers also commit suicide. The results of these studies have been mixed, with some researchers finding that killers who commit suicide kill more victims during their rampage (Lester, 2014). Other studies found that killers who were killed by police during the rampage killed more victims than those who committed suicide. This may or may not be an artifact of having been killed or caught before they were able to kill more people or commit suicide. The studies clearly indicate that many mass killers are also suicidal (Blair & Martindale, 2013) and suggest that policymakers must be aware of this connection.

Most people in the United States work away from their homes and accept the stressors of their occupations with resignation, if not actual satisfaction and some amount of pleasure. The routine of work is generally seen as engaged in or endured to earn money for the private portions of life in society. Many people will agree to work extra hours at times to receive additional pay when needed, or they may seek out transfers and promotions that come with pay increases. Stress at work and the organizational causes and consequences has been the subject of study by researchers in many disciplines. Modern practices within human resources have resulted in most employers providing access to an **Employee Assistance Program** (EAP) to assist troubled employees.

Viewing a workplace as fair and using just personnel practices may also mitigate the frustration felt by many employees. Even though many experience stress at work, few individuals react to the stress by acting out violently; even fewer go to the extreme of killing coworkers.

There have been those individuals who do not accept the stressors and who may project the blame for their disappointments and losses onto supervisors and fellow employees. Over the last several decades, we have been accustomed to the news media grabbing and keeping our attention with terrible reports of the likes of James Huberty, Patrick Sherrill, Patrick Edward Purdy, Mark Barton, Michael McDermott, Nidal Malik Hasan, James Holmes, and Aaron Alexis. All the names became quite familiar for a time after they carried out workplace mass murder. The names of the victims are, quite frankly, far more important to all those who loved them and are left wondering why the murders happened and how to cope with the losses. We name and discuss some of the killers only in the hope of understanding their individual paths or trajectories that culminated in harming and killing others. Many of these are viewed as the stereotypical workplace killer. Research reveals that people killed in a work setting are more likely to be killed by a stranger than by someone known to them.

Law enforcement and emergency medical responders have varying levels of training in disaster situations. Employers and facilities where people may visit in some numbers, such as hospitals, restaurants, places of worship, and movie theaters, must also develop policies and responses to what many consider to be the unthinkable and rare incidence of mass murder. This challenging scenario is faced by human resources regarding employees and customers and security in those companies or facilities that have access to such personnel.

While the beginning of this chapter provides quite a few statistics on various aspects of mass and workplace violence, our intention is to give the reader simply an overview of the frequency and impact. There are estimates of two million workers who are victims of workplace violence each year in the United States, with billions lost in time and productivity, litigation expenses, and security measures (Occupational

Table 9.1 Intentional Workplace Fatalities 2011–2017	
Year	Fatalities
• 2011	• 468
• 2012	• 475
• 2013	• 404
• 2014	• 409
• 2015	• 417
• 2016	• 500
• 2017	• 458

Source: U.S. Department of Labor, Bureau of Labor Statistics, Census of Fatal Occupational Injuries (2018).

Safety and Health Administration, n.d.). There are various governmental organizations that track and tabulate workplace violence, including the **Occupational Safety and Health Administration** (OSHA), the **Bureau of Labor Statistics** (BLS), and the previously discussed National Crime Victimization Survey, completed by the Bureau of the Census.

Each year, the U.S. Department of Labor's Bureau of Labor Statistics (2018) conducts the Census of Fatal Occupational Injuries. The preliminary total reported for 2017 was 5,147, up from the 2013 number of 4,405 fatal work injuries but down slightly from the 2016 figure of 5,190. The CFOI includes all workplace injuries, not homicide alone. Within the initial figures for 2017, 458 people died as a result of workplace violence and 275 by suicide. Findings of the CFOI included the following year-to-year intentional fatalities figures:

For more than 15 years, strangers have committed the greatest proportion of violence in the workplaces around the nation, with 53% of incidents perpetrated against males and 41% against females (Harrell, 2011). The survey results also show that the most likely person to commit assault was a coworker; most commonly, there had been a relationship between an assailant and victim, or they were known to one another. "Current or former coworkers committed 16%

of workplace violence against males and about 14% against females" (Harrell, 2011, p. 6).

It is helpful to separate aspects of workplace violence to better examine the dynamics of the incidents. Holmes and Holmes (2001) wrote that violence committed in the workplace usually takes one of three forms:

1. The violence is committed by people who work or used to work in the company where the crime occurred.

2. The violence is committed by someone who is or was a customer of the company where the crime occurred.

3. The violence is committed by people who have no relationship with the company. (p. 64)

In 2011, the Bureau of Justice Statistics (BJS) completed a special report of workplace violence crimes occurring against people at work between 1993 and 2009. More than 1,000 workplace deaths occurred annually. Some highlights from the report are as follows:

- From 2002 to 2009, the rate of nonfatal workplace violence declined by 35%, following a 62% decline in the rate from 1993 to 2002.

- The average annual rate of workplace violence between 2005 and 2009 (5 violent crimes per 1,000 employed persons age 16 or older) was about one-third the rate of non-workplace violence (16 violent crimes per 1,000 employed persons age 16 or older) and violence against persons not employed (17 violent crimes per 1,000 persons age 16 or older).

- Between 2005 and 2009, law enforcement officers, security guards, and bartenders had the highest rates of nonfatal workplace violence.

- Strangers committed the greatest proportion of nonfatal workplace violence against males (53%) and females (41%) between 2005 and 2009.

- Among workplace homicides that occurred between 2005 and 2009, about 28% involved victims in sales and related occupations and about 17% involved victims in protective service occupations.

- About 70% of workplace homicides were committed by robbers and other assailants, while about 21% were committed by work associates between 2005 and 2009.

- Between 2005 and 2009, while firearms were used in 5% of nonfatal workplace violence, shootings accounted for 80% of workplace homicides. (Harrell, 2011, p. 1)

According to the U.S. Department of Labor's Bureau of Labor Statistics (2018), in 2017, homicide was the fifth leading cause of death in the workplace behind the leading causes: transportation incidents—2,077 combined circumstances; falls, slips, and trips at 887; contact with an object or equipment at 695; and exposure to harmful substances or environments resulting in 531 deaths. Intentional homicides numbered 458. Between 1993 and 2009, workplace homicides decreased by 51% (Harrell, 2011). Ongoing efforts by the Occupational Safety and Health Administration (OSHA), worker groups, and a risk management approach to the workplace are seen as major contributors to the decline, in addition to the overall decline in U.S. homicide. Because the drop is so large, there may also be some aspect of data gathering that accounts for some percentage of the apparent decline.

WORKPLACE VICTIMS

Who are the victims of workplace homicides? Research from the Bureau of Labor Statistics' CFOI shows workplace homicide victims decreasing by 39% from 1993 to 1999 (Harrell, 2011). Decreases in workplace homicide occurred again in 2004 and in 2009. Statistics show that from 2005 to 2009, 81.6% of the victims of workplace homicide were males (Harrell, 2011). In 2016, 82% of victims were males (BLS, 2018). Without examination of the worker demographics of the different places where workplace homicides occur, we are limited in drawing conclusions from this. Recall that men are more aggressive and seen as more of a threat in most conflict situations, and a male supervisor may be the one whom the killer believes denied him something due him. Triggers for workplace homicides could well tie to the maleness of the majority of victims and offenders.

Women killed in the workplace may reflect their assignment in human resources or as a cashier, where a disgruntled worker or a customer may begin his rampage. Additionally, service workers or those who greet customers may disproportionately be women, and therefore, be vulnerable to angry customers arriving at a place to vent their anger. BLS (2018) data for 2016 showed that cashiers suffered the greatest number of homicides by occupation at 54. This was up from 35 homicides of cashiers in 2015. It is important to consider that in addition to women victimized during robberies or other assaults in workplace killings (39%), following closely and significantly were women killed by a personal relation (33%). The majority of these murders (78%) were by intimate partners, often in a parking lot or public building (Tiesman, Gurka, Konda, & Amandus, 2012). Other occupations experiencing relatively higher numbers of homicide in 2016 were "first-line supervisors of retail sales workers" (50) and "police and sheriff's patrol officers" (50) (BLS, 2018).

Victim ages for workplace homicides were tabulated in frequency distributions. Combining the youngest victims, just fewer than 10% of victims were under age 24. Age groupings of 25–34, 35–44, and 45–54 account for 69% of victims of workplace homicide, with the numbers roughly one third in each of these brackets. Victim race from 2005 to 2009 was distributed as follows: white, 48.9%; black, 21.7%; Hispanic, 16.2%; American Indian, 0.4%; and Asian and Pacific Islander making up 11.2% of the victims (Harrell, 2011). The ages and racial or ethnic categories may not be telling or provide any immediate insights.

Researchers find regional differences in the rates and numbers of workplace homicides regionally, with the majority of the deaths occurring in the South of the United States. The West followed but with a significantly lower rate, and then came the Midwest and Northeast regions.

THE WORKPLACE KILLER

Mass murder is a rare event. Workplace violence is a continuum of acts, including threats, intimidation, harassment (including sexual), and physical and emotional abuse (Rugala & Isaacs, 2002). In the FBI's 2002 report on workplace violence they state that

> It is the threats, harassment, bullying, domestic violence, stalking, emotional abuse, intimidation, and other forms of behavior and physical violence that, if left unchecked, may result in more serious violent behavior. These are the behaviors that supervisors and managers have to deal with every day. (Rugala & Isaacs, 2002, p. 6)

The acts of serial killers have often been made infamous in novels, movies, and even television series, and so the public perhaps fears falling victim to such a killer. While still a rare occurrence, being the victim in a mass shooting or workplace attack may be far more likely. And workplace violence is a problem worldwide. The World Health Organization (WHO) released its world report on violence and health more than a decade ago and chronicled the types of violence and its impacts in every country. Within the single category of workplace killings, there are subtypes to discuss. While the tragic result may be the same, the dynamics of who kills in the workplace have variations.

Employees

The most frequently documented mass workplace killer is a middle-aged white male, though within this broad brushstroke lies quite of bit of nuanced age and race or ethnicity variation (Harrell, 2011). This average age places the workplace killer as older than the average murder suspect in the United States, who is between 18 and 34 (Harrell, 2011).

One of the prime motivations for the workplace killer seems to push to the front of the line: revenge. Fox and Levin (2015) included this category in their earlier typologies of mass murder. Dietz (1986) used the category of the pseudocommando to describe someone who armed himself well and planned his attack. It may be known that the killer had a keen interest in weapons, just as many school shooters do. The disgruntled employee described by Holmes and Holmes (2001) is self-explanatory. As with the school shooter, we note here that the typologies developed by various researchers who examine mass murder overlap, and a killer may be described as fitting into more than one.

The workplace murder often follows a firing, demotion, disappointment, or argument at work. The perpetrator may also be on medical leave or disability. A 2004 article in *USA Today* examined 224 fatal attack cases across the United States covering the period from 1975 to 2003 and observed that the most commonly identified motive in workplace killings was that the attacker had been fired. Firings occurred in approximately 60 of the 224 attacks. Workplace arguments were identified by the journalist as the second leading motive (Armour, 2004).

If a murder, single or multiple, immediately follows an argument at the workplace, the killer may go to his car, which is parked outside the business, and retrieve a firearm. The laws vary by state regarding keeping a firearm in your vehicle at the workplace. Loomis, Marshall, and Ta (2005) published a study in which they state, "Workplaces where guns were permitted were about 5 times as likely to experience a homicide as those where all weapons were prohibited" (p. 830). In 2016 there were 500 workplace homicides, an increase from 2015 of 83 deaths. Seventy-nine percent of the 2016 homicides (394) were by shooting (BLS, 2018). Their study controlled for other risk factors and found that the association remained. As with many deadly incidents, if the attack is planned and the person

disregards the rule, no one may know until it is too late. The murderer may act immediately following an argument, also bringing the potential for confrontational violence discussed earlier in the book. An angry or delusional individual may come back years later and kill people at the place he had worked. The workplace killer typically uses some type of firearm.

The firearm is easily acquired, legally or illegally, in the United States, making it practical as a way to kill and injure many people quickly. While other weapons have been used in workplace violence and homicide, the firearm remains the most common weapon employed. For the majority of workplace mass murders, the killer's rampage will end in his taking his own life, being killed by police, or forcing police to end his life. Armour stated in her 2004 *USA Today* article that most mass workplace killers die at the scene (Armour, 2004). She went on to explain that while many are people killed by the gunfire of some of the murderers already mentioned, the common incident involves only a few persons killed. Armour cites a common number of two employees killed in each workplace homicide. She reminds us that if someone is in the way, he or she can become a victim as well. As stated, the vast majority of workplace homicides are committed with a firearm. From 2005 to 2009, 80% of the murders were done by shooting (Harrell, 2011).

The killer may go inside to target specific people but then continue to shoot others at random. The victims may have been known to the killer or have merely been *convenient* coworkers. For the employee or former employee, the setting will be his workplace, which supports the idea that such killers are *geographically stable*, remaining in the area where they were living while employed. The mass killer in such instances is considered *local*. The *disgruntled* employee who commits single or mass workplace homicide is rare but does captivate the news media and seemingly, the public attention. The underlying dynamic of violent response to frustration may explain what can appear to be disproportionate research and media focus on the employee who kills.

Nonemployees

A mass murder or shooting may be carried out by a person not employed at the business or organization. The individual may be a former employee but may also be a disgruntled customer or someone with an unknown motive for choosing the location of his lethal attack. Of course, one or more employees or customers are killed in many work locations by an armed robber who overreacts to a perceived obstruction to the robbery or who simply has no qualms about killing witnesses. The workplace homicides committed by robbers in the years 2005–2009 were 38.3%, with "other assailants" making up 32% (Harrell, 2011). This makes robbery the largest category of workplace homicide. This held true for 2016, when the Bureau of Labor Statistics (BLS) recorded 33% of men and 16% of women were killed by robbers (BLS, 2018). This is a surprise to many people who think of the disgruntled worker storming into the workplace to exact his revenge for real or imagined slights. The BJS data from 2005 to 2009 show homicides committed by coworkers and former coworkers at 11.4% and those committed by customers and clients at 10%. In other words, the category of work associates represents less than one-third the number of homicide offenders who were robbers or other assailants.

ASSESSING VIOLENCE POTENTIAL

Considering the continuum of workplace violence, with homicide as only the most serious of many acts, it is not wasted effort to continue researching and refining violence assessment and intervention methods. Many workplace murderers are believed to have suffered from some mental instability. The individual may be a loner on medications. He may be receiving counseling and be diagnosed as paranoid. The gain for this killer is psychological and expressive, not material or instrumental, such as in a robbery where the killing is a means to an end. If he does not survive his rampage, this may only be guessed at from examining evidence left behind and the statements of people who knew the killer. Investigating who commits workplace killings has received research attention but not to the extent that prediction is reliable. The suggestion of serious mental illness would lead many people to think that a dangerous worker or customer would be easy to spot. The practice of determining threat assessment and risk assessment is not quite so straightforward.

Threat assessment involves the analysis of the specific individual who made the threat. Assessment of risk is a common concept and practice in many industries. The high-stakes *forecasting* of whether and when a human is dangerous is a complex matter, to say the least. Most agree that all humans hold the potential to be violent. Violent behavior may only occur when faced with threat or extreme provocation. Protecting loved ones can elicit an aggressive response from many people. But what about acting with violence against coworkers or strangers for reasons intrinsically justified by an individual with no legitimate indication of an immediate threat from those persons?

WHY WOULD THEY DO IT?

On August 27, 2003, in Chicago, recently fired Salvador Tapia, aged 36, shot and killed six former coworkers. Tapia worked at an auto parts warehouse and had been fired for failing to come in for work. Salvador Tapia had several past arrests for intimate partner violence and weapons charges. In this final incident, Tapia came to his former workplace and tied up one employee before shooting others. Police were called by two employees who had escaped the location, and when they arrived, Tapia fired on them before he was ultimately shot dead by officers.

WHY WOULD THEY DO IT?

On August 3, 2010, Omar Thornton, a warehouse driver at a Manchester, Connecticut, beer distributor, shot and killed eight coworkers. Thornton had been called in for a disciplinary meeting after being caught on video stealing beer from the business. After locking himself in an office at the business and before committing suicide, Thornton called his mother and then 9-1-1. Thornton was reported to have told the 9-1-1 dispatcher that he killed his coworkers because of racism he had encountered and that he wished he had killed more of them.

In the chapter on school shootings, we mentioned the desire by many to have a *checklist* of behaviors or red flags that would quickly and accurately identify a student or employee posing an imminent threat of danger. This tool does not exist, and we may not move a great deal closer to such an early warning system, given the state of psychology, science, and the freedom of movement and expression enjoyed by democratic societies. If we know who has made threatening overtures, it remains to gauge the likelihood of a threat being carried out or a person escalating to acting. And then it falls to organizations as well as public-health and law enforcement agencies to respond within the law and protocols to manage the individual or situation.

Perhaps the most well-known example of addressing threatening speech or behavior is in the protection of the president and other high-profile potential targets. The Secret Service is tasked with assessing threats to the president and a number of other individuals. The agency expends a great deal of effort and resources tracking individuals who make their threats known to people. The various written or spoken threats are analyzed by intelligence members to assess potential likelihood of danger. Suspects and others with knowledge of suspects are interviewed and monitored. The volume of threats to the nation's leader is in a league of its own. But what school district or workplace has the resources to even properly assess occasional known threats? And to illustrate the challenge of dealing with the spontaneity of individual agency, in September 2014, an armed private citizen leaped a fence at the White House, ran across the front lawn, and avoided or bowled over several Secret Service members as he made his way *inside* the home of the most powerful and protected individual in the world before being stopped. This incident is clearly not representative of workplace violence or killing, but it does serve as an example of how even a setting thoroughly prepared for any act of aggression can be vulnerable on any given day. Whether the security breach represents a temporary lapse in vigilance or the knowledge that a goal-oriented individual holds the advantage of action over reaction may be academic.

Companies will often turn over concerns about known troubled employees or former employees to their human resources department and the security department if they have one. For the majority of businesses, human resources may still be the personnel model that deals with hiring and benefits, and there is no security department. This reality leaves businesses to call upon local law enforcement agencies, themselves understaffed, when there is need for members with the specialized training and resources to perform risk assessments. Companies and businesses may be proactive in training employees in various emergency procedures and the installation of some security technology to deter or document potential problems.

It is appropriate to mention that while employers have created policies and provided training about threats and potential violence, the typical workplace killer has received the same training. The eventual killer may have no idea what action he may someday commit, and the training and policies may act as either a deterrent or intervention. It is difficult to know what violent acts have been prevented through policy and training, but the need for such organizational programs and mechanisms is clear.

Warning signs about the worker may have existed prior to a workplace shooting. The shooter may have exhausted already limited coping skills as he struggled with his incompletely developed set of attachments to persons, his employing business, and the community as a whole. The outcome may turn lethal in the turmoil that exists in the shooter's mind and world.

The National Center for the Analysis of Violent Crime at the FBI convened the **Critical Incident Response Group** (CIRG) in 2001 to examine workplace violence and offer information about the dynamics and factors involved. The document notes the challenge presented by subtle, non-explicit threats that nonetheless exist. Again, we all want clear and definitive statements by potential killers that they are about to massacre others. We would also like the day and time of the attack. This is simply not possible and so, unfortunately, many organizations fail to put forth robust efforts. Exhibit 9.1 lists employee warning signs compiled by the CIRG. Remember that the typical workplace killer will exhibit a combination of many of these factors, as you can see from the numerous examples we have provided throughout the chapter.

Many individuals seem to share some characteristics that may help employers identify potentially violent employees. Some workplace killers show no warning signs prior to the killing, but these are in the minority of studied incidents (Lieber, 2007).

Less specific *red flags* that Miller (2008) notes may indicate an impending loss of control by an employee. These include

> disorganized physical appearance and dress; tense facial expression or other distressed body language; signs of intoxication or inappropriate use of dark glasses or breath mints to mask alcohol or substance abuse; severe agitation, verbal argumentativeness, or outright threats, especially to specific persons; and/or the presence or evidence of weapons. (p. 262)

The U.S. Department of Labor website for their Workplace Violence Program has a somewhat different list of indicators and the caveat that the presence of any of them does not equate to a certainty of violence.

Performance/Conduct Indicators

Being aware of performance and/or conduct problems which may be warning signs of potential trouble is good prevention strategy. These signs may show up in perpetrators of violence, those who are victims, and those involved in domestic violence. Although it is possible that only one of these indicators will occur, it is more likely that a pattern will occur or that they will represent a change from normal behavior. **Remember that the presence of any of these characteristics does not necessarily mean a violent act will occur. They may be indicators of another type of problem such as being ill, depressed, bereaved, etc.** Some examples of performance and/or conduct indicators are listed below (listing is not intended to be all inclusive):

- **attendance problems** – excessive sick leave, excessive tardiness, leaving work early, improbable excuses for absences;

EXHIBIT 9.1

RISK FACTORS ASSOCIATED WITH POTENTIAL VIOLENCE

Personality conflicts with coworkers
Mishandled termination or discipline
Bringing weapons to workplace
Alcohol or drug use at work
Real or perceived grudge
Break up of a relationship
Financial or legal problems
Emotional disturbance
Increasing belligerence
Ominous, specific threats
Hypersensitivity to criticism
Recent acquisition/fascination with weapons
Apparent obsession with a supervisor or coworker or employee grievance
Preoccupation with violent themes
Interest in recently publicized violent events
Outbursts of anger
Extreme disorganization
Noticeable changes in behavior
Homicidal/suicidal comments or threats

Source: Federal Bureau of Investigation, United States Department of Justice, Critical Incident Response Group. (2001). *Workplace violence: Issues in response,* pp. 21–22.

- **adverse impact on supervisor's time** – supervisor spends an inordinate amount of time coaching and/or counseling employee about personal problems, re-doing the employee's work, dealing with co-worker concerns, etc.;

- **decreased productivity** – making excessive mistakes, poor judgment, missed deadlines, wasting work time and materials;

- **inconsistent work patterns** – alternating periods of high and low productivity and quality of work, inappropriate reactions, overreaction to criticism, and mood swings;

- **concentration problems** – easily distracted and often has trouble recalling instructions, project details, and deadline requirements;

- **safety issues** – more accident prone, disregard for personal safety as well as equipment and machinery safety, needless risks;

- **poor health and hygiene** – marked changes in personal grooming habits;

- **unusual/changed behavior** – inappropriate comments, threats, throwing objects;

- **evidence of possible drug or alcohol use/abuse**;

- **evidence of serious stress in the employee's personal life** – crying, excessive phone calls, recent separation;

- **continual excuses/blame** – inability to accept responsibility for even the most inconsequential errors; and/or

- **unshakable depression** – low energy, little enthusiasm, despair. (U.S. Department of Labor, n.d.)

As with school-age youth exhibiting various behaviors, an individual exhibiting behavior labeled as a red flag will rarely become a killer. Threat assessment takes note of all warning signs and attempts to weigh the individual and cumulative acts. The ongoing assessment is in service of gauging the chances of an employee (or customer) becoming violent in the workplace. A triggering event may retrospectively appear to have been the straw that broke the camel's back for some killers or violent individuals in mass killings. But we know that the vast majority of individuals do not resort to horrendous violence in response to perceived injustice or disappointment. That last straw or trigger may be the employee being fired or not receiving a promotion he thought was due, a failed workplace romance, intimate partner violence that culminates in a workplace attack, a bad health prognosis coupled with perceived unjust work treatment, a work evaluation that is seen as unfair, or criticism from the employee's supervisor or a coworker (Lieber, 2007). A decision by the individual to act out his rage through murder in the workplace may build over time. Planning is evident, even if somewhat hasty, in certain cases. The killer does not simply *snap* and pick up an object to attack other employees. The revenge is planned over a period of days, weeks, or months. To the killer, carrying out the murders is the only acceptable solution.

The variations of workplace homicide run from single attacker and single victim through the mass murder that garners a great deal of media attention. The inevitable retrospective examination of the killer will comment on the setbacks he suffered and who survivors believe he blamed for his difficulties. Death at the hands of a known coworker is statistically not as likely as a lethal assault by a stranger or customer. Yet the fear of danger from a coworker is the worry that many employees hold (Forte, 2006).

The term *going postal* is not a statistically accurate reflection of the relative danger to post office employees of a rampage killer. Nonetheless, in 1986, postal worker Patrick Sherrill became known nationally for his attack on coworkers that left 14 dead. Sherrill killed himself at the end of his rampage. *Going postal* entered the American lexicon as a way of referring to an overwrought employee who strikes out at fellow employees. In Sherrill's case, he had been terminated from the postal service for incompetence but had been rehired to work part time (Forte, 2006). Sherrill had been labeled odd by coworkers and others who had known him over the course of his life. The challenge for threat assessment is not if someone is dangerous since everyone is capable of violence. The high-stakes evaluation of behavior goes to who is likely *in specific circumstances* to act out violently. As is typical in many workplace mass murderers, Sherrill believed that his supervisors and other employees had it in for him.

Mark Barton worked for Momentum Securities in Atlanta. On July 29, 1999, he walked onto the trading floor at Momentum and began to execute his coworkers, firing at them from close range. He killed four and then went across the street to a second trading firm, All-Tech Investment, and killed five more people. His attempt at being a day trader failed as he went heavily into debt. Barton killed his wife and their two children over a two-day period prior to his rampage at Momentum and All-Tech. Mark Barton was also suspected of having killed his first wife and her mother years before. The case of Mark Barton illustrates that his acts could classify him as not only a mass murderer but as a spree killer. While his murders at Momentum Securities were those of a mass murderer, having killed his family over two previous days and then going to All-Tech fit the pattern of a spree killing. The murders ended when Barton was cornered by police following a chase. He committed suicide, rather than be taken into custody.

WHY WOULD THEY DO IT?

Michael McDermott graduated from high school in 1976 and served in the U.S. Navy until 1982. He was unable to successfully turn his Navy training into a career at a nuclear power plant in New England. McDermott married and divorced and was considered by most who knew him as a bit odd and someone who did not socialize with others. After his various personal and professional failures, he ended up working for Edgewater Technology. On December 26, 2000, McDermott killed seven of his coworkers as he made his way through the Edgewater Technology facilities. He came to work that day with a bag that held an AK-47, a shotgun, a pistol, and ammunition. McDermott fits the description of the *typical* workplace mass murderer. He had conflicts with management and in his personal relationships and struggled financially. The IRS had garnished his wages to pay back taxes, and it appeared that his car was to be repossessed. McDermott's final rampage was the culmination of frustration over many years. He blamed his employers for his financial situation, another frequent component of many workplace mass murderers. McDermott had planned his rampage, and when he was captured, he pursued an insanity defense, though he was convicted of seven counts of first-degree murder.

POLICY IMPLICATIONS

In the Workplace

Preventing random acts of violence by employees, customers, or complete strangers is a tall order. A workplace rampage killer has likely had a long period of time to plan and prepare. Action always beats reaction, and it is hard to defend against what you cannot see coming. It is with this realization that organizations must approach their policy formulation and planning (Fox & DeLateur, 2014). The business selected by a robber will not know to stop that one apparent customer from walking through the front door. How employees are trained to respond to a robber or even a difficult customer will go far in determining the outcome of an incident—even a deadly one. And while policies can be implemented that direct employee behavior, these same dictates will hold no sway with an outside criminal or attacker. The spontaneity of a workplace murder sets off a chain of reactions and responses to minimize the impact of the action initiated by the killer.

Proper preemployment screening and training programs, as well as effective and accessible Employee Assistance Programs, are components of proactive recruitment and retention of quality employees. These practices also serve as cornerstones of proactive workplace violence policies. A rigorous background check of applicants is always important, though not sufficient, to ward off all issues of workplace violence. Many in business shortcut this critical area in an attempt to get people hired quickly or simply out of ignorance of the potential ramifications of poor hiring decisions. Thorough background work includes inquiring of applicants about gaps in their employment history; contacting the applicant's previous employers to verify all available information, including dates of employment; drug screening; credit checks; driving record checks; and verification of Social Security numbers (Lieber, 2007). A candidate's potential for violence may not be uncovered through a thorough background check, but it sets a tone for employees, follows industry best practices, and may even deter some unsuitable candidates.

The probationary period is designed, in part, to be a further level of filtering against unproductive employees who may also reveal a propensity for dysfunctional workplace behavior during the time that they may be appropriately dismissed with no stated cause. Supervisors and managers must be trained in what to look for by way of interpersonal conflict behaviors by employees as well as effective approaches to disciplinary and other personnel actions, including terminations, layoffs, and demotions. As these have been seen as potential triggering events for workplace homicide, key personnel should be properly trained and prepared on the sensitive nature of taking these actions. An unfortunate number of companies and organizations do not competently face these concerns with workplace violence and a proactive approach. Some do not see a cost–benefit ratio favoring laborious efforts to hire employees. What could happen? As few as 25% of companies are estimated to offer formal training on these issues to their employees (Miller, 2008b). Yes, proper recruitment, selection, hiring, and retention cost money. The efforts at proper hiring and training are effective and can help in reducing violence. The costs for failures in these activities can be devastating (Forte, 2006).

Policies that aim to prevent or reduce workplace violence must be clear, fair, and properly implemented, with ongoing review and revision as needed. The procedures should be followed consistently and treat all employees with respect and equality. Communicating with employees about the policies and procedures of the organization is good for business and is a pillar of support for morale, which is also implicated in workplace violence prevention. Employers should never use a one-size-fits-all approach to personnel issues such as conflict (Forte, 2006). Workforce involvement in designing methods to cope with or mitigate contributors to workplace stress helps ensure the desired outcomes are achieved.

Due to the attention given to workplace homicides that have occurred in the United States, organizations are creating policies and training practices in ever-increasing number to help prepare and protect employees from violence. Agencies must educate employees about the various types or forms of workplace violence and the precursors to violent behavior. Clear, concise policies must be put into place and training provided to employees, with the requirement that employees acknowledge their responsibility to follow the policies. Bruce and Nowlin (2011) outline a three-stage approach consisting of "(a) pre-incident strategy, (b) pre-incident/management strategy, and (c) post incident strategy" (p. 297). They say that in the pre-incident stage, zero tolerance for any violent behavior has to be put in place first. This is important to set expectations for employees. As with any well-constructed organizational policy, the document should include clear and concise definitions of acceptable and unacceptable behaviors. This stage should contain the strategies and actions to immediately respond to situations to reinforce to employees that expectations regarding behavior must be met.

In the pre-incident stage, employees must report the behavior of others that may be a potential threat. In this stage is the preemployment process that, among other things, contains screening and psychological testing in many organizations. Site analysis of potential threats and hazards should occur in the continuous pre-incident stage, akin to the total quality management (TQM) philosophy that began in earnest in the 1980s. Contingency plans must exist to contemplate failures in any of the proactive procedures. As with most emergency planning, the incident itself has been planned for and incorporates positive actions by various employees or team members. This will almost certainly include coordinating with human resources and possibly notification of security or law enforcement. Employees, during their training, must be sensitized to early warning signals of behavior issues by coworkers. "Training should include interpersonal communication, conflict resolution techniques and hostage survival skills" (Bruce & Nowlin, 2011, p. 297). The post-incident stage will include a debriefing of how a situation unfolded. During this type of after-action review and report, each person involved will document and discuss what they did in response to the plan. As with reviews in most industries and organizations, the focus is improvement in subsequent situations.

Outside the Workplace

Those who walk in and out of the doors of a business or organization may be known employees or unknown customers. Someone entering a religious facility or non-employment location or public event is not always known to those already at the location. How then to assess threat or formulate a policy of prevention? The confluence of factors in society, such as a culture of violence and gun ownership, the consequences of historically significant areas of poverty and unequal access, and individual factors of mental

WHY WOULD THEY DO IT?

On February 12, 2010, biology professor Amy Bishop of the University of Alabama at Hunstville started shooting her colleagues while at a routine faculty meeting. Bishop had been denied tenure the year before, seen by her as a devastating setback to her career. Amy Bishop had brought a 9mm pistol to the university, and she stood up in the meeting and began shooting those closest to her.

Following Bishop's murders, her background was examined, and it was learned that years earlier, in 1986, she had shot and killed her brother in an incident that, at the time, was ruled accidental. She and her husband had also been questioned regarding an incident of a pipe bomb mailed to her supervisor in the lab where she was working in 1993.

health, emotions, or predisposition, go together to preclude meaningful large-scale threat assessment, let alone specific prediction about someone entering a geo-temporal space.

Churches, mosques, synagogues, and other places to gather for spiritual purposes are known to be open and welcoming to newcomers. Many such religious institutions have introduced security officers or physical and technical measures to deter or intervene. This approach is not uncommon in many countries. As a policy matter these steps seem prudent. As a practical issue, having the resources to accomplish these enhancements can be problematic. This observation echoes the discussion in the chapter on school shootings. Troubled people go to places of worship and it is challenging to know who enters with malice in addition to their troubled views or emotions.

Fully public venues such as market places, marathon routes, and outdoor music festivals do not even have the physical construction that allows for design elements to aid in deterring or preventing attacks. A mix of tactics designed with consideration of bomb placement has communities or businesses removing mailboxes and trash cans near potential targets, bollards added to prevent vehicle entry to certain areas, and technology such as acoustic gunshot sensors to alert officials to gunfire and hasten a response. Designers work to make measures that are unobtrusive so as to keep the spaces open and approachable. Security sweeps and physical site assessment before a planned event can allow organizers to deploy scanners, K-9s, and extra personnel. Drone technology is already aiding in observation of locations covering large areas or many avenues of ingress and egress. Such practices, and the accompanying policies guiding their use, will continue to evolve.

SUMMARY

Non-family mass killings are infrequent, but they cause great concern among the public and law enforcement. Preventing such a crime is daunting and only likely to occur if someone notices behavior of a coworker or acquaintance that is abnormal or alarming in a way that the observer can connect it to a potential to do violence. People kill at places of worship for religious or ethnic motivations, or as in the case of the attack at a church in Sutherland Spring, Texas, the killer knew that family and friends of his ex-wife would be there.

Law enforcement response to an active shooter has undoubtedly ended some incidents more quickly than otherwise might have been the case, and workplace awareness and training has helped.

The workplace killer is often goal oriented and has planned out his attack for some time. The middle-class white male, the typical perpetrator of such mass killings, has dealt with personal and professional failures but has not coped adequately with these setbacks. The workplace mass murder is a rare event, but the killer frequently kills randomly at the worksite before or after locating his intended target(s). The individuals targeted by the killer are people the attacker blames for his most recent failures. They become the focus of his revenge. After dispatching his intended victim, the killer may randomly murder others in the work setting. Workplace homicide is also committed by customers. A challenge for management is to create effective policies to monitor employee behavior and intervene with various strategies to offer meaningful redress of perceived injustices by a complaining employee while being proactive in protecting coworkers.

The field and practice of threat and risk assessment continues to develop. Determining the level of threat posed by an individual or by a specific threat is important but illusive. The risk associated with employee behaviors and violence and the potential for customer violence against employees can be prepared for with sound policies, ongoing training, and attention to design and layout of physical facilities. But even with conscientious and competent planning, usually only the attacker knows when he plans to carry out his attack, and this leaves employers and organizations in a reactionary mode to a great extent.

KEY TERMS

Workplace homicide 138
Mass murder 138
Serious Mental
   Illness 138
Rampage 139
Active shooter 139
Workplace violence 140

Census of Fatal Occupational
   Injuries (CFOI) 140
Employee Assistance
   Program 141
Occupational Safety and
   Health Administration
   (OSHA) 141

Bureau of Labor Statistics 141
Threat assessment 146
Critical Incident Response
   Group (CIRG) 147

DISCUSSION QUESTIONS

1. Compare and contrast the types of mass killings and where they occur.
2. Discuss the types and levels of workplace violence in the United States.
3. Describe the typical workplace killer in terms of demographics.
4. Why do individuals from within and outside of an organization commit workplace murders?

5. Who becomes a victim of workplace shootings?
6. Discuss the challenges to assessing threats and risks of workplace violence and homicide.
7. Describe what components a policy on workplace violence should contain.
8. In a workplace killing, the victim is more likely to be killed by a stranger. Since this seems counterintuitive, explain why this happens.

TRY THIS

Go to the news article

The terrible numbers that grow with each mass shooting at https://www.washingtonpost.com/graphics/2018/national/mass-shootings-in-america/? utm_term=.aa429393f126. Read over some of the incidents summarized in this reporting. Discuss in class some of the information that you found to be surprising.

Go to the document Predicting Violent Behavior by the Department of Defense at https://www.acq.osd.mil/dsb/reports/2010s/PredictingViolentBehavior.pdf

Read the section on overall conclusions and consider the challenges to prevention of such acts.

10

KILLINGS BY GROUPS
Gangs and Cults

"A general loathing of a gang or sect usually has some sound basis in instinct."

—Ezra Pound

"The less reasonable a cult is, the more men seek to establish it by force."

—Jean-Jacques Rousseau

"The difference between a cult and an established religion is sometimes about one generation."

—Scott McLemee

CHAPTER OUTLINE

Student Learning Outcomes

Students will be able to:

- define and give examples of gangs.

- explain the gang-homicide connection.

- describe the motivations of gang members.

- identify gang activities that may lead to killing.

- evaluate reasons why people join criminal gangs.

- discuss instances of gang murder and what purpose they are intended to serve for a gang or gang member.

- define and give examples of cults and new religious movements (NRM).

- explain the role of violence in the few NRMs that use it.

- analyze the policy options available in a democratic society for dealing with potential violence by NRMs.

INTRODUCTION

Gangs have been a part of the American society since at least the end of the Civil War. The use of violence by gang members is well documented. Motives or instrumental use of violence is typically to intimidate, eliminate competition, or send a message to another gang or their own members. Communities expect law enforcement agencies to suppress gang activity and make their neighborhoods safe. Jail and prison officials must track and address the problems caused by prison gangs, also known as *security threat groups* (STG).

The number of gangs and gang members are not small, though they have decreased (Reynolds & Carlson, 2018). Gangs, and the challenges they bring, can exist in any city or community: urban, suburban, or rural. Gang members often know to keep a low profile so they do not draw the attention of law enforcement. Historically, many gangs were exclusive by gender or ethnicity. Today that is no longer true with hybrid gangs collaborating for the business of making money, such as a local drug gang cooperating with an outlaw biker gang to distribute their product. Because of the emphasis by gangs on demanding respect from others, not being shown respect often results in violence.

On the edge of most people's awareness and sense of reality lies the subject of cults. Why discuss gangs and cults in the same chapter? Cults and new religious movements (NRM) are responsible for a very small percentage or number of homicides, whereas gangs are estimated to account for perhaps more than 10% of all murders in the United States. Yet the topic of cults has been addressed in the literature and textbooks as deserving attention if only to inform the masses as well as those who study crime and responses to crime that exaggeration of the risk posed by such groups may not be appropriate. Killing perpetrated by groups of people with a central leader or figure is considered through a different perspective than one-on-one killing.

The term **cult** is understood by the average person as a group of glassy-eyed zealots following a charismatic leader who portends the end of days but promises salvation through him (or her). This portrait, at times exaggerated, is not a new picture, nor one unique to the United States. New religious movements (NRMs), which are considered by some as cults, are often simply groups with (largely religious or spiritual) views different than those of the majority in a community. The followers may see themselves as following the individual or following a philosophy. The phrase "cult following," colloquially, is applied to many loose followings of a person or group, such as a popular actor, politician, or musical band. When someone speaks specifically about a group formed around religious tenets typically with a charismatic leader, the term cult is often applied pejoratively. For many people, when they imagine cults, they think of violence and mind control. Even though cult killings are very rare, the public attention to such occurrences requires our examination of the phenomenon. Many incidents of mass death in cults are the result of a combination of murder and suicide. The leader may instruct followers to kill themselves and order the murder of the unwilling members of the group. We can never know how many followers died willingly or who the victims of murder were.

GANGS AND KILLING

Gangs come in a variety of forms and demographics, but our interest is mainly in those that commit violent crime. Street gangs, prison gangs, skinheads, and bikers or outlaw motorcycle gangs (OMGs) may threaten and intimidate, assault, rob, and occasionally kill while conducting drug or other illicit business, to declare a territory as their own, or to further their reputation. Most gang-related murders are considered in a category all their own, not in official statistics but based on the dynamics of gang violence. Some could be considered confrontational homicides, as when a conflict between or among rival (or same gang) members escalates. In fact, in the chapter on confrontational homicide, we briefly discussed gang violence. Gang violence is directed at rival gangs, and this is reflected in local news accounts in many communities as well as in fictional dramas like the former series *The Wire*, *Sons of Anarchy*, or the former show *Gangland*, the documentary series

A recent case filed in federal court in Chicago alleges that members of the Goonie Boss faction of the Gangster Disciples gang carried out numerous crimes including 11 murders, six attempted murders, other violent crimes, and racketeering over a three year period in the Engelwood community of Chicago. The charges resulted from the efforts of joint investigations by federal and state law enforcement agencies and were filed under federal statutes aimed at racketeering conspiracies. Many of the victims had no ties to the gang members and were innocent bystanders who were simply in the wrong place at the wrong time. The investigation revealed that unlike many other gang murders, most of these murders were not carried out to settle a score but were instead committed to help bolster the gang's social media status. Law enforcement agencies gathered evidence for the crimes mainly from social media and jail calls. The social media accounts included a Facebook Live video after one of the murders where about a dozen gang members, including some as young as 14 years old, waved guns and boasted about shooting the victim in the head.

on the History Channel. Violence also occurs within gangs as members are recruited, developed, and disciplined, often through violent acts. Law enforcement officers have been hurt and killed when investigating or encountering members and affiliates of gangs, and innocent bystanders are all too often victims.

But many researchers and scholars also note a similarity between the dynamics of some gang structures and cult or NRM structures. We would add that the centrality of a leader and the recruitment methods bear similarities to many terror groups. One similarity can be seen in the recruitment of followers from the disenfranchised or disillusioned who are looking for someone or something to align with. And we also address this theme in the chapter on terrorism and killing, which includes the complex dynamics of the recruitment of followers. Regardless of how local law enforcement or others may categorize a murder committed by a gang member, membership in gangs is recognized as a risk factor for a member to be involved in a homicide incident (DeLisi, Spruill, Vaughn, & Trulson, 2014). Gang homicides seem particularly intractable, and they account for many of the youth murders in the United States (Egley, Logan, & McDaniel, 2012).

The environment of most gangs is rife with factors that drive deviance and criminal or delinquent activity. Violence specifically by or within gangs is an important component of gang identity and activity, even if the violence is not what takes up the majority of a gang's time. In other words, gang members are not injuring or killing one another or others very often, but the acts are integral to who they are and how they do business (Gibson, Swatt, Miller, Jennings, & Gover, 2012). The violence more often takes place in a street setting than nongang homicides and overwhelmingly involves a gun.

But law enforcement and researcher assumptions can gloss over the distinctions and nuances of gang-involved individuals killing or being killed. As pointed out by Pizarro (2017), "The reliance on a gang-related definition limits the examination of the actual processes that spark gang violence, since gang-related homicides could occur for a host of reasons and not necessarily due to gang dynamics" (p. 78). In other words, a gang member may be killed, or may kill somebody, in an event that is not related to his gang involvement, or only tangentially so. Pizarro goes on to state, "It is still unclear how the various individual, situational, and structural factors interact to culminate in violence" (p. 84).

The number of gangs and gang members in the United States has fluctuated in the last 20 years, but there are currently estimated to be about 30,000 gangs with close to 800,000 members nationwide (Office of Juvenile Justice, 2014). Homicides in dense urban areas, such as Chicago and Los Angeles, may include a higher proportion of gang-related killings than rural and suburban areas. The partial increase of homicides in certain large cities is thought by many to be attributed to gang violence. One of the ongoing challenges is that such gang killings may go unsolved, leaving the numbers ambiguous. One of the important projects undertaken by the *Washington Post* newspaper (2019) tracked nearly 55,000 homicides in 55 cities through July 2018. The figures feed graphic representations of the different cities showing numbers of homicides and percentages of cases with arrests. While the arrest rate across all 55 cities was 50%, arrest rates varied widely. The reporting noted that almost all of the cities have a racial disparity in the cases with arrests. Among their conclusions is that there are "areas where murder is common but arrests are rare" (Washington Post Investigative Team, 2019). Often these areas are populated by minorities.

Gangs often are held in sway by the influence of a powerful or charismatic central figure. Entry to a gang and the socialization that acculturates a member to violent acts is documented (Engel, Tillyer, & Corsaro, 2013) and may suggest strategies for impeding gang violence. This is not universally so, as evidenced by the contemporary Goliath of gang threats in America, **MS-13**. MS-13, which stands for Mara Salvatrucha, is a gang that began as a social group in Los Angeles banding together for protection against other urban gangs. Efforts to deport Salvadoran members who made up the group resulted in the spread and growth of what is now seen as the most brutal gang in the United States. MS-13 does not claim a national hierarchy or central leadership as most other gangs do. At the same time, even though such gangs claim no central hierarchy, the local level or cliques typically do have a *shot-caller*. The federal government has been able to mount successful prosecutions, however, against MS-13 under the Racketeering Influenced and Corrupt Organizations Act (RICO), which relies on treating a series of crimes as part of an ongoing criminal organization. The suasion exercised through business savvy, ruthlessness, or both may keep this leader in place for some time. The followers will hold various roles and statuses with the gang and may commit violent acts (among other crimes) to impress the leader and as a way to gain full-member status in the gang.

Recruiting members has the familiar theme of trying to attract individuals from poor backgrounds and socially disorganized areas who lack any of the attachments, discussed earlier in the book, that increase a community's stability. Unemployment marks most areas where gangs draw their membership. Racial and ethnic identity is a common structural aspect of gangs in many countries. For example, recent national estimates (such as the National Gang

---

WHY WOULD THEY DO IT?

In May 2015, members of several rival biker gangs, including the Bandidos and the Cossacks, engaged in a melee escalating out of the already tense conditions between the groups and someone's foot being run over in a parking space dispute, according to reports. The deadly fight broke out at a Twin Peaks restaurant in Waco, Texas, where law enforcement had staged nearby to monitor the gathering.

Nine bikers were killed by gunfire and 18 more were injured. Some of the wounds were likely caused by officers returning gunfire from the gang members. Law enforcement confiscated more than 300 weapons after gaining control of the crime scene. The weapons included guns, knives, and brass knuckles. More than 100 motorcycles and cars were seized by police after the incident. Criticism came from some attorneys for the motorcycle gang members because of the high bond amounts the arrested were held on. It was asserted that the restaurant owner and franchisee of Twin Peaks ignored warnings about the potential for trouble as a result of the ongoing gatherings of biker gang members at the location.

It is evident that a fight of this size would result in chaos and take time to filter through. What is obvious is that a number of potential factors were in place for an altercation, and when it happened, people died.

Center (NGC), 2014), cite that half of all gang members are Hispanic/Latino, 32% are African American/black, and 11% are classified as white. Because of racial divides, many gang killings and much of their violence is deemed both gang behavior and hate crime behavior. Gangs have long held various initiation rites for prospective members, and for the more dangerous gangs, this will often involve committing a violent crime against a rival gang member or an innocent citizen. Gangs are increasingly using social media to recruit, coordinate, and brag about their operations and crimes.

There was an estimated increase of more than 23% in gang killings, going from 1,975 to 2,363 from 2007 to 2012, according to the National Gang Center (2014; latest report as of 2019) (see Table 10.1). While the increase is significant, it almost certainly does not reflect all gang killings because many such murders cannot be definitely attributed to gang activity based on a lack of witnesses or actionable information from sources. The NGC (2014) notes the estimated number of homicides attributed to gang violence accounts for approximately 13% of annual homicides in the United States. The NGC analysis reflects that two thirds of the gang-related homicides documented in 2012 occurred in cities with populations over 100,000. Many jurisdictions and communities are aware they have a gang problem while some deny it, either to themselves or through reporting practices by criminal justice agencies. Many law enforcement agencies do not label a homicide as gang-related when it is or when they do not know with certainty. Many agencies fail to respond to surveys, such as the annual **National Youth Gang Survey (NYGS)**, which reported,

> In 2012, there were an estimated 30,700 gangs (an increase from 29,900 in 2011) and 850,000 gang members (an increase from 782,500 in 2011) throughout 3,100 jurisdictions with gang problems (down from 3,300 in 2011). The number of reported gang-related homicides increased 20 percent from 1,824 in 2011 to 2,363 in 2012. (Egley, Howell, & Harris, 2014, p. 1)

Prison-based gangs are frequently referred to as **security threat groups (STGs)**. Some of the groups have members on the outside in street gangs, some form alliances with other gangs, and some are primarily prison-based. Just as violence is utilized for "business" purposes in a street gang, prison gangs enforce rules, discipline members, or establish turf in some prison environments the same way, which includes murder. Harsh rivalries lead to the groups planning assaults against enemy gang members or spontaneously reacting with aggression to any affront they perceive inside the prison walls. The Florida Department of Corrections (n.d.), the third-largest state prison system in the country, identifies the following groups as the six prison gangs most known for participating in violence: Neta, Aryan Brotherhood, Black Guerilla Family, Mexican Mafia, La Nuestra Familia, and the Texas Syndicate. The challenge of prison gangs includes the control many of them have over street gangs and their ability to coordinate criminal operations from behind bars (National Gang Intelligence Center, 2016).

Delaney (2014), in his book *American Street Gangs* (Second Edition), discusses the modern drive-by shooting, familiar to the general public in TV and movies and on the news and more intimately familiar to the residents of many urban neighborhoods. Delaney conceptualizes the reincarnation of Al Capone-era "Tommy Gun" killing from a car as replacing "the fair fight" of an earlier time, when gangs used less firepower and members did not have as much of the "win-at-any-cost" mentality. Delaney (2014) states that the shootings serve, among others, the following purposes:

1. They provide individual members an opportunity to prove themselves.

2. They may be used as part of an initiation rite for a new member.

3. They are a means of resolving an argument.

4. They can be viewed as preemptive attacks to intimidate rival gangs to not try the same thing.

5. They are used to eliminate competition in illegal businesses.

Table 10.1 Number of Gang-Related Homicides

	2007		2008		2009		2010		2011		2012		Percent Change, Previous Five-Year Average to 2012
	N	% Total	N	% Total	N	% Total	N	% Total	N	% Total	N	% Total	
Agencies reporting gang activity	992	—	921	—	1,050	—	1,026	—	928	—	999	—	—
Agencies reporting gang homicide statistics	890	—	768	—	910	—	860	—	739	—	829	—	—
Coverage rate (%)	—	89.7%	—	83.4%	—	86.7%	—	83.8%	—	79.6%	—	83.0%	—
Total gang homicides	1,975	100.0%	1,659	100.0%	2,083	100.0%	2,020	100.0%	1,824	100.0%	2,363	100.0%	23.6
Cities with populations over 100,000	1,215	61.5%	1,022	61.6%	1,123	53.9%	1,272	63.0%	1,242	68.1%	1,587	67.2%	35.1
Suburban counties	477	24.2%	357	21.5%	597	28.7%	439	21.7%	338	18.5%	408	17.3%	−7.6
Cities with populations of 50,000–100,000	215	10.9%	204	12.3%	274	13.2%	209	10.3%	198	10.9%	255	10.8%	15.9
Smaller areas*	68	3.4%	76	4.6%	89	4.3%	100	5.0%	46	2.5%	113	4.8%	**

Note: Because of the many issues surrounding the maintenance and collection of gang-crime data, caution is urged when interpreting the results presented in this figure.

* "Smaller Areas" refers to all cities with populations below 50,000 and rural counties combined.

**Not presented because of small base rate.

Note: Most recent data available

Source: National Gang Center. *National Youth Gang Survey Analysis.* Retrieved from http://www.nationalgangcenter.gov/Survey-Analysis.

6. They are used to settle turf fights.

7. They are used as a means of retaliation against rivals for a previous attack.

8. The "shooting fish in a barrel" mentality provides gang members with an adrenaline rush and provides them with the "courage" to strike against rivals.

9. Drive-bys are, in a sense, safer for gang members because they go into a rival turf and surprise attack targets. (p. 279)

Many government agencies and the nonprofit sector are working on a wide variety of prevention and suppression efforts. The Office of Juvenile Justice Delinquency and Prevention (OJJDP) has long worked to provide an array of services and documents to many sectors to help in the education and prevention effort. Braga (2017) has written about his examination and involvement with the Ceasefire project in Boston that leaned heavily on the lever-pulling strategy.

WHY WOULD THEY DO IT?

In May 2014, German Lisandro Benites Moreno traveled from Texas to New Jersey to recruit members to start a new MS-13 gang chapter. Moreno, two teenagers from Elizabeth, New Jersey, and two other gang members found a member of a rival gang. In an initiation to the MS-13 chapter, one of the two local teens shot the unarmed rival gang member twice in the head as the second team looked on to *verify* the act as a component of the initiation. After a five-month investigation by the county's homicide task force, all five of the individuals involved were arrested and charged in the murder. The gang initiation was to signal to the gang that the initiates were committed to the group's lifestyle and obedient to the leader.

CULTS AND NEW RELIGIOUS MOVEMENTS (NRM)

In defining a cult, we first have to consider the viewpoint of the person who creates the definition. Different academic researchers and journalists as well as anticult movement activists will have varied and nuanced definitions that emphasize key points of interest to the respective observers. Academic researchers might look objectively at the structure and dynamics of the people inside the cult or **new religious movement**. In constructing a description that captures the roles, functions, and purposes of a group, a sociologist, anthropologist, or researcher will highlight or describe the structure of the group in generally objective terms. Journalists may choose to highlight bizarre, violent, or unusual behavior by one or more members in a group with the aim of gaining further readership or viewership. The anticult activist may look at what he believes may harm someone who follows a particular leader or group. This may reflect the view that the new group is not aligned with his own views as much as it actually aims to warn potential followers of some danger.

The Merriam-Webster online dictionary offers the following brief definitions of the term cult:

- A small religious group that is not part of a larger and more accepted religion and that has beliefs *regarded by many people as extreme or dangerous* [emphasis added]

- A situation in which people admire and care about something or someone very much or too much

- A small group of very devoted supporters or fans

The website Urban Dictionary states that a cult is defined as follows:

- A religious group which promotes worship of a human leader and devotion of one's life to a specific purpose

- Some have members practice certain rituals or follow a set of principle rules. The group usually believes its way is the only correct way to live life, and all non-members are doomed to some horrible fate if they cannot be persuaded to join.

The website Christianity Today provides the following Q and A regarding the definition of a cult:

Q. What is a cult? And how does someone know if the faith they are following is harmful?

A. The word cult has three definitions. First of all, it can simply be a group that loves something. When people refer to an "Elvis cult" or "The O.C. cult," they mean really devoted fans. (Shelley, n.d., n.p.)

The second definition is that of a religious group whose beliefs differ from the majority around them. In the Roman Empire, Christians were sometimes considered a cult because they worshiped Jesus rather than the Roman gods.

The third and most commonly used definition refers to a religious group that meets three criteria:

1. *Exclusive.* They may say, "We're the only ones with the truth; everyone else is wrong; and if you leave our group your salvation is in danger."

2. *Secretive.* Certain teachings are not available to outsiders or they're presented only to certain members, sometimes after taking vows of confidentiality.

3. *Authoritarian.* A human leader expects total loyalty and unquestioned obedience. (Shelley, n.d., n.p.)

Some cults or new religious movements are considered millennial or following a variety of **millenarianism**, meaning that the group believes a major and transformative change in society is approaching. Many religions hold such beliefs, and this is not specific to groups considered cults or NRMs. Many millenarian groups believe that those in power in a society are acting against the good of the people and will be done away with when the millennial event happens.

Each of these definitions may confirm the view that someone had of cults, or they may suggest certain dimensions (e.g., exclusive, secretive, and authoritarian) that have clearly pejorative connotations.

Bob Larson, a controversial Christian counter-cult activist, defines cults in the following way: "The term cult . . . is generally understood to have a negative connotation that indicates morally reprehensible practices or beliefs that depart from historic Christianity" (as quoted in Cowan & Bromley, 2015, p. xiv). Cowan and Bromley (2015) have appropriately tried to transition from the singularly understood term *cult* to the broader and more value-neutral concept of *new religious movement*. The NRM

WHY WOULD THEY DO IT?

The Order of the Solar Temple was a group possessed of the idea that death had to be passed to reach life on a different planet. Their founders combined Christian, occult, and New Age philosophies as part of the basis of their cult's theology. In 1994, in Quebec, the cult murdered an infant because one of the group's founders said the child was the Antichrist. A few days later, in Switzerland, this founder and 12 members held a "last supper," and several days after that, some 50 members either committed suicide or were murdered. In 1995, another 16 individuals from the group died in France and were arranged in a start formation emblematic of the order's rituals. There were other incidents linked or identified with the group. Running counter to stereotyped impressions of cults, the Order of the Solar Temple had a number of successful and well-to-do members who joined and died in the order's rituals.

Table 10.2   Examples of Cult Deaths Worldwide

1969	United States	The (Manson) Family	Murdered several people in California
1978	Guyana	The People's Temple	Murder/suicide of more than 900 members and others
1987	South Korea	Paradise	Murder/suicide of 33 people linked to a religious cult
1993	United States	Branch Davidians	Shootout with law enforcement and subsequent fire kill more than 80
1994	Canada/ Switzerland	Order of the Solar Temple	Suicide/murder of 53 members of group
1995	Japan	Aum Shinrikyo	Gas attack on Japanese subway system
1997	United States	Heaven's Gate	Suicide of 39 members of group
2000	Uganda	The Movement for the Restoration of the Ten Commandments of God	Murder of 500 followers after leader's prediction of apocalypse did not occur

will surely include the odd group or individual who utilizes dominance over followers and the potential for violence in various forms. But the majority of such NRMs will pursue their vision of the working of the world or universe with no malicious or violent intent.

New religious movement is the current term used to describe most groups heretofore referred to as cults. Cowan and Bromley (2015) note that the evangelical and secular anticult advocates as well as the news media have different views than the academic community.

> Unlike the evangelical countercult, the secular anticult, or the mainstream media, most social scientists and religious studies scholars are interested in understanding new religions in their social, cultural, and historical contexts. Where do they come from? Why do they emerge at particular times and in specific places? How do they develop, and what contributes to their evolution, success, and, not infrequently, their decline? Rather than convince adherents to change their allegiances, these scholars want to understand the processes of recruitment and defection,

of experimentation and maturation, and of affiliation and disaffiliation. Why do people join and why do they believe? Are new religious movements, in fact, as dangerous as they are often portrayed in the mass media? (p. 4)

Most people get their information from the media, and this source is not subject to the same peer-review or extensive fact-checking of a scholarly journal or text. In the constant drive for readership, viewership, or their own followership, media organizations present titillating accounts of violent or lurid goings-on that may be short on context. Yet we all want summary information, and we want it fast. As we have explained throughout the text, this sense of immediacy among information consumers leads to untold numbers of inaccurate views on all manner of topics. This is certainly true when it comes to cults or NRMs.

Another component of the mythology and misunderstanding that people have regarding NRMs is the concept of brainwashing or thought control. In a 2000 article in the *FBI Law Enforcement Bulletin*, which is written mainly for law enforcement consumption, Szubin, Jensen, and Gregg (2000) pointed out the need for law enforcement involvement where clear physical coercion existed. They also noted that most NRMs likely conduct many of the same types of recruitment tactics as other more accepted groups. They go on to talk about the impression some people may have that anyone who seeks to join or joins a NRM must have been manipulated, rather than be motivated by the benefits the group members perceive they gain by joining. Misinterpreting motivations can lead to poor decision-making by law enforcement and others. The authors remind law enforcement agencies that they can turn to the **FBI's National Center for the Analysis of Violent Crime (NCAVC)** by contacting the nearest field office to request assistance in assessing a group's threat potential. Anticult activists and family members have used techniques designed to *deprogram* people who they believe

were brainwashed or influenced by cult members. The efforts of deprogrammers have been depicted as sometimes taking a person against his will from the cult environment and then using their own coercion techniques to change the views and thought process of the cult adherent. The practice of deprogramming has also been called *exit counseling* and *debriefing*.

Szubin et al. (2000), in their article, created a table of risk, neutral, and protective factors that they describe as being adapted from general threat assessment guidelines but tailored to aspects of NRMs that officers may encounter. These three sets of factors are listed in Exhibit 10.1 and help one conduct **threat assessment for cults or NRMs**. The authors emphasize that "no single factor, with the possible exception of a history of violence, will determine a group's threat potential" (p. 20).

EXHIBIT 10.1

RISK, NEUTRAL, AND PROTECTIVE FACTORS

Risk Factors

Certain characteristics provide indications of a new religious movement's instability and potential for violence. While some of these factors may prove more significant than others, many may signal a marked shift in a group's attitude, orientation, or behavior toward violent activity.

- History of violent episodes or clashes with law enforcement

- Leader's past or current condition (e.g., history of violence, drug or alcohol abuse, or mental illness; increasing amounts of paranoia; onset of real or perceived serious illness; or recent death)

- Any abrupt reversal of direction, whether the change appears positive or negative (e.g., stops recruiting new members or suddenly changes its message from doom to optimism)

- Recent attempts to obtain the knowledge to carry out a violent act (e.g., recruitment of military or ex-military personnel

or those with knowledge of chemical/biological weapons) and intelligence gathering against specific persons, organizations, or locations

- Recent purchases of weapons, poison, or unusual amounts of drugs or drug accessories

- Training in the use of weapons and rehearsals of suicide (e.g., performing ritualistic ceremonies where members jointly consume a single food or drink)

- Instances of violence within the group (e.g., child abuse, sexual abuse, ritualistic violence, violence as a form of social/religious punishment, or violence as a rite of passage)

- Setting an exact date for the imminent transformation of life on earth

- Moving the date for transformation forward, or closer to the present. Conversely, officers can view a group that pushes this date back as less of a threat.

- Phrasing its prophecies or predictions in a detailed manner (e.g., the general

---

claim that "a day will come when evil will be punished" represents less of a risk factor than the more specific claim that "a day will come when America's institutions will burn and its officials will be slain")

- Envisioning an active role for the NRM in the coming transformation (e.g., predictions that "God's chosen people will be taken up," which is phrased passively, versus a prediction that "God's chosen people will shed their mortal bodies and transport themselves to heaven")

- Having the knowledge, means, and ability to carry out a plan that makes sense operationally

Neutral Factors

Because new religious movements exhibit many unfamiliar traits, it becomes difficult to distinguish between risk indicators and characteristics that appear strange but are not necessarily dangerous. Several traits common to these groups exist but are not, in and of themselves, danger signals.

- Members offer absolute and unquestioning adherence to their leader and the belief system. In the absence of other risk indicators, this does not indicate a propensity toward violence or other criminal activity. Indeed, total devotion is the hallmark of new religious movements.

- The group physically segregates itself from others. This also is a common characteristic of many new religious movements and says little about a group's attitude toward violence or suicide.

- Members adopt unfamiliar customs or rituals, which may involve diet, dress, language, or family and social organization.

Protective Factors

The presence of some characteristics may indicate that a new religious movement is comparatively stable or is becoming more stable and, hence, less of a danger.

- Members take practical steps to plan for the future (e.g., send their children to school, work at permanent jobs, or make medium to long-term investments in commodities or real estate).

- The group adopts bureaucratic processes that routinize its affairs (e.g., transcribes its leader's teachings to writing for dissemination or appoints a committee to handle such aspects as outreach, finances, or general management).

- When the leader dies, a more conventional style of governance, involving voting or a committee structure, replaces autocratic decision making. Often, this causes outsiders to change their opinion of the group and view it as a religious denomination or mainstream religious organization rather than a new religious movement.

Source: Szubin, A., Jensen, C. J., and Gregg, R. (2000). Interacting with "cults": A policing model. *FBI Law Enforcement Bulletin*, 69(9), 16–24.

CULT LEADERS AND FOLLOWERS

The former television series *The Following* provided a graphically violent Hollywood vision of not just one cult but at times, competing cult groups. The leaders are shown to have their own agenda, which includes components not shared with the entire group, except perhaps only a few of the followers, while the remainder of the group performs tasks and shows obedience to the central figure. The tasks set before group members may include sacrificing a group member through some type of ritual killing by other members, thereby constituting a cult killing.

The *Crime Classification Manual* (1992) written by retired FBI Special Agent John Douglas and others, notes that at a cult death scene, there may be the use of artifacts or symbols intended to meet the ritualistic dictates of the group and to influence either the internal group or people external to the cult.

A number of the examples held out to the American public as proof of cult violence highlight a long-examined aspect of religious groups, new or not so new: that of charisma. The well-known image of a cult leader typically involves such charisma, which results in the ability to get people to follow him. And the following of a charismatic leader has less to do with the beliefs as it does the unquestioning devotion to the central leader. Jim Jones had been a controversial pastor of a San Francisco church before moving in 1978 with those who would follow him to a remote area in Guyana he called the Peoples Temple. Preaching that his group's way of life was under attack, Jones eventually exhorted some 900 of his followers to commit what he called *revolutionary suicide*. Extremism within a traditional religious belief or apparently unstable behavior has led to several such ministers being pushed out of the established group.

Cult killings are not frequent, and when they do occur, they are quick to draw media and public attention. This goes part of the way in explaining the *information* and certainly the perception that we have about groups labeled as cults. Given the rarity of such violence, it is quite important that scholars continue to examine these cases to determine what sets them apart, in the same way that most workplace disappointment does not end in a rampage shooting and school-age angst rarely ends in the killing of classmates.

Yet dismissing or pigeonholing all new religious movements denies our ability to understand those who have chosen a different set of spiritual concepts and precepts. If they do not espouse violence, they may likely be just one more tile in the mosaic of the U.S. cultural reality. If a self-defined group does exhort members to harm, abuse, or coerce others to join in condemnation of those not like themselves, then a society typically takes steps to pursue legal avenues to address the group's activities.

People are often wary or fearful about groups or movements that they do not understand or that are different from their own experience. We often process *different* as *bad*. Acceptance of a group falls to society as a whole. This acceptance may come over time. In the media age, the public has a greater ability to know something about a group or its members, which may bring about acceptance sooner than we would have seen in earlier days.

Many religions were first viewed as cults. Some still are, depending on whom you ask. For example, in the United States, Mormons and other Christian sects, in their early years, were considered cults. **Scientology**, based on the science fiction writings of L. Ron Hubbard, is still hotly debated by scholars and critics to be either a legitimate religion or a massively successful cult. Religions have had one or more

WHY WOULD THEY DO IT?

Although the killings happened many years ago, many people are still somewhat familiar with the horrific murders committed by the followers of **Charles Manson**. Manson, a criminal and sometime musician, started something of a communal group referred to as the Manson Family, who he directed in the murders of seven people over a two-day period in California. Manson was believed to have involvement with a satanic cult, and he ordered ritualistic killings by his followers. Such killings can be considered *team killings*, involving two or more people to carry out a murder. This illustrates the psychological role of mutual accountability and the dynamic of group behavior, lending some degree of anonymity or deniability

to individual participants as they rationalize that they did not commit the murder(s) themselves as individuals; they are not responsible. In the case of Charles Manson, he provided direction, and his cult followers went off to commit the actual murders. Though convicted of first degree murder and sentenced to death, his sentence was commuted to life in prison where he died in November 2017.

One of the Manson Family members, Leslie Van Houten, in her confession of the stabbing death of one of the Family's victims, said she committed the murder because she thought that was what Manson wanted. The influence of a charismatic leader is again seen here in the actions of a *disciple*.

In 1993, agents of the Bureau of Alcohol, Tobacco, and Firearms (ATF) tried to serve a warrant and were fired upon by members of a breakaway group from the Seventh-day Adventist Church called the **Branch Davidians**. Vernon Wayne Howell, who changed his name to David Koresh in hopes of boosting his music career, was the self-proclaimed leader of the Branch Davidian group. Howell/Koresh claimed to be a prophet, advocated polygamy, and was accused of having sex with many young female members of the group.

During the problematic initial attempt to serve the ATF warrant, four agents and six Davidian members were killed, with others wounded. Subsequently, federal officers from several agencies surrounded the compound and tried unsuccessfully for almost two months to get the group to surrender and come out.

Howell/Koresh had stockpiled weapons, including large-caliber rifles capable of piercing some of the armored defense of the law enforcement personnel. During the FBI assault on the compound, the buildings caught fire, and 76 Branch Davidians died. Government investigations revealed that the Branch members started the fire. Two years after the Branch Davidian compound fire, two men claimed the government's actions toward the Branch Davidians provided their motivation for setting off a bomb that destroyed the Murrah Federal Building in Oklahoma City, killing 168 men, women, and children.

charismatic leaders who gather followers as they spread the message or philosophy of their faith. But while the religion has one or more leaders, the cult has a focus on a particular leader, rather than on the precepts of the emerging movement. This difference in how key adherents are viewed is an important distinction. This leads many to consider the actions of the leader and how that leader is viewed by followers as a potential red flag to suspicious or insincere motivations.

This suspicion of cults or new religious movements appears to be quite common. Violent behavior may in fact come from the reactions of people to a new group. History is replete with such examples. And so the *problem* of such groups can be from the countermovement, rather than the group itself.

ASSESSING IMPACTS

We opened the chapter introduction by noting that cult killings are not frequent. It is a rare and unique form of homicide. The violence perpetrated by members of cults or NRMs is significant in the impact it has on group members, victims, families, and the society as a whole when they do occur. The impacts on people in each of these categories can be observed and commented on in ways similar to other murders. Yet the lingering sense of unrest that comes to a community touched by cult violence goes beyond the questioning of individual family members when a loved one is killed in a robbery or so-called crime of passion. Cult killings scare people because they can be harder to understand and explain than other types of homicide.

Groups who had no contact or connection with a violent movement may come under suspicion or monitoring simply because they are different from the prevailing social entities in a community. **Anticult movements (ACM)** often include members of other, more established religions or advocacy groups, sometimes founded or resourced by the families of people who have joined cults or NRMs. Some entities may also be components of an educational or therapeutic institution observing the movement and behavior of such groups or offering services to persons concerned about or leaving an NRM or cult. Monitoring of NRMs may also take place through the auspices of law enforcement or other governmental agencies on the lookout for potential danger to citizens.

Melton and Bromley (2002) challenge what they say are commonly held misconceptions about the connection of NRMs and violence. These misconceptions include the following assertions:

- Violence involving new religions is pervasive.

- New religions are violence prone.

Jonestown

Jim Jones was a pastor in a church in San Francisco in the 1970s. While he had initially been well regarded in the community, he also claimed to be Jesus and Lenin reincarnated. Jones also advocated mass suicide to protest racism and what he described as fascism. In 1977, he moved with many of his followers to Jonestown, Guyana, in South America. Jones, who had been under increasing pressure and media scrutiny in the United States, described his Peoples Temple in Guyana as a benevolent communist community. Eventually, close to 1,000 members occupied Jonestown, partly as a result of paying immigration officials in Guyana to look the other way to allow the mass migration. There were reports of many abuses of followers, and those who chose to leave were blocked. Jones had members practice various strategies, including mass suicide, in the event that the commune was attacked by those conspiring against them.

Congressman Leo Ryan of California traveled with others to Jonestown to examine for themselves the claims and counterclaims about Jones's activities and treatment of followers. While it appeared that some members wished to leave, most continued to show solidarity with Jones and claimed that all was well. Jones took even this modest amount of dissent as a signal that his utopia was failing. As Congressman Ryan and others went to the local airport to leave, they were attacked by Jones's Red Brigade security force, and several, including the congressman, were killed.

Jones ordered his followers to take a prepared drink containing poison. Over 900 people died, and Jones apparently shot himself in the head, dying at the compound he created.

Heaven's Gate

Heaven's Gate was another millenarian group that formed in the 1970s. One of the two founders claimed a near-death experience revelation led to him and his nurse forming a New Age group that coupled Christian elements and the existence of aliens. The group believed they had to leave Earth before it was devastated, only to be begun again. They believed they had to give up all earthly material possessions and bonds with friends and family outside of the group.

The group's leader spoke of a spacecraft that was following the trail of the comet Hale-Bopp and convinced 38 members to commit suicide along with him so that their souls could be transported by the spaceship to the next level of existence. They rented a mansion near San Diego, and in 1997, they were all found dead dressed in identical black clothing and lying in bunks at the mansion. They had all taken phenobarbital in applesauce. They apparently drank vodka to wash down the poisonous mixture.

Aum Shinrikyo

Aum Shinrikyo, a religious movement in Japan, released poisonous sarin gas on the subway in Tokyo on March 20, 1995. Members of the religious movement coordinated the release of the gas in five sections of the subway system, killing 13 people and injuring many more, some seriously. Three years before the attack in 1992, the founder of the group had declared himself to be Christ. Over the time prior to the attack, the self-proclaimed enlightened leader had described an end-of-the-world prophecy. He identified various groups and people from other countries as fomenters of conspiracies. The movement's leader, Asahara, stated a familiar theme of external persecution of the group and led the group to increasingly secretive and insular behavior. In another often observed aspect of groups that act out with violence, Asahara also claimed the sole ability to bring spiritual enlightenment to followers.

It is well known that Japanese society is far more homogenous than U.S. society. Various academics have examined how Aum being different in a culture that valued sameness affected the perception of Aum members and leadership (Simons, 2006). Central to our concern is that the group chose to kill and harm people outside of their group in furtherance of their *religious* activities or agenda.

- New religions provoke violence.

- Violence by new religions cannot be averted. (p. 43)

In their discussion, the authors point out that few actual *new* religions are begun. Most are adaptations of established religions. They also note that the frame of reference for violence by new religions is typically a comparison to established religions. There are problems disentangling the various types of violence and abuse in many religious groups or by individuals associated or identified with a religious group. Through a thoughtful recitation of historical and contemporary examples, the authors refute these major points that often lead members of the larger society to stereotype groups as dangerous. Given the relatively few violent episodes involving new religious movements balanced against the estimated thousands or tens of thousands of such groups worldwide and the small number of adherents in groups that have typically perpetrated multiple homicide or suicide, it is a challenging prospect to identify precursors to violence in such groups.

Melton and Bromley (2002), in addressing these four misconceptions regarding NRMs and violence, point out that not only are violent incidents rare but also that assigning *proneness* to such groups is problematic. A common aspect of many groups is the presence of a charismatic leader. Charismatic leadership is not in itself unusual, suspicious, or dangerous. Fixating on a charismatic figure within a NRM may divert attention from deeper and "more complex social dynamics." As to proving violence, the authors attribute this impression to faulty news reports or rumors far more often than actual incidents, citing instead that many NRMs are themselves the targets of provocation. Finally, as to the inevitability of violence by new religions, Melton and Bromley point to limited actual incidents of violence relative to the number of new religions and cults and that repressive social control or absence of any social control may each lead to episodic violence. They again suggest that examining the complex dynamics may be productive to prevent violence. If these assertions are indeed the salient ones, it seems clear that many people overreact to the existence and activities of many spiritually oriented groups.

POLICY IMPLICATIONS

Responses to the presence of various groups in a society run the gamut from mild interest to alarm. Media reports will often make people in a community aware of a group labeled as a cult or new religious movement. The tone of a story can certainly affect the way in which people process the existence or activities of such a group within the community. This means that if the media outlet adopts a posture of suspicion or implies that the group is secretive, public sentiment may be steered toward a negative view of the group.

Most people will not seek out further information to confirm whether or not an NRM poses some type of problem for the community. Where would someone ask about such a thing? A telephone call to a law enforcement agency will result in a statement of fact regarding whether there were any reported issues of a criminal nature. Some people may be more attuned to information that would tend to confirm a suspicious view of a group.

While official responses to perceived or potential groups are also influenced, at times, by media reports, there is an expectation that government will perform its due diligence in researching or examining a group and its actions before determining if a response is warranted. The protections of the First Amendment against government interference with religious practice remain an important aspect of the manner in which such groups are treated. The public looks to law enforcement agencies for leadership in assessing the danger posed by a group that is not viewed as traditional by a majority of a population. This underscores the challenging and complex role held by law enforcement in a democratic society. Police are often inserted at the point of social friction. How the police act toward groups and individuals and how they react to the actions of group members and others who voice a concern can ameliorate or inflame public reaction.

Many countries do, however, enact laws that curtail or outlaw various religious groups. The U.S. courts have encountered the question of when a religion is *legitimate* in the effort by some prison inmates to form their own religions with the intention of claiming various accommodations to their living conditions based on religious freedom.

SUMMARY

Gang violence and homicide has been present for a long time in the United States. Legislation addresses gang-related crimes and enhanced penalties for gang-affiliated criminals. Law enforcement and correctional authorities form specialized units and task forces to include federal authorities to monitor and investigate gang crime. Murders of and by gang members are not uncommon and are often some of the more difficult to successfully investigate and prosecute. Retribution is handled within the gang culture, and witnesses are reluctant or nonexistent. Many researchers point to the dynamics of the increased gang killings over the years to partly explain the decreased clearance rates of homicide in the United States.

Gangs, like other organized-crime groups, often use violence to claim territory, make money, and establish individual and group reputation. Small and large gangs frequently have a central charismatic figure who holds sway over the operation of the gang and actions of its members. Individuals may join gangs for physical and financial security and to feel they belong to a group. Sometimes the reasons are similar to the motivations of NRM followers. Gangs also make use of the instant communication available through social media.

In this chapter we reviewed gangs, cults, and new religious movements, but we did not examine the circumstance of terrorism, which has also involved killing, often on a massive scale. The use of violence in established religions down through recorded history has been responsible for more killing than any other cause. In the separate chapter, "Tool of Terror," we examine the planned murder of others as a way to try to influence public sentiment, political policies, and religious conversion. Terrorist groups are generally viewed as primarily political rather than religious, as opposed to the groups covered in this chapter, which are more religious than political.

Defining cults or new religious movements is difficult. This arises from the varying perspectives of those who wish to define such groups. NRMs are not inherently violent or dangerous. Clearly, the vast majority of *different* or new movements have no interest or inclination to violence but only wish to pursue their beliefs in ways that suit their membership. When the practices and beliefs of a group are different from that of a majority group, the majority group members may be uncomfortable, suspicious, and hostile. People may fear a cult or NRM because they have been socialized to react with fear, rather than respond with curiosity. Law enforcement agencies are most often tasked with investigating reported acts of impropriety or alleged crime by groups or individuals.

The consideration of NRMs is of interest to many groups. Academically, NRMs are examined by researchers in a variety of disciplines. The media will normally take an interest only if there is something they deem newsworthy, such as violent behavior involving a group. Anticult activists monitor and often work to intervene with the activities of and recruiting by NRMs. Legal response by legislative bodies is complex, with the overarching concern not to violate First Amendment rights. There is often a role for individual therapists and deprogramming counselors if someone has left a cult or NRM and seeks assistance in dealing with the psychological challenges the exit may bring on. Finally, law enforcement agencies play a role not only when a group violates laws but in opening and maintaining a dialogue with the many groups who have no violent agendas or tendencies and simply need the protection that any group in a democratic society needs.

KEY TERMS

Cult 156

Gangs 156

MS-13 158

National Youth
  Gang Survey
  (NYGS) 159

Security threat
  groups
  (STGs) 159

DISCUSSION QUESTIONS

1. What are some of the causes of gang violence and homicide?
2. What policy challenges exist for addressing gangs in a country such as the United States?
3. How is a violent gang similar to a cult or NRM? How are gang homicides similar to other types of homicide?
4. How can law enforcement agencies or schools use the data on gangs to implement policies?

5. How do cults and NRMs develop?
6. What are the benefits and challenges of charismatic leaders in NRMs?
7. Why do people join cults?
8. Explain why NRMs are incorrectly stereotyped as violent.

TRY THIS

Visit the National Gang Center at https://www.nationalgangcenter.gov/Resources, and select two to three sections to read. Familiarize yourself with some of the ways law enforcement deals with the challenges of gang violence.

Research new religious movements in the United States, and examine their web presence. Look at the stated mission or activities of two or more groups, and then compare these to one or more of what you consider to be traditional religious groups.

11

TOOL OF TERROR

"Demoralize the enemy from within by surprise, terror, sabotage, assassination. This is the war of the future."

—Adolf Hitler

"With guns you can kill terrorists, with education you can kill terrorism."

—Malala Yousafzai, *Pakistani activist, and at age 17, in October 2014, youngest winner of the Nobel Peace Prize*

CHAPTER OUTLINE

Student Learning Outcomes

Students will be able to:

- differentiate between domestic and international terrorist acts.

- explain the motivations of terrorist groups and individuals.

- discuss the factors necessary in policy formulation and implementation related to terrorist acts.

- define hate crimes and analyze how these differ from other terrorist acts.

INTRODUCTION

The goal of a terrorist, whether domestic or international, is to influence the views of people and the actions of governments. The *logic* of terror attacks is often lost on citizens in many Western democracies, who do not see such acts as effectively influencing government policies or public sentiment. Terrorist attacks may also be carried out to attract recruits and finance and raise the profile of the group that carries out the attack. Society, through laws and law enforcement agencies, sets about preventing terrorist acts and ameliorating societal conditions that may bring about violent terrorist behavior. The American public has had an ongoing exposure to, if not structured education about, terrorist groups, individuals, and actions over the last decade and a half. As we are all aware, terrorist acts often result in homicide.

Hate homicide fits within this chapter due to the connecting motivation of committing offenses against people for a purpose beyond single victimization, such as a felony murder, confrontational homicide, and intimate partner homicide. As specified by the U.S. Congress, an attacker's animus for his victim in a **hate crime** (including homicide) may stem from a bias against "the actual or perceived religion, national origin, gender, sexual orientation, gender identity, or disability of any

person" (Matthew Shepard and James Byrd, Jr. Hate Crimes Prevention Act of 2009). If the commission of a crime includes the potential violation of federal civil rights statutes, the FBI will investigate solely or in cooperation with state or local law enforcement agencies.

We do not offer a comprehensive examination of the typologies and groups identified with contemporary terrorism. That task is handled quite well by a number of current books solely addressing terrorism. Our aim is to provide some context for the reader about a form of murder that represents one type of motivation that may lead someone to kill a fellow human. Like serial killings, cult killings, and school shootings, terroristic murders inside the United States represent a small number and percentage of all homicides committed. Nevertheless, an examination of terrorism and homicide will help you better understand its causes and consequences.

DEFINITION AND HISTORY

The public in America and in most countries has a common understanding of contemporary terrorism. For U.S. citizens, most acts of terrorism seem geographically remote even though

WHY WOULD THEY DO IT?

The September 11, 2001 (9/11), attacks etched an indelible mark on the consciousness of this generation of Americans. Four attacks were coordinated and carried out by members of the terror group al-Qaeda in New York City and the Washington, D.C., area.

The 19 terrorists hijacked four commercial passenger jets with the intention of crashing them into several targets. Two of the planes were flown into the World Trade Center towers in New York and one into the Pentagon

in D.C. Terrorists were not able to fly the fourth plane into the unknown third target because passengers fought the terrorists, and the airliner crashed in a field in Pennsylvania.

Nearly 3,000 people died in the terrorist attacks. These attacks galvanized America's efforts to deal with terrorism through multiple initiatives, including the creation of the Department of Homeland Security (DHS) and the passage of the U.S.A. Patriot Act.

EXHIBIT 11.1

DEFINITIONS OF TERRORISM IN THE U.S. CODE

18 U.S.C. § 2331 defines **international terrorism and domestic terrorism** for purposes of Chapter 113B of the Code, entitled "Terrorism": "International terrorism" means activities with the following three characteristics:

- Involve violent acts or acts dangerous to human life that violate federal or state law;

- Appear to be intended (i) to intimidate or coerce a civilian population; (ii) to influence the policy of a government by intimidation or coercion; or (iii) to affect the conduct of a government by mass destruction, assassination, or kidnapping; and

- Occur primarily outside the territorial jurisdiction of the United States, or transcend national boundaries in terms of the means by which they are accomplished, the persons they appear intended to intimidate or coerce, or the locale in which their perpetrators operate or seek asylum.*

"Domestic terrorism" means activities with the following three characteristics:

- Involve acts dangerous to human life that violate federal or state law;

- Appear intended (i) to intimidate or coerce a civilian population; (ii) to influence the policy of a government by intimidation or coercion; or (iii) to affect the conduct of a government by mass destruction, assassination, or kidnapping; and

- Occur primarily within the territorial jurisdiction of the U.S.

18 U.S.C. § 2332b defines the term "federal crime of terrorism" as an offense that:

- Is calculated to influence or affect the conduct of government by intimidation or coercion, or to retaliate against government conduct; and

- Is a violation of one of several listed statutes, including § 930(c) (relating to killing or attempted killing during an attack on a federal facility with a dangerous weapon); and § 1114 (relating to killing or attempted killing of officers and employees of the U.S.).

*FISA defines "international terrorism" in a nearly identical way, replacing "primarily" outside the United States with "totally" outside the United States 50 U.S.C. § 1801(c).

Source: Federal Bureau of Investigation, United States Department of Justice. "Definitions of Terrorism in the U.S. Code," http://www.fbi.gov/about-us/investigate/terrorism/terrorism-definition

the incidents are disturbing. Political rhetoric is supplanted by suicide bombings or incidents of mass murder using firearms, machetes, and even bludgeoning many people to death in single incidents. As we write this chapter, we are aware of numerous acts that have occurred in the preceding day, week, and month. No country is immune to violent acts perpetrated by individuals and groups claiming a particular worldview or ideology. Acts can be perpetrated by subnational political groups or supported by sovereign countries. The violence is intentionally aimed at civilians and not military targets. A group may carry out parallel attacks against governmental or military locations. The focus is on striking fear into the civilian population and showing that the government cannot keep them safe.

The use of terror as a tactic is not a new one. Going back more than 2,000 years, we see the **Sicarii** as the earliest recorded group to use terrorism. The Sicarii and Jewish Zealots resisted the oppressive control of Roman rulers in the first century A.D. The Sicarii members would attack prominent Romans or moderate Jewish leaders in public for the instrumental reason of showing that no one was safe from their terror attacks. These groups had initially used nonviolent resistance to gain supporters. The Roman military cracked down on demonstrators, which resulted in an escalation to violent tactics. Such **assassinations** for political or religious reasons typically targeted someone of significance in a community or society. Since that time, and around the world, the pattern of nonviolent resistance followed by violent attacks has occurred.

The Romans too, for their part, used operatives, often women, to poison enemies. How do we compare this to *contract killings* in more recent times, wherein an organized crime boss orders a *hit* on a rival or enemy? There have also been groups of killers organized into secret societies in countries around the world. Today's groups may avoid a central hierarchy and simply carry out acts that follow the guiding tenets of the movement.

With the variety of groups claiming responsibility for killings and the destruction that often accompanies such killings, it is challenging for the average citizen of most countries to keep them straight, let alone understand the fundamental motivations of the groups. In addition to the directed or sanctioned terror acts by groups and members, there are other single individuals who claim affiliation with a group where none exists or simply state their support for a movement as they carry out a terror act. We look at independent actors later in the chapter.

How does a murder considered as part of a terrorist act differ from the various other homicides we discuss? Many murders are spur-of-the-moment actions or occur after a brief exchange or escalation of an argument. A bomber, sniper, or weapon-wielding assailant carrying out a terror attack has planned and prepared in advance. You would be right to note that many murders are planned ahead of time but involve revenge, greed, jealousy, or a longstanding grievance. The man accused of orchestrating the 2012 attack on the U.S. consulate in Benghazi, Libya, was tried in federal court in Washington, DC in 2017—prosecutors said that he had planned the attack for some time. The man was convicted in the United States for crimes of terrorism, but he was acquitted of murder charges, though U. S. Ambassador

Christopher Stevens and three other Americans were killed (Siegel, 2017).

Some murderers kill with no expectation of getting away with the crime or even surviving the encounter. Beyond this ambivalence about escaping capture or death, the terrorist is focused on the act being a *message*. His dramatic act is intended to reach the whole society or the entire world. It is this drama that experts and observers point to as a distinguishing characteristic of terrorism. Poland (2011) aptly observes that, "Today, terrorism is a global theater" (p. 9).

Domestic

Working from the definition supplied by the FBI, we can examine events and attacks that occur inside U.S. borders to distinguish geography, if not always motive, from international and transnational terrorist acts. The FBI definition, consistent with the USA Patriot Act, notes that the act occurs within the territorial jurisdiction of the United States. Most acts of terrorism are domestic, and both the attackers and the attacked have the same nationality. The public is generally unaware of how many acts occur each year in the United States that are considered terrorism.

Consider the following known groups and their aims: the Animal Liberation Front (ALF) acts against those they believe are harming animals; the Army of God (AOG) acts against those offering abortion counseling or services; the Aryan Nations (AN) white supremacist organization promotes the belief that people of all races other than white are inferior; and the Earth Liberation Front (ELF) commits acts of property and personal violence against those they see as damaging the environment. This is a small sampling of groups that have formed, broken up, and reformed over the years in the United States. Sometimes, group members will damage property and claim responsibility to gain notoriety for their cause. Some group members have also committed violent acts, including murder, against individuals they see as opposed to or acting inconsistently with the group's worldview.

The Oklahoma City bombing was an attack carried out in April 1995 by Timothy McVeigh and Terry Nichols at the Alfred P. Murrah Federal Building. The two had been unhappy with how the federal government had handled the 1993 siege of the Branch Davidian's compound in Waco, Texas, and other investigations carried out by federal investigators. McVeigh decided to bomb a federal building in retaliation for these previous incidents.

McVeigh and Nichols gathered supplies to create a large bomb, and they placed these in the back of a rental truck that they parked in front of the federal building that housed multiple agencies, including the FBI, DEA, and ATF. McVeigh detonated the bomb, which destroyed or damaged more than 300 buildings and resulted in the deaths of 168 people and the injury of hundreds more. Nineteen of the victims were children, most of whom were in the day care center at the federal building. This remains one of the deadliest mass killings in U.S. history.

International

U.S. citizens and property have been attacked abroad on several occasions in recent history. These terrorist attacks outside U.S. territory have resulted in the murder of many American citizens. There is symbolic and consequently often strategic value in attacking Americans. Neumayer and Plümper (2011) examined attacks against Americans with the belief that such attacks would benefit the terrorists in their attempts to influence politics within *their own* countries.

Neumayer and Plümper (2011) continued their analysis by asserting that the majority of terrorist attacks on Americans are by groups who are in conflict with their own governments. Further, they found that the terrorists' home countries are typically receiving military aid from the United States. They point out a number of strategic reasons for attacking foreigners: media coverage of attacks is a function of the nationality of terror victims; the acknowledgment of peers in the terrorist's home country or region; and governments accepting U.S. (or Western) aid may take unpopular measures at home that increase friction with the attacking terror group.

Genocide

As a society, we are greatly concerned when a person or group attacks other people because of the victims' racial, ethnic, or national identity. Such *hate crimes* are often investigated by multiple agencies, including federal law enforcement, and the sanctions for such crimes are enhanced through legislation. When a government or group attempts to exterminate an entire group simply because of their intended victims' affiliation or identity, this is called **genocide**.

The Office of the United Nations Special Adviser on the Prevention of Genocide (OSAPG) provides this definition of genocide from Article 2 of the Convention on the Prevention and Punishment of the Crime of Genocide (1948):

> any of the following acts committed with intent to destroy, in whole or in part, a national, ethnical, racial or religious group, as such: killing members of the group; causing serious bodily or mental harm to members of the group; deliberately inflicting on the group conditions of life calculated to bring about its physical destruction in whole or in part; imposing measures intended to prevent births within the group; [and] forcibly transferring children of the group to another group.

The OSAPG commentary adds that the following is the aim of the Genocide Convention:

> to prevent the intentional destruction of entire human groups, and the part targeted must be significant enough (substantial) to have an impact on the group as a whole. The substantiality

requirement both captures genocide's defining character as a crime of massive proportions (numbers) and reflects the Convention's concern with the impact the destruction of the targeted part will have on the overall survival of the group (emblematic).

Acts of genocide within the boundaries of the United States are not a contemporary focus of government intervention. More frequently, the United States is engaged with other countries in trying to address instances of potential genocide perpetrated in other parts of the world. In historical context, an act of genocide has been debated by those who perpetrated acts so labeled and those who apply the label. History is replete with the efforts of one group to eliminate, dominate, or obscure the existence of another group. The most notorious act of genocide known in modern times was the Holocaust. The political party in power under Adolf Hitler attempted to exterminate all European Jews. The Nazis and their subordinate groups murdered approximately six million Jews.

ACTS OF TERROR

Terrorists are known for committing brutal acts. These acts are intended to strike fear into a civilian population. Violent attacks against specific groups can underscore the vulnerability of the population and attract the media coverage needed to maintain the terror group's public profile. Actions against individuals by terrorists include kidnappings and murder. Kidnapping or hostage-taking in this context involves political motivation or furtherance of a professed religious movement by holding one or more people for a ransom. This differs from a straightforward criminal kidnapping, where money is the end rather than the means to finance further group acts.

We have witnessed a dramatic increase in the killing of people by terrorists through the use of ever-evolving weaponry. A lone Sicarii or zealot with a knife could have only limited effectiveness beyond a single target. One or several attackers with automatic weapons, a suicide bomber, or the release of a biologic or radiologic weapon can kill so many more victims. A tragic example was a December 2015 mass shooting in California that law enforcement and the White House labelled a terrorist incident. A radicalized American, Syed Rizwan Farook, and his wife, Tashfeen Malik, killed 14 and wounded 21 other people at a holiday party of Farook's coworkers in San Bernardino. The couple supported ISIS, though they may never have met nor communicated with any of its members.

Suicide Bombings

We have established that over the course of history, various individuals and groups have been willing to use violent methods to further their agendas or attempt to influence the views and

WHY WOULD THEY DO IT?

On November 13, 2015, in Paris and the northern suburb Saint-Denis, France, a series of coordinated terrorist attacks including suicide bombings and mass shootings at several locations resulted in the deaths of 130 people and injuries to over 400 more. The attacks included the mass shootings of people attending the Eagles of Death Metal concert at the Bataclan Theater where three heavily armed men entered the building about 30 minutes after the concert had begun. The attacks were the deadliest in France since the Second World War and were the deadliest in Europe since the Madrid train bombings in 2004. France had been in a high state of alert since the Charlie Hebdo attacks earlier in the year. The Islamic State of Iraq and the Levant (ISIL) took responsibility for the attack which had been planned in Syria and carried out by an organized terror cell in Belgium. Following the attacks, the French government declared a three month state of emergency during which time it carried out numerous measures focused on fighting terrorism across the country.

actions of those in power and of normal civilians. Media coverage can be intense, and the burgeoning use of social media augments and sometimes exaggerates the destructive magnitude of an attack. That these violent methods often include the acceptance of the attackers' deaths through their own actions has also been common. Explosives are concealed in various ways and delivered by vehicles as well as directly on someone's body. The deaths and injuries can be significant as well as destruction of property and disruption to social activity, schools, and commerce.

Violence by those labeled terrorists is used to demoralize the public. When terrorists kill civilians, such as those murdered in the Oklahoma City bombing in 1995, the 9/11 attacks, or the Boston Marathon bombing in 2013, the effects are often not what the terrorists intended. In the short term, we observed many Americans avoiding going into federal buildings after Oklahoma City. People canceled or avoided commercial flights after 9/11. But this was only for a while. "Boston Strong" became more than a catchphrase as runners from America as well as other countries flocked to participate in the subsequent 2014 Boston Marathon as a show of solidarity for the citizens of Boston. One World Trade Center was built on the site of the World Trade Center destruction, and the building opened in November 2014.

The use of murder as a tool of terror is observed to impact the citizenry of different countries or regions within countries in different ways. If the country does not have a strong governmental structure or a stable political and economic system and citizens feel disenfranchised on the whole, terror attacks may indeed have a demoralizing effect and lead people to believe they may benefit by not resisting terrorists. If the protection of citizens is generally sound and the government is viewed as legitimate and relatively competent, there is far less likelihood that terrorists will achieve significant or any progress with their agenda. As an example, on May 22, 2017, American pop star Ariana Grande was performing a concert in Manchester, England. Salman Abedi, a British citizen of Libyan ancestry, detonated an improvised explosive device and killed 22 people and injured over 500 others in attendance at the concert. On June 4, 13 days later, Grande and other artists hosted One Love Manchester at a different venue in Manchester to raise money for the victims and to demonstrate solidarity in response to acts of terrorism. The Greater Manchester Police Department and the U.K. government devoted increased security resources and personnel for the concert. Following the One Love concert, British Prime Minster Theresa May made public statements that the citizens of Manchester had joined together to demonstrate strength and resilience against terrorists.

Various explosive compounds and devices have been refined over more than 1,000 years, and as the materials became more stable and the delivery mechanisms more discriminate, the use of explosives increased. The use of explosives to wreak havoc and kill innocent civilians has been seen worldwide. Small and innocuous items can conceal lethal amounts of explosive materials. Increased fear of the use of nuclear material to construct bombs or to function as a contaminating component of conventional bombs has caused governments to focus on ways to contain

The Moscow theater hostage crisis occurred in October 2002. Approximately 50 Chechens took control of a theater containing 800 people in central Moscow. The hostage-takers were armed and possessed explosives. While the Chechens demanded that Russia cease trying to again force their dominance over Chechnya, the Chechens threatened the death of the hostages to show their determination.

The Russians responded by attempting a rescue using gas pumped into the theater to render everyone unconscious. The Russians killed the unconscious hostage-takers and disarmed the explosives. The use of the narcotic gas by the Russians killed more than 100 of the hostages.

or control the technologies and materials that can enable terrorist organizations to construct such devices.

ISIS Beheadings

Attacks using edged weapons have, as we have already mentioned, a long history in terror attacks. While the use of swords and daggers is well known in warfare, the use of such weapons to kill civilians in the current day is often intended to increase the dramatic effect of the murders. In 2014 and 2015, many people, including Americans, were murdered by the group the Islamic State of Iraq and Syria, also known as ISIS, ISIL, and the Islamic State.

The beheadings of many people captured by ISIS, including Westerners, has met with widespread condemnation. Such a brutal method of killing is seen as a way to strike back at the United States for military action it has taken against ISIS. This brutality, while shocking, may seem to be a small act compared to the powerful military strikes that can be delivered by formal armed forces. Such killings, however, may be some of the only actions ISIS can take. The use of beheadings and the like are also employed as a tactic of recruitment to their group. In addition, terror groups seek to establish their reputation and garner media attention by the use of brutality.

Criminal Terrorism

Alvarez and Bachman (2014) discuss the use of terror tactics to further a criminal enterprise. They cite a potent example in the acts perpetrated by the Medellín drug cartel, operating primarily in Mexico. The cartel stymied the efforts of the Mexican government and military through asymmetrical warfare using bombings and assassinations. These actions were to protect the financial interests of the drug cartel.

The use of various tactics to acquire funding for terrorist organizations is ongoing. Al-Qaeda and other groups use credit card fraud to gain money. Kidnapping for ransom is notably employed by Boko Haram in Africa, al-Qaeda

and its affiliates, Abu Sayyaf in the Philippines, and many others. The use of kidnapping for ransom, like many tactics of terrorists and organized-crime groups, is nothing new.

WHO ARE TERRORISTS?

Those who would be recruited to groups such as ISIS are often stereotyped as possessed of specific demographic characteristics. But Laqueur (1999) and others have pointed out that no single profile exists. The characteristics of one group, at one point in time, in one location, with one set of grievances, may differ markedly from others similarly labeled terrorist. In fact, most contemporary groups and individuals would reject the term and self-identify as a "freedom fighter, a guerrilla, a militant, an insurgent, a rebel, a revolutionary—anything but a terrorist, a killer of random innocents" (Laqueur, 2006, para. 22). While there is no universal terrorist profile, the commonality remains the willingness to kill civilians as a way to intimidate and to draw media coverage.

Terrorist actions in the United States and in other countries have historically been aimed at maintaining the status quo, augmenting nationalistic political rhetoric, changing conditions for labor, alleviating perceived relative deprivation, and advancing a twisted view of one religion or another. Extremist ideology and the violent pursuit of a political agenda are not new in the United States or in other countries. The United States has encountered groups identified as left-wing, right-wing, and single-issue terrorists. The distinctions among the various ideologies and issues of differing groups are important to understanding and countering violent crime.

Left Wing

Left-wing terrorist groups formed in the United States from the 1960s through the 1980s and arose from some of the student movements opposed to the Vietnam War. A dwindling number of student activists resulted in the decline of a central national issue and a move to more and smaller single-issue activities. Some of the single-issue causes that have used destruction of property as a mainstay tactic include animal rights groups, such as the Animal Liberation Front (ALF) and People for the Ethical Treatment of Animals (PETA), and ecological groups, like the Earth Liberation Front (ELF) and Greenpeace. While these particular groups have caused significant damage to equipment and cost individuals and corporations huge sums of money, they have generally avoided personal violence.

A number of groups arising in the 1960s and 1970s were not averse to the use of violence. The Revolutionary Armed Task Force (RATF) of the early 1980s arose from remnants of some of the groups from the 60s and 70s, such as the Weather Underground and the Black Liberation Army. Whites and blacks espousing a Marxist-Leninist ideology of anti-capitalism worked together through committing robberies, assassinations, and bombings to bring about an end to U.S. political and social institutions. The end of the Vietnam War, and a failure to agree on a guiding philosophy, saw the decline and eventually cessation of most of the groups involved in the movements of the previous two decades.

Right Wing

Right-wing terrorist groups in the past several decades have clung to extremist religious ideologies and national and international conspiracy theories of economic controls. Groups resisting state and federal government actions remain active and are seen in militias, white supremacist organizations, and others. The use of a perverted form of Christianity has drawn followers within the United States as many detached individuals struggle to find a purpose or guidance or give a coherent shape through a group to some of their own views. The bombing of the Murrah Federal Building in Oklahoma City by Timothy McVeigh and Terry Nichols is an example of an attack associated with a right-wing ideology. White supremacists who have murdered African Americans also fall under this category of terrorism or hate crime.

The extremist practices of groups like the Ku Klux Klan (KKK) have been responsible for many deaths and terrorizing citizens from just after the Civil War and continue today through various militias, skinheads, and others. Many of the members of such organizations train in military tactics and weapons use for eventual use in what they see as a religious and racial war within the country. The criminal justice system must deal with the crimes and dangers posed by such groups all across the United States. To this end, government and nonprofit groups track and document the activities of hundreds of groups labelled as hate groups throughout the United States.

Lone Wolf or Lonely Guy?

So-called **lone-wolf terrorists** act outside the structure of a terrorist organization or even the small-cell format of many groups. This modus operandi has several implications. For law enforcement, it is far more challenging to intervene and prevent the actions of someone who is not working in concert with others. There are no communications to intercept and no pattern of behaviors among associates to triangulate. Great strides have been made by law enforcement and intelligence organizations to disrupt and prevent hostile actions, but the concern about homegrown terrorists in the United States challenges the methods of authorities. If an individual is not part of or responsive to a group, his strike may be without warning and can only be defended by physical security measures in place at an intended target.

Aside from this practical concern, another aspect of individuals at least initially identified as lone wolves is the true motivation or mindset of the person. In other words, are they truly committed to an organization's cause, or are they looking to claim an affiliation to point to when they commit acts of violence? It is simplistic and largely inaccurate to say that terrorists are crazy. While some individuals within different movements or groups are surely burdened by mental illness, most studies do not find that this is a major characteristic of rank-and-file terrorists. More commonly, the members of such groups view their actions as rational and consistent with their aims. On the other hand, several lone-wolf perpetrators of violence have been identified as having

In October 2014, Zale Thompson of New York City attacked four police officers with a hatchet. The self-radicalized convert to Islam was ubiquitously seen on video across the country as he began his daylight assault on the police officers.

Former New York City Police Commissioner Bill Bratton labeled the incident a terrorist attack. Deputy Commissioner John Miller, in charge of intelligence and counter-terrorism for the NYPD, said that Thompson was self-directed and was not affiliated with a particular terrorist group. Law enforcement review of the man's Internet activity showed searches for ISIS, al-Qaeda, and beheadings. His social-media postings were described as anti-Western.

The attack came within days of two apparent lone-wolf terrorist attacks on soldiers in Canada. All of the attacks were in public places during daylight hours. Some of the ways that large law enforcement agencies in cities that have been or are potential targets work to prevent attacks is assigning officers to foreign locations. The NYPD has officers embedded in more than ten locations around the globe to monitor and analyze activities that may pose a threat to New York City.

suffered mental illness. Whether an individual's mental state influenced a lone-wolf-type attack or he wanted to commit a violent act and attribute the motivation to a cause, such incidents are shocking and hard, if not impossible, to predict.

At the end of 2014, separate attacks in the United States, Australia, and Canada illustrated the lone-wolf phenomenon. It is apparent that some of the individuals had been radicalized abroad or by groups in the West, while others had been self-radicalized through the messages of groups such as ISIS. Al-Qaeda and ISIS have told followers to commit such independent attacks since larger, more involved efforts are difficult to carry out in Western nations.

In October 2014, a 32-year-old New York man described as a *Muslim extremist* attacked four police officers with a hatchet, injuring two of the officers before being shot dead by the police. Important in such instances is not to too hastily categorize an attack or killing as the result of a devotion to a religion or movement. The hatchet-wielding assailant in this case was described as having issues of mental illness and had only in the past two years converted to Islam and then self-radicalized. Consideration of such an event raises a discussion of what the motivation of an attack actually stems from. Is an individual with a serious mental illness who aligns himself with his perception of a religion or movement but is not steeped in a particular religion a religious zealot carrying out a message of hate? Or are the person's actions to be interpreted as more complex or, at the least, not correctly identified as stemming from a religion? Mercier, Norris, and Shariff (2018) conducted research about whether average citizens may see certain people committing terrorist acts to be more likely mentally ill if they were identified as Muslim. Their findings showed that "Muslim shooters were seen as less mentally ill than non-Muslim shooters, but only by those with negative views toward Muslims" (p. 772).

The December 2014 incident in Sydney, Australia, involved a man who took a number of people hostage in a cafe. The standoff lasted approximately 17 hours before police and military special forces entered the cafe and killed the hostage-taker. Also in October of that year, two separate individuals attacked Canadian soldiers in Montreal and Ottawa. In the first attack, a man believed by authorities to have become radicalized ran down two soldiers using a car. One of the soldiers died as a result of the injuries, and the man fled in his car, was chased by police before wrecking, and was shot after getting out of his car with a knife. In the same week, a Canadian soldier was gunned down at the Canadian War Memorial where he was guarding the Tomb of the Unknown Soldier. After shooting the soldier, the gunman walked the short distance to the Canadian Parliament building, entered, and was subsequently shot and killed by a security officer.

In the United States, examples of well-known lone-wolf attacks are included in Table 11.1.

Table 11.1 Sample of Lone-Wolf Attacks in the United States

1995	Oklahoma City, OK	Timothy McVeigh	Killed 168 and injured hundreds more
1978–1995	Various	Theodore Kaczynski	Known as the "Unabomber"; mailed bombs that killed three and wounded 23
1996–1998	Various in Southeast	Eric Rudolph	Bombings killed three and injured at least 150
1999	Los Angeles, CA	Buford Furrow	White supremacist injured five at Jewish daycare and then shot and killed a mail carrier
2006	Chapel Hill, NC	Mohammed Reza Taheri-azar	Drove a vehicle into a crowd of students at UNC injuring nine
2009	Little Rock, AR	Abdul Mujahid Muhammad	Shot two soldiers at the recruiting office, killing one
2009	Fort Hood, TX	Nidal Malik Hassan	Shot and killed 13 and wounded 30 others
2010	Austin, TX	Joseph Stack	Flew small airplane into IRS building, killing one and injuring 13
2013	Boston, MA	Dzhokhar and Tamerlan Tsarnaev	Set off two homemade bombs at finish line of Boston Marathon, killing three and wounding 260 others
2014	New York, NY	Zale Thompson	Attacked four police officers with a hatchet before being shot dead
2015	Merced, CA	Faisal Mohammad	ISIS-inspired attack, shot and killed by University of California police after stabbing four people on the campus
2016	Philadelphia, PA	Edward Archer	Rushed the squad car of a patrol officer and fired 13 shots, wounding the officer severely; officer was able to chase the man and return fire before he was taken into custody
2016	Orlando, FL	Omar Mateen	Killed 49 people and wounded 53 more at a nightclub; claimed he was motivated by American involvement in Iraq and Syria
2017	Las Vegas, NV	Stephen Paddock	Described by police as a lone wolf, he used automatic-style rifles to kill 59 and wound hundreds, firing on them from the 32nd floor of a casino hotel
2018	Florida resident	Cesar Altieri Sayoc	Mailed 16 improvised explosive devices (IEDs) to 13 victims around the U. S.

Source: Compiled from various news sources.

It is important to consider international context when discussing murder by those categorized as terrorist. In January 2015, an apparent sleeper cell of al-Qaeda in the Arabian Peninsula (AQAP) attacked the French satirical magazine *Charlie Hebdo*, killing 12 people. The attack was motivated by what AQAP considered offensive references to the Muslim Prophet Muhammad. Around this same time, another even more horrific act took place when Islamist militants of Boko Haram killed an estimated 2,000 or more children, women, and men in several villages in Nigeria. This was part of a continuing effort by Boko Haram to create an Islamist state from their beginnings as a group opposing Western education for people in various regions of Africa. And then in October 2015, terrorists planted a bomb on a Russian airliner filled with tourists returning from Egypt. On November 13 of the same year, terrorists launched numerous simultaneous attacks in Paris, resulting in at least 130 deaths and more than 400 injured.

HATE CRIMES AND KILLING

Extremist groups, including those who commit crimes of violence against others based on some aspect of the victim's identity such as race, ethnicity, or religion, are not to be considered cults or even new religious movements (NRMs). Some of these groups may try to claim the mantle of religion by perverting the dictates of established religions. We mention hate crimes here because we do not want to ignore the murders committed by individuals and groups who use hatred toward another group as the basis of their actions, with the intent of terrorizing a group of individuals, not just the immediate victim(s). Many of the groups that espouse hatred of others also assert a nonviolent message, though some followers are inspired by the hate rhetoric to do violence. We recognize the scholarly debate about *where* to place the discussion of hate homicide. The categorization in law of hate crime represents the need to call attention to those who target entire groups for violence.

Our aim is to provide the student a broad understanding of the use of homicide to influence or terrorize others.

Many groups or movements have a driving or central theme without necessarily having a well-defined or consensus leader. This is evident in the ways that some may express their views (including hatred) about people of a certain category defined by the antagonist or hate group. The murder-suicide by a white supremacist at a Sikh temple in Oak Creek, Wisconsin, in 2012, is an example of a hate crime that also blurs the boundary or shows the dual category of **domestic terrorism**. The killer shot 10 victims, killing five, before he killed himself after being wounded in a shootout with police. The perpetrator had evidence of a troubled past and participation in a number of groups who espoused white power. The FBI did not describe this killer's actions, however, as being tied to a group or other people of like mind.

In 1999, at a Jewish community center in Los Angeles, another individual described as a white supremacist entered the center and started shooting. He wounded five people, including three children, before fleeing. After his rampage, the suspect, who had been treated previously for mental illness, shot and killed a postal worker near the Jewish center. He then abandoned his vehicle and fled by taxi, ending up in Las Vegas, where he turned himself in at an FBI field office. The motivation to harm or kill those who are *different* from the assailant or who appear to represent something the assailant hates crosses most boundaries and results in many homicides in this and other countries.

Legislative action has enhanced the penalties for crimes that are identified as being bias or hate based. The particular bias of someone committing an act may be racial, but it may also be based on gender, sexual identity, religion, or other factors. Society considers such crimes as more serious than the underlying charges alone because they are directed at groups of people. Violent hate crimes in the United States are tracked by many states and the federal government, in part due to federal and state laws mandating such collection. Many states, however, do not collect such data,

Pulse Nightclub Shooting

In Orlando, an attack on the Pulse nightclub came suddenly and brutally. Twenty-nine-year-old security guard Omar Mateen had apparently intended to target a shopping and entertainment complex, but after learning about the security measures in place, decided to attack a nightclub instead. He killed 49 people and wounded 53 more.

Mateen entered the largely LGBTQ nightclub on June 11, 2016. The evening's "Latin Night" had drawn a largely Hispanic group of patrons, and it was initially thought the attack may have been motivated for homophobic reasons. The killer was armed with a semi-automatic rifle and a semi-automatic pistol and entered the club before last call in the early hours of June 12th. Mateen was initially encountered by an Orlando police officer working security at the nightclub before making his way further into the bar where he began shooting patrons.

Nearly 200 law enforcement, EMS, and firefighter first responders arrived, and most of the injured and dying were transported to a nearby hospital over the course of the hostage situation that resulted. Law enforcement officers eventually breached the building using explosives, engaged the gunman, and killed him. In the trial of Mateen's wife on charges that she aided and abetted her husband and obstructed justice, evidence was produced that indicated Mateen's desire for revenge against the United States for its efforts against ISIS and ISIL.

Emanuel African Methodist Episcopal Church Shooting

On June 17, 2015, at the Emanuel African Methodist Episcopal Church in Charleston, South Carolina, a 21-year-old white man came to a Bible study meeting and participated for an hour with the assembled group. The shooter, Dylann Roof, took a .45-caliber handgun out of a pack, and while shouting racial epithets, began firing on the church members.

Nine people were murdered, and three others were injured before the killer fled. Roof was arrested the day after the mass shooting. He has been shown in photographs with white supremacy paraphernalia, and it appears he posted a website with his racial enmity obvious in comments. The Charleston police chief called the shooting a hate crime. The prosecutor announced plans to seek the death penalty in the case.

do not have hate crime legislation, and do not have civil remedies. In 2017, the FBI documented 7,106 single-bias incidents with the following breakdown:

- 59.6 percent were race/ethnicity/ancestry motivated

- 15.8 percent resulted from sexual-orientation bias

- 20.6 percent were motivated by religious bias

- 1.9 percent were prompted by disability bias

- 1.6 percent were motivated by gender-identity bias

- 0.6 percent resulted from gender bias (FBI, 2018)

ROLE OF THE MEDIA

An important theme in our analysis of homicide in America throughout this textbook is the role that the media plays in our understanding of such violence. The media impact is especially evident in the general public's view of terrorism. Terrorist organizations hope for media coverage but also utilize various forms of electronic communication via the Internet. They arrange and hold meetings in chat rooms, they post training and propaganda materials at URLs, and they recruit followers using the medium. Attacks are carried out with a primary purpose of attracting attention and publicizing the group's agenda through the media.

Media coverage is often designed to dramatize an event. This includes the use of language and terms that can present a misperception to the public about the motivations and legitimacy of people committing acts of violence. Poland (2011) points out that "groups and individuals are often referred to as rebels, freedom fighters, commandos, guerillas, protestors, dissidents, rioters, extremists, or jihadists" (p. 52) and that the variety of terms confuse many people. He says, and we agree, that the connotation of many terms may provide an air of legitimacy to the actions of some such groups, both in their own minds and in those of the various publics who receive news accounts of violence.

News accounts also serve the intended purpose of informing people of acts in their community, region, nation, and the world. Information can help us put violence and the motives of people who commit violence into perspective. Raising awareness of hate crimes helps mobilize public opinion and brings about legislative action and direct law enforcement efforts. Thorough and conscientious journalism is a hallmark of a free society and an institution rooted in the U.S. Constitution and valued in most countries around the world. The media can facilitate warning citizens of potential hazards and urge them to contact authorities with information about possible criminal activity.

STOPPING TERRORISTS

The individual pathway to a planned murder is, well, individual. The type of planned murder addressed in this chapter involves killing another human (or many of them) based upon a bias against some demographic not like you (hate homicide) and those philosophically inconsistent with your own worldview (terrorism). We began the chapter noting that we would not endeavor to talk at length about terrorism, leaving that to others who focus more specifically on this important area of study. Our observations and examples illustrate the use of homicide mainly against civilians by people and groups to forward their efforts regardless of compassion or effectiveness. Some individuals come to a belief system or political movement at a point in their lives that makes them susceptible to the fervor of rhetoric. Some cling to the message or to the messenger. Some terrorists come from poor backgrounds and choose to join a group perhaps based on limited options. Other terrorists come from middle or even upper-class socioeconomic groups in their respective societies.

WHY WOULD THEY DO IT?

The Boston Marathon bombings occurred on April 15, 2013, near the finish line of the race. Two Chechen brothers, Dzhokhar and Tamerlan Tsarnaev, set off two homemade pressure-cooker bombs placed about 200 yards apart. The bombs killed three people and injured approximately 260 more. After leaving the scene, the brothers murdered a local police officer, stole a car, and exchanged gunfire with police, during which Tamerlan was wounded and Dzhokhar fled in the stolen vehicle. Tamerlan died at the scene of the firefight.

In a massive manhunt for Dzhokhar Tsarnaev, 20 blocks of Watertown, Massachusetts, were closed down, and well over 1,000 officers went door to door. Many more officers fanned out across the Boston area on the possibility that the homegrown terrorist had escaped the cordon or that other individuals might commit another act. Dzhokhar Tsarnaev was captured and claimed that his brother Tamerlan had been self-radicalized and was the one who initiated the bombings.

Dzhokhar Tsarnaev was convicted in early 2015, and in May sentenced to death.

The 2008 Mumbai, India, attacks evoked the fear of what many people believe can happen and what Hollywood can depict—coordinated multiple attacks in dense urban areas of civilians. Over a span of four days in November 2008, terrorists identified as members of Lashkare-Taiba struck in 12 locations, shooting people and detonating bombs. In the attacks, 164 people died and more than 300 were injured.

The one attacker captured alive was a Pakistani citizen and claimed that the Pakistan InterServices Intelligence (ISI) agency supported the attacks. Pakistan denied the assertion, though it was confirmed that planning of the attacks was at least partly carried out in Pakistan. The 10 terrorists received continued instructions via cell phone from inside Pakistan during the attacks.

History is replete with examples of the use of murder and violence to further the aims of groups and individuals. The use of instrumental violence as a means to an end for political movements may not represent an effective strategy as much as a propaganda one. Government efforts to deter, interrupt, or, if necessary, retroactively investigate acts of terrorist violence face several challenges. Deterrence is pursued through intelligence gathering, physical security measures, and programs that attempt to address some societal conditions that give rise to groups that would use violence.

SUMMARY

Several of the categories of murderers we discuss here and elsewhere in the book differ from *ordinary* homicides in society. Terrorists, cult adherents, and hate crime offenders are typically committed to a person or a cause and kill based on the instructions of the leader or consistent with the espoused ideology. If there is coordination and communication within a group, there are opportunities for law enforcement and intelligence efforts to discover some activities of a terrorist organization and perhaps intervene. Less vulnerable to deterrent efforts are lone-wolf attackers who operate outside any group and who do not answer to a central authority. Communicating with no one, the lone-wolf attacker can plan and execute an attack at will, with only already-in-place security measures to counter a spontaneous attack.

Terrorist attacks employ all manner of weaponry, from edged weapons to firearms, biological and chemical agents, explosives, cars, and airplanes. Following different attacks, there has been legislative action to limit the means and methods of terrorists.

Tracking of explosives, including fertilizer, after the Oklahoma City bombing became more tightly regulated. Methods of financing terrorist activities have been dramatically reduced through changes in the law. Cockpit doors were reinforced following the 9/11 attacks. Federal agencies, including the Department of Homeland Security (DHS) and the Transportation Safety Administration (TSA), were created to deploy comprehensive measures aimed at prevention and interdiction of terrorist activities.

Domestic terrorism as well as the perhaps more well-known **international terrorism** present specific challenges for the many agencies tasked with addressing the problem. **Single-issue terrorists**, such as those acting to call attention to animal rights, ecological concerns, or abortion, commit crimes against property as well as people. Some groups see violence as an effective or the only viable tactic to draw attention to their issues.

Violence will likely always draw media attention, and this serves the purpose of terrorists, even if it is not effective in the pursuit of their goals.

Media coverage can also assist the public and law enforcement in disseminating and gathering information. Legislation is used to deter terrorist violence by regulating acts and access to materials and methods used to carry out violence. Law enforcement agencies, including the Department of Homeland Security, employ a wide variety of intelligence gathering and preventive strategies. DHS recognizes that the public and local-level police agencies are often best positioned to notice irregularities in their own communities that may indicate the actions of would-be terrorists.

Hate killings have dwindled but not gone away in the United States. The legacy of such crimes is a part of the story of our country. The underlying biases and emotions that lead a person to hate or disregard another human based on some demographic characteristic remain a present and troubling aspect of contemporary life in many countries. The hate-based actions of someone are often intended to *send a message* to others. Such behavior reinforces reciprocal emotions in some and resolve to end hate-based enmity in others.

KEY TERMS

Hate crime 174
Sicarii 175
Assassinations 176
Genocide 177

Left-wing terrorist groups 180
Right-wing terrorist
   groups 181
Lone-wolf terrorists 181

Domestic terrorism 184
International terrorism 187
Single-issue terrorists 187

DISCUSSION QUESTIONS

1. Why do groups and individuals carry out homicide credited to their terror group?
2. What are some of the motivations of domestic terrorists?
3. Why are lone-wolf terrorists particularly difficult for law enforcement to interdict?
4. Define hate crimes. How do these differ from terrorist acts?
5. Describe and discuss the effects of media in covering terrorists and terror organizations.
6. How do government agencies in the United States address terrorism? How do they coordinate with the law enforcement agencies of other countries?
7. Discuss the rationale of those who commit hate crimes.

TRY THIS

Examine the definition of terrorism stated by several government and not-for-profit agencies. Compare the similarities and differences as you consider the mission of the respective agency. Discuss how the agency missions are reflected in the terrorism definitions they use.

The FBI works on investigating acts of terrorism affecting U.S. citizens. Go to http://www.fbi.gov/about-us/history/famous-cases/anthrax-amerithrax/amerithrax-investigation and review several of the famous terrorism cases listed there. How do these groups share the motivations and methods described in this chapter?

Visit the "Special Feature: Hate Crime" page of the National Criminal Justice Reference Service (NCJRS) at https://www.ncjrs.gov/spotlight/hate_crimes/summary.html. Look through the topical resources and talk about some of the resources available to help agencies and communities deal with hate crime.

12

SERIAL KILLING

"There are very few people who are going to look into the mirror and say, 'That person I see is a savage monster'; instead, they make up some construction that justifies what they do."

—Noam Chomsky

CHAPTER OUTLINE

Introduction

Myth and Mayhem

    Race and Serial Killings

    Gangs, Organized Crime, and Serial Killing

Typologies

Profiling Serial Killers

Female Serial Killers

Medical or Health Care Serial Killers

Team Serial Killers

Catching Serial Killers

Summary

Key Terms

Discussion Questions

Try This

Student Learning Outcomes

Students will be able to:

- define serial killing.

- compare and contrast the common typologies within serial murder.

- describe the motivations of various types of serial killers.

- explain the role of research and data in identifying and catching serial killers.

INTRODUCTION

Most criminal homicide in the United States is the result of an argument or secondary to a different crime. A person who kills one individual may do it on impulse in the moment, not through premeditation. **Serial murders** are rare. Regardless of the comparative infrequency of serial killings to confrontational murder or intimate partner homicide (IPH), both of which we discuss fully in other chapters, it is this manner of sequential and often seemingly random murder that enthralls us beyond most others. While the tragic results of a serial killer's work are horrifying, we cannot help being interested in the person responsible for such mayhem.

We need only look at the proliferation of fiction novels, movies, and television to gauge the popularity of the *story line* of serial killers. Another measure of the fascination with individuals who commit multiple murders is the increased study and attention paid to them by academic researchers. Serial killing has been defined by different researchers or groups as either two or more, three or more, or even four or more people killed over at least one month with a cooling off period between each of the murders. In defining serial killing, we consider the *point* of the definition. Academic researchers and law enforcement examine cases with a purpose of better understanding the creation or development of individuals who commit these crimes and with the intention to prevent or catch killers, respectively. Journalists also are keenly interested in the case of a serial killer for the reader interest such stories generate.

Settling on three versus four victims is not so important, we believe, as the fact of the cooling off period in between. The interim period allows and ensures that the person has the opportunity to reflect on what he did. We know that for many serial killers, this period of reflection may include a number of different emotions and thoughts. The killer may dwell on the pleasure he felt at his treatment of and ultimate murder of another human. Further, he may contemplate the *effectiveness* of his approach to his victim and the tactics he used to achieve the ends he desired. This aspect of the post-event behavior gave rise to the observation by members of the FBI's Behavioral Science Unit that serial killers may be categorized as *organized* or *disorganized* killers (Ressler, Burgess, & Douglas, 1988). The concept is straightforward enough to summarize as follows: The organized killer plans out the crime and clears away evidence to prevent discovery of his identity; the scene of a murder by the disorganized killer exhibits spontaneity of the crime and little or haphazard attempts at concealment of evidence. The utility and accuracy of such a dichotomous classification has long been questioned, and objections have grown as researchers have gained deeper understanding of motives and behavior of serial killers (Taylor, Lambeth, Green, Bone, & Cahillane, 2012).

Entire books have been written on the topic, by academic researchers (see Fox, Levin, & Fridel, 2018; Hickey, 2015; Holmes & Holmes, 2010), novelists, and journalists (e.g., Truman Capote's *In Cold Blood* or Ann Rule's *The Stranger Beside Me*). Some focus on telling the stories of select serial killers while others present a more comprehensive treatment of potential pathways of the offenders, investigative efforts to catch such killers, and ideas of how to identify active or budding serial killers. There are few adults in America who could not name one or more serial killers. If murder intrigues us, then serial killing holds an even higher level of fascination. With this said, serial murder is rare (Cooper & Smith, 2011). This partly explains the lack of attention to the crime by academic researchers until relatively recently.

The murder investigation is arguably the most important type of criminal investigation. Identifying a person or persons responsible for the ongoing selection and killing of victims then becomes even more important. Technological progress in forensics aids the effort at early identification and intervention with serial criminals (White, Lester, Gentile, & Rosenbleeth, 2011).

Serial murder is not new. There are historical commentaries on the use of poison as a method of disposing of many enemies of Roman rulers (Kaufman, 1932; Retief & Cilliers, 2004). Reasons explored or asserted for serial murder have been many and diverse, including demonic possession, biological factors, emotional detachment, childhood trauma, lack of infant attachment to mother, watching sex and violence on television, sexual arousal, vigilantism, lack of available psychiatric

Dennis Rader was a U.S. Air Force veteran, who then worked in a variety of vocations, including as a supermarket employee, at a supply company, working with alarm systems, catching dogs, and serving as a code compliance officer. Rader earned a bachelor's degree in justice administration, was on his church council, and had served as a Cub Scout leader.

From 1974 to 1991, Rader killed 10 people in Kansas, strangling and suffocating most and earning the moniker "BTK" for the bind, torture, kill method he used. Rader stopped killing but apparently missed the limelight, and so he began to communicate with news outlets in 2004. These communications led to his capture in February 2005. Rader was convicted and sentenced to serve 10 life sentences because Kansas had no death penalty.

treatment, and so on (Bartels & Parsons, 2009; Henson & Olson, 2010; Warf & Waddell, 2002; Whitman & Akutagawa, 2004). Serial murder may occur as a result of the tried-and-true motive of greed, as in the case of John Allen Muhammad and Lee Boyd Malvo. The so-called D.C. Snipers killed 10 people and injured others in the Beltway area around D.C. while demanding money to halt their killings. The chronic violent offender who kills over time is rare, but he or she has been with us for a very long time.

MYTH AND MAYHEM

Myths of any kind may often be found to have some component of accuracy. People learn what they believe to be accurate about serial murder largely from the entertainment media. The public (and students) thus informed likely have a fairly monochrome view of serial killers. Researchers too have often relied on individual case studies to illustrate or explain serial killers (Hodgkinson, Prins & Stuart-Bennett, 2017). What we know is that there are a number of reasons for multiple, sequential killing, and it is carried out in various ways. In addition, serial killers come in all shapes and sizes; there is no tried-and-true description of killers (Arndt, Hietpas, & Kim, 2004).

Race and Serial Killings

Crime statistics provide the parameters for our conceptualization of criminals, explaining who commits what type of crime and in what numbers. These figures are helpful for research and policy development when they are accurate and their limitations are noted. We recognize, for example, that many crimes are significantly underreported. We have come to realize that an early limitation of crime statistics, including the consideration of serial murders, was race-based. Many law enforcement personnel and criminologists likely did not believe that blacks committed the crime of serial killing. This resulted, in part, from various challenges of early data gathering in crime and from the bias of underenforcement in minority communities that typified past law enforcement practices. If the crime is not recognized, it does not get counted.

Gangs, Organized Crime, and Serial Killing

In the chapter that examines cults, we discuss some similarities in the social structure or organization of gangs and cults. We have also mentioned several times that there are overlaps among the various types of violence, including murders, that people commit. One similarity between gang murders and serial killing is that some gang and organized-crime members kill sequentially over time. The number of gang and organized-crime members who commit multiple murders over time is not large in comparison to other types and categories of killers, yet the unique dynamics of such enforcers or zealous members of a criminal organization deserve attention.

Gang recruitment, for many groups, has certainly involved initiations of violence, either committing violent crime or being subjected to violence. Few such sequential murders can be seen from existing research and only very few from self-reports by captured individuals. Whether a gang member repeatedly uses violence, including murder, as a subcultural practice of his group or upon the orders of a charismatic gang leader, the technical result may be a *serial* killer. Contract killings arranged and ordered by mafia leaders or other organized-crime members bring the same outcome: serialized murder by a hit man or assassin. There is historical precedence, of course, for eliminating one's rivals or enemies through the use of assassination, as discussed in the chapter where we examined murder as a tool of terror.

Table 12.1 Myths of Serial Murder

Myth	Fact
1. They are nearly all white.	One in five serial killers is black.
2. They are all male.	Nearly 17% are female.
3. They are insane.	Insanity is a legal term. Very few offenders (2–4%) are legally insane.
4. They are all lust killers.	Many are lust killers, but several cases do not involve sexual assaults, torture, or sexual mutilations.
5. They kill dozens of victims.	A few have high body counts, but most kill under 10 victims.
6. They kill alone.	About one in four have one or more partners in murder.
7. Victims are beaten, stabbed, strangled, or tortured to death.	Some victims are poisoned or shot.
8. They are all very intelligent.	Most are of average intelligence.
9. They have high mobility in the United States.	Most offenders remain in a local area.
10. They are driven to kill because they were sexually abused as children.	Many kill as a result of rejection and abandonment in childhood.
11. Most serial murderers cannot stop killing.	Some serial killers have stopped killing for several years before they killed again or until they were caught, including Dennis Rader (BTK), Jeffrey Gorton, Jeffrey Dahmer, and Theodore Kaczynski. Such offenders often substitute paraphilic behaviors or other diversions in lieu of killing.
12. Most serial killers want to be caught.	Like anyone, they learn and gain confidence from experience. Many want-to-be serial killers end up in prison after their first murder. Some become adept at concealing their identities and may feel as if they will never be caught.

Source: Hickey (2013).

In May 2018, convicted killer Samuel Little agreed to be interviewed by Texas homicide detectives and offered information about numerous unsolved killings that he claims he committed from 1970 until 2005. In 2014, Little was convicted of three murders and was sentenced to three consecutive life sentences. During his murder trial, while he maintained his innocence, several women testified that he had attempted to kill them and that they were barely able to escape his violent attacks. Little was a former boxer who officers believe knocked out his victims and then strangled them. Investigators from Texas were attempting to solve a cold case and believed that Little may have been involved. They reached out to him to ask him to be interviewed, and he agreed because he wanted to be moved from his prison in California to one in Texas. Over the course of numerous interviews, he confessed to killing close to 90 women across the United States, most of whom were involved in prostitution or drugs. Even though he is in his late 70's and the murders spanned decades, he has provided numerous specific details to investigators about the murders including descriptions of the cars he drove, pictures of the victims, and locations. While he has been connected to at least 34 murders so far, the FBI's Violent Criminal Apprehension Program (ViCAP) is still working to corroborate his confessions on the others. If his confessions prove true, Little would be considered the most prolific serial killer in U.S. history.

TYPOLOGIES

Motive and method then arise as key aspects of how we label serial killers for the purpose of studying them. As we begin to discuss the different categories that researchers and law enforcement have described to examine serial killers, it is important to warn that the categories are likely not exhaustive. As we have noted elsewhere in the book, the types overlap at times in regard to individual killers' motivations. Different serial killers have different motives for their deeds. While many of the infamous killers identified as serial killers have a component of sexual sadism (erotophonophilia) in their crimes (Wilmott, Boduszek, & Robinson, 2018), others do not seem to (Bartels & Parsons, 2009; Knight, 2006, 2007). This also goes back to the challenge of defining serial murder in a way that is inclusive, while also providing structure for discrete types along the continuum of those who kill sequentially over time. Categories have been established by examining perceived causes of and outcomes to the killings.

Jack the Ripper, who terrorized London in the 1800s, can be categorized a *mission* serial killer. This historical killer targeted a specific type of victim: prostitutes. While we cannot know his personal reasons for killing prostitutes, we can speculate on his motives. He may have seen prostitutes as immoral, and it was therefore his responsibility to rid society of them. His satisfaction may have been psychological as he performed what he considered worthy work in his mission of ridding the streets of the wicked. Alternatively, he may have sought sex through rape and then wanted to ensure that there were no witnesses. Sexual satisfaction remains a prominent motivation of many serial killers. Power and anger also fuels the behavior of some of the serial killers who seek sexual pleasure (Myers, Husted, Safarik, & O'Toole, 2006).

Colombian serial killer Luis Garavito was convicted of murdering 189 boys. Garavito, who was abused as a boy, had psychiatric illness and alcohol problems (Jenkins, 2014). He tricked boys between the ages of 8 and 16 to come with him, and he then raped the boys and mutilated their bodies. Because many of the children lived in very poor areas or did not live with their families, it is believed that many of the missing children had no one trying hard to find them.

Holmes and DeBurger (1988) created one of the first classifications of serial killers. The organization by types helps understand the *why* of such killings and killers. The four categories

Gary Leon Ridgway came to be known as the Green River Killer before he was identified or captured. Ridgway was eventually convicted of killing 49 women. Ridgway confessed to killing 71, though he says he lost count of how many he actually murdered, and there is speculation that the number of his victims was substantially higher than 49 or 71.

As a boy, Ridgway was assessed as having lower-than-average intelligence, though he graduated from high school. At the age of 16, he stabbed a 6-year-old, who survived the attack. Ridgway served in the Navy and began to frequent prostitutes during that time. He was married and divorced three times, and his wives and others said that his desire for sex was continual.

Ridgway chose prostitutes because of their accessibility, and he said that he had sex with his victims before and after killing them. In a plea arrangement, Ridgway received sentences totaling 480 years in prison rather than the death penalty in exchange for his cooperation in identifying his victims and providing information to help locate many of their remains.

developed by Holmes and DeBurger were visionary, mission, hedonistic, and power and control. Holmes and Holmes (2010) modified or expanded this list to include three subtypes of the **hedonistic killer**: *lust*, *thrill*, and *comfort*. They noted the hedonistic killer's commission of the acts as "fun and enjoyable."

The **visionary killer** may seem similar to the mission serial killer in selecting a certain type of victim. The visionary serial killer may be psychotic, resulting in some breaks with reality. The killer may hear voices or experience hallucinations where he is told to kill. The murder is generally not planned, and the killer may not bring a weapon with him. In keeping with the label of a disorganized killer, the murder scene will likely be chaotic. The visionary serial killer is often presented by the entertainment media as the archetypical, or *classic*, serial killer (Holmes & Holmes, 2010). Prosecution and trial can be complicated by the question of whether the killer should be in a psychiatric or other treatment facility or in prison.

The *mission* serial killer may regard his victims as useless to society or even blights that must be removed. The killer may believe it his responsibility to cleanse society of the meaningless creatures (Holmes & Holmes, 2010). A misguided religious zealot may consider prostitutes morally repugnant to an extent that it is only through his killings that society will be made right. Because the mission serial killer holds himself up as god-like in his quest to rid society of an evil, very few mission serial killers commit suicide (Lester & White, 2012). This killer demeans his victim to nonhuman status.

In the three distinct forms of killers, *lust* killers are regarded as having a purely sexual motivation. Sexual pleasure is the goal, and the killer may torture the victim and sexually abuse the body post mortem. For example, Gary Leon Ridgway, the Green River Killer, is considered a lust killer because after dumping the bodies of his victims, he would often return to have sex with the corpses. The kill is a thrill, but the pleasure seeking extends beyond the victim's death. Ridgway was undetected for many years, kept a job, had a home, and was married. Such killers will go to great lengths to avoid detection so that they may continue to kill.

Fictional television gives us an *entertaining* example of a **mission killer** mixed with a *hedonistic thrill* killer in the character Dexter. While the character, who is a police department employee in the series, is not a real serial killer, the example helps illustrate the motivations. Thrill serial killers get excitement from the murder. Unlike the lust killer, who may return to the body after death, this killer takes time to dispose of the body so as to remain undetected. The TV character Dexter targets other murderers, which categorizes him as a mission serial killer with a story line that he believes he is benefiting society by doing away with those who commit murder. He satisfies his own desire to kill at the same time. As with other such *thrill* killers, once the character commits the murder,

From 1979 to 1981, Wayne Williams murdered at least 22 young, black males in Atlanta. While under-enforcement of crime against African American victims had long been documented in many communities, no one could ignore the continuing disappearance of so many young, black males, ranging from 7 to 28 years old. Twenty-nine victims were believed to have been murdered in the same series of crimes attributed to the Atlanta Child Killer. The killings stopped after Williams was arrested in June 1981.

Williams fancied himself a freelance photographer and talent scout, and it is believed he used this ploy to entice young people to go with him. He had developed an interest in journalism while in high school.

Law enforcement linked fiber evidence from Williams's home and car to several of the victims. After that information was leaked to the media and widely reported there, Williams changed his M.O. and began to dump his victims into moving bodies of water in an attempt to wash away the fiber evidence. Williams volunteered to take polygraph tests during the investigation before his trial. He failed all of the tests. Individuals who worked with Williams reported that around the time of the murders, they had seen scratches on Williams's face and arms.

Williams was convicted of two of the murders and was sentenced to two life terms in prison.

---

he expends great effort to clean up a crime scene to avoid being detected. The satisfaction for this killer comes from the pain he inflicts on his victims.

Finally in this category is the *comfort* killer. Material gain is the overarching goal, though the killer may derive other satisfaction from his or her murders. The killer carefully selects the victim as compared to the random victim of opportunity of other serial-killer types (Holmes & Holmes, 2010).

A **power/control killer** known to most Americans is Ted Bundy. Bundy sought out an ideal victim type and received pleasure from exercising complete control over the person's life. This life-and-death decision by Bundy gave him sexual satisfaction. If such killers cannot find someone of their ideal victim type, and they feel the desire to kill is strong enough, a person who the killer encounters and is vulnerable may become the next victim. The power/control serial killer displays the need to be in control or manipulate his victims. This characteristic or feeling is arguably present in most or all serial killers but is a more pronounced aspect of the power/control killer. Another distinctive drive of this killer is his or her fantasy life and fulfilling those sexual fantasies through killing (Holmes & Holmes, 2010).

PROFILING SERIAL KILLERS

The general public certainly has a skewed view of forensic-science methods and how profiling actually works in the search for serial (and other) killers. Examining the different personalities, traits, and characteristics of serial killers can aid in understanding how investigations into the killers' actions are actually carried out. Many believe that the keys to adult serial killers can be found in their troubled youths. One cluster of behaviors is used by many as shorthand of sorts for a child destined for trouble. The behaviors, known as the MacDonald Triad, are chronic bed-wetting, fire-starting, and abuse of animals. This grouping, if present in a child, is certainly no guarantee of becoming a serial killer or even engaging in crime when older, but the presence of the factors in the case histories of many adult serial killers leads many to continue noting early warning signs of maladaptive behavior ahead. Recent research has also explored the relationship of these factors in connection with physical or psychological parental abuse (Leary, Southard, Hill, & Ashman, 2017).

The different types of serial killers exhibit some variety in motivations and anticipated gains. The methods of killing differ as do the locations of finding victims, murdering them, and disposing of the bodies, if the killer has the time or inclination to do so. These choices and habits can tell a good deal about the individual killer. Whether or not the scene is organized or disorganized can be important in the work of typing or profiling the serial killer. Gary Ridgway, the Green River Killer, murdered his victims in different locations yet disposed of their bodies in the same place so that he could return to the victims. In the case of Ridgway, he wanted to relive the crimes, and so he needed access. The profiling that people are somewhat familiar with is a mix of crime scene work and psychology, with a goal of creating a personality description of the killer. The level of detail about an individual killer is generally exaggerated on TV and in the movies since the data-driven profile is based in large part on percentages of what has been seen in similar cases and extrapolated to the instant case, along with any unique information.

The *Crime Classification Manual*, written by retired FBI Special Agent John Douglas and others (1992), notes that many serial killers can be categorized as organized or disorganized. While organized killers may have an outward appearance of normalcy, this is a façade that allows them to perhaps be more effective in their terrible pastime. The disorganized killer may be psychotic, kill with a spontaneity that belies concern for covering up the evidence, use available weapons rather than selecting them ahead of time, and live close to the scene of the crime (Warf & Waddell, 2002). The recognition of a murder that appears to represent the actions of a disorganized killer may help focus investigative efforts on a geographically close area and on someone who knew the victim.

The demographics of serial killers are, of course, varied, yet there are also several overlapping similarities. Hickey's (2006) studies show that the majority of identified serial killers are lower-class white males in their twenties or thirties. As noted, there are many different serial killers, including racial-minority offenders and women. Many serial killers are believed to have been abused by a family member. Also, according to Skeem, Polaschek, Patrick, and Lilienfeld (2011), many are believed to have a degree of mental illness or psychopathy.

Psychopathy is a condition characterized by personality traits that include the inability to feel guilt, deceitfulness, and poor impulse control. A distinction is generally drawn between psychopathy and **antisocial personality disorder (ASPD)**, with psychopathy seen as primarily behavior-based and ASPD as more personality-based. Persons with psychopathic personalities are not seen as necessarily aggressive. Psychopathy should not be confused with psychosis, which is a disconnection from reality (Berg et al., 2013). Not all serial killers are psychopaths. Psychopathy is more condition than category. And while some infamous serial killers have been identified or diagnosed with some mental illness, a psychopathic personality is not always a prominent feature. The psychopathic personality can encompass ASPD or other antisocial tendencies.

Identifying a typology can help understand the killer's motivations and allow law enforcement to deploy resources accordingly. Serial-killing investigations are reactive, and investigators may see several murders before enough of a pattern of evidence is compiled to apprehend a suspect. The commonalities of serial-killer characteristics may be what laypeople refer to as a profile. Profiles are not exact by any means and, in fairness to the FBI and others, were never held out to be exact. In 2008, the FBI released a report on serial murder to try to define and explain serial murder. The article discusses common myths of serial homicide and debunks them. The article acknowledges the link between psychopathy and serial killers but points out that this is not established as a sole causal factor (FBI, 2008).

Most murderers knew their victims, if only briefly or as an acquaintance. Serial-murder victims are typically strangers to their killers. Most serial killers—but not all—are males. Most are from the lower socioeconomic strata of society and are in their twenties or thirties (Hickey, 2013).

According to Skeem et al. (2011), most serial killers have some degree of mental illness or psychopathy. Some serial killers were emotionally, physically, or sexually abused by a family member. A study of 95 serial killers for whom IQs were known showed a mean IQ of 103 and a median IQ of 102, placing them in the average range (Aamodt et al., 2007). Only serial killers who had used bombs had an average IQ above the population mean. Most serial killers were not raised in a traditional nuclear family, and many were adopted (Keeney & Heide, 1994). Keeney and Heide (1994) argue that many serial killers had parents or legal guardians who were addicted to drugs and even alcohol. These factors occur with varying frequency across the different killers, but none act as a single red flag for a future serial killer.

FEMALE SERIAL KILLERS

Kelleher and Kelleher (1998) argue that "female serial killers are so different from male serial killers that the standard serial killer typologies [Holmes and DeBurger's four categories] fail to categorize female serial killers adequately" (p. 221). Kelleher and Kelleher (1998) devised nine female serial-killer types. The types are (1) the **black widows** who kill their spouses or other family members; (2) the **angels of death** who kill those in a health care setting; (3) the *sexual predator* who murders in acts of sexual homicide; (4) the female *revenge serial killer* who kills from a sense of passion and revenge; (5) the *profit for crime* female killers who do so for financial gain; (6) the *team killers* who kill with a partner; (7) the *question of sanity* types who are legally insane; (8) the *unexplained* category for female serial killers who kill for an undetermined reason; and (9) the *unsolved category* for serial killing that is believed to have been perpetrated by a female (p. 11). We note that the angel of death type also fits the male nurse or other healthcare worker (Yardley & Wilson, 2016).

Female serial killers compose a group that is small by comparison to men but that also demands the attention of researchers. Farrell, Keppel, and Titterington (2011) note that the definition of serial murder has often excluded women, which in turn limited early study of the cases of serial murder by females. The rarity of serial homicide by females makes the identity of women serial killers hard to locate and study. These authors examined newspaper article accounts of 10 different female serial killers and generally found that information about their cases was scarce. The public often views women who commit serial murder (and other crimes) differently than it does men. Society is more apt to see the woman as a victim. This orientation has been reflected in many media stories that emphasize early life mistreatment of a woman as mitigating or explanatory for heinous violence. Little mention is made in such news accounts of the infinitesimal number of such female killers out of those who have suffered abuse.

Motivations of those females who are labeled as serial killers have often been found to be for personal gain and the instant gratification many serial killers have described (Frei, Vollm, Graf, & Dittman, 2006). Some claim to have committed these murders because of sexual abuse they had suffered early in their lives. The sadistic female serial killer appears to be rare as are those who claim sexual motivation. If an offender confesses, we can gain some insight regarding motive. Again, with relatively small numbers studied in-depth to date, a consistent theory of female serial killing is elusive.

Aileen Wuornos was called the first female serial killer in America by the FBI when she was linked to the killing of seven men. While she was certainly not the first female serial killer in this country, her method was unique in that Wuornos used a firearm for her murders, shooting her victims in the body. She had a history of physical and sexual abuse and family dysfunction. Wuornos had abused drugs and alcohol and had brain damage from the abuse. Wuornos lacked a stable family in her childhood years and began to live on the street after age 15. She got by panhandling and through prostitution.

She was arrested several times for various crimes but was brought in on murder charges in 1991. She was convicted and executed in Florida in 2002 after serving 10 years on death row.

WHY WOULD THEY DO IT?

Stacey Castor, one of several female killers dubbed "Black Widow" for killing a husband, was convicted of killing her husband David Castor by poisoning him with antifreeze. Stacey Castor tried to frame and murder her daughter to cover the killing and to remove suspicion that she (Stacey) had also killed her first husband, David Wallace, by the same method.

In the same way that an aggravated assault or battery may be considered an unsuccessful murder, a case where the subject has a record of one attempted murder, one conviction for murder, and strong indications of committing an earlier murder points to someone who, if they escaped detection, would be a serial killer.

Among the serial-killer types, the comfort killer is chilling because she kills her own family members, motivated by financial or material gain. The female comfort killer is not rare among serial killers who are women. Children and adolescents under the age of 18 are an even rarer subset of serial killers. Perhaps lacking the capacity to organize the thoughts and actions necessary to carry out such crimes, there have been few documented cases. Myers (2004) analyzed six such serial murders identified in the last 150 years. Each of the located cases exhibited sexual-homicide characteristics. The killers used their hands to strangle or stab their victims.

With the most commonly identified motive of women who commit serial homicide being for personal gain, men commit the crimes typically for more violent reasons, like sexual compulsion. There are several women who acted on sexual compulsion or their violent nature when they murdered (Ramsland, 2007). Several of the female killers describe the same *rush* from committing the murder as that described by many men. Even after the academic *discovery* of female serial killers, there was little thought that they killed out of pleasure. The *normal* female comfort serial killer commits the crime for some type of gain, often financial. Other types of female serial killer have been categorized as visionary, hedonistic, power seeker, and disciple (Frei, Vollm, Graf, & Dittman, 2006). And like men, a female serial killer might be influenced by biological, genetic, psychological, or social factors.

MEDICAL OR HEALTH CARE SERIAL KILLERS

In September 2014, a nurse in Italy was captured and was investigated in the deaths of up to 96 patients over a one-year period at a hospital where she was working. The suspect, who had been a nurse for 17 years, had recently been transferred to the day shift after administrators became concerned over the number of patients dying on Daniela Poggiali's shift. She then, according to the investigating magistrate, found the move to the day shift a challenge, killing patients when there was greater activity and more people around (Farrell, 2014). This is one of many **medical murders**. The motivation to kill those who are in a person's care speaks to issues of power and control as well as a fundamental objectification of people. Some claim to end the lives of patients out a sense of mercy for their suffering. In the case of Poggiali, investigators believe the murders were simply because the patients irritated the nurse.

A type of serial killer who can avoid detection, apparently with a great deal of success, is the murderer employed in the medical or health care field. **Healthcare serial killers (HSKs)**, including several nurses and physicians, have murdered their patients while ostensibly treating them, with no one the wiser. With a ready supply of potential victims in a hospital, convalescent center, or retirement home, this killer's hunting ground is remarkably convenient. The victims may be ill or elderly to an extent that their deaths do not appear unexpected or unusual. If the killer is a physician and has already documented the victim's health problems, he may then sign the death certificate, which will generally preclude an autopsy being performed. Medical *surveillance* in the United States has reached a point where a volume of such death cases under the care of one doctor may be noticed. The rationalization of some medical serial killers is that they are saving people from suffering. This type of killer is sometimes called an *angel of death* by claiming to help end the victim's pain.

Interestingly, health care professionals or workers, as a group, account for more serial killers than any other single profession (Holmes & Holmes, 2010; Kaplan, 2007). Homicide has certainly been committed by medical doctors over the years, and as a profession, they have produced double the number of identified serial killers of any other profession or vocation (Kinnell, 2000). Kinnell observes that this may relate to the observation that some doctors already possess a complex regarding control of life and death with patients. There have been cases documented in a number of countries. The United States seems to have more such killers, which may simply be a function of more sophisticated medical monitoring that leads to discovery of such crimes. Given our reliance on health care workers to care for us when we are ill or vulnerable, the discovery of such serial killers from time to time is profoundly disturbing. Predatory murderers in the medical profession are able to target vulnerable patients (Soothill & Wilson, 2007).

It is entirely plausible that many or most such killers have gone undetected in the past. Detecting a medical serial killer is quite difficult, even in comparison with other serial killers. The person who dies at the hands of a medical worker may have been *expected* to die, or at least, given their circumstances, it was not unexpected. A doctor or nurse may hold another person's life in his or her hands and make the decision of whether the patient lives or dies. We do not want to believe that the doctors who take the Hippocratic Oath to "do no harm" may be capable of killing people intentionally and repeatedly (Soothill & Wilson, 2007). Noting a pattern of questionable deaths in a medical facility may only happen through database programs, an alert coworker, or perhaps an intended victim. Without a clear reason to go back and examine the cases of hospital deaths, such cases may simply never be identified as murders. "Hospitals seldom rely on a centralized database to keep track of suspected offenders, nor do they communicate with one another and share information" (Curtain, 2004, p. 5).

Lubaszka and Shon (2013) state that

> some of these serial killers exhibit an inordinate amount of pleasure in taunting and psychologically abusing the primary victim's family and other staff members in the healthcare environment through unwanted, sometimes duplicitous, contact long after the victims have been killed. (p. 69)

Serial killer Dr. Harold Shipman was from the United Kingdom. His mother died of cancer when he was 17 years old, and possibly as a result, Shipman became interested in medicine. He graduated from medical school and eventually started his own practice. As an independent family practitioner, little notice was paid to how many of Shipman's patients were dying, especially when he came to call at their homes. Shipman was confirmed of killing 15 people and was linked to more than 20 others but is suspected of killing possibly 200 or more people (Ramsay, 2001). One of the ways that law enforcement confirmed the 15 deaths was using toxicology reports, which showed none of the deaths were natural. Shipman injected many of his patient-victims with large doses of heroin.

TEAM SERIAL KILLERS

Two or more people working together to commit serial murders is infrequent. Fox and Levin (2015) estimate perhaps 20% of serial killers murder in teams of two (or more). Teamwork has advantages in many domains of life. "Many hands make light work" may be especially true when moving a body. Distracting a victim before abducting him or her can be facilitated by two people working together as well as increasing the physical ability to overpower a potential victim. **Team serial killers** have consisted of two males as well as a male and a female and the very rare female-only team. There is generally found to be one member of the team who is dominant and guides the actions of the pair (Holmes & Holmes, 2010). Fox and Levin (2015) also note that one partner is significantly older in almost 50% of team serial killers. It would be only guesswork to speculate about whether one or both members of a serial-killing team would have killed or killed sequentially had they been working independently. Examining the backgrounds of the killers gives insights and information about their violent responses to past situations but not an absolute conclusion about what their future trajectory would have been absent a partner. And of course, each partner, if caught, may point to the other to place the majority of the blame.

WHY WOULD THEY DO IT?

A couple from France, Michel Fourniret and Monique Olivier, were involved in the killing of at least nine young girls. Fourniret admitted to murdering the nine, and his wife was his accomplice. Olivier was convicted of killing one of the girls and being complicit in three of the other killings. Fourniret's primary motive to kill these young girls was that they were virgins. Fourniret, however, also raped his victims, revealing that a sexual fantasy was also present (Leistedt, Linkowski, & Bongaerts, 2011).

Another aspect of team serial murder is the concept of mutual accountability. Partners in murder may certainly encourage one another as well as share the emotional experience they derive from murders. Each may also support the other to follow through and commit the act(s). Whether one goes on a diet, starts an exercise regimen, or apparently sets about to kill people, having a partner may facilitate the effort.

CATCHING SERIAL KILLERS

Serial murder is a rare phenomenon, and it is a difficult crime to explain or to solve. Part of the challenge of explaining and solving such murders is the low number of incidents and paucity of available and cooperative killers who have been caught. Researchers are limited, therefore, in the information sources from which to gain insight. Aside from the lack of suspects to question and study, serial killers typically conceal the nature of their crimes. The targeted population is often composed of fringe members of society. Serial killers use various methods in their murders, but most work to hide their efforts and avoid capture.

To this end of avoiding discovery, most serial killers murder victims in their homes or some other location that provides concealment. The fringe nature of the victims means the killer will select people who will not soon be missed or that historically did not generate intense law enforcement interest initially. Most serial killers dispose of their victims' bodies in a manner that would prevent any but an accidental discovery. The lust killer may keep the bodies near his home so that they can be in close proximity and be accessible (Holmes & Holmes, 2010).

The thoroughness of scene observation and documentation cannot be overemphasized. Details that may seem at first glance to be unimportant may later prove to be vital. The recording and gathering of all potential evidence is never time or effort wasted. The seemingly trivial details often result in a case that is successfully resolved. The entire crime scene is important. Minor details may yield leads for investigators. Crime scene clues may provide insights into the type of killer police are in search of. Knowing the type of killer may give insight into the killer's motivation. In many matters, including serial killers, the best indicator of future behavior is past behavior (Hazelwood & Burgess, 2009). Developing patterns may lead to identification of the killer or aid in linking crimes that otherwise might seem unconnected. The pattern recognized may lead to an understanding of the killer's aims and, in turn, lead to the killer's identity. The typologies discussed earlier in the chapter can help suggest avenues for the detectives to travel.

A widely used method to find or narrow the likely region where an offender is based is referred to as the **circle hypothesis** or theory (Canter & Gregory, 1994; Canter & Larkin, 1993). Known offenses of a suspected serial killer are plotted, and the area where the killer may reside is approximated by a circle drawn with a diameter based on the two offenses or body dump sites farthest apart (Canter, Coffey, Huntley, & Missen, 2000). This area can be further reduced by door-to-door questioning of residents about suspicious activity in the area. Also, local law enforcement will likely identify some areas more likely and some less based on topography and land use known to them. This is a helpful method used for those serial killers who choose to target victims in their local area.

Mapping the locations associated with murders can also help the investigation. Keppel and Weis (1994) note that the more information available about "the location of the original contact between the victim and the killer, where the assault occurred, the murder site, and the body recovery site the more likely a murder case will be solved" (p. 386). The serial killer will not typically leave the body where he killed his victim, and so, analyzing the time and distance between the associated locations for the crime can be important to understanding the pattern of movement of the person. This, in turn, may help focus the resources of law enforcement in their investigation. Using the routine activities theory (RAT) to understand victim target selection has also been examined by various researchers. Godwin (1998) explains in detail and provides a useful graphic representation of his victim targeting networks and asserts that the approach begins with the assumption that serial killers carry geographical templates in their mind. They have a certain kind of place in mind where experience has taught them where suitable victims can be found. Each subsequent trip to these crime locations forms something of an analogy with previous successes, modified by experience and perhaps intelligence gained from previous murders. (p. 79)

These various techniques and views of the relevance of geography are helpful in some cases. Not all serial killers or serial criminals of any crime type will follow a pattern vulnerable to such analysis. This same limitation of the number of available cases is true of other theoretical lenses that have been used to achieve more insight into the motivations and behaviors of this small subset of killers (Chassy, 2017; Reid, 2017).

A roughly accurate truism in crime is the 80/20 rule. The idea, while not statistically accurate, says that 80% of crime is committed by 20% of offenders—the high-capacity criminals. Thus, if these few big-volume perpetrators could be identified and incapacitated via repeat-offender sentencing schemes, crime reduction would be significant and cost-effective. Economists cite this rule of thumb as the **Pareto principle**, and we see the concept used in many fields. So if serial killers disproportionately destroy lives and bring misery to communities, their identification and removal would be quite important. In the past, crime *linkage* was more difficult, though law enforcement agencies are still dependent on physical and testimonial evidence to attach a person to a crime and a scene. Labuschagne (2006) discusses the use of linkage analysis to help law enforcement locate serial offenders. Law enforcement examines various characteristics of a crime to determine if one offender may have committed several crimes. Think modus operandi plus advanced forensics. Efforts such as those of the FBI's Violent Criminal Apprehension Program (ViCAP), the Homicide Information Tracking System (HITS) begun in Washington State, and others increase the ability of authorities to discover patterns.

The killer is always at some risk of detection through the investigative efforts of law enforcement and the chance discovery by a witness or a victim who escapes before being killed. There are serial killers who become overconfident and hasten their identification and capture. An example of this would be Dennis Rader, the serial killer discussed earlier in the chapter, known as BTK, which stood for "bind, torture, kill." He killed at least 10 people in the local area, and then the murders stopped. Since the reason for the string of murders ending was unknown, there was speculation that BTK may have left the area or died. Years later, when Rader learned that authorities thought he might be dead, he began communicating with law enforcement by sending in evidence of his killings. This was Rader's need to be known, even if not named, by his deeds. These actions included sending a computer disk to a news station that was able to be traced to his computer. Rader was caught, and DNA evidence was also used in convicting him. Arrogance by Rader, investigation, and science kept a serial killer from going free. DNA use in forensic investigations has been a boon in linking suspects to persons or places. The evidentiary value of DNA identification is accepted with little objection. DNA joins fingerprints, facial recognition technology, and other biometrics in solving violent crimes.

Like Rader, many serial killers have jobs and families, are known by their neighbors, and, in most ways, seem quite normal. This complicates the job of catching them and can delay it for years, if not prevent it altogether. Many of these individuals are quite careful in their efforts to avoid detection. Many technologies have helped law enforcement identify and catch killers. The increased abilities have not translated to an increased rate of arrests for such cases as serial murder or murder generally. This is partly attributed to gang rivalries and other confrontational homicide without the benefit of witnesses or discernible physical evidence.

The power and ubiquitous nature of recorded video has been instrumental in solving many crimes. The recent Boston Marathon bombing and the Mother's Day shootings in New Orleans were both broken or greatly aided by the gathering of video from the fixed camera systems of businesses and public places as well as the footage recorded by various witnesses using smartphones and recorders (Grier, 2013; Johnson, 2013). In November 2014, video captured the disturbing images of a 22-year-old Philadelphia woman being kidnapped right off the street. The footage showed the suspect park a car by the curb before abducting the woman. The video led authorities to spot the vehicle, arrest the subject, and rescue the woman relatively unharmed.

Contract killer and self-professed drug cartel enforcer Jose Manuel Martinez was arrested in April 2014 and initially charged with nine killings. Martinez has confessed to 40 such murders while working as an enforcer. From 1980 until 2011, Martinez murdered individuals in a number of jurisdictions, and investigators are questioning him to try to verify as many of the murders as they can. He is suspected of committing killings in California, Alabama, and Florida.

Researchers and writers have not always thought of contract killers, hit men, enforcers, or assassins as serial killers. Yet a broad definition of someone who has murdered many people over a period of time, with breaks in between the killings, would include them.

SUMMARY

Many factors lead to the *development* of a serial killer. No single theory or causal pathway to what makes a serial killer has been identified. The complexity of human emotion and motivation as well as the seemingly endless combination of branching factors and influences in a person's life may mean that we will never have a thorough or even workable theory that could explain, let alone lead to prevention, of a progression to serial killing. We possess historic, statistical, and psychological information about people who have killed sequentially and over extended periods of time. Researchers have not identified specific characteristics or a genetic template that predisposes an individual to be a serial killer, but they have identified several combinations of factors that appear to be contributors. Studying past crimes and convicted killers can suggest avenues of investigation. Victim types and characteristics can provide clues about what a killer looks for in a potential victim. Specific victim vulnerabilities are not the least of these characteristics.

That many find serial killing and the killers to be interesting is understandable. To try to prevent people from following a pathway to violent repeat offending, society needs to understand why individuals follow such a path. Law enforcement agencies too must gain as much understanding as they can to better detect and apprehend this type of violent criminal. The need for cooperation among agencies is clear when dealing with individuals who not only repeat violent crime but who may move around while doing so in an attempt to thwart investigative efforts. As evidenced by the Samuel Little case, where federal, state, and local agencies worked together utilizing ViCAP and other methods to tie together unsolved murders across the country. As we see technology improve the chances of catching many criminals, the advancements have been a boon to crime linkage, allowing quicker identification of a serial criminal.

The true number of serial killers and victims is unknown. Murders are sometimes misidentified as accidental or natural, and missing persons may have actually been victims of murder. Forensics and the use of DNA evidence along with advanced techniques of investigation, including profiling, have provided law enforcement with improved odds of identifying and catching serial killers. A recent notorious example is the decades old Golden State Killer case solved, in part, through the use of a publicly available DNA database and genealogical research. While serial killers certainly do not all leave telltale *signatures* in their killings, the value of physical evidence is tremendous and must be pursued through appropriate technology and effective investigative technique. A lack of evidence at the scene where a victim's body is discovered may itself be an indication of a so-called organized killer, at least insofar as he took the body to a secondary location to reduce the possibility of leaving trace evidence.

Serial killers may inadvertently leave evidence to be found later by police, or they may take great care and leave little in the way of evidence. The killer may use a *dump site* separate from where the killing took place. The murderer may wash his victim's body, wear gloves, and attempt various efforts to defeat forensics through lessons learned from television and movies. The police, for their part, use fingerprints, blood, hair, laboratory analysis, witness canvassing, geographic profiling, and other tools to identify the killer. The victim typology and interviews with friends, coworkers, and families of the victims may lead to clues. The use of video footage from fixed cameras or lucky smartphone recordings may reveal important bits of information or even the killer's identity.

KEY TERMS

Serial murders 190
Hedonistic killer 194
Visionary killer 194
Mission killer 194
Power/control killer 195
Psychopathy 196

Antisocial personality disorder (ASPD) 196
Black widows 197
Angels of death 197
Medical murders 198

Healthcare serial killer (HSK) 198
Team serial killers 200
Circle hypothesis 201
Pareto principle 201

1. Why are people fascinated with serial killers?
2. How do we best determine the number of serial killers in a particular country and how many victims they have?
3. What are the most common myths about serial killers?
4. What common experiences or traits do many serial killers share?
5. Describe and discuss the motivations of serial killers.
6. How are *organized* and *disorganized* serial killers described?
7. What techniques do law enforcement officers employ to identify and catch serial killers?

TRY THIS

Visit the serial murder report of the FBI at http://www.fbi.gov/stats-services/publications/serial-murder. Examine the section "Investigative Issues and Best Practices" to grasp the challenges in the investigation of serial homicides. Think about how policy should be developed to address murder investigations once it is determined that crimes are the responsibility of a serial killer.

The FBI's online ViCAP database is the largest repository for data on violent crimes in the United States. Go to the section of the website on homicides and sexual assaults here: https://www.fbi.gov/wanted/vicap/homicides-and-sexual-assaults. How might this tool assist in determining crimes of a possible serial killer?

13

SOLVING HOMICIDES

"You know my method. It is founded upon the observation of trifles."

—Arthur Conan Doyle, *"The Boscombe Valley Mystery"*

"Supposing is good, but finding out is better."

—Mark Twain

CHAPTER OUTLINE

Student Learning Outcomes

Students will be able to:

- explain the duties of the first officer on the scene of a suspected homicide.

- describe the functions of the homicide investigator.

- explain the process of documenting a homicide case.

- discuss the methods of collecting evidence in a murder case.

- identify the contributions and involvement of the medical examiner in a homicide case.

- list the various homicide case personnel and explain their duties.

- analyze the challenges of working with the media on homicide cases.

INTRODUCTION

It is not overstating to say that if the initial steps taken in a suspected homicide are mishandled, the case may well fail to reach a successful conclusion. The critical nature of the preliminary work done in any criminal investigation, let alone ones involving death, also explains the volume of writing that has been done on the subject. We use an amalgam of the steps various authors, agencies, and investigators have identified as important in the preliminary homicide investigation. Many of the steps apply equally to most crimes.

While TV and movies give the impression that most homicide responses involve a legion of officers and technicians, this is hardly representative of all cases. The number of personnel assigned varies by jurisdiction and resources available. Small agencies or ones that deal infrequently with death investigations often call upon larger local departments or state agencies for assistance with murder investigations. When a law enforcement agency knows the event in question is homicide, the initial officer(s) will make haste in getting to the reported scene. If the initial call is to an unknown event, one officer may be dispatched. If that officer arrives to discover a violent assault or completed murder, more personnel will be summoned as quickly as they are available.

We should note at this point that a homicide may have multiple *scenes*. Think of a person being initially assaulted in one location. They may then be taken somewhere else. The final acts of a murder may take place at the second location. The deceased may then be transported to yet another location—and in a different vehicle! Each location where the victim was during the course of

the eventual murder becomes a relevant scene that investigators will want to process if they can.

While each scene requires the same attention and effort, we will focus on activities typically involved in any violent crime scene and refer to the *primary* scene in discussing preliminary investigation. This will be the location where the deceased victim is found. Geberth (2008) and others have authored extensive and detailed procedures and checklists to guide officers and investigators in crime scene duties specific to homicide. While checklists are useful, they should not be relied upon as the single template for investigating crimes.

The National Institute of Justice, too, has published various guides, including significant works in 1999 and 2009 addressing general crime scene investigation. Other police and government entities have published documents such as the 2013 report "10 Things Law Enforcement Executives Can Do to Positively Impact Homicide Investigation Outcomes," a collaboration between the Bureau of Justice Assistance (BJA), the International Association of Chiefs of Police (IACP), and the Institute for Intergovernmental Research (IIR), also resulting in "Homicide Process Mapping" prepared by David Carter, and the 2007 Police Executive Research Forum (PERF) publication of "Promoting Effective Homicide Investigations."

With the attention paid to murder and the efforts of officers and agencies to solve cases, it would not be unreasonable to expect investigative success in these cases. Unfortunately, the United States has seen declining homicide clearance rates. In the 1960s, about 90% of homicide cases were cleared. While the murder rate has declined

Chicagocide

The Washington Post tracked nearly 55,000 murders in 55 cities that occurred in the last ten years and found that half of those crimes did not produce an arrest (Murder with Impunity, June 6, 2018, https://www.washingtonpost.com/graphics/2018/investigations/unsolved-homicide-database/? utm_term=.98ee4e70118f&city=chicago). In Chicago, the percentage of murder cases with no arrest was a staggering 74%. The journalists mapped data on areas where the murders occurred as well as where there were low arrest rates, resulting in a series of layered maps providing graphic illustrations. The article points out as a comparison that in Austin, TX over the same time period, more than 70% resulted in arrests. Recent comparisons to former homicide stand-outs New York and Los Angeles underscore drops in homicide cases and significantly better clearance rates in those two cities and leave more questions about Chicago's response to murder. A *Chicago Tribune* story looked at 39,000 homicides over the past 60 years. The article contributors note the significance of the crime spike since 2016, and what that means for Chicago in particular (39,000 homicides: Retracing 60 years of murder in Chicago, January 9, 2018, https://www.chicagotribune.com/news/local/breaking/ct-history-of-chicago-homicides-htmlstory.html). The Chicago Police Department has used data to direct their tactical efforts at crime suppression as well as sometimes adding resources to the units that combat the significant gang challenges in the Windy City. A U.S. Department of Justice investigation declared that adequate training and the improper use of force were both problems within the police department. A *Chicago Sun Time* article points to various explanations for the low clearance rate, including a poor relationship between police and the residents of high-crime areas and a reduction in the number of detectives in the police department from 1,252 in 2008, to 922 in 2016 (Murder 'clearance' rate in Chicago hit new low in 2017, February 9, 2017, https://chicago.suntimes.com/news/murder-clearance-rate-in-chicago-hit-new-low-in-2017/).

in the United States, the percent of cases cleared in 2016 was just 59.4 (FBI, 2017), and increased slightly to 61.6% in 2017 (FBI, 2018). Researchers examine the factors associated with case clearance, and police remain frustrated over the stable but low clearance rate of homicide investigations. Whether a case is solved depends on a complex array and interplay of characteristics involving the victim, offender, dynamics of the incident, as well as the investigator and available resources.

FIRST OFFICER ON THE SCENE

Responding to the Scene

Most suspected homicide investigations begin with an officer responding to the reported scene. Rapid response to a homicide call is important if the crime has just occurred or is in progress. If the crime has just been discovered and no official yet knows when it occurred, getting there quickly to protect the scene and evidence is also important. While haste is important, safely arriving is obviously the most important aspect of the initial response.

The preliminary investigation is conducted by the primary officer, who is typically the officer assigned by dispatch to respond to the initial call. Whatever officer is in the assigned geographic zone of the jurisdiction will be primary unless a field training officer (FTO) with an officer in training is working at the time and is assigned to the case for training purposes. The actions of the first officer(s) begin with receiving the call itself and quickly planning the route to the reported scene. This act of choosing which way to get there is based on the fastest route but may also involve assigning other responding officers to come by way of different routes that could be escape paths for a suspect.

When the officers arrive on the scene, they must think simultaneously about their own safety and whether there is anyone at the scene in need of immediate assistance medically or due to the threat of a still-present offender. Sometimes, responding officers will know victims or suspects are present, but more often, they will not know this. Caution, therefore, is always the order of the day when approaching. If the scene appears deserted save for a victim, the officers do not let down their guard as an offender may be nearby and possibly lying in wait. Offenders also may return to scenes they have left. In some cases, officers and additional victims have been killed or injured when a killer returns. When the scene is relatively secured, the officer begins to immediately further secure the scene, notify dispatch and supervisors, and summon additional resources.

Arriving

After arriving safely at the reported crime scene, the initial officer will approach the scene, remaining alert for danger and also using his senses to note any relevant sounds, smells, or activity. The officer has duties in aiding anyone in need of medical assistance, identifying the nature of the crime, determining if a suspect is still present, establishing scene boundaries and protecting what is inside the scene, and notifying supervisors and calling for appropriate assistance. Given the location, layout, and physical condition (weather, night or day, etc.) of the scene as well as people present, this process can happen very quickly or be more protracted. Even if initial steps occur rapidly, they can be accomplished with caution and competence. While weather may compromise the scene and available evidence, people may also create difficulties for scene security and management.

When the officer first arrives, there may be emergency or dangerous circumstances to be controlled or contained. There may be one or more injured persons who need assistance. An officer must ensure that if the suspect is still present, he is secured so that he does not assault the officer or victim(s) further while the officer turns her attention to the injured. If a suspect is at the scene and is identified as a suspect, then it is not likely the officer will conduct an interrogation. This is typically left to the investigator, following the reading of constitutional rights, or *Miranda* warning. If the suspect makes extemporaneous statements, the officer should, however, note these as accurately as possible. Detaining and removing the suspect also keeps him from possibly altering the scene in some way. As with almost any crime, if the suspect recently left the scene, the primary officer or a backup officer should broadcast a description via the communications center to alert patrolling officers to be on the lookout (BOLO) for the person(s).

ARRIVING WITH CAUTION

Officers are taught to be cautious when responding to virtually any reported crime, but arriving at a suspected homicide scene can be especially dangerous. In July 2014, deputies were responding to a call of an assault with a deadly weapon in Moreno Valley, California, when the apparent shooter fired upon one of the officers who had just arrived. Two victims were found by police when they responded to separate crime scenes in the chaos that is not uncommon when receiving calls of an in-progress violent crime. A city surveillance camera showed a vehicle fleeing one of the scenes, a gas station. The shooter abandoned the car, and when an officer tried to make contact with a man thought possibly to be the suspect walking in a nearby neighborhood, the individual opened fire on the officer, wounding him. The suspected killer was found dead hours later with an assault rifle next to him near where police had set up a manhunt for the killer. The suspect had also been wearing body armor.

Fire or rescue personnel may be at the scene or arrive shortly. Personnel should be alerted to items identified as possible evidence to help ensure that there is not needless **contamination** of the scene. If a victim or suspect is seriously injured and must be taken by ambulance from the scene, an officer should accompany the person to try to speak with him. Medical personnel should be told to listen for any statements made and relate them as completely and accurately as they can as well as include such statements in their own reporting. Another situation that is sometimes applicable is a **dying declaration** by the victim or a suspect. While later admissibility will be determined by the court, it is generally the case that a person who dies after making a statement must have sincerely believed or known he was dying. Officers should always write down or record all statements made. Officers should always obtain the identifying information from the EMS crew and vehicle as well as what hospital a victim is taken to. Documenting these statements carefully in the report can assist the prosecution later with the admissibility of such evidence in court.

Given the need that officers often have to quickly bring a scene under control, they may fail to discern some important aspect of the scene—something that may be fleeting. Officers must still use their experience-enhanced observations to note potentially odd activity or persons. Are there several upset witnesses and people in attendance but one person who seems still and quiet? Generally, are there actions that are not consistent with the scene? If an officer allows her focus to become too quickly fixated on the victim, she may miss potential evidence or threats.

Establishing and Securing the Scene

Once any potential danger or medical needs are mitigated or accomplished, the officer(s) must establish the perimeter of the scene. It is a maxim in crime scenes that you cannot set the boundaries too broadly. While the officer can contract the scene as necessary after processing it, it is difficult and open to criticism to expand a scene after people have already been circulating in unprotected areas. However, if a reason is found to expand the scene, it is recommended that officers do it. Officers should also document the circumstances that lead to establishing a broader perimeter and note any persons who were clearly inside the earlier perimeter.

Ultimately, a court will decide if evidence was compromised to an extent that makes it inadmissible, so every effort must be made to collect available evidence and protect the integrity of a scene that can still yield information to investigators. The scene boundaries should include potential ways into and out of the location where evidence is obvious. The body of the victim is the single most important source of evidence that links the killer to the crime. Evidence is also discarded by killers in many cases. This evidence may be located at the scene(s) of the incident(s) of a case or along routes of flight from a scene. Often, such discarded evidence is quite close to the scene.

The scene may be cordoned off with crime scene tape or a similar method. Officers may need to be posted to help guard against persons entering the scene without authorization. There have been numerous instances when a witness or suspect who was inside a crime scene but unknown to officers was only discovered when he began to leave. If the length of time on scene is going to be lengthy, law enforcement reserve officers or cadets may be used to help in securing or searching. Before officers arrive initially, dispatchers may ask the person who discovered a crime to remain and *protect* the scene, if possible, through making people aware they should not enter the area. A complainant should not be asked to endanger himself in any way if he remains at the scene.

Various individuals can compromise the scene and for various reasons. Family members who are upset may disturb the body or the scene, either unintentionally or in an attempt to cover embarrassing or incriminating evidence. Media members may ignore crime scene tape or stated scene limits in attempts to record or photograph people or evidence at a scene. While addressed elsewhere in the book, these types of intrusions may be more than annoying as release of information prematurely can compromise an investigation. **First responders** from fire departments or EMS may also inadvertently trample or otherwise contaminate scene evidence in efforts to provide aid. General knowledge of evidence and increased training have greatly improved the care taken at potential crime scenes by fire and

While not as familiar now to many college-age students, the murder investigation centering on former professional football player O.J. Simpson still carries echoes of a poorly handled crime scene by a large agency with little excuse to perform so badly.

Nicole Brown, Simpson's former spouse, and her friend Ron Goldman were murdered at her home in Los Angeles. Simpson, previously charged with spouse abuse against Nicole, was arrested for the two murders after fleeing from police. Simpson claimed his innocence and was acquitted based on reasonable doubt being cast from the notable errors in crime scene procedure.

At the initial crime scene of Brown's home, fiber evidence was mixed together, rendering it all but useless; a bloody fingerprint never got recorded properly or collected; other blood samples were packaged together and placed in a hot vehicle; and the blood evidence was gathered using already used evidence gloves.

Physical evidence cannot "speak for itself" when it has been shouted down by the incompetent actions of personnel assigned to the critical task of evidence collection and processing. Simpson, who was acquitted in the criminal trial, was ordered by a civil court to pay $33.5 million to the families of Nicole Brown and Ronald Goldman for their deaths.

EMS personnel. Additionally, perhaps the most pervasive and frequently damaging are other law enforcement personnel who are used to being around the *action* who enter the scene believing they belong there or have the authority or *right* to be in the scene.

Control of these various personnel and interlopers is essential. In addition to potential damage or removal of evidence, precious time is wasted determining if evidence or conditions at a scene are a result of the crime or from foot traffic after the crime. An agency and officers inexperienced in death investigations have long been criticized for the initial scene handling of the JonBenét Ramsey case in December 1996 in Boulder, Colorado. Extra **documentation** of unnecessary personnel in the scene must be completed, and difficult questions by attorneys lie ahead regarding the need for various people in the crime scene and what potential damage was done. An assigned officer or crime scene technician (CST) should have responsibility for logging in and out all persons who enter the crime scene. Crime scene tape is carried by most officers, supervisors, and technicians, and this is often used to establish a boundary to keep people back. Officers and investigators must be mindful of the capability of media and personal cameras to view the scene from significant distances. As mentioned, details of the scene should not be prematurely released as the investigation may be compromised. In addition to investigative challenges, there is often the need and responsibility to protect the privacy of victims or family members.

LOCARD'S EXCHANGE PRINCIPLE

Edmond Locard was born in France in 1877 and obtained both a PhD in medicine and a law degree. Locard is credited with creating the first official police crime laboratory in 1910–1912 in Lyon, France. Dr. Locard wrote many publications about the use of medicine and forensic science in solving crimes. Locard is probably best known for the concept that every contact between two objects leaves a trace on each from the other. This *exchange principle* has heavily influenced criminalistics and forensic science ever since. As technology has increased the ability to locate, gather, and measure trace evidence, we have also expanded our understanding of the types of microscopic matter that are available to be gathered. Based on Locard's principle, criminalistics experts seek the trace evidence that may have passed between a crime scene and a person. As new technologies and methods are developed, standards under the *Daubert* rule raise issues for the admission of new or novel scientific findings and the experts who testify about them. Experts must be able to demonstrate reliable scientific principles to have evidence admitted in court during a criminal prosecution.

While working with the media is addressed elsewhere, we note that contact should be made by the detective to encourage the media to provide any information they develop while near the scene or afterward in their story production. First responders should typically not be the ones to interact with media. Likewise, first responders should not tell family, witnesses, or others about the case or about the scene. Family members and friends of the victim may be present, and they too must be controlled, albeit with sensitivity, to avoid unnecessary scene contamination. There may be other available witnesses at or near the scene. The officers will seek information, but be cautious about giving out any information as this may compromise the investigation or influence witnesses.

Some passersby may have some level of knowledge from observing what happened. Some are unknowing witnesses. Frequently people are cognizant of some aspect of a crime that they are not aware of at the time of the occurrence. They may not realize that they were witnessing perhaps an abduction or another crime. In those cases where there was a physical description of a killer before that killer was identified, the case clearance rates have been higher. Eyewitness identification of a suspect must be carried out with great care by police and investigators. States and the federal government have altered policies in recent years to reflect best practices in eyewitness identification procedures. The challenges of faulty witness memory and the witness being influenced by the identification process and those who conduct it has caused problems for the integrity of many cases. Always important is the fact that once the opportunity to gather initial information has been lost, it may never be available again, and a case may not be solved as a result. Spending the time and energy during this preliminary part of the investigation is always important. Talking to every available person and even returning to the area later to try to locate additional people with information or insights can be the key to determining who is responsible for a homicide.

A proven tool and method in major case investigations is the neighborhood **canvass**. The canvass is a door-to-door interviewing of all residents within a logically determined radius from the identified scene(s). This is often completed by patrol officers because they are the available resource. The key consideration is that officers are briefed as to the importance of this role and of gathering thorough information, including facts that may not seem relevant but may rise to the mere level of *odd*. Additionally, communication to the lead investigator or coordinating detective or supervisor may determine the need to return to certain addresses for further interviewing. This is also very important regarding residences or businesses where no one was present when the officer visited. Increasingly, businesses and private residences may have digital or video camera recordings of an area that can prove helpful or instrumental in producing leads.

The necessity for the canvass and the designation of responsibility for conducting the canvass should be specified in agency and unit policies. Determining the area to be canvassed is based on the physical environment and geography of the scene in conjunction with the experience of the various team members. One person must be assigned specific overall responsibility to coordinate and document the conduct of the canvass. The assignment of follow-up on leads arising from the canvass must also be meticulously documented and integrated into the ongoing case progress review.

During the initial canvass as well as during follow-up canvasses, a supplemental report form or specific canvass form should be used to identify all people who live or routinely visit a location or who might have been visiting. This consideration is similar to identifying and taking even a brief statement from everyone at any scene. It has unfortunately been the case that a bystander has claimed he "didn't see anything" and was dismissed without having given a formal statement or perhaps even identification only to appear sometime later in a case as a defense witness who claims to have seen a number of things but asserts that he was not interviewed by law enforcement.

Noting, again, the value of the neighborhood canvass, witnesses at or near the scene must be interviewed. Officers should separate witnesses to increase the ability to get independent observations and statements. Separating a number of people can be challenging, and the officer should be clearly instructing everyone that it is important for people not to influence others or *check* their perception against another person. The officer can hand people pieces of paper or witness statements and ask them to simply start writing what they saw or what they know. Some people will not want to do this. The officer must be persuasive. He must also gain identification and accurate information about how to contact the person. If the officer is persistent, she will find everyone has a way to be contacted—a relative, a neighbor, a place of work, or a street where they hang out. The officer should never write in his report that the contact information is "none," "unknown," or "n/a."

An area search where a victim was assaulted may yield physical evidence. The area search differs from the neighborhood canvass in that it is a more general search for items of evidence that may also identify witnesses in the area. The preliminary investigation involves observation and documentation, which will already have been started by the officer as he arrived. There will likely be some level of search by the preliminary officer on the scene and possibly collection of evidence. The search and evidence identification and collection generally waits until enough personnel are on scene to conduct the search in an orderly manner and assign tasks to those who will document evidence and those who will collect evidence. Weather, chaotic conditions with crowds, or the danger of persons in the immediate area may create an exigency that forces the officer to quickly gather perishable evidence and secure it, even if this means removing it from the spot where it was first observed. All of these actions must be thoroughly described in the officer's reporting, and all evidence collected must be bagged and tagged to protect the required chain of custody that law enforcement officers must demonstrate.

Each of the tasks carried out by first responders during the preliminary investigation involves a number of steps to be carried out carefully and thoroughly. Whoever performs the preliminary investigation will also need to brief others on all of the information gathered up to the point of relinquishing the primary investigation responsibility to the follow-up investigator, typically a homicide or *persons crimes* detective.

WHY WOULD THEY DO IT?

Neighborhood Canvass

On August 25, 2014, the body part remains of a 28-year-old man were found in bags near dumpsters at an apartment complex in Laurel, Maryland. The next day detectives were going door to door in the apartment complex, talking to residents and handing out flyers. The case initially was a mystery until the witness interviews and efforts by investigators revealed that the victim had shared an apartment with two other men. The murder that ended in the dismemberment of the victim was apparently the result of an argument over money.

Door-to-door canvassing at and near the scene of a crime is often an effective method of obtaining information. Unfortunately, canvassing is often overlooked or put aside due to lack of resources or the pursuit of other leads. Many crimes, including murder, are committed by someone who lives or works near the scene. Often residents or others who frequent an area will have knowledge of the comings and goings of people and whether someone in the neighborhood stands out as a possible suspect. If no one is present when a location is checked, the address should be noted and assigned to an investigator for follow-up.

In late 2017, Tampa, Florida police faced a brazen killer who seemed to be killing random individuals in an area with a small circumference in the Seminole Heights neighborhood. Each of the four victims was shot and killed, and police were able to use ballistics to connect the first two murders. The realization that someone was perhaps continuing to kill, led to law enforcement devoting resources to the immediate area, including carrying out a door-to-door canvass of the neighborhoods and posting a $25,000 reward through Crime Stoppers. Surveillance video from a private home gave a poor image of the possible killer, but approximately five weeks after his murders began, the alleged suspect gave a gun to a McDonald's restaurant manager, saying he was going to a nearby business. The manager called police who were waiting when Howell Emanuel Donaldson III, a 22-year-old African American, returned to the restaurant. The gun was seized along with possible blood-stained clothing in Donaldson's car and his cell phone, which gave further indication that he had been in the area at the times of the murders.

INVESTIGATOR ARRIVES

A detective or investigator should be contacted to respond to the scene as soon as possible after the homicide is discovered. When possible, more than one detective will at least initially be assigned to work a homicide case. Some studies have shown a correlation between case clearance in homicides and the number of detectives assigned. This may not seem surprising. What is quite important, however, is that the investigators all receive specific assignments of what to do relative to the investigation. The homicide event has many aspects that must be explored to determine what happened and who is accountable. Analogous to reducing the size of an initially large crime scene, the number of detectives taking part in a homicide investigation can be tapered off as functions are handled. While one or more detectives respond to the primary scene, other detectives may go to the hospital to interview other victims or medical personnel, canvass the vicinity of the crime along with patrol officers, begin interviews with anyone with potential knowledge about the case, conduct background research on possible suspects, and more. At least one detective should attend the postmortem examination of the victim.

We are fans of the A&E television program *The First 48*. Why? Because the show provides a compressed but authentic view of many of the activities of actual homicide investigators and other justice system professionals involved in a typical murder investigation. Given the inaccuracies and dramatization provided by Hollywood, the show allows viewers a reality check into some of the more mundane aspects of a criminal investigation as well as the reality of being faced with interrogating an offender who will have a series of fairly predictable responses. A point often illustrated in the show is that as time passes, emotions cool, and suspects and witnesses rethink cooperating. The show also reminds us that many cases are never solved. Evidence may deteriorate or be obliterated by weather, people, or lack of discovery. Suspects have time to develop an alibi.

The initial arrival at the scene by patrol officers may result in a search for any other victims or the offender at the crime scene. Once the scene is stable and the detective arrives, the status of the scene and any subsequent search should be reviewed to determine if a search warrant or a signed consent to search by a party with *standing* to do so is needed. A family member or someone who lives in the home may have such legal standing to sign a form for *consent to search*. Contact with the prosecutor by the detective should be occurring to determine what is needed legally to ensure the integrity of the search authority. Courts have held that after emergency conditions have passed, a search warrant based on probable cause or consent is needed to conduct most searches.

The assigned detective will assess the scene and coordinate with any other involved personnel for immediate steps to be taken in the case. Crime scene investigators (CSI) or technicians will provide their input, and a plan of action will be decided upon for processing the scene.

Before concluding the preliminary investigation at the scene and releasing the scene, the primary investigator should conduct a scene debriefing. This may be relatively informal and touch base with all personnel performing a duty in the case. The investigator should keep his notes up to date with who has been assigned what task and what the status of the tasks are when leaving the scene. This is also a time to direct personnel as to what additional tasks they should perform. They should set up opportunities to review the investigation's progress throughout the case. Detective supervisors should also maintain a role, monitoring progress and directing certain activities as well as ensuring needed resources are provided to the investigators.

DOCUMENTATION

The primary patrol officer, other responding patrol officers, and the investigator(s) will be compiling many observations, pieces of information, and initial reports. Observations will include information about the scene and any leads developed there. Information will potentially be from witnesses, victims, and suspects. In the case of the assigned investigator, there will also be a number of supplemental reports over the course of the investigation. All other officers and investigators who responded to the scene or had any role whatsoever in the initial call or subsequent assigned task must complete supplemental reports even if their actions did not result in developing evidence. To ensure the integrity of the overall investigative process, this must be done. Failure to properly document everyone's actions and involvement can provide a later opportunity for raising questions about how competently the investigation was handled. While officers and investigators will take notes throughout the investigation, reports should be written as soon as possible

to ensure the information is preserved in permanent form according to formal agency procedures. Many cases have been compromised and many law enforcement personnel embarrassed from failing to document details in written form and follow up properly on the many aspects of an investigation.

Writing a brief supplement may be all that is required if an officer was only tasked with checking certain residences or businesses to determine if any witnesses were present. However, what may come of this task is follow-up by a detective or the actual taking of a statement by the initial officer. If no one is located at neighborhood homes or businesses, this must also be documented so that during the ongoing case management process, investigators or officers can return to these addresses until someone is reached. In cold-case investigations, it has often been revealed that there were failures to re-canvass or go back to locations where no one was first located. This proves to hamper many investigations needlessly. A question left unanswered, such as whether anyone was present or was talked to at a specific address can significantly increase effort later on.

The assigned investigator will describe the scene in great detail. The appearance of the scene and location when the investigator first arrives is important. The detective will provide a description of the dead body, including the position of the body in relation to the surroundings. Each member of the team working the crime scene will include individual descriptions of relevant scene observations. Crime scene conditions on the arrival of the investigator may or may not be the same as when first responders arrived. All should describe what they observe and what they perceive through their various senses. Responders and witnesses may have heard or smelled something unique or important in addition to what they saw. The initial officer should inform the detective of any changes that occurred at the scene before the detective arrived and why. The detective, for her part, should inquire if there have been any changes at the scene and why.

At the homicide crime scene and throughout a death investigation, documentation is critical. Photography is one of the first applications of technology that takes place at a scene to document what has been found. The advent of digital photography and recording of images have been invaluable in crime scene reconstruction as well as documenting individual items of evidence. Even the booking of arrestees and the management of incarcerated offenders has benefited from the improvements that digital photography and recording have provided. On the street, police officers take photographs of suspects, witnesses, and informants. They also take pictures of tattoos or distinguishing marks. These stored images can be instrumental in later identification of offenders, gang affiliations, and even unidentified bodies.

Photographs are still used for many applications in crime scene and investigative work. Photos have the benefits of being immediate and accurate. Presentation of photographs in court continues to be a mainstay of communicating information to juries. Experienced prosecutors know that a weakness of scene photography can be its inclusion of too much detail, which can distract from the relevant items in a picture. Some agencies still have crime scene technicians trained in still and black-and-white photography methods to develop their eye for effective and accurate documentation of scenes and evidence.

Like photos, video has benefits and challenges. Digital or video recording of scenes adds a measure of depth and perspective that individual photographs cannot provide. A thorough walkthrough of the scene with recording equipment can capture most evidence and provide context. Videography, like photography, is vulnerable to poor technique and distracting camera movements by untrained or careless operators. Two added benefits that scene recordings and photos provide are case review for follow-up and prosecution preparation and the use of recordings for training purposes. Basic and advanced in-service training of law enforcement officers and crime scene technicians is made more effective by visuals as illustrations.

The follow-up and case preparation is aided by the ability to display the photos in various ways to get the *big picture* of the scene and what activities took place during the crime and by various actors after discovery of the crime. Software programs can attach pictures together in a panoramic view, allowing observers to move through the scene virtually. Seen on several reality TV programs are digital-capture devices that provide photographic mapping of a scene to allow three-dimensional playback and interaction.

Photography is also used for surveillance of suspects, aerial search of large areas, mug shots, and lineups. Once again, the storage capabilities of software programs and computers allow for efficient management of individual-person images as well as rapid construction of photo lineups. The availability of mobile computer terminals allows responding officers to take their assigned laptop computers into a scene with them to facilitate report writing and computer files research. Crime scene technicians are able to compile evidence inventories more efficiently on site as well as input measurements from a scene into various software programs. Analysis of a scene is facilitated by use of ever-more sophisticated devices that occasionally make appearances in various television series.

Just like computers, software programs to coordinate, automate, analyze, and manage investigative functions have proliferated. The use of applications will provide even greater flexibility for crime scene and law enforcement personnel. Dictation is nothing new to the crime scene technician or investigator, but the advent of voice recognition has elevated the use of the method.

COLLECTION OF EVIDENCE

After determining whether the scene is intact, the investigator will conduct a **walk-through** of the scene so he or she can develop a sense of the event and the condition, location, and position of the body and other evidence in the crime scene. This provides the homicide detective with the ability to form an initial investigative hypothesis (Cook & Tattersall, 2016). This hypothesis should not act as a tool to exclude contradictory information. Rather, it is the beginning of a process that is dynamic over the course of the investigation, especially in this early period. The initial hypothesis can assist by assessing whether various bits of evidence or information are consistent with the initial assessment or whether they tend to contradict the hypothesis.

Some initial observations may go to contemplating motive and whether the victim and offender were known to one another. Did the homicide occur on a street or in a business where valuables were taken? Did the homicide occur in a home and appear to have an inordinate amount of physical trauma with no valuables taken? Many bits of information will be considered as the investigator remains open to increasing understanding of the event and surrounding circumstances.

In homicide cases, evidence and the condition of a scene not only aid in identifying how a murder occurred, but they can also assist in understanding why it may have happened and certainly who was responsible. In many cases, the *who* is not apparent. Even given this, investigators may learn things that give them insight into what contributed to the occurrence. A local law enforcement agency will, on occasion, seek assistance from a state agency or a specific federal government agency. The FBI has resources that can assist in cases that involve indications of a serial perpetrator or those with unique artifacts or *signature* behavior at the scene.

Although widely misunderstood, the FBI's Crime Scene Analysis Unit does sophisticated work in developing possible profiles of suspects based on a careful examination of inputs from the scene. The analysis and suspect profile allow investigators to see if there are common characteristics among homicide suspects (Miller, 2008). The first step is creating profiling inputs in which all the evidence from the crime scene is collected. The process moves to identifying any linkages between crime and offender. An assessment in the form of a reconstruction to assist in understanding the dynamics at the scene is next. After that, analysts create a profile in order to guide or suggest strategies for interviews with suspects. In the investigation, the suspect profile is used by investigators to assist in identifying the suspect. If apprehended, the suspect is compared to the profile. Miller suggests that a suspect profile is important during the preliminary investigation of a homicide as detectives try to determine if there is a certain characteristic of a homicide suspect.

Biological Evidence

While some of the technology that makes its way into movies and shows may exist, the availability is either not absolute or has a waiting time that may render the test irrelevant. Consider **DNA** samples waiting six months or more to be tested. An investigation may have concluded based on other factors, or a suspect may flee because sufficient probable cause does not exist without the test results. The idea of DNA

WHY WOULD THEY DO IT?

Mishandled evidence can easily ruin the criminal case against a suspect or thwart the effort to locate a suspect to begin with. The murder of 6-year-old JonBenét Ramsey happened 20 years ago, and yet it remains a touchstone of what can happen when inattentive or inexperienced personnel arrive on the scene of a serious crime.

Former Boulder, Colorado, Police Chief Mark Beckner said in candid remarks in early 2015 that the officers on the scene of the Ramsey murder mishandled the scene and investigation. Chief Beckner pointed to being understaffed and frankly unfamiliar with

such a case as leading to missteps at every turn in the case.

JonBenét was reported missing by her mother, who claimed a ransom note was also found at the family home. JonBenét's body was found in the home's basement. Police failed to separate the parents to take statements and did not stop a variety of friends and family from coming into and out of the active crime scene. Chief Beckner also cited "interference" by the district attorney's office. Unknown until documents were unsealed in 2013, the grand jury in the case had recommended indictments against both parents.

comparison results in less than a day is not realistic. A television show may use a computer that automatically scans fingerprints to find a match. This device is the Automated Fingerprint Identification System, or AFIS. In real life, once a *hit* or match is located, a trained technician must still examine and compare the prints to determine a match. We do know that the availability of DNA evidence allows for the reopening of **cold cases** and increased potential for solving cases that previously had little physical evidence to lead to a suspect (Kirsch, 2006).

The increased use of technology brings moral as well as practical and legal questions and challenges. The general public may have little concern about defendants and convicted persons when it comes to matters such as seizing DNA samples from all or some arrestees. Some states are taking DNA samples from arrestees, no matter what the crime (Cole, 2007). Increased use of DNA evidence and information obtained through genealogical websites have led to the solving of numerous cold cases that had little other than biological evidence maintained in evidence storage. This may reflect unequal treatment of defendants, implying that

people who commit a crime are going to offend again. While this view may be cynical regarding the use of DNA and its effect on the system as a whole, unintended consequences can occur. This may be especially true in the criminal justice system. Methods of obtaining DNA samples from suspects remain debated as questions of Fourth Amendment boundaries are analyzed (Maclin, 2006).

It is also notable that new advances in analysis of DNA have led to the exoneration of some individuals wrongly convicted of crimes. DNA identification, digital fingerprinting, and digital lineups have improved the investigation process and, in turn, made it more effective through the use of technologies. Although more effective, such technologies have come with a cost to the criminal justice system and the public. If jurors do not understand the evidence being presented, they may default to evaluating the experience credentials or presentation of the expert witness (Singer, Miller, & Adya, 2007). This is problematic as the expert's testimony is still an opinion despite his or her status as an expert. The ***Daubert* standard**, which is the standard that applies to the admissibility of scientific evidence

The Golden State Killer was a murderer, rapist, and burglar who was active in California for a dozen years through the mid-1980s. More than 30 years later, in April of 2018, police charged Joseph James DeAngelo, a Navy veteran and former police officer, with eight murder charges. DNA evidence linked DeAngelo with the cases, helped clear several other suspects in crimes eventually tied to DeAngelo, and is seen as perhaps the best example of the utility of California's DNA database that seeks DNA samples from all accused and convicted felons in the state.

The killer's modus operandi also linked him to a number of other killings, and he has been named the attacker in more than 50 rapes. Until all of DeAngelo's crimes were connected, his activities earned him the moniker of the Original Night Stalker for crimes between 1979 and 1986, designation as the

Visalia Ransacker for crimes in 1974 and 1975, and he was known as the East Area Rapist for offenses in the Sacramento area between 1976 and 1979.

Investigators utilized the personal genomics and genealogy website GEDmatch in their renewed search for the Golden State Killer. The search revealed 10–20 relatives of a family that was then family-tree mapped by police working with an experienced genealogist to identify two suspects—one was DeAngelo. In 2018, GEDmatch and genealogical work is credited with identifying suspects in 28 cold murder and rape cases. The website can use profiles uploaded from companies such as 23andMe and Ancestry. These two companies work with law enforcement if presented with a court order, whereas the public database GEDmatch is available widely and free.

WHY WOULD THEY DO IT?

in federal court and in many state courts, requires that an expert's testimony be reliable and relevant. The responsibility to determine such reliability and relevance rests with the trial judge, who will determine whether an expert will be allowed to testify in a case.

Even though DNA evidence is not an exact science, it can be very strong evidence that jurors expect to hear in serious cases. DNA profiles are measured in probabilities, not hard figures. This reflects the reality and nature of all physical sciences. The use of DNA in the court system continues to evolve as jurors and the general public think through how exonerations of convicted persons call into question the use of the death penalty. DNA can be compromised simply because of human error in the process of sampling or analysis (Aronson & Cole, 2009). The DNA matching process to the CODIS (Combined DNA Index System) or other database is not exact. However, the 1 in 7,000,000,000 chance of being wrongly identified is a standard most jurors have been willing to accept.

As with any technology or method used by the state, there is a balance between individual rights guaranteed by the Constitution and the public interest of crime control. There continues to be controversy over obtaining DNA samples widely from suspects as well as offenders convicted of minor crimes. An example of the controversy is in Orange County, California. There are differences between the national DNA database and the DNA database for Orange County, California (Putrill, 2011). The Orange County database was started and is maintained by the district attorney's office. It is argued that the prosecutor's office has created rules regarding when a DNA sample may be taken that are not in keeping with the Fourth Amendment. For example, a man found trespassing and due for trial was offered a plea bargain of taking a DNA test for the local DNA database in exchange for dropping the misdemeanor charge. While the trespass defendant agreed to the submission, this would be considered unethical in many other states and jurisdictions. The district attorney in Orange County approves of taking these samples even in misdemeanor cases because he and others believe that this will help deter crime and be a useful tool for investigations. There is debate about the ethics of such DNA sampling, with some asserting that the 14th and Fourth Amendments are compromised. After charges are dropped, the offender's DNA is still maintained in the database. This is a locally run program but an example of one controversy that DNA sampling methods have brought on.

The **National DNA Index System** (NDIS) and CODIS help police solve crimes more efficiently. Because of the volume of requests and the shortage of staff at laboratories, the system is, unfortunately, backlogged far more than people realize, and the category organization of the database further lengthens the time it takes to complete a database search (Gabriel, Boland, & Holt, 2010). Clearly, more offenders are being caught as a result of DNA samples in these databases. There is no evidence to suggest that offenders are deterred knowing their DNA is stored in one or more databases.

While there are a number of methods to analyze DNA samples, the FBI currently uses short-tandem repeat, or STR, analysis. This procedure takes a sample of DNA and compares its double helix pattern with a known sample from their CODIS. The CODIS can have difficulty in analyzing evidence from a crime scene because the sample is not always a clean, uncontaminated sample (Widyanto, Soedarsono, Katayama, & Nakao, 2010). This challenge is why it is proposed that the FBI examine other methods or systems to reduce or eliminate any uncertainty with the comparison.

ME OR NO ME?

The **medical examiner** or coroner (ME/C) is a necessary component of a homicide investigation. In a murder case, the finding of a forensic pathologist is necessary to establish the cause of death and that the manner was criminal. Determining cause and manner of death relies on facts from the scene, witness accounts, and investigator information as well as the results of the postmortem examination. While the identity of most victims is not difficult to determine, the pathologist and other medical specialists, such as a forensic odontologist, may be needed in cases where identity is not readily discernible. Other specialized medical personnel routinely or sometimes involved in a death investigation include the forensic entomologist, toxicologist, and the occasional forensic anthropologist.

Our question here is whether an ME/C or one of their investigators needs to attend the scene of the homicide. The requirement to respond to the scene will vary with the policy of the respective ME/C office. The desirability of having a **death scene investigator** (DSI) from the ME/C respond is more dependent on local custom and communication between law enforcement and the ME/C. State statutes cover many death circumstances where the ME/C office will be involved. Since criminal homicide is not always readily apparent, early involvement of additional trained investigators is generally recommended. Like crime scene technicians, DSIs will have varied education, training, and backgrounds. The DSI will gather demographic information for their agency reporting purposes.

If the DSI does respond to the scene of a suspected criminal death, he will gather information on the circumstances of the death along with law enforcement personnel. This coordination is necessary to avoid duplication of effort and to help ensure that both agencies have all available information regarding the death. While the personnel will cooperate in assessing the scene, the DSI has specific interest in the body of the deceased, including preparing the body for transport to the morgue facility.

PROSECUTORS: WHO NEEDS 'EM?

We address the specifics of the prosecutor's role in murder cases later in the chapter on homicide in court. Detectives know that while the gathering of physical evidence often correlates to the solving of a homicide case, the physical evidence in and of itself does not ensure prosecution or case clearance. Many cases are, for various reasons, unable to proceed to an arrest or to trial. Detectives often coordinate early in a case with prosecutors so that they can receive guidance on legal matters such as establishing sufficient probable cause, writing search warrants, and preparing lineups. The prosecutor is in the best position to assist in objectively advising the investigators on Fourth and Fifth Amendment issues to be mindful of. Some specialized homicide prosecutors also decide to visit the crime scene during the investigation of a homicide so that they can be more prepared to prosecute the case later. Coordination between the detective and the prosecutor can increase the likelihood of successful case development, prosecution, and conviction of the responsible person.

TECHNOLOGY

It would be impossible to overestimate the impact that technology has had on the investigation of crime in general and homicide specifically. The applications of science and the scientific method are no longer new to criminal justice, and the awareness of the benefits of these applications is now universal. The last few generations of TV and movie watchers are awash in offerings that highlight, if often exaggerate, the capabilities of technology and those who wield it to solve crime. The techno-optimism of those who have seen the modern march of equipment-enhanced existence exists alongside the techno-expectation of a younger generation who has known little else.

A concern that many people voice is the way that TV dramas, such as *CSI*, and reality shows, such as A&E's *First 48*, can educate criminals in ways to limit the presence of or destroy evidence or otherwise foil attempts to gather the evidence through forensic technology. While a certain level of concern is reasonable on this account, many criminal homicides are the result of a rapid escalation of circumstances that do not involve preplanning. An attempt to clean up all evidence afterward is often evidence in itself that a suspect knew his actions were criminal. We must rely on the increasing sophistication of the technology and the skill of technicians and investigators to locate, collect, analyze, and present the available evidence.

The use of technology can initially be broken into two main sections—preliminary and follow-up—just as investigations are. Preliminary investigation takes place most often at a crime scene, and it is here we find patrol officers, crime scene technicians, and detectives first observing and examining the area for physical evidence. Follow-up investigation is conducted by investigators while follow-up testing or initial advanced testing of items or substances gathered at the scene are conducted by criminalists at a laboratory.

The testing that occurs at the crime scene may include **presumptive tests** for blood and other fluids, flammable substances, fingerprints, drugs, explosives, and gunshot residue. Many of these tests consist of exposing the suspect substance to a reagent and observing if a telltale reaction occurs. Even with a positive presumptive test, the substance will be sent on to the laboratory for further testing. Given the need for more conclusive follow-up testing, some question the need for presumptive testing. The reasons for the initial tests are to determine if probable cause may be established through presumptive identification of a substance and the elimination of a substance or person from consideration if a test shows a negative result.

Case management software programs are tools that improve the organization of an investigation, and, as such, their use is always an advantage. In addition to software programs for organizing and tracking the details of an investigation, there has been a proliferation of programs that map and analyze crime data. The data can include powerful search capabilities to identify linkages among associates of known criminals or wanted individuals.

As computers continue to change much of how business and life are conducted in most countries, the specific changes in criminal justice and investigations have been significant. Computers are now ubiquitous in criminal justice settings. Officers utilize laptop computers at calls for service and at crime scenes. Crime scene technicians use computer-aided drawing (CAD) programs to render crime scene sketches. The previously mentioned case management programs allow investigators to organize details and look for information connections while supervisors follow the progress of a case or determine when additional resources are needed. From relational database management of suspect and victim information to inventory of evidence, digital storage and retrieval of information has made investigations more effective. Crime analysis and mapping joined with accountability programs, such as COMPSTAT (Computer Statistics), which began at the NYPD, have changed how crime is tracked and resources allocated.

Computers allow dispatchers, patrol officers, investigators, prosecutors, and court personnel to append audio and video clips and update files with greater ease, frequency, and speed than at any previous time. The sharing of intelligence and raw data among jurisdictions has had a multiplier effect that results in identifying and arresting offenders who would have simply slipped out of a jurisdiction and away from being held accountable for their crimes. With the realization that most people follow identifiable patterns, Geographic Information Systems (GIS) assist investigators in narrowing search parameters for the locations and activities of suspects. Social media will continue to impact homicide and other investigations. Researching the social media posts of victims, suspects, and contacts can provide a trove of information—which must then be sorted and analyzed by investigators or support technicians. This modern analog of poring over records raises the challenge of receiving an avalanche of information such as that which has long existed when police open a tip-line. Police will often acquire and post to their own social media sites the CCTV and digital footage from private and public sources as a use of video information to elicit public tips in cases. Citizens have assisted law enforcement by sharing their own digital pictures and video. A number of cities have introduced local ordinances requiring businesses to share their video under specific investigative circumstances.

The police lab in the television show or movie is equipped with almost every imaginable technology while, in reality, most crime labs typically do not have the tools and devices depicted. Agencies often have to send their evidence to state or private labs to perform routine and critical tests. This testing takes time, unlike what we see on television, where mobile crime labs sometimes solve the crime in a matter of minutes. When test results do return, they may not link a suspect to the scene or a key piece of evidence (Roane, 2005). Jurors expecting fast-paced, exciting, technologically slick, graphics-filled court presentations are sure to be disappointed. More importantly, this disappointment may lead to faulty decisions by jurors. Many prosecutors attempt to address this unrealistic juror expectation during jury selection to make sure that jurors understand that what they have watched on crime shows does not reflect reality.

The exaggerated capabilities of movie and television investigators have resulted in a phenomenon known as the **CSI effect**. This effect imbues ordinary citizens with the impression that they grasp the scope and detail of forensic technologies and the potential outcomes of using the sciences in criminal investigations. This happens because so many television shows and movies portray each serious crime being responded to by numerous detectives, crime scene investigators (CSI), and coordinating supervisory personnel. To be blunt, this is not the typical response by most agencies.

The CSI effect bears mention in several chapters of this text, but the full discussion belongs here, as we examine the realities of technology's role in criminal justice. In addition to the citizen on the street, the CSI effect leads jurors largely to mistakenly believe they possess thorough knowledge about the methods of crime scene and laboratory investigation and analysis. This state of affairs creates a need for prosecutors to thoroughly explain this effect and disabuse jurors of the notion that all crime investigations are capable of providing conclusive physical evidence (Lovgren, 2004). At the same time, when such evidence does exist, both prosecutors and defense attorneys must be conversant with the technology so that they can put the gathering and testing of evidence in the context of contemporary capabilities. Prosecutors realize that the awareness of technology by the general public requires the state's case to incorporate the testimony of experts to address the significance of gathered evidence.

A homicide scene can be a bloody mess. While such crime scenes often provide an abundance of evidence, locating and collecting trace evidence is challenging and sometimes impossible. Crime scene technicians and investigators must be able to clearly explain the methods and equipment used and why such methods and equipment did or did not produce demonstrable evidence. The relative lack of physical evidence is not in itself an indication of poor investigative effort but often merely the reality of little evidence left behind at a scene. The unrealistic assumption in the minds of jurors is frequently about the quantity and quality of evidence that will be presented. If seemingly significant evidence is not present, there may be more of an inclination to acquit the defendant. Jurors may hold defense attorneys to similar and possibly unrealistic standards when it comes to evidence and testing. If defense attorneys do not appear to aggressively argue down each item of evidence presented, jurors may wonder why and interpret this as guilt (Mann, 2006). This has dictated a change in how many attorneys handle criminal cases (Smith, Patry, & Stinson, 2007). Many prosecutors feel that jurors are influenced by television shows and movies. Television and movies show many real and some fanciful scientific instruments and procedures, often not practical for most cases investigated in the real world. Prosecutors worry that without a mountain of scientific evidence that jurors see on television, they may not convict guilty defendants.

While the CSI effect may cause jurors to unreasonably expect certain evidence or testing to be performed, others assert that the effect may be creating more informed jurors, which may, in turn, result in improved outcomes (Heinrick, 2006). Some have viewed the use of technology as prosecutors attempting to *trick* jurors into giving guilty verdicts. It can be the case that a jury does not see evidence interpretation as variable, viewing the evidence as black or white. Many of the techniques on *CSI*-type shows would not pass the reliability standards established by courts and used to determine that scientific processes are widely accepted within the scientific community. If methods do not pass these standards, they cannot be used in court proceedings.

Biometrics

Biometrics allow for recognizing people based on measureable biological criteria. In this way, government agencies are using the power of technology to identify wanted persons in public places with facial-recognition devices. Devices have also been used for quite some time to control ingress and egress to secure facilities. These same algorithms that can control secure access can be used to ensure the correct inmate in a facility is being moved, transported, or released.

Because of television and movies, most people are familiar with the use of biometrics for secure-access applications. Retinal and iris scans as well as fingerprint scans are shown to confirm the identity of an individual and provide him entry to a building or room or the opening of a vault or secure storage area. Some retinal-scanning concerns revolve around long-term exposure to the scanner light source as well as inconsistent performance based on changes to the eye from age or disease. Iris scans have an advantage over retinal scanning in the distance from the scanning device that a person may be accurately scanned.

Voice recognition software has been joined by hand geometry that relies on the measurements of a person's fingers and hand. While retinal scanning and hand geometry have some errors, voice recognition is still considered the least reliable of the available identification methods. Voiceprints rely on the energy of the human voice. Like polygraphs, the use of voiceprints in criminal trials is controversial because the technology is not as reliable as other methods.

CASE PERSONNEL

We noted that patrol officers are typically the first official people to encounter the homicide scene or call. It cannot be overstated how important the role and functions of patrol officers are as they give medical aid, secure the scene, document evidence and witnesses, and work closely with investigators in the myriad functions that must be handled in homicide investigations. When the homicide or major crimes investigator arrives to take the lead on a death case, he becomes the central coordinating point for what can be a nearly overwhelming volume of information. Working within a team of people handling various aspects of the event, the detective works to ensure that everyone addresses their areas thoroughly, and then documents their actions just as completely.

The story of technology and forensics is also the story of the professionals who conduct investigations and examinations. Markedly different from the *triple-threat* fictional characters from television shows such as *CSI*, these real-life professionals do not simultaneously work crime scenes, conduct laboratory analyses, and interrogate suspects. They also do not generally wear high heels or tight suits while visiting crime scenes. We hope you are not surprised by this. Many undergraduate college students enter course or degree programs believing that this type of omni-skilled, high-fashion career awaits them. Each role in forensics is fascinating and important and requires a singular focus on the requisite skill sets and functions.

At the first line of initial scene examination are crime scene technicians who often locate, document, and collect evidence at the various scene locations. Patrol officers frequently fill this role as well. The job of crime scene technician has gradually transitioned from one occupied by a certified law enforcement officer to one taken on by highly trained civilian employees of an agency. This follows the civilianization trend of other positions, including communications specialists (dispatchers and call-takers). This evolution recognizes that the higher salary cost of certified officers is not needed for crime scene work and that by having personnel who only conduct scene investigations, the level of specialization increases and results in higher quality work at scenes.

The variance in qualifications for the job is based on factors such as departmental budget, crime rate and volume, top-management philosophy, or available interagency assistance. Undergraduate students with various related degrees have had success in acquiring crime scene technician positions. Some retired officers also seek out the job of technician. Hands-on training after joining an agency can be the primary source of training in the various functions of the job.

Crime scene technicians may perform virtually all documentation and evidence collection functions, or there may be role separation, resulting in crime scene photographers distinct from technicians, who locate and collect evidence as well as perform limited presumptive testing. The photographer may also perform digital mapping of a crime scene or sketching as appropriate. Once again, this varies with available resources and personnel.

Beginning in the early 1900s, crime laboratories began to be established, though these were available to relatively few agencies. The FBI established a laboratory in 1932 to make forensic science available to law enforcement agencies around the country. While this marked a step forward in the use of science in criminal investigations, the general lack of sophistication of medium and small-sized agencies in applying science meant that fully exploiting new and developing capabilities was still some time off.

Personnel who analyze evidence in the lab are generally referred to as **criminalists**. Some crime scene technicians choose to eventually transition to laboratory work. The qualifications for criminalist typically include at least a bachelor's degree in biology, chemistry, biochemistry, pharmacology, or a related core forensic discipline. In some cases, a person with a degree in criminal justice who completed a diverse selection of courses in the hard sciences may be accepted to laboratory training programs.

In the laboratory setting, criminalists may work in any of a number of sciences, including anatomy, anthropology, bacteriology, biology, chemistry, entomology, pharmacology, and even psychology. Different labs provide different services around the country. Just as with other key areas of public safety resources, the federal government has been a leader in establishing and funding laboratory services.

Crime laboratory growth has been significant, but there is much concern that insufficient national standards exist to ensure the thoroughness of qualifications for personnel and solid integrity of testing protocols for the labs. Supreme Court decisions over the second half of the 20th century required law enforcement agencies to rely more on physical evidence and science in building cases against suspects. This too led to the proliferation of laboratories in the United States. No doubt, the tremendous volume of drug cases inundates labs with testing as has the rapid increase in the use of DNA in forensic identification since the mid-1980s.

Technology and forensic capabilities for testing may or may not be readily available to various sized agencies. Large local agencies routinely assist smaller agencies. State law enforcement agencies similarly assist local-level departments in large or complex cases. Additionally, the FBI has various programs and personnel available to assist with coordination, training, and other forms of assistance. The National Center for the Analysis of Violent Crime (NCAVC) is the central entity to facilitate assistance. Within the NCAVC, there are three units that perform various functions and assist in investigations: the Child Abduction and Serial Murder Investigative Resources Center (CASMIRC), the Violent Criminal Apprehension Program (ViCAP), and the Behavioral Analysis Unit (BAU). Various federal, state, and some local agency laboratory facilities assist in analysing the evidence gathered from the field and various other sources. One example that saw expansion of access in 2018 is the National Integrated Ballistic Information Network (NIBIN). The Bureau of Alcohol, Tobacco, Firearms and Explosives (ATF) furnished the equipment to 22 state and local agencies to aid in the comparisons between bullet casing and firearms recovered by law enforcement.

Many cases have certainly benefited from not only the application of forensic identification through DNA but from all manner of technological innovation. With that said, not all cases have a direct application of sophisticated technology or testing to stand in for the responsibility of a jury to comprehend and apply the reasonable-doubt standard. In other words, not all cases have available items to be tested, nor do criminal cases require a long list of items of physical evidence. In the closing argument of the trial in the accompanying boxed-story case of the murder of 2-year-old Caylee Anthony, the defense attorney went on at length about what forensic evidence the prosecution did not show.

Casey Anthony was put on trial for the murder of her 2-year-old daughter Caylee. Dubbed the "Social Media Trial of the Century" by *Time* magazine, the nation was captivated and horrified at the facts of the case. Most were further stunned at the acquittal of the accused killer on charges of first-degree murder, aggravated child abuse, and more. Casey and Caylee lived with Casey's mother and stepfather, Cindy and George Anthony, in Orlando, Florida. After four weeks, Casey Anthony told her mother that she had not seen her daughter Caylee for a month. Cindy Anthony called the police and told them of Caylee's disappearance and that her daughter's car smelled as though a dead body had been in the trunk. Casey Anthony told law enforcement officers a variety of lies regarding Caylee's disappearance. Caylee's remains were found buried near the house inside a garbage bag six months later. Prosecutors presented hundreds of items of evidence during the trial that police had collected during the investigation of the crime, including computer searches on a computer accessible to the defendant on how to make chloroform and break someone's neck.

This was the result not of a poor investigation but because the remains of the deceased child had been buried for some six months, compromising virtually all evidence that may have tied the suspect to her.

WORKING WITH THE MEDIA

Virtually everybody is interested in murders. And while the average citizen has curiosity, the media finds such cases important as they package information for public consumption. As news organizations rush to scoop their competition in bringing the often gory details of a murder to the attention of the public, these outlets and individual reporters may take actions that can compromise ongoing investigations (Hough & Tatum, 2014). These acts can be intentional under the asserted right to inform the public, but they can also be questionable from an ethical standpoint as the release of certain information can tangibly damage investigations. The hurried and overly broad provision of details by the media can be viewed alternately as the irresponsible or simply aggressive pursuit of a story of interest.

Law enforcement, for their part, can be secretive in providing information on murder cases to the media. This may include withholding information that may not be sensitive to an active case. Many agencies and news organization recognize there is a middle ground that allows both to pursue their organizational functions as well as to often facilitate the goals of the other. The media can be of help to investigators by alerting the public to a suspect, asking the public's assistance in identifying unknown victims, and asking people to come forward to provide information about a case. Cold-case investigations will frequently call upon the media to recap old or unsolved crimes. The law enforcement and media relationship is often challenging. This is the result of the tension created by the pursuit of different goals. When the common ground is found, both can benefit.

COLD CASE INVESTIGATIONS

A great deal of crime is never reported or discovered. Of the crime that is reported to authorities, much presents little in the way of physical or witness evidence. When this happens, police may have little recourse but to await information to come in from the victim or another source. Frequently that help never comes and a case is closed or held inactive. In cases of homicide and sexual battery, due to the seriousness of these crimes, the term cold case has come to be applied.

Not all homicide cases are solved quickly or easily. If a suspect is not readily identified,

In December of 1992, Christy Mirack, a 25-year-old Pennsylvania teacher was brutally assaulted, raped, and murdered in her home. The person responsible was never identified—until after 25 years a combination of genetic genealogy and an increasingly utilized investigative technique identified Raymond Rowe, a DJ, as the killer. Following the celebrated arrest of the so-called "Golden State Killer" as a result of the use of DNA to trace a suspect's family tree, the murder of Christy Mirack was solved using the same method. The now 50-year-old Rowe was working as a DJ at an elementary school when police were able to obtain his DNA from chewing gum and a bottle of water and then connect it to DNA found at the crime scene. Rowe pleaded guilty to first-degree murder, rape, and other charges in exchange for a sentence of life without the possibility of parole.

or insufficient evidence exists to connect the suspect to the crime, an open case of homicide may languish, sometimes for years. The formation of a unit, task force with other agencies, or even assignment of a sole investigator to review inactive cases can yield results. Victims matter, as do their families and more broadly the community's sense of safety. For these and other reasons, addressing cold cases is beneficial. Whether DNA comparison from a long-closed case leads to a killer, or witnesses find the resolve to finally speak with police, the fact that a case has been unsolved does not mean it will always remain so.

Some agencies have found or devoted the resources to conduct cold case investigations into matters that seemed unsolvable. Funding these efforts is no mean feat. The federal government has at times made start-up funding or grant money available to begin or continue the work of a local agency or a collaboration of multiple agencies. The additional resources include selection and additional training of investigators to carry out the work of the cold case unit. Groups such as ViCAP have done much to facilitate efforts aimed at solving older cases as well as identifying potential connected cases that may suggest the work of a serial criminal. In the process to *warm up* an old case, detectives go through all existing reports and evidence, hoping that the work done initially was competent and that a case may have just been waiting for a key piece of information or evidence to come to light. This last part is an important assumption when we examine the varying clearance rates of agencies around the country.

SUMMARY

There are a number of important investigative challenges in homicide investigations. These include securing witness cooperation, crime scene processing, having adequate initial resources, video interrogations, eyewitness identification, documentation, forensic evidence, and homicide team communication. These issues and others represent investigative challenges and ultimately challenges to successful case outcomes.

The arrival and actions of the first responding officer in a homicide investigation are critical. When the patrol officer gets to the scene, he must quickly determine if medical aid is needed by anyone, while staying alert for the presence of the killer or any other dangers. The officer has to identify who the victim is and begin carefully observing the homicide scene. As quickly as possible, the initial officer(s) must block off the crime scene to protect obvious or potential evidence.

The scene may be relatively static, with a dead body and no other witnesses or participants present. On the other hand, there may be numerous people, who may or may not be involved, and a dynamic environment. In either case, the officer must work efficiently to control and protect the scene and identify the roles of the people who are present. Scovell (2010) notes that at the scene of a homicide, you may be faced with a "study in conflicting agendas." The officer needs to secure the scene, EMS needs to check the injured, and witnesses, additional victims, and suspects may be trying to leave or be disruptive due to the emotion of the situation. The initial personnel must truly manage the scene and then move to organizing the actions for what may be a long and involved investigation.

Documenting the scene, activities, and statements is an important function of the primary officer. Thorough and accurate recording of all the officer finds is a must. The patrol officer generally is the preliminary investigator. He must be able to effectively brief the homicide investigator who arrives to carry on the investigation. We have noted that many personnel typically arrive at a scene. Most are given specific duties or tasks to carry out. Some personnel may be assigned to less glamorous roles and should be reminded to be vigilant, observant, and document thoroughly all relevant observations.

An integral component of any death investigation is the collection of evidence, whether physical or testimonial. In the early stages of an investigation, it may be unclear what things or statements may turn out to be important. Great care must be taken to completely document all potential items of evidence, and statements and information must be gathered from any and all people, whether they witnessed the actual act or not. Many witnesses do not realize that they possess important information about an event. The preliminary officer must seek out information so that the investigators who take up the investigation have everything they can to move the case forward. When homicides become cold cases, a long time may pass before witnesses come forward or advances in medical and forensic technology bring to light a connection between a victim and a suspect who may have cloaked themselves in obscurity or been hiding in plain sight. This highlights the importance of law enforcement agencies maintaining a focus on investigating cold cases.

KEY TERMS

DISCUSSION QUESTIONS

1. Discuss the initial concerns of a patrol officer arriving at the scene of a reported homicide.
2. List and describe the roles of the personnel who might respond to a scene that has been identified as one involving a homicide.
3. Why should investigators get information and statements from people at the scene even if they said they did not witness anything?
4. What are some items of evidence at a homicide scene that should go to the laboratory for testing?

5. Describe and discuss the ways in which a prosecutor can aid a preliminary investigation.
6. What are some functions that a death scene investigator from the medical examiner's office might conduct?
7. Law enforcement agencies have policies of various length and content. What should be covered in a homicide investigation policy?

TRY THIS

Examine several news reports for a murder case. Imagine yourself in the role of the preliminary officer responding to the initial scene. List with brief explanations the various steps you would take when you arrive at the scene.

The National Institute of Justice offers a number of free online training programs. Go to https://www.nij.gov/training/Pages/training-detail.aspx?itemid=72, and try the "Crime Scene and DNA Basics for Forensic Analysts" course.

14

MURDER IN COURT

Some circumstantial evidence is very strong, as when you find a trout in the milk.

—Henry David Thoreau

"Murder may pass unpunished for a time,

But tardy justice will o'ertake the crime."

—J. Dryden

CHAPTER OUTLINE

Student Learning Outcomes

Students will be able to:

- explain the stages of the court process involved in criminal homicide cases.

- articulate the different legal definitions and levels of homicide crimes.

- describe the most common defenses used in homicide cases.

- discuss the process of sentencing, including the use of mitigation evidence, in homicide cases.

INTRODUCTION

Everyone growing up or living in America has more than a passing familiarity with the steps of the criminal justice system, especially when it comes to a criminal court case and trial. An unending stream of television shows, movies, and podcasts present to us the process of a murder suspect arrested and then taken to court where a hardnosed prosecutor faces a determined criminal defense lawyer. Okay, but this seems to leave quite a bit out, doesn't it?

As discussed earlier in the book, the interest that we all have in not just cases of criminal homicide but even more broadly the criminal justice system has been shaped and is fed by this steady diet of Hollywood creations and embellishments. The reality is sometimes far less gripping and unquestionably tragic. Notorious cases of murder or homicides involving people well known to the general public can drive a significant amount of media coverage. But the vast majority of homicide cases are rarely covered past an initial mention on the local news or in a local newspaper. By the time the average homicide case goes to trial, there is little interest from the public, save for the immediate friends and family of the people affected by the event.

Homicide is the most serious violent crime in a culture. Defined as the killing of one human by another, homicide is categorized in several ways. The ones that most people think of when they hear about murder are those cases where someone has intentionally killed another person and, in many cases, has what is referred to as **malice aforethought**, meaning that the intention to harm existed before the moment the act occurred. **Manslaughter**, as a legally lesser category, includes homicides that occur in a moment of extreme anger or recklessness without previous ill intent. There are also accidental homicides, which will be investigated before determining a legal outcome, and excusable and noncriminal homicides as well as deaths resulting from negligence.

The decision about what specific charge to file in response to the actions of someone who has killed another person is the province of the prosecutor. Some state jurisdictions call this individual the district attorney and some refer to the position as the state attorney. At the federal level this person is called a U.S. attorney. The attorney representing the people wields significant power through the charging system, and he must conduct himself with great integrity (Corrigan, 1986). In any event, the prosecutor will look at the known facts of the case and decide which category of murder or manslaughter and what level or degree of seriousness will be formally charged. The prosecutor must always consider what can be proven during trial as prosecutors have ethical duties to pursue charges which they believe the evidence supports. Each stage of a homicide case is important in our adversarial system and falls in a specific sequence of stages that ultimately dispose of a case via one of the options available by law. Multiple crimes committed within one incident can bring multiple charges. Often, the charges do not carry as heavy a penalty as murder or manslaughter and may be used to negotiate a plea arrangement with the defendant.

STAGES IN HOMICIDE CASES

Following the arrest of a suspect, the pretrial stage begins. The prosecutor conducts an assessment to gauge whether the case has potential to succeed in court. If the prosecutor does not believe the evidence is sufficient to prove the case **beyond a reasonable doubt**, she may use discretion to dismiss charges. In some cases, as mentioned, the prosecutor may file additional charges beyond those initially listed by law enforcement, which may serve as leverage for an eventual plea arrangement. An initial court appearance follows within 24 to 48 hour of the arrest, during which the accused individual is made aware of the charges brought against him, and if the person cannot afford to hire an attorney, the court will appoint one to represent the defendant. The U.S. Constitution guarantees defendants who are facing the potential loss of liberty the right to have an attorney represent them even if they cannot afford one. The court will also determine, based on legislative guidelines, if a defendant is eligible to be released prior to trial and will set the amount and conditions of bail or release to ensure the defendant's appearance for future court dates. If ordered by the court, the amount of bail for a murder suspect is usually significant, given the seriousness of the charge. A Bureau of Justice Statistics (BJS) special report in 2007 noted that just 19% of murder defendants in state courts nationwide were granted pretrial release. The report identifies a decreasing number of pretrial releases, partially caused by rising bail amounts, and notes that when bail rose above $100,000, only 1 in 10 defendants was able to post bail (Cohen & Reaves, 2007). This level of pretrial release denial for murder defendants is not surprising and reflects the court's assessment of risk to the public or flight by the defendant.

About half of the states and the federal criminal courts utilize a **grand jury** system. The grand jury meets behind closed doors and hears from only the prosecution. The grand jury's role is to determine if there is sufficient evidence to move forward with a trial. The grand jury does not determine guilt. If the grand jury members determine there is enough evidence and probable cause that an individual committed a specific crime, an indictment or *true bill* is rendered. Fewer rules apply to the conduct of the jury, and the hearing is held behind closed doors. Given the manner by which the grand jury operates and the low standard of proof required at this stage, it is nearly a foregone conclusion in American jurisprudence that a prosecutor seeking a grand jury indictment will get one.

If charges go forward against an individual, an **arraignment** will follow where the defendant can enter a plea. The plea can be guilty, not guilty, or *nolo contendere*, or no contest. If a guilty or no-contest plea is entered and accepted by the court, a sentencing hearing will come next, and there will not be a trial. The defendant may enter a plea of not guilty as a result of believing himself innocent of the crime for which he is charged or to force the prosecutor to fulfill his role and prove the case against the defendant. A defendant in a serious case often enters a not guilty plea at the arraignment stage to give his

lawyer more time to investigate the case and to seek a **plea agreement** with the prosecutor. A plea can be agreed upon at any time during the process. If a plea cannot be arranged, a trial will take place. The defense counsel must provide his client with information regarding all offers of a plea deal by the prosecution. If the defendant wishes to accept a plea, it is the responsibility of the court to ensure the defendant has accepted the plea willingly and knowingly, with no promises or threats to do so (Ehrhard-Dietzel, 2012). Increased sentence severity in cases showing a greater likelihood of conviction reduces the chances that a prosecutor will offer a plea bargain and increases the probability that the defendant's attorney will seek one (Baumer, Messner, & Felson, 2000).

Following the pretrial stages, the prosecution and defense will offer various pretrial motions requesting the court suppress or allow evidence in the trial. In serious criminal cases like homicide, there may be a number of legal issues for the court to address before the trial including whether certain scientific evidence should be admitted, whether there were any constitutional violations by the police in the investigation, and the admissibility of confessions. And then, before the trial can begin, a jury must be seated. A group of citizens is selected to weigh the evidence presented and render a verdict. This panel of prospective jurors is known as the **venire**. Choosing jurors is important to the integrity of the process, and the court searches for citizens who can be impartial. Lawyers from both sides directly question prospective jurors in what is called *voir dire*. Ideally, jurors will not favor either the prosecution or the defense in their views. Lawyers on both sides are allowed a set number of **peremptory challenges** to remove a prospective juror. These can be used for almost any reason other than a juror's race, religion, disability, or other protected class. Lawyers can also use **challenges for cause**, which are strikes that can be used when it is apparent that a juror cannot be fair and impartial. An example of a challenge for cause in a capital murder case would be a prospective juror stating that he would be unable to vote for the death penalty (in a case where the death penalty was authorized by statute) under any circumstance based on his personal beliefs. Judges must rule on all challenges to make sure they are lawful. In some cases, mainly significant civil trials, so-called scientific jury selection has been used. The potentially high dollar amounts of settlements in such cases and the resources available to defendants make the use of the jury consultant more likely. The process of scientific jury selection (SJS) involves the use of a trial consultant, who is often a social scientist, to conduct survey research of the profiles of eligible jurors and assess the most suitable ones for one side or the other. Research is mixed regarding scientific jury selection as jurors still rely predominantly on the evidence presented.

The homicide trial begins with opening statements in which the prosecutor and defense attorney briefly summarize their positions to the jury. The attorneys will generally outline for the jury what they will show during the trial as well as the evidence and testimony they will present. Lawyers often try to present a "roadmap" in the opening statement to preview how the case will proceed and to help the jurors see the big picture. Presentation of evidence by the prosecution follows the opening statements. The applicable rules of evidence guide the trial process and determine what is admissible. The prosecution seeks to establish that the defendant is accountable through the presentation of the evidence. The defense works to show the court or jury that there is reasonable doubt of the defendant's guilt. The defense strategy may include making the case that the defendant is guilty of a lesser crime. This is a common strategy in homicide cases where the lower levels of homicide crime can carry much lower penalties than the more serious levels. Attorneys on both sides may present what is called **direct evidence** and **circumstantial evidence**. While direct evidence tends to prove a fact directly and includes evidence like eyewitness testimony or the defendant's admissions or confessions, circumstantial evidence is considered indirect and, therefore, calls for

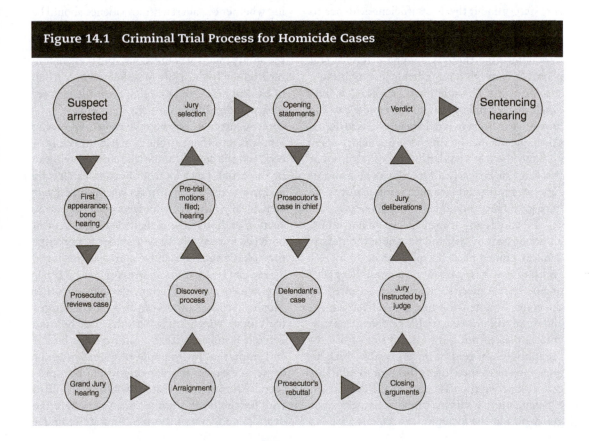

Figure 14.1   Criminal Trial Process for Homicide Cases

inferences of what happened. But circumstantial evidence can still be extremely powerful proof of criminal actions, and many homicide defendants have been convicted based on strong circumstantial evidence.

Both sides have an opportunity to ask questions of witnesses. When an attorney questions a witness for his side, this is called direct examination. Direct examination can be thought of as storytelling wherein the attorneys explain a version of events using the testimony of witnesses. The American Bar Association (ABA) and many legal writers over the years have provided guidelines and advice on controlling the testimony of witnesses. During direct examination of witnesses, the attorney for the prosecution is attempting to present evidence that meets the burden of proof and to convince jurors that the evidence and the witness are reliable. Attorneys for both the prosecution and the defense in murder cases must be well organized and have their presentations reflect that organization (Twiss, 2007). During a direct examination, the attorney generally asks specific questions to establish the foundation of the case. Once a witness has been directly examined, the opposing counsel will cross-examine to clarify and validate or attempt to discredit and impeach all or parts of the witness's testimony. The cross-examination allows opposing counsel to probe issues raised during the direct examination that may benefit their side of a case. This may come as the result of showing weaknesses in the opposing attorney's case (Wheatcroft & Ellison, 2012). It is the role of the jury to weigh the testimony of all witnesses and to determine what evidence is believable. This is why the jury in American legal system is referred to as the fact-finder.

EXPERT WITNESS TESTIMONY

In many homicide cases, prosecutors and defense attorneys rely on the use of **expert witnesses** to help them prove their cases and to present **forensic evidence**, which can be defined as evidence obtained through the use of the scientific method. Rule 702 of the **Federal Rules of Evidence**, which is very similar to evidence rules under every state's evidence rules, requires the following:

Rule 702. Testimony by Expert Witnesses

A witness who is qualified as an expert by knowledge, skill, experience, training, or education may testify in the form of an opinion or otherwise if:

a. the expert's scientific, technical, or other specialized knowledge will help the trier of fact to understand the evidence or to determine a fact in issue;

b. the testimony is based on sufficient facts or data;

c. the testimony is the product of reliable principles and methods; and

d. the expert has reliably applied the principles and methods to the facts of the case.

This rule was amended after the U.S. Supreme Court decided the **Daubert** case, and applied more flexible standards to the use of expert testimony at trial. In order for attorneys to use expert witnesses to provide scientific testimony related to DNA, ballistics, autopsy findings, blood spatter, hair follicle analysis, fingerprints, mental health diagnoses, and other scientific matters, they must lay a proper foundation that the expert witness is qualified to provide an opinion, and also that the area is based on reliable scientific principles. If either side in a criminal case wants to keep the other side's expert from testifying, they will typically file a pre-trial motion and assert that under this evidence rule, the expert is not qualified or the area of the proposed testimony has been sufficiently tested in the scientific community.

As the trial nears its completion, both sides offer closing arguments. The prosecution confidently tells the jury that it has proven beyond a reasonable doubt that the defendant committed the crime. The defense points out weaknesses of the case and assures the jury that the evidence is not convincing. Following the closing arguments the judge instructs the jury on the available verdicts and the relevant law that applies. The jury retires to deliberate and discuss the case. In a homicide trial, in order for the jury to find the defendant guilty, the verdict must be unanimous. Depending on the jurisdiction and the seriousness of the crime charged, homicide juries can range from six to 12 members.

Researchers have noted that jury verdicts are affected by numerous extralegal factors, including individual juror factors as well as characteristics of the defendant, the victim, or criminal justice players in the case (Stauffer, Smith, Cochran, Fogel, & Bjerregaard, 2006). When jurors have a higher socioeconomic status than the defendant, there is a tendency to deliver a verdict harsher than otherwise expected (Foley & Powell, 1982). A harsh verdict may reflect a perceived threat of economic encroachment by the defendant (Litwin, 2004). It has long been noted that when there is a white victim in a homicide case, a death penalty recommendation results more frequently than for black victims, and if the victim is a white female, the chances of the death penalty verdict are even higher (Stauffer et al., 2006). And while religious references or imagery are often frowned upon in a trial, attorneys have been known to use various biblical or religious references in an attempt to sway jurors (Chavez & Miller, 2009).

If a defendant is found guilty, sentencing will follow. In most homicide cases, judges will set sentencing hearings and request detailed sentencing reports to give both sides sufficient time to prepare for sentencing. In capital cases where the death penalty is sought, separate sentencing hearings are required. Victim impact statements would be presented at this stage of the proceedings. It is common for family members or friends to testify about how their loved one's murder has affected them (Newman, 1995). The victim impact statement has been shown to greatly influence jury recommendations in sentencing, and this calls for the mitigating or controlling practice by the judge in providing victim impact instructions to jurors (Berman, Narby, & Cutler, 1995; Newman, 1995; Plantania & Berman,

2006). It should also be pointed out that victims of crime and their family members in homicide cases may feel insecure submitting statements (de Mesmaecker, 2012). Murder cases are hard on family members of the deceased as well as the family of the defendant. The victim's family members may have to testify and endure media attention, no matter how sympathetic it may be.

BUILDING THE CASE AND CHARGING DECISIONS

After the investigative phase and the arrest, prosecutors must make charging decisions in homicide cases. Most students of criminal justice know that there are varying levels or categories of criminal homicide, ranging from the most serious to the less serious. Every state has detailed criminal statutes that define the level of the homicide and explain the minimum and maximum penalties for the crime. Law enforcement officers and prosecutors often work together to review the details and circumstances of the crimes so that prosecutors can determine appropriate charges. In some jurisdictions, prosecutors must present first-degree murder charges to a grand jury before filing the charge. The grand jury must present an indictment for first-degree murder cases to proceed. The categories of homicide include the following:

Murder. The most serious form of homicide is murder. In most states, murder is defined as a killing that results from **premeditation** or malice aforethought. In states that have the death penalty, first-degree murder is considered a capital felony. In order to prove premeditation, it is not required to show that the defendant planned the murder far in advance of the killing. Instead, there must be evidence that the defendant formed the conscious intent to complete the deliberate act at any time *before* the killing.

Felony murder. Felony murder is a killing that results when a person is engaged in the commission of a very serious felony and also constitutes a capital felony just as first-degree murder does. The legal reasoning supporting felony murder cases as capital cases is that the premeditation element is satisfied by the defendant's intent to commit the dangerous felony enumerated in the statutes. In Florida, for example, these qualifying felonies include the following:

1. Trafficking offense,

2. Arson,

3. Sexual battery,

4. Robbery,

5. Burglary,

6. Kidnapping,

7. Escape,

8. Aggravated child abuse,

9. Aggravated abuse of an elderly person or disabled adult,

10. Aircraft piracy,

11. Unlawful throwing, placing, or discharging of a destructive device or bomb,

12. Carjacking,

13. Home-invasion robbery,

14. Aggravated stalking,

15. Murder of another human being,

16. Resisting an officer with violence to his or her person,

17. Aggravated fleeing or eluding with serious bodily injury or death,

18. Felony that is an act of terrorism or is in furtherance of an act of terrorism. (Fla. Stat. § 782.04-2, 2014)

Second-degree murder. Second-degree murder is generally defined as a killing that results without premeditation but with a *depraved mind* and is generally punishable by a term of up to life in prison, but it is not considered a capital offense.

Manslaughter. Manslaughter includes all other killings, including those that occur through what is termed *culpable negligence*. Some states continue to make the distinction between voluntary and involuntary manslaughter. But others, like Florida, do not and instead enumerate other less serious forms of manslaughter, which carry lesser penalties.

Vehicular or vessel homicide. Some killings occur during the reckless operation of motor vehicles or boats, often when the driver or operator is impaired. Many states now have separate categories for these types of killings. These homicides carry serious penalties, including up to life imprisonment for the most serious offenses.

Something known to those who study criminal justice is the concept of the crime funnel. In all criminal cases, there are many more cases investigated than charged and even fewer still that make it all the way to a jury trial. This reflects the reality that in our system, prosecutors have not only a high burden of proof but also a great deal of discretion. O'Neill (2004) examined declinations to prosecute in federal prosecution offices. He noted that the reason given by prosecutors for some declinations is a lack of investigative resources, but he also commented on the hesitancy by some prosecutors to devote effort to low-level cases. On the other hand, news coverage and an increased profile that comes from involvement in a homicide case also require a great deal of effort and resources, including the writing of search warrants, the subpoenaing and managing of witnesses, and ongoing coordination with law enforcement and other criminal justice system actors. While caseload can certainly be a factor, the message O'Neill derives also has to do with the value or lack of value placed on crimes considered low level, such as drug cases. Prosecutors must also carefully evaluate the decision to prosecute based on **double-jeopardy** concerns. The double-jeopardy clause of the U.S. Constitution holds that defendants cannot be tried for the same crime twice. This means that if a defendant is acquitted at a jury trial, the state is barred from trying him a second time, even if new evidence is later discovered. The prosecution gets no second bite at the apple, so they must be sure they are ready for a trial when the case is filed.

As an investigation proceeds, the prosecutor has a dual role of advising and assisting law enforcement and conducting specific duties as the people's representative. Pope (2011) addressed the prosecutorial investigation standards to which attorneys should adhere. The American Bar Association (ABA) developed a set of five overarching principles to guide prosecutors and followed with detailed factors to consider along the way in a criminal case. The principles that Pope (2011) noted are as follows:

1. The prosecutor has a duty to view the facts with completely disinterested eyes during an investigation. Much injustice is done when a prosecutor falls in love with a case or a solution, and ignores the truth in favor of a pet theory.

2. A prosecutor must understand the potential harmful collateral consequences of an investigation, consider them in choosing investigative steps, and attempt to minimize or mitigate them.

3. A prosecutor should use a sense of proportionality in choosing investigative steps, much in the same way discretion informs prosecutive decisions. Particularly intrusive or damaging choices may not be warranted in less serious cases. Not everything that can be done should be done.

4. A prosecutor is not a free-lancer, but a member of an office and a tradition that existed before the line assistant and will exist after the line assistant leaves. Any individual prosecutor is no more than a temporary custodian of the powerful and intrusive tools placed in his or her hands. It is, consequently, the prosecutor's duty to continually consult with supervisors and peers, and learn and follow the rules and mores of the office.

5. A prosecutor's craft and ethics are inseparable. Good craft leads to better truth finding and the prevention of unwarranted intrusions on privacy and liberty. (p. 5)

The prosecutor has the power to file or drop a case in part based on the evidence assembled by law enforcement during their investigation. This power is often unchecked and presents the classic risk of abuse that wide discretion holds (Van Patten, 2010). The prosecutor evaluates whether he can secure a guilty verdict by the fruits of the investigation, including witness accounts and any physical evidence. The prosecutor should never pursue a case based solely on the belief of being able to gain a conviction but rather on being convinced of the defendant's guilt.

> Conviction rates at trial (convictions/ prosecutions) do not tell us about the strength of the prosecutors' cases generally. Instead, the rates tell us only about the strength of those few cases the prosecutor chooses to pursue and the defendant chooses to contest. (Rasmusen, Raghav, & Ramseyer, 2008, p. 49)

Given the prosecutor's decision to pursue a case based in large part on what the police assemble, it is clear that a high level of cooperation is called for. Vecchi (2009) describes it this way:

> No matter how well conceived and successful the investigation, the investigator must be able to articulate the facts of the case in a manner that enables prosecution. Prosecutors are the gatekeepers of the courts who ultimately determine whether a case is accepted and prosecuted. As such, it is essential that the investigator coordinate and collaborate with the prosecutor early on in the investigation in order to provide the prosecutor with a sense of ownership and participation throughout the investigation. In this way, the prosecutor becomes a stakeholder in the success of the investigation and will be more willing to see it through even if weaknesses exist. (p. 10)

The role of the prosecutor has not always been agreed upon. Some of the inconsistency surrounding this role comes from the lack of legislative direction provided by states as to specifics guiding the prosecutor's quest for justice. The gaps in the law that allow a prosecutor latitude in charging decisions are rarely a subject of intense public scrutiny. This lack of legislative direction is a key component of the prosecutor's fairly unrestricted decision-making power (Green & Zacharias, 2008; Levenson, 1998). Discussed but rarely pursued is placing meaningful limits on a prosecutor's discretion in plea bargains as well as in charging. However much prosecutorial behavior and guidelines are addressed through legislation, communities frequently grade their local prosecutor on the statistics or *batting average* he or she compiles.

Having an elected prosecutor can have pros and cons. While the prosecutor's office is held accountable for delivering results in the prosecution of crimes, this measuring stick may also lead to selective choices of cases that are winnable while less promising matters are dismissed with no fanfare (Nugent-Borakove & Worrall, 2008). The negative press that can arise from a citizen falsely imprisoned or an apparent violation of someone's due-process rights can have a tremendous impact on the official's next trip to the polls.

Many jurisdictions have experimented with or committed to the use of specialized prosecution units to focus on one single crime type or grouping. Many of these are well known, such as those dealing with drugs, domestic violence, gun violence, and gang crime. Pyrooz, Wolfe, and Spohn (2011) noted in their examination of a gang prosecution unit in Los Angeles that the use of specialized units and the seriousness of the crimes involved do affect charging decisions. There are also specialized homicide units in prosecutors' offices. Prosecutors who work in these units are typically the most experienced lawyers in the office.

Both sides in a criminal case must prepare their witnesses for deposition and potential courtroom testimony. And each side prepares differently. Prosecution witnesses, including homicide investigators and medical examiners, often have trial testimony experience, allowing for potentially more impactful performance (Campbell, 2007). The defense witnesses are often less experienced or familiar with court procedures. The lack of trial experience on the part of defense witnesses can provide the opportunity for the attorneys to construe the testimony as lacking reliability or appearing inconsistent with previous testimony (Campbell, 2007; Wheatcroft & Ellison, 2012). The weight given to any witness's testimony is a decision for the juror, which underscores the need for witness preparation. Preparation must be within ethical guidelines and must not merely be coaching a witness what to say (Campbell, 2007). Proper witness preparation is not likely to cause the witness to alter his testimony. And as long as the defense attorney does not rehearse the defendant's testimony, there is less likelihood that the defendant will at some point accuse the defense attorney of telling him what to say on the stand (Campbell, 2007). Juries assess a case through the actions of lawyers. Who used the evidence most effectively, and who made the most compelling argument? The jury makes the final decision based on the presentations of both legal teams, who are doing their best to effectively put forth their side of a case.

EVIDENTIARY ISSUES

The lay public often thinks of a weapon with the suspect's fingerprints on it when evidence is mentioned. In fact there are a number of forms of evidence. Cases are routinely decided on the basis of circumstantial evidence, which does not directly link a defendant to a victim but does so indirectly. The value or weight of circumstantial evidence is a matter for the jury to decide, or, if the case is a judge trial, the judge determines if the evidence is believable. There is generally not an abundance of direct evidence in cases that go to trial. Direct evidence includes eyewitness testimony, confessions, or video evidence. In criminal cases such as homicide, the burden of proof rests on the prosecution.

Throughout the course of a trial, various challenges to or complications with evidence can arise. Anyone who has watched a crime drama in the last 50 years is aware that law enforcement officers must read to suspects their warning of constitutional rights, colloquially referred to as the Miranda warning. If the police fail to

You may recall that we mentioned criminal defendant Casey Anthony in the investigations chapter earlier in the text. She was the Orlando mother accused of killing her 2-year-old daughter Caylee in 2008 and acquitted by a jury. During the trial, the prosecution presented forensic and DNA evidence that included a strand of her daughter's hair found in Anthony's car trunk that showed decomposition and high levels of chloroform. The Anthony defense team challenged the strength and conclusions of the state's scientific evidence throughout the trial and called their own scientific experts. During the trial, an FBI forensics expert testified for the state about the decomposition signs from the hair strand, but she admitted that the science was still evolving when the defense attorneys questioned her on cross-examination. Additionally, the defense argued an alternative explanation for the child's death—that she accidentally drowned in the family pool and Casey and her father tried to cover it up—and argued that this was not inconsistent with the scientific evidence presented by the state. In the end, even though the state presented scientific evidence, the jury acquitted Anthony in the child's death.

do this or it is later shown that the suspect did not comprehend his rights, any information or statements gained from the suspect may be held inadmissible in court (Weiss, 2005). Any leads or further evidence discovered as the result of evidence initially obtained illegally or improperly may also be found inadmissible under the doctrine known as fruit of the poisonous tree. Such constitutional violations of a defendant's rights can also result in the case being dismissed (Weiss, 2005).

Evidence presented in court may take many forms, including witness testimony, which must be based on personal knowledge; various documents, including victim and witness statements; and the familiar physical evidence. Each state and the federal court system have rules of evidence that govern admissibility issues. In addition to the rules, the admissibility of different forms of evidence is guided by case precedents. Scientific standards for evidence address tests or observations offered by experts, which must conform to the scientific method. DNA evidence is one example. Judges must make the final decisions on the admissibility of evidence.

In our chapter on investigations, we discussed the CSI effect of lay people (and criminal justice actors) often believing they understand forensic and technical detection and analysis equipment and methods (such as DNA) more than they actually do. Curtis (2014) points out that since "there is relatively limited insight into the public perceptions and expectations of forensic DNA use" (p. 21), we have reason to be concerned about the impact on case outcomes. The presence of DNA evidence was previously shown to increase the chances that a case would reach court and the jury would convict (Briody, 2004). Juries are also influenced by the absence of DNA evidence in homicide cases (Briody, 2004). Because DNA evidence is viewed as so significant by jurors, the process of collection, storage, and analysis is critical to the integrity of DNA evidence. DNA evidence may be seen as compromised if strict procedural steps are not followed. As discussed earlier, prosecutors are keenly aware of the impact of the CSI effect on prospective jurors and spend time during jury selection addressing the realities of actual criminal cases, which may or may not include an abundance of scientific evidence.

DEFENSE ATTORNEY FUNCTIONS AND TACTICS

Federal or state prosecutors represent the people. Prosecutors at their best are also trying to get justice for the victim and the victim's family. Defense attorneys are essential in providing a vigorous defense for anyone accused of such a serious crime as causing the death of another person. Defense attorneys are required by the codes of legal ethics to provide their clients with zealous representation. Our adversarial system of justice is said to be effective as both sides advocate diligently to fully represent their clients within the bounds of the law. The checks and balances are key.

Whether private attorneys or public defenders, the defendant's legal representatives are there to provide fair and competent representation (Anderson & Heaton, 2012). Discussion continues over the relative benefit to a defendant of a public versus a private attorney to represent him (Hartley, Miller, & Spohn, 2010). History is replete with examples of insufficient or nonexistent legal representation of persons charged with a crime. Serious cases have been overturned on appeal when a defense attorney slept during trial or showed up intoxicated. The effectiveness of the public versus the private defense attorney is often a subject of commentary, and many view the public defender as an inferior lawyer. But it is important to recognize that public defenders have as their sole responsibility the representation of criminal defendants, usually those who are indigent. On the other hand, private-practice attorneys may assist clients in a wide range of legal matters.

The depth and familiarity with contemporary issues in criminal practice may favor the public defender in some instances, and some research on the effectiveness of public-defender representation has found this (Anderson & Heaton, 2013). What a private attorney may provide that is frequently unavailable to the public defender is the resource of time. The private attorney will typically have a lighter caseload, allowing him to focus more attention on his selected cases. In addition, he may have more investigators and staff to assist in preparing the defense case. It is also important to note that in some jurisdictions, private attorneys can also be assigned counsel when there is a shortage of public defenders to represent defendants charged in serious cases.

Hoffman, Rubin, and Shepherd (2005) examined case outcomes for all felony cases in Denver, Colorado, for the year 2002. Their findings indicate "that public defenders achieved poorer outcomes than their privately retained counterparts, measured by the actual sentences defendants received" (p. 223). The differences were significant. The study pointed out that the Supreme Court, more than 50 years ago, identified representation by counsel as a constitutional guarantee. The public-defender systems in most states evolved from this view. Implicit is that the counsel must be effective.

But research has been varied about whether public defenders or private counsel are more effective. As we mentioned, private attorneys often have greater resources (including time) available to mount a defense in a homicide case. The study supported the proposition that private attorneys achieve significantly more positive outcomes, measured in actual length of sentences, than public defenders. The authors raise the question of whether a partial explanation for the difference in outcomes has to do with clients "self-selecting." The idea goes that if a "marginally indigent" defendant has money available and is faced with a relatively more serious charge, he will hire a private attorney and gain the benefit of the attorney's lighter caseload and (hopefully) expanded resources. If the defendant who is marginally indigent is faced with the reality that the evidence of his guilt is substantial, he may hesitate to seek out money to hire an attorney that may be essentially of no great help. And so public defenders may be representing, on the whole, people with worse cases, which in turn leads to worse case outcomes. And so the authors assert, "Thus, in a system that tries only 5% of all criminal cases, the most important skill for a lawyer on either side is the ability to evaluate a case before entering into plea negotiations, not the ability to shine at trial" (Hoffman et al., 2005, p. 245).

The investigators and support staff for prosecutors or defense attorneys are important in assembling information, checking leads, and confirming facts. The team members locate and coordinate with witnesses for the attorneys to interview. The preparation of witnesses for depositions and trial is crucial as a case moves forward. Wheatcroft and Ellison (2012) say that this "familiarization of witnesses to cross-examination processes increased accurate responses and reduced errors" (p. 821). In the effort to arrive at the truth, witness familiarity with courtroom procedures and attorney tactics can reduce the discomfort of the witness and attendant lack of focus and accurate statements that come from feeling intimidated or unsure.

A challenge faced by the defense attorney is providing some type of explanation for his client's actions that might make sense to jurors. If the defense attorney can provide a scenario that makes some sense, the jury will be left to consider whether the defendant acted reasonably (Duck, 2009). The defense may argue that the defendant's mental state was such that he did not know right from wrong when he acted. This would often fall under a temporary insanity defense. An argument might be made that the killing was spur of the moment as the result of a distraught or emotional individual. Perhaps a claim of self-defense will be made, wherein the defendant asserts that he was in fear for his life and that he saw no other course of action but to take the life of someone else. The defense attorney still must make the case that the defendant's actions were reasonable and that most people (including the jurors) would have done the same thing in his place (Duck, 2009). While the prosecutor may depict the defendant as a remorseless killer, the defense often explains the actions of her client in the context of the defendant's life history (Costanzo & Peterson, 1994).

Defenses

As in all criminal cases, there are numerous legal defenses available to the criminal defendant charged with homicide. While there are many texts devoted to the detailed study of criminal law and procedure, we will provide a brief overview of the most common defenses used specifically in homicide cases. There are many ways to categorize criminal defenses, so we have used the following common categories for legal defenses: failure-of-proof defenses; alibi; justification defenses; and excuse defenses.

Failure-of-Proof Defenses

The failure-of-proof defense is asserted to show that the prosecution has failed to prove its case beyond a reasonable doubt and is used frequently by defendants in criminal cases. It is often used effectively in homicide cases, where prosecutors have many elements to prove beyond a reasonable doubt, which is a very high burden of proof. Skilled and experienced defense attorneys will continue to remind the jurors throughout the trial about how high this burden is. In first-degree murder cases, for instance, prosecutors must prove the element of premeditation, most often using circumstantial evidence to show that a defendant's actions before the crime prove deliberation. Defendants can argue that the evidence does not prove premeditation or planning and that the defendant should not be convicted of the crime charged but perhaps of a lesser included offense, like second-degree murder or manslaughter, instead.

Alibi

The word **alibi** comes from the Latin and literally means *elsewhere*. Defendants assert this defense when they claim that they could not have committed the crime because they were somewhere else when the crime was committed. The defendant attempts to prove that he was not present at the crime scene, at least during the commission of the crime. The defendant does not carry the burden of proof for an alibi defense. The government continues to bear the burden of proving that the crime was committed by the defendant beyond a reasonable doubt. Often, there will be conflicting testimony at trial about a defendant's possible alibi, with a defense witness testifying that he or she was with the defendant when the crime occurred and state's witnesses testifying that they saw the defendant near the crime scene. Many defendants assert alibi defenses at trial, but these defenses are not always effective, especially when the state offers other compelling evidence of the defendant's guilt.

Justification Defenses

The **justification defenses** include self-defense or the defense of others, defense of home and property (commonly known as stand-your-ground laws), consent, and necessity. A justification defense means that the defendant admits committing the act, but he asserts that he had just cause in committing the act and is therefore not criminally liable.

Most students are familiar with self-defense as a defense to homicide and other crimes. Self-defense statutes usually also include some language about defense of others and regarding the right to stand his ground, since these are related concepts in the criminal law. In most jurisdictions, a self-defense, defense-of-others, or stand-your-ground claim requires a defendant to show the following elements, such as those that are used in Florida's statute:

A person is justified in using or threatening to use deadly force if he or she reasonably believes that using or threatening to use such force is necessary to prevent imminent death or great bodily harm to himself or herself or another or to prevent the imminent commission of a forcible felony. A person who uses or threatens to use deadly force in accordance with this subsection does not have a duty to retreat and has the right to stand his or her ground if the person using or threatening to use the deadly force is not engaged in a criminal activity and is in a place where he or she has a right to be. (Fla. Stat. § 776.012-2, 2018)

The self-defense and defense-of-others claims are considered affirmative defenses, which require a defendant to prove that he used reasonable actions to protect himself or a third person and that his actions were necessary to protect himself or the third person. The burden of proof is on the defendant for this defense. It can be difficult to prove self-defense because a person has to prove that he did not cause or start the conflict that led to the event, and he must prove that his actions were reasonable given the circumstances he faced. The category of stand-your-ground laws, like the one in the Florida statute, is relatively recent, as Florida's law was enacted in 2005. These laws do not require people to retreat if they are in their homes or on their property and allow them to use deadly force. There has been wide concern and debate about these laws, with some commentators suggesting that we are returning to the Wild West and legalizing vigilante justice. Since Florida's enactment of the first stand- your-ground law, at least 25 states have now passed some form of this law.

The necessity defense is defined as "[a] justification defense for a person who acts in an emergency that he or she did not create and who commits a harm that is less severe than the harm that would have occurred but for the person's actions" (Garner, 1999, p. 1053). Generally, when a defendant asserts the necessity defense, the courts require him to demonstrate that the pressure arose from a physical force of nature and not from other human beings.

Excuse Defenses

There are also several defenses that are known as **excuse defenses**. These defenses may include age or infancy, involuntary intoxication, provocation, and insanity. Excuse defenses mean that the person admits to committing the criminal act at issue but claims he cannot be held legally responsible because he lacked the criminal intent necessary to be guilty of the crime. The age or infancy defense hails from the common law, where there was a strong belief that young children were incapable of forming the required **mens rea**, or guilty mind, to be guilty of a crime. Under the common law, there was a presumption that children under the age of 7 are incapable of forming the required mental state to form criminal intent, and there was rebuttable presumption that children between the ages of 7 and 14 could not do so.

Dr. Jack Kevorkian was arrested and convicted of second-degree murder for assisting a terminally ill patient in ending his life. The debate about voluntary euthanasia, or bringing about a painless death, is ongoing. In some countries and the U.S. states of Oregon and Washington, physician-assisted suicide is allowed by law and within guidelines. While the consent defense was unsuccessful in the case of Dr. Kevorkian, the case of the Michigan doctor moved the discussion of this social issue forward in America.

WHY WOULD THEY DO IT?

Physician-assisted suicide is now legal in 7 states and in the District of Columbia under specified circumstances.

Presenting adequate evidence to convince jurors that a person was involuntarily drugged or induced into a state of intoxication is challenging. If this threshold can be overcome, the defense hopes to show that the defendant was incapable of forming the requisite intent to commit the charged crime. Similarly, the defense of provocation seeks to excuse the defendant's behavior with the claim that any reasonable person would have lost control temporarily in the same circumstances and acted in a similar way to the defendant.

A well-known excuse defense in homicide crimes is the insanity defense, though infrequently used overall. Each state establishes its own definition of insanity in its criminal statutes. Currently, 26 states use the **M'Naghten rule** in their statutes, and this standard is often referred to as the *right/wrong test*. The M'Naghten rule is based on a British case from 1843 where a criminal defendant was found not guilty by reason of insanity and holds that offenders who did not know right from wrong at the time of the offense should not be held criminally responsible. Most states that do not use the M'Naghten standard instead use the **substantial capacity** test from the American Law Institute's Model Penal Code. Currently, 23 states use some version of the substantial capacity test. This test is considered a less stringent standard than M'Naghten and holds

> a person is not responsible for criminal conduct if at the time of such conduct as a result of mental disease or defect he lacks substantial capacity either to appreciate the criminality of his conduct or to conform his conduct to the requirements of the law. (American Law Institute, 2006, § 4.01)

It is important to note that in an insanity defense, the burden to prove the defense rests with the defendant. Defendants must prove insanity by clear and convincing evidence. Research suggests that juries are reluctant to find defendants not guilty by reason of insanity (Torry & Billick, 2010).

WHY WOULD THEY DO IT?

In 1979, 6-year-old Etan Patz disappeared on his way to school in New York City. His parents had allowed him to walk the two blocks from their home to his bus stop for the first time. The child's disappearance made international news and eventually led to systems to track missing children in this country. Although his body was never found, after 33 years, the police finally made an arrest in the case when they charged Pedro Hernandez with the crime. They made the arrest after receiving a tip from the brother-in-law of Mr. Hernandez that he had talked to a prayer group in 1979 about killing a child in the basement of a store where he worked. At the time of Etan's disappearance, Mr. Hernandez had worked as a store clerk at the bodega on Etan's route to his school bus. In the spring of 2015, Mr. Hernandez was tried over 10 weeks with over 50 witnesses for the state, and the trial included a confession Mr. Hernandez had made to the police. While the defense did not pursue a complete insanity defense, it did raise the issue of Mr. Hernandez's personality disorder and low IQ. Additionally, the defense team raised doubt by pointing out that the police had considered another suspect in the case for many years, a man who was a convicted child molester. After 18 days of deliberation, the jury was deadlocked, with 11 jurors in favor of conviction and one juror in favor of acquittal. In spite of the strong evidence presented by the prosecution at the trial, the jury was unable to reach a unanimous verdict. The judge finally declared a mistrial, and the prosecution has insisted that it will retry Mr. Hernandez for the murder of Etan. In 2017, after a second trial, Mr. Hernandez was convicted of kidnapping and killing Etan Patz and was sentenced to 25 to life in prison.

In November 2014, a judge found an Iowa teenager not guilty by reason of insanity during a judge trial on homicide charges stemming from the killing of his 5-year-old foster brother. Cody Metzker-Madsen was 17 years old when he killed his foster brother Dominic Elkins with a brick and drowned him. The teen's defense alleged that he attacked the child because he believed he was a goblin commander that he had to kill. The testimony during the trial by a forensic psychologist for the defense explained that the teen was in a psychotic state during the killing and that he showed no emotion after the event. In her ruling, the judge stated that she was convinced that he could not understand or appreciate the consequences of his actions, and based on testimony about his extensive history of emotional disturbances, she wrote, "This is a young man who has never been mentally normal." Under Iowa law, the teen will be evaluated in a correctional facility and held where he will receive psychiatric care and so that the court can determine whether he is a danger to himself or others. Some commentators suggest that defendants seeking an insanity defense may fare better with judges instead of juries as the judge may be more inclined to accept the defense.

Source: Rodgers (2014).

ETHICAL ISSUES

The legal systems of all countries have experienced examples of bias, perjury, the use of false evidence, and misconduct by different actors within the system. Ongoing improvements in the law, procedures, and professionalism and training of personnel throughout the criminal justice system have led to improved access to justice and equity in the American criminal justice system. None of the components of the criminal justice system are perfect, nor do they run flawlessly at all times. With that said, the American system of jurisprudence works fairly well and is examined, envied, and emulated by many other countries.

Planting evidence to incriminate a suspect is unlawful and weakens the faith people have in their legal system. Stories about such occurrences, while not frequent, appear in the media. Some officers have used what Delattre (1996) calls noble-cause corruption to attempt to achieve a conviction of a known criminal who, for various reasons, has not been held sufficiently accountable in the eyes of many people. The officers' rationale of trying to remove from society an offender is a flawed one because if citizens are expected to obey the law, they must feel confident that the officers they entrust with enforcing the law also respect and follow the law.

The prosecution and defense teams must both conduct themselves in accordance with case law and ethical principles governing the conduct of lawyers. When a prosecutor uncovers evidence that tends to exonerate a defendant, he or she is obliged to share this information with the defense. This is known as exculpatory evidence, and the ethical codes are very clear that prosecutors must share this information with defense counsel. For their part, as the defense team prepares their case, they may not claim ignorance of information made available to them or that they discovered during their own preparations. This also goes to the matter of counsel effectively representing their clients. If the defendant in a homicide case is found guilty, it is not uncommon to attempt to appeal his conviction based on a claim of ineffective counsel even if the defense attorney thoroughly and professionally carried out her duties and advised her client in the best way she could. There is an enormous amount of case law relating to ineffective assistance of counsel, especially in criminal felony cases like homicide.

We rightfully expect a high standard of conduct from attorneys working in the criminal justice system. In this most important of criminal justice venues, the capital case, prosecutors should be competent and receive ongoing training. Without high ethical standards and an awareness of the bounds of ethical behavior, the entire system suffers (Toryanski, 2007).

PLEA BARGAINING

Both prosecutors and defense attorneys face a difficult and resource-intensive task in cases of criminal homicide. One of the challenges facing the prosecutor, in addition to speaking for the deceased victim, is to weigh the costs and benefits to the community of going forward with a trial. As a result, some cases are resolved through plea bargaining.

It is common that members of the public misunderstand the full dimensions of the use of plea bargains. Plea bargains not only provide a lesser sanction for a defendant but also allow case resolution without expending unnecessary public resources and allow the prosecutor to move on to other cases. While different people have varying views on what a homicide case outcome should be, quicker justice and imposition of sentence may be helpful to a victim's family as compared to the ordeal of a lengthy trial. The plea bargain may result in a lesser sanction, but it also ensures *some* sanction. A clear incentive for the defendant is that fewer charges might be brought, and he would therefore receive a reduced sentence. In the Chris Watts' murder case discussed in the Intimate Partner Homicide chapter, we explained that he entered a plea to the murders of his pregnant wife and two daughters. His plea deal resulted in life sentences instead of the death penalty, and prevented the families from having to endure a lengthy and painful trial. Through no fault of either the prosecutor or the law enforcement officers who investigated a case, there simply may not be sufficient evidence to reasonably go to court and expect to win a conviction. In these cases, a plea bargain may be an appropriate action.

Plea bargaining is considered by some to be coercive and may result in false convictions from misuse of this mechanism. Plea bargaining, under certain circumstances, may induce self-incrimination and a plea of guilty in hopes of a lighter sentence. Even the death penalty is used in cases to leverage a plea bargain. It is understood that in order to avoid the potential imposition of a death penalty sentence, a defendant will often plea-bargain to a lesser offense to achieve a lesser sentence. This illustrates another controversy regarding their use. While the victim's family may feel the relief of avoiding an involved criminal trial, they may also be upset at the killer receiving less than the maximum. Controversy about plea bargains includes the defendant waiving his right to a jury trial, his right against self-incrimination, and his right to confront witnesses. Still, the Supreme Court has stated that plea bargaining passes constitutional muster. The courts insist that the defendant must knowingly and willingly plead guilty with full knowledge of the consequences. On balance, though plea bargaining has critics, its usage keeps the system moving, reducing cost to tax-payers, time and suffering for victims' families, and arguably making little difference in outcome in terms of sanctions imposed given that many cases, if proceeding to trial, would not have won convictions or resulted in more punishment.

Roberts (2013) comments in favor of further regulations on plea bargaining and efforts by counsel, saying that while some

> believe that regulating bargaining will open floodgates to future litigation . . . these are manageable challenges that do not outweigh the need to give meaning to the constitutional right to effective counsel. After all, in a criminal justice system that is largely composed of plea bargains, what is effective assistance of counsel if it does not encompass effectiveness within the plea negotiation process? (p. 2650)

A plea bargain must be approved by the defendant and by the court to guard against undue influence by the attorneys in the case.

SENTENCING

In order for a defendant to be convicted, the jury must find the defendant guilty by a unanimous verdict. If a defendant is found guilty of a death penalty–eligible crime, a second hearing follows to decide the penalty. This is referred to as a bifurcated trial, and the process arose after the Supreme Court's suspension of the death penalty during the mid-1970s following the Court's decision in *Furman v. Georgia*. The Court found that the imposition of the death penalty was arbitrary and inconsistent. They did not find the penalty cruel but rather *unusual* under an Eighth Amendment standard, based on the inconsistency of its use from state to state. Most states responded by adopting the two-phase bifurcated trial process of first determining guilt or innocence and then, in cases of a guilty verdict, moving on to the penalty phase of a trial. The same jury hears the evidence in both phases of the trial, and the jury decision is either binding or the final sentence is pronounced by the judge, taking the jury decision into account.

Jurors may be impacted in their decision not by the facts alone but the tactics of the attorneys in the case. Perhaps a victim fails to show "enough" emotion; jurors may see the victim as less sympathetic or deserving of justice (Rose, Nadler, & Clark, 2006). The defense attorney being friendly toward his client has been found to increase juror receptivity to **mitigation** in a case (Brewer, 2005). Homicide trials also see the victim blaming far too common in the criminal justice system. The defense may raise the issue of the victim's socioeconomic status in subtle ways or perhaps that the victim identified as LGBT to influence jurors to think of the victim as less deserving of justice (Gallagher, 2002).

Not only is the arrest and prosecution of individuals accused of murder important, but criminal sentencing is part of the sober process of making formal social-control decisions (Ulmer & Johnson, 2004). A conviction in a murder case can result in the harshest of sentences. Sentencing options, as we know, vary from state to state and even within jurisdictions, based in part on state guidelines enacted by legislatures but also from some discretion through judges acting within those state guidelines. A guilty verdict in a first-degree murder case in some states may bring the death penalty or life in prison without the possibility of parole based on any of a number of aggravating and mitigating factors. Seeking the death penalty in a particular case is a decision made by the prosecutor's office based on a variety of factors. In Florida, for example, first-degree murder statutes provide the option to assign the death penalty. Classification of the crime is the main consideration driving the charge. Three potential options are the death penalty (depending on if the state uses the death penalty), life in prison without the possibility of parole (LWOP), and, typically, a sentence of 20 to 25 years extending to life imprisonment. Disagreement on appropriate sentencing in homicide cases remains animated. Many students may not realize that the vast majority of defendants who commit homicide and are found guilty will serve a prison sentence of less than life in prison and will return to society.

In the spring of 2015, Dzhokhar Tsarnaev was tried for the Boston Marathon bombings that he and his brother Tamerlan orchestrated on April 15, 2013, and that resulted in the deaths of four people and the injuries of hundreds of others. He was tried and convicted in federal court in Boston, and then the court proceeded to the sentencing hearing. The 12 jurors deliberated for over 14 hours as they reviewed the mitigation evidence presented by the defense, which argued that Mr. Tsarnaev, who had been a good student with many friends, was heavily influenced by his older brother, who became a dominant negative influence in his life after his parents left for Russia in 2012. The jurors voted in favor of the death penalty for the crimes. The death sentence for Mr. Tsarnaev is the first death penalty verdict in a federal terrorism case in the post-9/11 era. This sentence has raised some debate among policymakers and scholars about the appropriateness of the death penalty in terror cases, specifically raising the question about whether sentencing a terrorist to death gives him the ability to have more sympathizers. The sentence also comes at a time when public support of the death penalty in the United States, as reported by the Pew Research Center polls, is at an all-time low, and many states are examining their death penalty statutes.

WHY WOULD THEY DO IT?

Mitigation

In discussing the role of mitigation and the mitigation expert in the trial, it is vital to understand the purpose of this phase of the trial. The mitigation phase occurs after the defendant has been found guilty of capital murder. The only issue in this phase of the trial is what sentence the defendant will receive. Therefore, nothing introduced as mitigation is intended to be an excuse for the defendant's committing the crime. Mitigating evidence is offered to assist the judge and jury in determining an appropriate sentence for this particular defendant.

The mitigation expert's role in the proceeding is to present a complete picture of the defendant. By the time this part of the trial is conducted, the defendant has often been portrayed as a brutal, almost inhuman monster who has committed a terrible crime. Mitigation evidence is introduced in an effort to humanize the defendant and to show that the defendant is more than the offense he or she has committed. The mitigation expert conducts extensive interviews with individuals who have known the defendant throughout his or her life. Information is collected regarding family, work, and school background; mental-health history, including substance abuse; military record; criminal background; and relationship history.

Interviews are conducted with numerous people who have known the defendant in these and other circumstances that may be considered relevant to an understanding of the defendant. Various records pertaining to each of these major areas are collected and reviewed. In addition, numerous interviews are conducted with the defendant. Expert professional assessments by psychologists, psychiatrists, social workers, and other professionals are completed and reviewed by the mitigation expert. There are several mitigating factors that may be considered in these cases, including

- Learning disabilities

- Psychiatric conditions occurring in young children, such as ADHD

- Inability to read

- Dropping out of school

- Major family issues, including divorce, domestic violence, and child abuse of the defendant

- Sexual abuse of the defendant at an early age

- Intergenerational patterns of abuse, neglect, or criminal behavior in the family

- Severe substance abuse by the defendant and intergenerational patterns of substance abuse in the family

- Intergenerational patterns of mental illness or mental disability in the family

- History of head trauma in the defendant

The mitigation expert collects volumes of data and shares the data with the defense attorneys. Testimony is generated from family members, teachers, former employers, and others who can bear witness to the presence of various mitigators. In some cases, expert witnesses are called to present facts related to their assessments and can render an opinion as to what those facts mean in terms of impairment.

Death Penalty

The most severe penalty for the most severe crime is a sentence of death. The use of the death penalty has been a part of the American response to murder and various other crimes, historically. A minority of countries continue to employ the death penalty, and support for its use in the United States has dropped over time, based on mixed attitudes toward taking life, even in response to the crime of murder. Currently 31 states, the federal government, and the military allow the use of the death penalty, which is down from an all-time high of 38 states in 1995. According to the Pew Research Center, 11 of those states have not used it in over a decade. Over the last couple of decades, the U.S. Supreme Court has also ruled that the death penalty cannot be imposed on juvenile offenders or those with mental illness. Some argue against the use of capital punishment because of the associated expense of a death penalty trial and appeals and the ensuing lengthy process. Another important factor for many people is the fact that scientific advances, such as the use of DNA, have revealed many cases of incorrect conviction and execution. The majority of research conducted in regard to the efficacy of the death penalty as a deterrent has not shown its use to reduce homicide. A society may still choose to impose the penalty of death as societal retribution for crime (Newton, Johnson, & Mulcahy, 2006). Recommendation or imposition of the death penalty is generally reserved for clearly premeditated murders or cases where there is little doubt of guilt, such as those with a confession, witnesses, and an abundance of physical evidence; where the defendant shows little remorse; and where the crime was particularly brutal.

Dr. Glenn Rohrer, along with his partner June Waller, LCSW, both licensed clinical social workers, served as mitigation specialists for over 10 years. Dr. Rohrer worked on over 100 capital murder cases and testified as an expert witness in substance abuse and family dynamics in 17 cases. Mitigation specialists generally have a background in the social sciences, and most do not testify in cases. One of the most compelling cases Dr. Rohrer worked on involved a 27-year-old man named Freddy, still living at home with his alcoholic mother at the time of his arrest. He had a full-scale IQ of 72 and had dropped out of school in the eighth grade. He was very isolated from his peers and only dated one woman in his life. The woman was 10 years older than Freddy, and he was in love with her. One night, Freddy discovered the woman in a bar with another man. Freddy was so angry with her that he went home, got a shotgun, and returned to the bar. He killed the man and the woman in front of several witnesses. He shot the woman and then reloaded the gun and shot her a second time with both barrels of the gun at very close range. Freddy was arrested at the scene and tried and convicted of capital murder. In the mitigation phase of the trial, the following mitigating evidence was presented:

- At the age of 6, Freddy's mother took him to various stores and taught him how to shoplift. For years after that, his mother would drive him around town and send him into stores to steal and bring the stolen goods to her.

Source: Interview with Dr. Glenn Rohrer.

- When Freddy was 7, his mother got mad at her brother and took Freddy over to his house and put him up on the roof. She gave him a large hand drill and had him drill several holes in the roof. A subsequent severe storm did significant water damage to the house.

- Freddy's mother got into an argument with a neighbor. She bought a 5-pound bag of sugar and had Freddy put the sugar in the man's gas tank. The sugar did major damage to the truck.

- Freddy's mother frequently went to another town to drink and party with her friends on the weekends. She would give Freddy some food and water and lock him alone in a shed over the weekend.

- Freddy's mother was very abusive to him, and he was removed to foster homes on several occasions but was always sent back home in a short time.

- Freddy was an alcoholic and drug addict but never went to treatment. He was convicted of breaking and entering four times and spent a total of 32 months in jail.

The mitigation evidence was presented through the testimony of several witnesses who knew Freddy and his mother, including family members, neighbors, teachers, Department of Social Services workers, and a local minister. The jury recommended and Freddy was sentenced to life in prison without parole instead of the death penalty.

There have also been concerns over the methods used to carry out a sentence of death. States and the federal government have variously used lethal injection, the electric chair, hanging, poisonous gas, and the firing squad to carry out the act. In a recent 5–4 decision by the U.S. Supreme Court, *Glossip v. Gross* (2015), the Court upheld the use of controversial lethal injection drugs and allowed states to continue their use in executions. The federal government and 32 states still utilize the death penalty in the United States, though even conservatives in the Nebraska legislature voted in 2015 to abolish its use. There, as elsewhere, the costs associated with the process and questionable deterrent value were at issue. Neither the District of Columbia nor Puerto Rico uses the death penalty.

SUMMARY

Most readers began this chapter with somewhat of a grasp of the process of how a homicide case makes its way through the court system, from arrest through arraignment and pretrial motions to an actual trial and, if a conviction occurs, to sentencing. We did not intend a state-by-state review of court rules and requirements and homicide cases but rather to familiarize you with the actual sequence of steps in homicide cases and point out the importance of various parts of the process.

We have again discussed the interest people have in the criminal justice process and certainly in cases of murder. This extends to the portion of the process involving the courts and trial preparation, process, and outcomes. Hollywood and the news media have certainly fanned the flames of sometimes misinformed interest in criminal trials, but unless the case is notorious, it often receives relatively little attention. The verdict in high-profile cases is often the single thing of interest to most members of the public.

Preparation and conduct of a homicide case for trial is not a simple or quick process. While most people are never aware of the tremendous amount of work that goes into such cases, the coordination required between the prosecution and law enforcement is substantial. Law enforcement enters a homicide investigation with the goal of finding out who is accountable for the killing and, along with other actors in the criminal justice system, determining whether the death was the result of a criminal act. Part of this goal is preparing each and every step of the way for a potential trial. To that end, law enforcement must always be thinking about the prosecutor's office and how best to help the prosecutors assemble the most complete case possible. The television-viewing public will typically see police dramas where law enforcement catches the killer. Some shows also provide an image of the high drama of a witness on the stand in a murder trial. We do well to remember, however, that the prosecution is also considering the public's resources in deciding whether or not to offer a plea arrangement with the defendant and considering whether the strength of available evidence would support going all the way through to a trial regardless of available resources. Whether or not a case actually goes all the way to the trial setting is not always a reflection of the work done by law enforcement or the prosecutor. There simply may be insufficient evidence to prove a case.

Homicide prosecutions are clearly of great importance in society. Reflecting the seriousness of the crime and the impact on victims and community, adequate evidence must be discovered and assembled to prove the case in court before a jury. The preparation of the case by both prosecution and defense involves a great deal of work with members of the criminal justice system, preparing lay and expert witnesses and presenting a coherent case to the jury. It is vital to the success of a case that the attorneys scrupulously pursue the work of representing either the people or the defendant and avoid any ethical lapse.

Malice aforethought 230

Manslaughter 230

Beyond a reasonable doubt 230

Grand jury 231

Arraignment 231

Plea agreement 231

Venire 231

Voir dire 231

Peremptory challenges 231

Challenges for cause 231

Direct evidence 232

Circumstantial evidence 232

Expert witnesses 233

Forensic evidence 233

Federal Rules of Evidence
Rule 702 233

Daubert 233

Murder 234

Premeditation 234

Felony murder 234

Second-degree murder 235

Manslaughter 235

Vehicular or vessel homicide 235

Double-jeopardy 235

Alibi 240

Justification defenses 240

Excuse defenses 241

Mens rea 241

M'Naghten rule 242

Substantial capacity 242

Furman v. Georgia 245

Mitigation 245

DISCUSSION QUESTIONS

1. How should a prosecutor evaluate a charging decision in a case of homicide?
2. What is the difference between direct and circumstantial evidence? Give an example of each.
3. Do the principles and rules guiding attorney behavior benefit the trial process in homicide cases? If so, how?
4. Describe and discuss the factors considered in plea bargaining.
5. What are aggravating or mitigating factors in deciding the sentence in a murder case?
6. Briefly discuss the activities at each stage of the homicide case process following an arrest.
7. What is mitigation and why is it important?

TRY THIS

Over 25 years ago, two lawyers founded The Innocence Project in an effort to assist those who may have been wrongfully convicted of serious crimes. Their work has brought attention to the need for the criminal justice system to enact reforms to ensure that the investigation and prosecution of crime is fair, transparent, and lawful. Go to their website at: https://25years.innocenceproject.org/

Examine the details of a case where their organization has assisted in the exoneration of a defendant through the use of DNA evidence. How has the work of their organization impacted public policy and reform efforts? What does this mean for prosecutors, defense attorneys, and courts in the handling of homicide cases?

15

VICTIMS, SOCIETY, AND THE FUTURE

"The only thing we know about the future is that it will be different."

—Peter Drucker,
American businessman, 1909–2005

"Research is to see what everybody else has seen, and to think what nobody else has thought."

—Albert Szent-Gyorgyi,
Hungarian scientist, 1893–1986

CHAPTER OUTLINE

Student Learning Outcomes

Students will be able to:

- discuss factors affecting victims and covictims of homicide.

- address the role of victims' rights in the prosecution of homicide cases.

- explain the roles of criminal justice system agencies and legislation in addressing homicide.

- describe the public health perspective on violent crime and homicide.

- explain the challenges of predicting violence and homicide.

- articulate promising trends in the study of and approach to addressing homicide.

INTRODUCTION

We have spent much of the book describing homicide and discussing factors involved in committing criminal homicide, the people who kill, and some policy and practical issues involved in the control and investigation of such crimes. The context of criminal homicide in the United States is important for criminal justice students, practitioners, and policymakers to understand. Many policymakers, researchers, and practitioners consider two large frames for examining response to homicide: prevention and retribution. Some view these two conceptual approaches as mutually exclusive or at least in tension. This would be similar to the crime control model versus the due-process model, which can illustrate differing approaches to criminal justice as a whole. Prevention, as we examine it in this concluding chapter, includes consideration of violence prediction, public health efforts, the use of technology, addressing guns, and deterrence. Retribution, on the other hand, clearly involves legislative initiatives that punish and possibly deter some offenders. Victims' rights, while not a clear component of retribution, may be considered in that broad frame as part of accounting for some of the damage caused by a homicide.

We have delivered a broad commentary and discussion of many types of homicide while pointing out that some types (e.g., serial, mass, and cult) are infrequent, and others are more common (confrontational and intimate partner homicide, to name two). The dichotomy of more and less frequent killing can be useful in focusing research and policy efforts. Homicides arising from arguments and confrontations and those resulting from an ongoing and escalating pattern of abuse of an intimate or family member are also the categories most susceptible to prevention and intervention efforts.

For criminology to be of broad use to society, it must offer usable information to policymakers. The theories and ideas arising from research are not in the form of policies ready for implementation. Completed policy involves the realm of valuing alternatives, weighing and comparing, assessing available resources, and making actual choices. The world of the academic is not this world. Students struggle with moving beyond many theoretical abstractions, concept definitions, and tabulations of crimes to the use of critical thinking to apply the various bits of information in concrete ways that reduce violence by increasing collective social efficacy in communities and prosocial skills in individuals.

The researcher relies on data to formulate models of behavior and to glean and articulate insights. Legislative bodies must enact laws to address all manner of actions and activities in society that mesh to accomplish different goals, including the prevention of crime and intervention in existing criminal acts. Social and justice system policies are important. Research has increasingly aided the development of policy. Recognition of the Pareto rule (the 80/20 Rule) led to a focus on repeat offenders. The terms intelligence-led and evidence-based are ubiquitous in the literature now as integral to formulating policies and creating programs to use limited criminal justice system resources.

The themes of the book point to what we believe are key issues in the examination of and response to homicide in America and, indeed, worldwide. Various statistics and resources describing homicide frequency and dynamics around the world remind the reader to maintain perspective. The work of Steven Pinker (2011) and others provides a solid empirical basis to view violence in its temporal dimension. In spite of the impression we might absorb from media immersion, we should understand that violence in general and homicide specifically have declined in the world and continue to do so. That does not mean to sit back and be content. On the contrary, we see this as a rallying cry to redouble our collective efforts. The historic, ongoing aspects of inequality, relative deprivation, job and career access challenges, and more can create a mountain that seems too high to climb. But the ascent must be made.

A focus on the most frequent types of homicide should guide research and subsequent evidence-based policies and programs. Legislative actions, educational approaches, public health initiatives, and criminal justice system efforts should coordinate to grasp and then grapple together with the factors involved in confrontational violence, intimate partner homicide, and the dramatically disproportionate homicide victimization and offense rate of African American males, men and women of meager means, and others. Indeed, race and economic status remain variables of considerable significance in many crimes (Sampson, Wilson, & Katz, 2018). We recognize that comparing the single number of murders committed does not illustrate the broader challenge of violence. Criminal homicide does not rank within the Top 10 as a cause of death in the United States. Violence, however, remains implicated in immeasurable suffering, countless losses in productive human action, the subsequent economic costs associated with this, the lack of security for millions of individuals, and the consequent reduction of stability in communities. Violent criminal victimization declined in the United States to 382.9 victimizations per

WHY WOULD THEY DO IT?

Chicago has been challenged by violent crime and continues to experience more than its proportional share of homicide. Early 2017 found the Chicago Police Department (CPD) underway with a new initiative to address shootings. CPD, in collaboration with the Urban Labs of the University of Chicago, developed Strategic Decision Support Centers (SDSCs) in precincts determined to be the locations where a disproportionate percentage of shootings occurred. The SDSCs use predictive software and the embedded analysts from the University's Crime Lab. The approach combined data analysis, human intelligence generated by CPD, and technology, through the teamwork of CPD officers and analysts from the Crime Lab. This latest effort by the city incorporates gunshot detection acoustic systems, additional access to cameras around the city, and direct telephone calls from the SDSCs to officers in the affected areas to allow a focused deployment.

CPD reported that between 2016 and 2017, homicides declined by 765, more than half in precincts where a SDSC was located. Both years showed a reduction in homicides over the previous year. This is some encouragement in a city that in 2016 saw more shootings and homicides than any year in the last 20, more homicides than in Los Angeles and New York City combined that year. The majority of Chicago homicides are the result of gun violence. The toll of gang homicide on the community is palpable in neighborhood after neighborhood, as seen through ongoing news coverage.

Operation Ceasefire Boston (no connection to the Chicago organization), also known as the Boston Gun Project, reflected an approach that had a central component that focused on bringing significant enforcement and prosecution resources to bear on gun violence. The Boston program utilizes a **lever-pulling strategy**, incorporating dialogue with gangs about the consequences that will be immediately directed at members following a violent incident.

100,000 in 2017, down 0.9 percent from 2016, but down 16.5 percent from 2008 (FBI, 2018). Serious violent crime—defined as murder, sexual assault, robbery, and aggravated assault—in 2017, had increased from 2013 by 3.7%, but as noted, was down significantly from a decade before. Over that same decade, domestic-violence rates also decreased.

We run the danger in this final chapter of following the pattern of much research, both summative and normative, that asserts simply that "more research is needed" and "this has implications for policy." We have tried throughout to comment on the continuing need to connect documented facts with concrete actions. Students often see this more plainly from their vantage point than many academics. Yes, what we know should influence what we do. Change is not fast, but you have to start somewhere. Legislators, practitioners, and academicians should continue to do what is truly quite hard—see the perspectives of others and incorporate those realities in their own calculations. We know that is hard, and many prefer the comfort of their own domains or perspectives, as narrow and unfettered by facts as these often are.

VICTIM IMPACT

The **victim impact** of homicide includes a larger number of people in America than most probably realize. In addition to the individuals who die at the hands of someone else each year are the loved ones, friends, coworkers, and others who are impacted in myriad ways by the loss of the actual victim. Risk management firms, management associations, insurance companies, and government accounting offices all provide data on the *cost* of a human life. Lost productivity, medical costs incurred leading up to one's death, and even impact on work in progress by some individuals is included in a calculation somewhere. These pieces of the impact puzzle do not count the homicide survivors or covictims. The **covictims** are loved ones of the victim, including parents, siblings, spouses, children, and other relatives (Simmons, Duckworth, & Tyler, 2014). If we

consider that 13,000 to 16,000 people are the victims of homicide each year, Simmons and his colleagues estimate that 6 to 10 survivors mourn each loss (Simmons et al., 2014). Given the permanent or lingering effects of the loss, covictims accumulate over time. The number of covictims in the 12 months during which their loved one was killed is not anchored to that year alone. Given this expanded but blurry effect of considering impacted persons, we can get an idea of the scope, if not a sharply focused view, of how people think, function, and respond to losses due to homicide.

Research shows the relative difficulty of coping by covictims based on the manner of a loved one's death (Simmons et al., 2014). The loss of the person by murder is a more complex challenge than the fact of death alone. Groups formed to assist those who have lost a loved one to criminal homicide have provided much-needed assistance. One such group is the National Organization of Parents of Murdered Children, Inc. (POMC). Founded in 1978, the POMC has been dedicated to helping all those who survive the loss of a loved one taken by an act of murder. The criminal justice system has only recently evolved to be more supportive of victims and survivors of crimes. The added frustrations that often accompany dealing with the legal system are trying. Advocacy and practitioner groups constantly work to ameliorate the challenges to covictims and to improve the outcomes of all those impacted by homicide. The importance of these groups cannot be overstated.

The Office for Victims of Crime (OVC) (http://www.ovc.gov/) helps direct compensation to victims throughout the United States. In addition to compensation and assistance to victims, OVC calls attention to service gaps for victims, provides training, and promotes public awareness. The OVC Resource Center (OVCRC) is an information clearinghouse and a component of the National Criminal Justice Reference Service (NCJRS). The OVCRC site (http://www.ovc.gov/resourcecenter/index .html) is a portal to publications and programs on victim services. Private non-profit groups, such as the Washington, D.C.-based National Center for Victims of Crime, perform advocacy, provide education and training, and act as an information source for policymakers. States also fund various victim advocacy and programming efforts to different degrees as the recognition of victims' rights has developed over the past 30+ years.

Victims' Rights

The homicide survivor will almost invariably be interviewed by detectives, either as a suspect or to gain information about the victim and his activities. Being questioned in this way can further alienate family and loved ones from the professionals working to handle a case of murder. Fortunately, the **victims' rights movement** in the United States gained momentum in the 1980s. This movement recognizes that crime victims have rights throughout the processing of a criminal case in the criminal justice system. These rights include the right to be notified of all proceedings, the right to attend the proceedings, and the right to be heard throughout the process. This movement has also resulted in the use of victim advocates by law enforcement agencies and prosecutors' offices. These personnel are specially trained to assist victims during the investigative and court processes.

Another right familiar to many people is the victim impact statement (VIS), which allows a victim or surviving covictim to present to the court a commentary on the impact the crime has had on his or her life. The victim impact statement is typically written by the covictims and read at sentencing. Participation in this way can benefit a survivor or victim of a crime other than homicide by letting him or her be heard (Englebrecht, Mason, & Adams, 2014). It has been found that at different stages in the criminal justice system process, symptoms of trauma, including those associated with **post-traumatic stress disorder (PTSD)**, may vary (Simmons et al., 2014). For example, those in the prosecution stage exhibited somewhat lower stress than those with a case in the investigation stage. Perhaps the feeling of movement or progress is at play when we think about court proceedings. In homicide cases specifically, victims often give input regarding whether the death penalty should be sought or whether a plea and a life sentence are acceptable. While many have recognized that our society has moved forward in addressing the rights of victims in the criminal justice system, we also recognize that more could be done to improve the experience for victims in the criminal justice system.

Restorative Justice

Homicide survivors, in some rare instances, may interact with the convicted killer through the restorative-justice concept (Ferrito, Needs, & Adshead, 2017; Zehr & Mika, 1998). Indeed, while many people can accept the logic of facilitated interactions between the victim and offender in, say, a robbery case, the appropriateness of such a meeting in cases of homicide gives some pause. **Restorative justice** is not as simple as some would make it; it is not just *making whole* the victim, community, and offender. Wemmers (2009) includes the components of "respect for the dignity of the individual," "inclusion or the participation of victims and offenders," and "reparation." Respect for the dignity of the individual is claimed by the contemporary criminal justice system, but that claim is not always evident in system practices. Historically, victims were often relegated to being witnesses for the state. The type of and manner in which questions were asked of victims by legal actors of the system made them feel as much on trial or as guilty as the accused in some instances. This can unfortunately be at the level of victim blaming and has many ramifications, including lack of desire by many to report being victimized, to cooperate with an investigation, or to remain available for protracted prosecutions.

The restorative-justice process that includes the participation by the victim and the offender enables the victim to communicate with the person who victimized him or her. The interaction, if it occurs, is mediated by a counselor and follows orientation sessions for both the victim and offender independently. Recognizing the offender as a person may allow a victim to adjust her perspective. For some, this can enable moving past the crime event or placing it within a broader context of how the victim sees the community and people in it. The offender is afforded

The use of restorative-justice principles has increased in the last several decades in the criminal justice system as an adjunct to the traditional retributive model. In the beginning of the movement, restorative-justice practices were used primarily with juveniles or in adult property crimes cases. With the increased use of restorative-justice practices in adult crimes, including facilitated prison conferences and prisoner training classes, some researchers have found increasing evidence that restorative justice does achieve its goals of holding offenders accountable and making victims more whole than the traditional criminal justice system process alone can do. Restorative justice focuses primarily on the concern for victims and how to meet their needs, repairing the harm as much as possible.

In his groundbreaking book *Transcending: Reflections of Crime Victims* (2001), Dr. Howard Zehr, the founder of contemporary restorative justice, interviewed 39 victims of violent crimes and murder to understand and detail the anguish and emotions that crime victims experience after the shattering loss of a loved one. The victims were part of restorative-justice programs that helped them connect with the offenders who harmed them to try to get information from the offenders that would help them heal and *transcend* their loss. As Zehr asserts, a restorative-justice model holds that violations create *obligations* for which offenders should be accountable. The restorative-justice model requires that we ask, "Who's been hurt, what are their needs, and whose obligations are they?" Using the restorative justice model, in the last several decades, in similar programs in prisons across the world, there have been opportunities for crime victims who want to participate to have an opportunity to confront offenders. As one facilitator from a New Zealand prison explained,

> For over four years now I have been facilitating restorative justice conferences, many of which have taken place within the confines of the prison environment where, despite the degradation and desolation, I have witnessed on numerous occasions examples of reconciliation, forgiveness and healing. (McElrea & Katounas, 2001, para. 6)

an opportunity and provided context to develop empathy for the victim or family. In many cases, victims simply want more information from the offender about the details of the crime so that they can use this information in healing. Reparation is also discussed by Wemmers (2009) as giving a *role* to the offender in the overall process. He is "encouraged to be accountable" in this way and to understand what he has done to others. For many crimes where restorative justice is used, reparation can often be paying restitution to the victim, contributing to the cost of correctional supervision, or making an apology. The aim is for the offender to accept responsibility for the crime, rather than projecting onto others blame for what he has done. Given that the majority of those convicted of homicide do eventually return to the community, the acceptance of accountability and working to create a robust system of reintegration into society are both of vital importance to communities.

With the efforts to *make whole* the victim, community, and offender, an overarching goal is to return society to a previous state not impacted by a crime. As noted, there are a limited number of practitioners or academics who would assert that the approach is very often appropriate or helpful in instances of homicide. On the other hand, given that most individuals convicted of killing someone will eventually be released back into society, restorative justice may be a viable component of reintegration. If the citizen who has completed his sentence is to become a functioning member of society, his adjustment to the reality of having taken a life is surely part of that process. Restorative justice is not for everyone or for every crime. Restorative-justice methods compose one tool in a box of many instruments.

PUBLIC HEALTH PERSPECTIVE

The public health of a community is often associated with this year's flu epidemic or an alert on tainted groceries. Dahlberg and Mercy (2009) discuss the evolution of thinking about violence as an issue of public health. The authors note that some time ago, people began to accept that violence was at least partly vulnerable to a public health approach. The medical community gained more and more ground in fighting diseases, and deaths subsequently declined. Homicide and suicide (a form of homicide) remain a significant, if not leading, cause of death in the United States. The rate of homicide varies of course by age, and while homicide is not in the Top 10 causes of death among all Americans, the risk of death by homicide for persons ages 15 to 24 is significant. In 2016, homicide deaths accounted for 20.1% of all deaths in this age group. For African American men, the homicide rate of 21.4 per 100,000 in 2016 compared to an overall U.S. rate of 6.2 per 100,000 (CDC, 2017). For all persons, the rate of suicide in 2016 was 13.9 per 100,000 (CDC, 2017) (see Figure 15.1).

At the beginning of the book, we said that the number and rate of homicide victims would be larger if our society's public servants were not receiving far more and better training than in years past and if innovations in technology, emergency medical services, hospitals, surgeons, and medicine had not continued. Many people would have died without penicillin, 9-1-1 availability, paramedics, and emergency room doctors, nurses, and technicians skilled in the science of emergency medicine. The likelihood of surviving a gunshot wound now greatly exceeds that chance in 1950, 1960, or 1970, though some researchers point out that the lethality and accuracy in the use of firearms sometimes precludes medical intervention (Eckberg, 2015). Medicine, technology, and training have saved lives and contributed to a decline in the homicide rate.

The criminal justice and public health systems pursue the "reduction and prevention of negative human outcomes" (Potter & Rosky, 2013, p. 276). Both may be seen as attempting to prevent and treat, as necessary, the problems people face. The Centers for Disease Control and Prevention (2018) states that public health systems should provide the following 10 "essential public health services":

1. Monitor health status to identify and solve community health problems.

2. Diagnose and investigate health problems and health hazards in the community.

3. Inform, educate, and empower people about health issues.

4. Mobilize community partnerships and action to identify and solve health problems.

5. Develop policies and plans that support individual and community health efforts.

6. Enforce laws and regulations that protect health and ensure safety.

7. Link people to needed personal health services and assure the provision of health care when otherwise unavailable.

8. Assure competent public and personal health care workforce.

9. Evaluate effectiveness, accessibility, and quality of personal and population-based health services.

10. Research for new insights and innovative solutions to health problems. (n.p.)

Examination of the list through a criminal justice system lens shows how the **public health perspective** of violence and homicide makes the problems amenable to strategies that can overlap with criminal justice approaches. This cooperative concept is logical and reminds us that the same need for a comprehensive strategy to prevent, reduce, and affect criminal behavior and the damage it causes to society must also include the educational system. Partnering between school districts and public health departments is not new. In fact, partnerships

Figure 15.1 10 Leading Causes of Death by Age Group, United States – 2016

						Age Groups					
Rank	<1	1-4	5-9	10-14	15-24	25-34	35-44	45-54	55-64	65+	Total
1	Congenital Anomalies 4,816	Unintentional Injury 1,261	Unintentional Injury 787	Unintentional Injury 847	Unintentional Injury 13,895	Unintentional Injury 23,984	Unintentional Injury 20,975	Malignant Neoplasms 41,291	Malignant Neoplasms 116,364	Heart Disease 507,118	Heart Disease 635,260
2	Short Gestation 3,927	Congenital Anomalies 433	Malignant Neoplasms 449	Suicide 436	Suicide 5,723	Suicide 7,366	Malignant Neoplasms 10,903	Heart Disease 34,027	Heart Disease 78,610	Malignant Neoplasms 422,927	Malignant Neoplasms 598,038
3	SIDS 1,500	Malignant Neoplasms 377	Congenital Anomalies 203	Malignant Neoplasms 431	Homicide 5,172	Homicide 5,376	Heart Disease 10,477	Unintentional Injury 23,377	Unintentional Injury 21,860	Chronic Low Respiratory Disease 131,002	Unintentional Injury 161,374
4	Maternal Pregnancy Comp. 1,402	Homicide 339	Homicide 139	Homicide 147	Malignant Neoplasms 1,431	Malignant Neoplasms 3,791	Suicide 7,030	Suicide 8,437	Chronic Low Respiratory Disease 17,810	Cerebrovascular 121,630	Chronic Low Respiratory Disease 154,596
5	Unintentional Injury 1,219	Heart Disease 118	Heart Disease 77	Congenital Anomalies 146	Heart Disease 949	Heart Disease 3,445	Homicide 3,369	Liver Disease 8,364	Diabetes Mellitus 14,251	Alzheimer's Disease 114,883	Cerebrovascular 142,142
6	Placenta Cord Membranes 841	Influenza & Pneumonia 103	Chronic Low Respiratory Disease 68	Heart Disease 111	Congenital Anomalies 388	Liver Disease 925	Liver Disease 2,851	Diabetes Mellitus 6,267	Liver Disease 13,448	Diabetes Mellitus 56,452	Alzheimer's Disease 116,103
7	Bacterial Sepsis 583	Septicemia 70	Influenza & Pneumonia 48	Chronic Low Respiratory Disease 75	Diabetes Mellitus 211	Diabetes Mellitus 792	Diabetes Mellitus 2,049	Cerebrovascular 5,353	Cerebrovascular 12,310	Unintentional Injury 53,141	Diabetes Mellitus 80,058
8	Respiratory Distress 488	Perinatal period 60	Septicemia 40	Cerebrovascular 50	Chronic Low Respiratory Disease 206	Cerebrovascular 575	Cerebrovascular 1,851	Chronic Low. Respiratory Disease 4,307	Suicide 7,759	Influenza & Pneumonia 42,479	Influenza & Pneumonia 51,537
9	Circulatory System Disease 460	Cerebrovascular 55	Cerebrovascular 38	Influenza & Pneumonia 39	Influenza & Pneumonia 189	HIV 546	HIV 971	Septicemia 2,472	Septicemia 5,941	Nephritis 41,095	Nephritis 50,046
10	Neonatal Hemorrhage 398	Chronic Low Respiratory Disease 51	Benign Neoplasms 31	Septicemia 31	Complicated Pregnancy 184	Complicated Pregnancy 472	Septicemia 897	Homicide 2,152	Nephritis 5,650	Septicemia 30,405	Suicide 44,965

Data Source: National Vital Statistics System, National Center for Health Statistics, CDC, 2017.
Produced by: National Center for Injury Prevention and Control, CDC using WISQARS™.

Figure 15.2 The 10 Essential Public Health Services

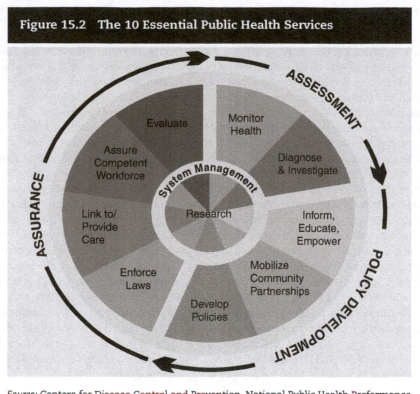

Source: Centers for Disease Control and Prevention, National Public Health Performance Standards, 2018.

involving criminal justice, public health, and education are not unique. Bonner, McLean, and Worden (2008) described Chicago's Cease-Fire program with language that illustrates all three groups working to identify the threat to life (public health), interdict with the agents of transmission (criminal justice), and affect group and peer behavior (education). As we said, there is a great deal of overlap, and this can be seen as a strength of a multidisciplinary approach, in much the way contemporary criminology eschews monotheory explanations or avenues to explain or investigate criminality. Public health research efforts have also highlighted the dangers of firearms present in the home and readily available on the street. Family doctors have recently been encouraged to inquire about firearm accessibility when performing checkups for patients, especially children.

CRIMINAL JUSTICE SYSTEM RESPONSE AND LEGISLATION

Role of Legislation

The criminal justice system's response to homicide and the murder rate in the United States has historically been limited to a few tools. The hope of deterrence, the time-bound restriction of incapacitation, targeted legislation, and programs to identify and punish those who commit criminal homicide have been some of the general approaches. Moving from prevention through deterrence to retribution, we see the lever-pulling strategy of coordinated local–federal action providing a swift and thorough response to violent crime, which has shown some positive

The contemporary focus on the brain's role in crime causation is due, in no small part, to the career-long efforts of biosocial researcher Adrian Raine. Dubbed neurocriminology, the new subfield created by Raine examines brain impairments that affect how a person deals with such cognitions as fear, decision-making, and guilt. These are constructs that Raine believes are steps on a pathway to violence. He notes that risk factors in children such as poor nutrition, brain trauma from abuse, and genetics lie outside the ability of the child to control and that these occur within a reality of social disadvantage and a society ill equipped to identify, assess, and treat those disadvantaged. The potential result, he asserts, is turning to crime.

Social factors are not ignored in this new incarnation of theory addressing the biological basis of crime. Raine (2013) explains, "Social factors are critical both in interacting with biological forces in causing crime, and in directly producing the biological changes that predispose a person to violence" (p. 9). He goes on to note that there are practical implications for the legal system and ethical considerations as we contemplate what this new and integrated interdisciplinary research means within a public health approach to crime.

Molecular and behavioral genetics are shown to be parts of the basis of behavior through our responses to our unique physiology. Neuroscience indicates emotions like fear may be in our nervous system through our genetics. Incredible advances in brain-scanning technology give scientists unprecedented access and ability to explore the biological basis of who we are and how we act. Advanced brain scan capabilities are also greatly aiding the diagnosis and treatment of traumatic brain injury (TBI) that results from a blow to the head or body and can lead to a variety of behaviors, including aggression. With much violence being expressive rather than instrumental, what does the future hold, for example, for addressing the anger–violence connection?

results (McGarrell, Chermak, Wilson, & Corsaro, 2006). Classically, the required components of effective deterrence are severity, certainty, and celerity, or being time-connected to the offense. Lever-pulling, such as in the Boston version of Ceasefire or the Cincinnati Initiative to Reduce Violence (CIRV), aimed for a robust response involving local authorities and federal prosecution, consistency in the form of responding to every instance of violent crime, and a fast track to ensure the timeliness or celerity (Engel, Tillyer, & Corsaro, 2013).

By comparison, so-called three-strikes-and-you-are-out retributive legislation has had mixed reviews on whether the various models are particularly effective (Baran, 2014). Most states and federal legislators enacted laws that called for lengthy prison sentences for second or third offenses involving guns or felonies. Given that many of those who commit crime do not believe they will get caught and many who commit murder are in the grip of emotion or under the influence of a substance, the deterrence potential of a sanction is weakened. In 1994, California enacted the harsh three-strikes legislation that led to thousands of offenders filling the already-strained prisons beyond any reasonable level of crowding. Twenty years on, in 2012, the voters approved significant changes to the law, which allowed a logical move toward decarceration and right-sizing sentences (Levine, 2014). These challenges to the efficacy of three-strikes laws call into question the use of capital punishment as well, if considered under the rubric of deterrence.

Capital punishment has been used in the United States and continues in most states as a response to the conviction of some individuals (not all and not consistently) for heinous crimes. Evidence is at best mixed as to whether the death penalty is a deterrent for someone who would commit murder (Durlauf, Fu, & Navarro, 2013, among others). Public opinion is mixed as well about the appropriateness of using capital punishment as retribution. Public views have also been affected by a number of executions that have encountered complications while being carried out (Brumfield, 2014).

Criminology and criminal justice researchers view murders committed in the heat of the moment as likely not to be impacted by the thought of capital punishment. When a society chooses to use a penalty of death for committing premeditated or brutal murders, it might be made clearer to the general public to cite the rationale as societal retribution and leave it at that. Moving forward, it will be necessary for legislators to incorporate research findings in the drafting of effective legislation designed to reduce violent crime, including homicide.

Role of the Investigator

Individual investigators of criminal homicide carry an awesome burden: discovering and assembling facts that indicate responsibility for the taking of a human life. The focus is, of necessity, one that is narrow and concerned with identifying persons responsible for the criminally wrongful death of another and assembling information to present to a prosecutor. The detective and other criminal justice actors then work collaboratively with the prosecutor to present the case through our adversarial process of criminal court.

In an earlier chapter, we discussed the contributions that technology and science have made to the investigation of violent crimes. The increasing power of the computer and the analysis of ever more minute trace evidence are facilitated by devices. Yet with the burgeoning of technological capabilities, it still remains central for the human investigator to piece together the actions of people. Equipment does not conduct interviews or interrogations in the social-process elements of an investigation. The homicide detective and many other professionals synthesize the most likely course of events resulting in a death. The image of the lone detective persevering against daunting odds and little concrete evidence to elicit a confession from the killer is largely Hollywood fiction. But the factual need for professional investigators with stamina and a strong sense of mission is on the mark.

EXHIBIT 15.1

EFFECTIVE HOMICIDE UNIT PRACTICES IN THE BOSTON POLICE DEPARTMENT

John M. Brown of the Boston Police Department has seen a lot in his years serving the citizens of Boston. In our interview with Brown, he listed a number of practices that he says the Boston Police Department (BPD) has found useful not only in solving homicides but in working with citizens and family survivors of homicide victims. This is important as police are called to handle the aftermath of criminal violence and certainly cases of homicide. Improvements in the processes and technologies that aid in the retroactive investigation of murder have contributed much to this grim but necessary endeavor. With the significant drop in homicide clearance rates nationwide over the past 50 years and more cases *going cold*, working effectively with community members to gain information is a focal concern in order to identify offenders and bring them to justice.

Deputy Brown's ongoing involvement from the early stages of his career in the gang unit and as a member of the homicide unit affirmed his conviction of reaching out to the community in as many ways as possible.

Boston Police Criminal Investigations Division (CID) Highlights

Homicide/DA Office Reviews. These monthly meetings review all cases from the year as well as any from previous years that have new developments or need some feedback.

Detective In-Service Training Modules. There is department-wide detective training focusing on forensics and evidence collection for all detectives in the department. Modules include portions of lectures and practical work.

(Continued)

(Continued)

Private Family Meetings. Investigators and surviving families (and the District Attorney's Office if necessary) have been meeting regarding case status upon request by either the investigators and squads or surviving families.

Survivor's Workshops & Educational Meetings. There are educational and therapeutic workshops that include the initial stages of the 9-1-1 call throughout the investigative process. Presentations include

- forensic units,

- ongoing investigation needs,

- DA's Office and criminal proceedings process, and

- focus on clinical support from experts who specialize in homicide bereavement.

Unsolved-Homicide Media.

- *Unsolved Herald Highlighted Homicides:* This began in October 2014 and is ongoing. It involves working with families and detectives to share details that may assist in bringing people forward with information.

- Local TV segments on unsolved homicides in collaboration with the Homicide Unit.

Source: Interview with John Brown, BPD.

- *Boston Globe* featured articles on various topics from homicides to witness protection and more.

Homicide Website. For the first time, the Boston Police Homicide Unit has created a website to provide information to the public directly. The information on the site covers the following:

- Current unsolved-homicide cases

- Current solved cases

- Previous years' cases

- Family and witness support

- Text-a-tip information

- FAQs

CID Community Partnerships. These focus on the quality of life for young people, with prevention, guidance, and leadership for youth impacted by violence on various levels that can ultimately lead to *deadly* paths. It includes the following:

- Teen empowerment

- Youth connect

- Youth–police dialogues

Investigators and many of the other technicians of a law enforcement agency work together in homicide units or across functional groups and agencies to coordinate and work a homicide case (Hough & McCorkle, 2015). The process of an investigation results in facts and findings that explain to various audiences what happened in a lethal event. Recreating a likely chronological sequence of events is an important portion of the work of detectives. Providing context and background can aid prosecutors, the court, and potentially a jury in understanding and reaching decisions about accountability in death cases.

Role of the Researcher

As the substance of this text indicates, the execution and subsequent compilation, summarization, and presentation of research is critical to our understanding of the dynamics of homicide. Additionally, we continue to make the case that such knowledge is crucial for the construction and implementation of policy through laws and agency initiatives to prevent and mitigate homicide or effectively identify and hold accountable those who commit homicide. All components of the foundation for these efforts are the province of researchers and policy analysts.

A January 2019 NBC News article sketched a picture of the movement around much of the United States to enhance security measures at churches. The article, titled "Guns and God: Growing number of churches want armed security, describes how many places of worship utilize 'volunteer-run security teams'" to provide a presence, generally armed, in a place historically kept free of firearms. One person interviewed for the story points to turmoil in the personal lives of congregants as what can lead to violence at a church gathering. Family discord and the culmination of intimate partner violence or domestic cases are among these. The gunman in the 2017 Sutherland Spring, Texas, church shooting killed 26 people, including members of his estranged wife's family and wounded 20 others. The man had been discharged from the military for assault on his wife and stepson and pointing a loaded gun at his wife. The man was later charged with cruelty to animals. Due to his military court-martial, he was not lawfully permitted to own or possess guns or ammunition, yet he purchased several in Texas before his deadly rampage.

Experimental design and experimentation are the tools of the criminologist and researcher. Making sense of the findings and illuminating connections among theoretical views are their bread and butter. Researchers put varying degrees of effort into placing these findings before actual policymakers. We long for the day that new findings are effectively channeled in a timely and comprehensible manner to greater numbers of practitioners and legislators. We are encouraged by the participation of researchers in organizations such as the International Association of Chiefs of Police (IACP) and the Police Executive Research Forum (PERF) as well as the unique Homicide Research Working Group (HRWG) that brings together researchers and practitioners to examine homicide as its sole focus. This new day will hopefully be matched by the eager consumption of said findings by enlightened politicians and administrators in service of trying new (and evidence-based) programs. Researchers should continue to make efforts to reach out to practitioners and policymakers to appropriately package and provide research that is useful to them.

Role of the Community and Citizens

In the era of community-oriented policing, there should be little argument that citizens individually and communities collectively compose an actual functioning component of the criminal justice system. Arguably, the victims' rights movement begun in the 1980s, the Homeland Security era that came about post-9/11, and the contemporary envisioning and attention paid to reintegration of offenders all strongly support the necessity to consider people and groups as partners of *official* criminal justice agencies. It would be difficult, to say the least, to provide an exhaustive list of community groups, let alone the many ways that individuals are available to agencies in the form of victims, witnesses (in the sense of anyone who can furnish information), and passive-security monitoring systems. All of these can aid the actors in the official system in their criminal, academic, and legislative investigations. As many law enforcement officers can attest, law enforcement agencies need citizen involvement to continue to solve and prevent crimes in communities. This requires both an engaged citizenry and a good relationship with law enforcement.

SOCIETAL ISSUES

Frequent violence and homicide may leave many residents of a community numb. The lived reality of neighborhood members is often remote or ignored altogether by those living in areas not similarly troubled. We wonder at how neighbors interviewed by the media sometimes do not appear emotional, even while we understand the shock the neighbors feel at how close violence is (Grant & Diehl, 2012). Some residents and onlookers appear at the crime scene not strictly out of curiosity but also to show support for each other or a victim's family or to attempt to process what is happening *in* and *to* their neighborhood. In areas where violence and murder are common, residents have lost faith in the criminal justice system. Homicide is a constant for many of them. The residents understand that a homicide may occur in a dyadic circumstance between two individuals in the neighborhood, but they also know that there are larger issues. In Chicago's South Side neighborhood, for example, residents routinely awake on a Monday morning to hear that multiple shootings and murders occurred just over the weekend. These are the failings in a society that seems to move forward all too slowly in improving the lot of the least of its members. Law enforcement knows, in turn, that the lack of trust results in poor or no communication with law enforcement agencies. We again note here that law enforcement is often inserted at the point of social friction. This is not to say that police do not, at times, add to the problems of community communication and trust. But without the sustained effort, day after day, to reach out to one another, portions of a community most in need of help and the law enforcers who strive to address violence are continually pulled apart by the tides of distrust and frustration.

Concentrated disadvantage and poverty continue to appropriately be studied in conjunction with violence in such areas (Stretesky, Schuck, & Hogan, 2004). The social, educational, environmental, and criminal factors that work together in these toxic areas to create a big part of the homicide problem in this country all need attention and action. Community, educational, economic, and police programs must have a substantial and positive presence where the need is greatest. No political orientation can or should own or disown this reality. It is practical and a money-saver to do what reduces crime and suffering. We caution students, politicians, and the public not to confuse correlation with causation. What may appear frequently alongside the problem itself may not indicate a cause-and-effect relationship. However, it bears mentioning that the center mass of much crime, including homicide, exists where other individual and community weaknesses flourish or persist.

Guns

There have been attempts at regulatory measures designed to reasonably limit the types of weapons intended to propel deadly projectiles facilitated by gunpowder. A component of such policy initiatives is a reasonable limit on certain individuals, not all of society, who could possess the designed-to-be-deadly firearm. So-called *gun control* measures are often intended to

WHY WOULD THEY DO IT?

While Houston police officers were recently executing a search warrant at a suspected drug house, four police officers were shot and two suspects were killed. Houston Police Chief Art Acevedo spoke about the incident and issued a call for action, "We don't elect people to pray for us. We elect people to lead us. I appreciate your prayers, but the question is, what are policymakers willing to do, besides prayers, to address a public-health epidemic?" The chief used a refrain that has recently become popular on social media after recent mass shootings, where many have expressed frustration that all elected leaders can offer to families of shooting victims is *thoughts and prayers*. The high profile police chief has been a proponent of gun safety measures, particularly in the wake of the mass killing in a Texas church that left 10 people dead. He has asserted that he supports the Second Amendment while also supporting some reasonable measures that would keep law enforcement and the public safer. He has been actively involved in national law enforcement organizations including the Major Cities Chiefs Association, which has supported assault weapons bans and increased background checks at gun shows.

accomplish appropriate people control. A reality of much of the intended criminal homicide by people using firearms in this country each year (as well as hundreds of accidental deaths and shootings of children and others) is that firearms are found in so many places. Interest groups and elected representatives, who frequently choose to act in ways not consistent with the larger group of citizens, provide substantial hostile opposition to seemingly *any* legislative effort at clear, transparent, and narrow limits on the killing power available to almost every person in society. The rhetoric and shouting that crowd out reasoned conversation are filled with fallacies and flawed numbers presented as *research* that can scare people into knee-jerk opinion, rather than a calm, balanced response reflective of the reality in the United States that government and society would not advocate nor set out to block everyone from firearm ownership.

Law enforcement officers are highly trained in not only the use of firearms but, more importantly, the dynamics of threat and danger assessment. Officers are tasked with protecting the rest of society from those who would harm people. And yet with all of these facts that describe the reality of law enforcement's use of force, laypeople who do not carry guns *professionally*, as police do to serve and protect the public, believe that they would know when to shoot someone dead when they perceive a threat. This conclusion is difficult to credibly support. Many avoidable homicides occur with regularity by citizens shooting other citizens in circumstances that objectively do not call for a killing response. Even the trained law enforcement professional gets it wrong sometimes. Emotional suggestions for airline pilots, schoolteachers, students on college campuses, and others to carry firearms also fail to pass the empirical test of utility and balanced response to actual threats.

Violence has many different components that need to be addressed before the problem can be fixed. An aspect of political debate is regulating the sale of firearms of certain kinds. While few people suggest a so-called ban on guns, those who resist any attention paid to firearms use this tired rhetoric. Specific requirements regarding who can and cannot own a firearm need the force of law to accompany the public

sentiment. The constitutional rights of citizens do not appear threatened in the United States on this matter. What remains in question is to what lengths elected representatives of those citizens are willing to go to in trying to reduce firearms-associated violence. For example, in the wake of several recent mass shootings, including at Sandy Hook Elementary School, there were promises of legislative action, but there has been very little progress to date.

Violence Prevention

Sociologist Leonard Beeghley (2003) expressed an important observation that elected officials should pay heed to when he said, "The dirty little secret of public policy in this country is that wars on crime do not deal with the sources of violence" (p. 7). Legislative efforts in the form of laws against violent acts and funding to programs aimed to address that violence have mixed effects. Traditional police efforts have been directed to suppression of violence. In late 2018, the Major Cities Chiefs Association in conjunction with the Bureau of Justice Assistance issued a Violent Crime Reduction Operations Guide addressed to law enforcement agency heads with a message that administrators must show leadership in dealing with violent crime (Flynn & Selletti, 2018). The Guide discusses *critical elements* that agency heads must consider as they assess capacity to effect change. The first element addressed is community engagement. Federal agencies from varied components of government have endorsed education for young people, supported strategies to combat violent crime, and emphasized the need for coordinated efforts to address the causes and consequences of violence. Figure 15.3 depicts the variety of groups and organizations contemplated in a public health approach to the challenge of violence. As you consider the figure, think about how each of the entities named could address some aspect of violence with an eye toward prevention and reduction.

There are many sources of violence and clearly a variety of forms that the violence takes in society. American author and activist Jackson Katz has devoted much of his focus on men and

Figure 15.3   The Public Health System

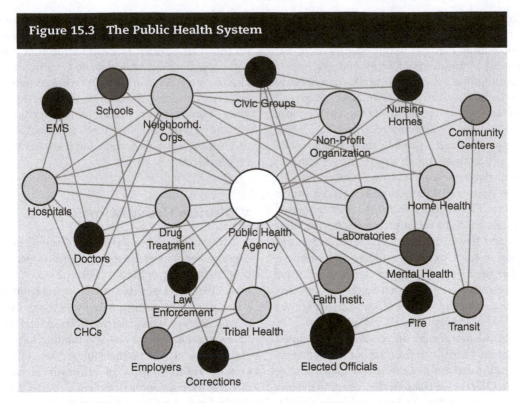

Source: Centers for Disease Control and Prevention, (2018). Public Health Systems & Best Practices. Retrieved from https://www.cdc.gov/publichealthgateway/publichealthservices/essentialhealthservices.html

male youths and the need to confront flawed aspects of male identity in regard to violence toward women and each other. As cofounder of the Mentors in Violence Prevention (MVP) program, Katz has long delivered the message that violence against women is a men's issue, and his popular TED Talk on the subject has been viewed by millions. Churches, non-profit organizations, schools and others have sporadically addressed similar issues but not always in a coordinated approach that might leverage more community resources to create a constant pressure to improve and do better together. One approach is to emphasize involvement in sports over gangs in areas that struggle with gang presence and kids who struggle with gang pressure.

There is an awful and immutable reality attached to an angry young man with a gun in his hand. The age-old phenomenon of wanting to save face has driven incalculable violence throughout history. It seems clear that it will take nothing less than the involvement of every segment of society to address violence and its causes.

PREDICTING VIOLENCE

Some violence and even increased likelihood of homicide is vulnerable to prediction. **Threat assessment,** as we have commented earlier in the book, has been examined by many authors and agencies. Much of the academic research surrounding the prediction of violence has dealt with the risk assessment of offenders released early from a sentence of incarceration or charged individuals allowed free on bond prior to trial. Often, this assessment is concerned with general threat to the community. Some studies show empirical support for this type of prediction (Liu, Yang, Ramsay, Li, & Coid, 2011; Neuilly, Zgoba, Tita, & Lee, 2011). There is obvious concern, as well, for determining the potential dangerousness of an individual to a specific person. Noted examples would be the threat to someone from an intimate partner, threats made against people such as celebrities or politicians, and the immediate threat posed by someone in an escalating face-to-face conflict.

EXHIBIT 15.2

RED FLAG LAWS

After the Parkland shootings in Florida, there was a renewed interest across the country in passing gun restrictions, and this resulted in more legislation enacted after Parkland than after the Newtown school shooting in 2012. An analysis of state laws revealed that in 2018, over half of states increased gun restrictions. The analysis further demonstrated that these measures passed in states with legislatures controlled by *both* parties. The legislation covered a variety of specific areas, but the most popular measures were related to increased restrictions on domestic violence offenders, bump stocks, urban gun violence, and **red flag laws**. Red flag laws have generated significant interest and support, as these laws allow police, family members, or others to petition a court to allow temporary removal of firearms from a person who is a danger to himself or others. As the investigation into the Parkland shooting revealed, family members of the shooter had contacted the FBI and local law enforcement prior to the shooting with concerns about his mental state and his access to guns. Since the passage of these laws in at least 13 states, many other states are considering similar measures. Some early studies have suggested there may be a correlation between red flag laws and a decrease in firearm homicides and suicides.

The stuff of prediction is neither certain nor consistent. We consider the homily that the best predictor of future behavior is past behavior (regression line) or that if a sufficient cluster of red flags is present in a given scenario, a violent outcome is far more likely. Experts and laypeople have a fair chance of increasing their *best guess* about a pathway to violence and possibly murder using these *methods*. Intimate partner homicide (IPH) presents important lessons about the turn-off points that are often present on the road to a lethal event. Gavin de Becker (1998) reminds us, however, that "only human beings can look directly at something, have all the information they need to make an accurate prediction, perhaps even momentarily make the accurate prediction, and then say that it isn't so" (p. 288). As we have pointed out, the dynamics of intimate partner violence are not simple, despite the inclination for the uninformed to assert that they are. De Becker's MOSAIC threat assessment systems have been applied to situations in the workplace and schools and with public officials and intimate partner violence.

Checklist prediction must be avoided. The use of validated assessment instruments can be helpful if they are used in conjunction with a human interviewer. On a bad day in Mrs. Brown's third grade class, the majority of kids may look to be heading to a life of crime if a simple checklist were used that tabulated deviant or disruptive behavior. The U.S. Secret Service and other groups devote significant time and resources to examining threats to the safety of prominent individuals. Determining who is a credible threat in a given situation can be quite difficult. Young people grow and learn in part through conflict. We can predict that many will engage in violence of some sort. We can even reasonably predict that many gang members will continue to engage in violence, for instance, and that their risk of committing murder or of being murdered is significantly higher than others in society or even people who are otherwise matched for age or economic position. This knowledge alone cannot stop violence. Programs must use this information to implement education and intervention strategies. Researchers should continue to work with practitioners to validate threat assessment tools when possible. Validation efforts, like those being done by Dr. Jacquelyn Campbell regarding the danger assessment instrument used in intimate partner violence situations discussed in the chapter on intimate partner homicide, show great promise.

In addition, as we consider the pace at which technology and data mining has stitched together a picture of who were are, we marvel at the accuracy that an algorithm may discern our actions or choice. Marketers are not the only beneficiaries of the insights gleaned from our web surfing, social media postings, and purchases. Health care professionals are able to assess and give feedback to us with greater specificity than ever before based on genetic mapping, early discovery of markers in our systems, and more. Why not threat assessment? Well, in part, the answer to this rhetorical musing about who is dangerous—and to whom—goes to a procedural justice and ethics concern. If someone has not done something yet, what action would government take if they suspected him or her of presenting a future threat? As researchers and policymakers cautiously make their way forward, mindful of ethical concerns, they may be able to harness data-informed factors that taken together give rise to concerns about a trajectory toward violence. Retrospectively, when we learn that a family annihilator had multiple firearms, arrests for violence, animal abuse incidents, the lay person may believe it was clear he would kill his family. We know that such high stakes predictions are never that simple. However, police departments have been able to give individuals feedback about the danger they may be in based on the aforementioned assessments and the data the departments themselves gather.

TECHNOLOGY

Technology is the basis for much of forensic examination and testing. From the comparison of tool marks to biological samples, laboratories have become quite effective in linking trace or other evidence from one person or place to another. Computers have been applied for several decades, and they will continue to power aspects of analysis. Social media can be utilized to educate the public and seek assistance that is so critically needed following a violent event.

Some concern has been voiced that the universal awareness of forensic methods can lead criminals to be better at covering their tracks. However, the professionalism and expertise of criminalists and investigators in addition to the sensitivity of equipment and testing methods makes us believe that law enforcement will stay ahead in this race. The specialties and subspecialties in forensic personnel and laboratory examination will likely increase. In our brief treatment of technology and forensic examination, we did not, for instance, discuss glass fragments, soils and minerals, documents, digital evidence, drugs, hair and fiber evidence, and many other items and corresponding analyses.

Technology plays an important role at the scene and later in the laboratory. At various scenes, technology allows technicians to thoroughly search for and gather evidence and then document it. At the laboratory, criminalists employ many devices and databases to analyze and compare evidence gathered and establish links or connections between objects and suspects. The human genome project, brain scan technologies, and important research by Adrian Raine and others offer insights through neurocriminology.

The technology of detection has certainly been a boon to law enforcement, whose job it is to retroactively find those who have committed murder. Similarly, technology and other scientific advances have aided the would-be victims of homicide or other violent crimes. The potential for a victim of traumatic injury to survive has increased dramatically in the last half-century. First responders have better and more extensive training; emergency medicine has become a specialized field within the medical community; there are increased numbers of designated trauma centers in addition to other hospital emergency rooms; the inevitable advances and methods improved through wartime have come through the experiences in Iraq and Afghanistan; and medicines and diagnostic tools have provided powerful methods to pull life back from the jaws of impending death. Witness, too, the ubiquitous cellular telephone, GPS locating, and the development of personally worn vital-signs devices and digital medical records carried on one's person. The context here is that while crime, including violent crime, has declined in some categories in most of the last 20 years, the homicide rate and numbers would be higher without the advances in technology and medicine, though how much can be debated.

An interest in homicide will always exist in society. Curiosity about homicide is normal, and learning about causes and solutions informs citizens and may give them the perspective needed to approach the topic with a rational rather than an emotional mind-set. Knowing how to predict violence before it occurs is not a perfect science. Risk assessment in intimate partner relationships has advanced due to the work of Jacquelyn Campbell, Gavin de Becker, and others, but the tools must be used and more effectively applied to people at risk. Nonetheless, knowledge about homicide is an important component of the foundation for construction of sound policies and programs to reduce violence in society.

A discussion of homicide in various countries and cultures around the world helps provide some context for the level of violence and homicide here in the United States. In recent years, the effort at compiling data from different countries has expanded. *The European Sourcebook of Crime and Criminal Justice Statistics* (Aebi et al., 2014) was published in its fifth edition in 2014, collecting and validating crime information from 41 countries. The data in the fifth edition covers the period 2007–2011, and it shows homicide declining in almost every country over that period of time. *The Global Study on Homicide 2013*, created by the United Nations Office on Drugs and Crime (UNODC), reflects a never-before-seen effort to tabulate and compare homicide across countries.

The report emphasizes, as we do, that, "unlike other forms of homicide, which vary significantly across regions and from year to year, intimate partner and family-related homicide remains persistent and prevalent" (UNODC, 2014, p. 5). The U.S.-based international Homicide Research Working Group formed in 1992 to join academics of many disciplines and practitioners to "discover the best ways to measure and reduce rates of lethal violence" (HRWG, n.d., n.p.). The HRWG members work to understand the dynamics of homicides and share the research with others in hopes of affecting policy and reducing lethal violence. We must do better at understanding the dynamics of family and intimate partner violence and educating families and agencies about those dynamics and how to channel outcomes away from violence and abuse. We are not there yet.

Confrontational violence and lethal incidents arising from arguments or perceived insults represent perhaps the single largest category of homicide. Such violence and murder is the province of young men, many caught up in gangs, others caught up in testosterone, angry responses, and the pitfalls along the inevitable path to maturity that sadly comes too late for some who kill. The chance to reach maturity may never come for those who die at the hands of someone who generally looks in all ways just like them. Medical technology holds down some of the numbers for would-be homicide when people survive wounds they would have succumbed to only a few years ago. With aggravated assault rates showing us that violent attacks are still the ultimate conflict resolution that some people see, continued efforts and resources have to go to parenting programs, early-childhood programs, school programs, and intervention methods that emphasize nonviolent strategies, especially for young people. These have to be realistic strategies that will find an audience with the disillusioned and prematurely hardened 14-year-old on an urban street or the marginalized 16-year-old in small-town America. His reality is not the reality of many policymakers. Our efforts should continue to focus on ways to address the comparatively high rates of confrontational homicide and violence.

We conclude the book with a note of optimism, even if that optimism is tempered by the knowledge that homicide remains a serious and far-too-frequent outcome of some human interactions.

KEY TERMS

Lever-pulling strategy 253
Victim impact 254
Covictims 254
Victims' rights movement 255

Post-traumatic stress disorder
 (PTSD) 255
Restorative justice 255
Public health perspective 257

Threat assessment 266
Red flag laws 267

DISCUSSION QUESTIONS

1. How does the public health perspective contribute to society's understanding and response to homicide?
2. Name and discuss an evidence-based strategy for homicide or violence reduction.
3. Explain how a lever-pulling strategy works to address violent crime.
4. What is a covictim of homicide, and how is he or she impacted by homicide?

5. How can the restorative-justice approach be applied to homicide?
6. What benefits and limitations exist for threat assessment?
7. What areas remain for policymakers and researchers in addressing homicide in the United States?

TRY THIS

After recent high profile killings by offenders who should not have had access to guns, homicide prevention strategies have included efforts to remove guns from those who should not lawfully possess them. Go to the NPR article on the law enforcement efforts in Seattle to enforce these orders here: https://www.jhsph.edu/research/centers-and-institutes/johns-hopkins-center-for-gun-policy-and-research/publications/

Law enforcement agencies in large jurisdictions with high homicide rates like Baltimore have attempted a variety of strategies to reduce violence and homicide. Go to the Johns Hopkins Center for Gun Policy and Research here: https://www.jhsph.edu/research/centers-and-institutes/johns-hopkins-center-for-gun-policy-and-research/publications/

Read the 2018 report related to the intervention efforts in Baltimore. What were these strategies and were they effective?

Aamodt, M. G., Moberg, J. L., Nash, T. M., Pendleton, G. B., Hommema, D. A., & Walker, C. E. (2007, September). *Profiling serial killers: When science and the media collide*. Poster session presented at the annual meeting of the Society for Police and Criminal Psychology, Springfield, MA.

Adams, D. (2007). *Why do they kill? Men who murder their intimate partners*. Nashville, TN: Vanderbilt University Press.

Adams, D. (2009). Predisposing childhood factors for men who kill their intimate partners. *Victims & Offenders, 4*(3), 215–229.

Adler, F. (1975). *Sisters in crime: The rise of the new female criminal*. New York, NY: McGraw-Hill.

Aebi, M. F., Akdeniz, G., Barclay, G., Campistol, C., Caneppele, S., Gruszczynska, B. . . . Þórisdóttir, R. (2014). *The European Sourcebook of Crime and Criminal Justice Statistics* (Fifth Ed.). Helsinki, Finland: Hakapaino Oy.

Agnew, R. (1992). Foundation for a general strain theory of crime and delinquency. *Criminology, 30*(1), 47–87.

Agnich, L. (2015). A comparative analysis of attempted and completed school-based mass murder attacks. *American Journal of Criminal Justice, 40*(1), 1–22.

Akiba, M., Baker, D., Goesling, B., & LeTendre, G. (2002). Student victimization: National and school system effects on school violence in 37 nations. *American Educational Research Journal, 39*(4), 829–853.

Alder, C., & Polk, K. (2001). *Child victims of homicide*. Cambridge, UK: Cambridge University Press.

Alvarez, A., & Bachman, R. (2003). *Murder American style*. Belmont, CA: Wadsworth, Cengage Learning.

Alvarez, A., & Bachman, R. (2014). *Violence: The enduring problem* (2nd ed.). Thousand Oaks, CA: Sage.

Alvarez, A., & Bachman, R. (2016). *Violence: The enduring problem* (3rd ed.). Thousand Oaks, CA: Sage.

American Law Institute. (2006). *Model penal code: Sentencing* [Discussion draft]. Philadelphia, PA: Author.

Anderson, E. (1994, May). The code of the streets. *Atlantic Monthly, 273*(5), 80–94.

Anderson, J. M., & Heaton, P. (2012). How much difference does the lawyer make? The effect of defense counsel on murder case outcomes. *The Yale Law Journal, 122*(1), 154–217.

Anderson, J. M., & Heaton, P. (2013). *Measuring the effect of defense counsel on homicide case outcomes*. Washington, DC: U. S. Department of Justice.

Armour, S. (2004, July 15). The mind of a killer: Death in the workplace. *USA Today*, p. 1A.

Arndt, W., Hietpas, T., & Kim, J. (2004). Critical characteristics of male serial murderers. *American Journal of Criminal Justice, 29*(1), 117–131.

Aronson, J., & Cole, S. A. (2009). Science and the death penalty: DNA, innocence, and the debate over capital punishment in the United States. *Law and Social Inquiry, 34*(3), 603–633.

Asbridge, M., Smart, R. G., & Mann, R. E. (2003). The "homogamy" of road rage: Understanding the relationship between victimization and offending among aggressive and violent motorists. *Violence and Victims, 18*(5), 517–531.

Associated Press. (2006, July 27). Woman not guilty in retrial in the deaths of her 5 children. *The New York Times*. Retrieved from http://www.nytimes.com/2006/07/27/us/27yates.html

Aujla, W., & Gill, A. K. (2014). Conceptualizing 'honour' killings in Canada: An extreme form of domestic violence? *International Journal of Criminal Justice Sciences, 9*(1), 153–166.

Averdijk, M. (2014). Methodological challenges in the study of age-victimization patterns. Can we use the accelerated design of the NCVS to reconstruct victim careers? *International Review of Victimology, 20*, 265–288.

Ayar, A. A. (2006). Road rage: Recognizing a psychological disorder. *Journal of Psychiatry & Law, 34*(2), 123–150.

Bagalman, E., & Napili, A. (2014). *Prevalence of mental illness in the United States: Data sources and estimates*. Washington, DC: Congressional Research Service.

Baird, A. A., Roellke, E. V., & Zeifman, D. M. (2017). Alone and adrift: The association between mass school shootings, school size, and student support. *The Social Science Journal*, *54*(3), 261–270.

Baker, K., Gartner, R., & Pampel, C. (1990). Gender stratification and the gender gap in homicide victimization. *Social Problems*, *37*(4), 593–612.

Baran, K. A. (2014). A felonious strikeout: The preventative benefits of the "three strikes law" in Massachusetts. *New England Journal on Criminal & Civil Confinement*, *40*(2), 403–425.

Bartels, R., & Parsons, C. (2009). The social construction of a serial killer. *Feminism & Psychology*, *19*(2), 267–280.

Bartol, C. R., & Bartol, A. M. (2011). *Criminal behavior: A psychological approach* (9th ed.). Upper Saddle River, NJ: Pearson.

Bartol, C. R., & Bartol, A. M. (2013). *Criminal & behavioral profiling: Theory, research, and practice.* Thousand Oaks, CA: Sage.

Baumer, E. P., Messner, S. F., & Felson, R. B. (2000). Role of victim characteristics in the disposition of murder cases. *Justice Quarterly*, *17*(2), 281–307.

Beaver, K. M. (2010). The biochemistry of violent crime. In C. J. Ferguson (Ed.), *Violent crime: Clinical and social implications* (pp. 75–98). Thousand Oaks, CA: Sage.

Beeghley, L. (2003). *Homicide: A sociological explanation.* Lanham, MD: Rowman & Littlefield.

Berg, J. M., Smith, S. F., Watts, A. L., Ammirati, R., Green, S. E., & Lilienfeld, S. O. (2013). Misconceptions regarding psychopathic personality: Implications for clinical practice and research. *Neuropsychiatry*, *3*(1), 63–81.

Berman, G., Narby, D. J., & Cutler, B. L. (1995). Effects of inconsistent eyewitness statements on mock-jurors' evaluations of the eyewitness, perceptions of defendant culpability and verdicts. *Law and Human Behavior*, *19*(1), 79–88.

Bernhardt, P. C. (1997). Influences of serotonin and testosterone in aggression and dominance: Convergence with social psychology. *Current Directions in Psychological Science*, *6*(2), 44–48. doi:10.1111/1467-8721.ep11512620

Blair, J. P., & Martindale, M. H. (2013). *United States active shooter events from 2000 to 2010: Training and equipment implications.* Texas State University. Retrieved from https://rems.ed.gov/docs/United-StatesActiveShooterEventsFrom2000to2010.pdf

Blair, J. P., & Schweit, K. W. (2014). *A study of active shooter incidents between 2000 and 2013.* Washington, DC: Federal Bureau of Investigation and Texas State University.

Bonner, H. S., McLean, S. J., & Worden, R. E. (2008). *CeaseFire-Chicago: A synopsis.* Albany, NY: The John F. Finn Institute for Public Safety.

Braga, A. A. (2017). Focused deterrence and the reduction of gang homicide. In F. Brookman, E. R. Maguire, & M. Maguire (Eds.), *The Handbook of Homicide* (pp. 197–212). Sussex, UK: John Wiley & Sons.

Braga, A. A., & Dusseault, D. (2018). Can homicide detectives improve homicide clearance rates? *Crime and Delinquency*, *64*(3), 283–315.

Breitman, N., Shackelford, T. K., & Block, C. R. (2004). Couple age discrepancy and risk of intimate partner homicide. *Violence and Victims*, *19*(3), 321–342.

Brewer, T. (2005). The attorney-client relationship in capital cases and its impact on juror receptivity to mitigation evidence. *Justice Quarterly*, *20*(2), 74–88.

Briody, M. (2004). The effects of DNA evidence on homicide cases in court. *Australian & New Zealand Journal of Criminology*, *37*(2), 231–252.

Brookman, F. (2003). Confrontational and revenge homicides among men in England and Wales. *The Australian and New Zealand Journal of Criminology*, *36*(1), 34–59.

Brookman, F., & Maguire, M. (2004). Reducing homicide: A review of the possibilities. *Crime, Law & Social Change*, *42*(4-5), 325–403.

Brown, C. H. (2018). The role of leadership in surviving a school shooting. *Journal of Cases in Educational Leadership*, *21*(2), 3–14.

Bruce, M. D., & Nowlin, W. A. (2011). Workplace violence: Awareness, prevention, and response. *Public Personnel Management*, *40*(4), 293–308.

Brumfield, B. (2014, September 8). 15 injections used in controversial Arizona execution, documents show. *CNN.* Retrieved from http://www.cnn.com/2014/08/02/justice/arizona-execution-controversy/

Buck v. Bell, 274 U.S. 200 (1927).

Buerger, M. E., & Buerger, G. E. (2010, September). Those terrible first few minutes: Revisiting active-shooter protocols for schools. *FBI Law Enforcement Bulletin.*

Bureau of Justice Statistics. (2011). *Homicide trends in the United States, 1980–2008* [NCJ 236018]. Retrieved from http://www.bjs.gov/content/pub/pdf/htus8008.pdf

Bureau of Justice Statistics. (2018). *Criminal victimization, 2017.* Retrieved from http://www.bjs.gov/index.cfm?ty=pbdetail&iid=6466

Bureau of Labor Statistics, U.S. Department of Labor. (2018, January 23). *TED: The Economics Daily: There were 500 workplace homicides in the United States in 2016 on the internet.* Retrieved from https://www.bls.gov/opub/ted/2018/there-were-500-workplace-homicides-in-the-united-states-in-2016.htm

Buzawa, E. S., Buzawa, C. G., & Stark, E. (2012). *Responding to domestic violence: The integration of criminal justice and human services* (4th ed.). Thousand Oaks, CA: Sage.

Buzawa, E. S., Buzawa, C. G., & Stark, E. (2015). *Responding to domestic violence: The integration of criminal justice and human services* (5th ed.). Thousand Oaks, CA: Sage.

Caldwell, M. F., Calhoun, V. D., & Kiehl, K. A. (2014). Abnormal brain structure in youth who commit homicide. *Neuroimage: Clinical, 4,* 800–807.

Campbell, J. C. (2002). Health consequences of intimate partner violence. *The Lancet, 359*(9314), 1331–1336.

Campbell, J. C. (2004). *Danger assessment.* Retrieved from http://www.dangerassessment.org

Campbell, J. C., Glass, N., Sharps, P. W., Laughon, K., & Bloom, T. (2007). Intimate partner homicide: Review and implications of research and policy. *Trauma, Violence and Abuse, 8*(3), 246–269.

Campbell, J. C., Webster, D. W., & Glass, N. (2009). The danger assessment: Validation of a lethality risk assessment instrument for intimate partner femicide. *Journal of Interpersonal Violence, 24*(4), 653–674.

Campbell, J. F. (2007). Ethical concerns in grooming the criminal defendant for the witness stand. *Hofstra Law Review, 36*(2), 265–274.

Campobasso, C. P., Laviola, D., Grattagliano, I., Strada, L., & Dell'Erba, A. S. (2015). Undetected patricide: Inaccuracy of cause of death determination without an autopsy. *Journal of Forensic and Legal Medicine, 34,* 67–72.

Canter, D., Coffey, T., Huntley, M., & Missen, C. (2000). Predicting serial killers' home base using a decision support system. *Journal of Quantitative Criminology, 16*(4), 457–478.

Canter, D., & Gregory, A. (1994). Identifying the residual location of rapists. *Journal of Forensics Sciences Society, 34*(3), 169–175.

Canter, D., & Larkin, P. (1993). The environmental range of serial rapists. *Journal of Environmental Psychology, 13*(1), 63–69.

Carbone-Lopez, K., Kruttschnitt, C., & Macmillan, R. (2006). Patterns of intimate partner violence and their associations with physical health, psychological distress, and substance abuse. *Public Health Reports, 121*(4), 382–392.

Carter, T. (1999). Equality with a vengeance. *ABA Journal, 85*(11), 22–24.

Catalano, S. (2013). *Intimate partner violence: Attributes of victimization, 1993–2011.* Washington, DC: U.S. Department of Justice.

Cauffman, E. (2008). Understanding the female offender. *The Future of Children, 18*(2), 119–142.

CDC/National Center for Health Statistics. (2017). *About the National Vital Statistics System.* Retrieved from https://www.cdc.gov/nchs/nvss/about_nvss.htm

Centers for Disease Control and Prevention. (2011). *National vital statistics system.* Retrieved from http://www.cdc.gov/nchs/nvss.htm

Centers for Disease Control and Prevention. (2013). Homicide rates among persons aged 10–24 years—United States, 1981–2010. *Morbidity and Mortality Weekly Report, 62*(27), 545–548.

Centers for Disease Control and Prevention. (2015). *FastStats—injuries.* Retrieved from http://www.cdc.gov/nchs/fastats/injury.htm

Centers for Disease Control and Prevention. (2018). *The public health system and the 10 essential public health services.* Retrieved from http://www.cdc.gov/nphpsp/essentialservices.html

Centers for Disease Control, (2019). NVDRS Overview Fact Sheet. National Violent Death Reporting System. Available at https://www.cdc.gov/violenceprevention/datasources/nvdrs/index.html

Chapin, J. (2008). Youth perceptions of their school violence risks. *Adolescence, 43*(171), 461–471.

Chassy, P. (2017). The neural signature of emotional memories in serial crimes. *Medical Hypotheses, 108,* 31–34.

Chavez, L., & Miller, M. (2009). Religious references in death sentence phases of trial: Two psychological theories that suggest judicial rulings and assumptions may affect jurors. *Criminal Justice Periodicals, 13*(4), 1037–1083.

Chesler, P. (2009). Are honor killings simply domestic violence? *Middle East Quarterly, 16*(2), 61–69.

Cheung, G., Hatters Friedman, S., & Sundram, F. (2015). Late-life homicide-suicide: A national case series in New Zealand [Epub ahead of print]. *Psychogeriatrics.*

Children's Hospital of Philadelphia, Center for Injury Research and Prevention. (2019). *Gun violence: Facts and statistics*. Retrieved from https://injury .research.chop.edu/violence-prevention-initiative/ types-violence-involving-youth/gun-violence/ gun-violence-facts-and

Chilton, R., & Jarvis, J. (1999). Using the National Incident-Based Reporting System (NIBRS) to test estimates of arrestee and offender characteristics. *Journal of Quantitative Criminology, 15*(2), 207–224.

Cohen, T. H., & Reaves, B. A. (2007). *Pretrial release of felony defendants in state courts*. Washington, DC: U.S. Department of Justice.

Cole, S. A. (2007). How much justice can technology afford? The impact of DNA technology on equal criminal justice. *Science and Public Policy, 34*(2), 95–107.

Cook, T., & Tattersall, A. (2016). *Blackstone's senior investigating officers' handbook*. Oxford, UK: Oxford University Press.

Cooke, G. (2001). Parricide. *Journal of Threat Assessment, 1*(1), 35–45.

Cooper, A., & Smith, E. L. (2011). *Homicide trends in the United States, 1980–2008*. Washington, DC: Bureau of Justice Statistics. Retrieved from http:// www.bjs.gov/content/pub/pdf/htus8008.pdf

Cope, L. M., Ermer, E., Gaudet, L. M., Steele, V. R., Eckhardt, A. L., Arababshirani, M. R., Caldwell, M. F., Calhoun, V. D., & Kiehl, K. A. (2014). Abnormal brain structure in youth who commit homicide. *Neuroimage: Clinical, 4*, 800–807.

Corrigan, C. A. (1986). On prosecutorial ethics. *Hastings Constitutional Law Quarterly, 13*(3), 537–543.

Costanzo, M., & Peterson, J. (1994). Attorney persuasion in the capital penalty phase. *Journal of Social Issues, 3*, 305–316.

Cowan, D. E., & Bromley, D. G. (2015). *Cults and new religions: A brief history* (2nd ed.). Malden, MA: Blackwell Publishing.

Crabbe, A., Decoene, S., & Vertommen, H. (2008). Profiling homicide offenders: A review of assumptions and theories. *Aggression and Violent Behavior, 13*(2008), 88–106.

Curtain, L. (2004). On serial killers and job references. *Clinical Systems Management, 6*(2), 5.

Curtis, C. (2014). Public understandings of the forensic use of DNA: Positivity, misunderstandings, and cultural concerns. *Bulletin of Science, Technology & Society, 34*(1–2), 21–32.

Dahlberg, L. L., & Mercy, J. A. (2009). History of violence as a public health problem. *Virtual Mentor, 11*(2), 167–172.

Daly, M., & Wilson, M. (1988). *Homicide*. New Brunswick, NJ: Transaction Publishers.

Daly, M., & Wilson, M. (1994). Evolutionary psychology of male violence. In J. Archer (Ed.), *Male violence* (pp. 253–288). London, UK: Routledge.

Davies, K. (2008). *The murder book: Examining homicide*. Upper Saddle River, NJ: Pearson.

de Becker, G. (1997). *The gift of fear*. New York, NY: Random House.

de Becker, G. (1998). *The gift of fear: Survival signals that protect us from violence*. New York, NY: Dell.

de Mesmaecker, V. (2012). Antidotes to injustice? Victim statements' impact on victims' sense of security. *International Review of Victimology, 18*(2), 133–153.

Deadman, D., & MacDonald, Z. (2004). Offenders as victims of crime? An investigation into the relationship between criminal behavior and victimization. *Journal of the Royal Statistical Society, 167*(1), 53–67.

Declercq, F., & Audenaert, K. (2011). Predatory violence aiming at relief in a case of mass murder: Meloy's criteria for applied forensic practice. *Behavioral Sciences & the Law, 29*(4), 578–591. doi:10.1002/bsl.994

Delaney, T. (2014). *American street gangs* (2nd ed.). Upper Saddle River, NJ: Pearson.

Delattre, E. J. (1996). *Character and cops*. Washington, DC: AEI Press.

DeLisi, M., Spruill, J., Vaughn, M., & Trulson, C. (2014). Do gang members commit abnormal homicide? *American Journal of Criminal Justice, 39*(1), 125–138.

Department of Homeland Security, United States Secret Service, National Threat Assessment Center. (2018). Mass Attacks in Public Spaces. Retrieved from https://www.secretservice.gov/forms/USSS_NTAC-Mass_Attacks_in_Public_Spaces-2017.pdf

Diem, C., & Pizarro, J. M. (2010). Social structure and family homicides. *Journal of Family Violence, 25*(5), 521–532.

Dietz, P. E. (1986). Mass, serial and sensational homicides. *Bulletin of the New York Academy of Medicine, 62*(5), 477–491.

Dobash, R. E., & Dobash, R. P. (1978). Wives: The appropriate victims of marital assault. *Victimology: An International Journal, 2*(3/4), 426–442.

Doğan, R. (2013). Honour killings in the UK communities: Adherence to tradition and resistance to change. *Journal of Muslim Minority Affairs, 33*(3), 401–417.

Douglas, J. E., Burgess, A. W., Burgess, A. G., & Ressler, R. K. (1992). *Crime classification manual: A standard system for investigating and classifying violent crimes*. New York, NY: Macmillan.

Douglas, J. E., Burgess, A. W., Burgess, A. G., & Ressler, R. K. (2013). *Crime classification manual: A standard system for investigating and classifying violent crime* (3rd ed.). Hoboken, NJ: John Wiley & Sons.

Drake, D. S. (2004). Confronting and managing GLBT homicide and its associated phenomena. In W. Swan (Ed.), *Handbook of gay, lesbian, bisexual, and transgender administration and policy* (pp. 311–348). New York, NY: Marcel Dekker.

Drake, D. S. (2015). Understanding economic power dynamics as a method to combat lesbian, gay, bisexual, and transgender homicides. In W. Swan (Ed.), *Gay, lesbian, bisexual and transgender civil rights: A public policy agenda for uniting a divided America* (pp. 297–331). Boca Raton, FL: Taylor & Francis.

Duck, W. (2009). "Senseless violence": Making sense of murder. *Ethnography, 10*(4), 417–434.

Dugan, L., Nagin, D. S., & Rosenfeld, R. (2003). Exposure reduction or retaliation? The effects of domestic violence resources on intimate-partner homicide. *Law & Society Review, 37*(1), 169–198.

Durlauf, S., Fu, C., & Navarro, S. (2013). Capital punishment and deterrence: Understanding disparate results. *Journal of Quantitative Criminology, 29*(1), 103–121. doi:10.1007/s10940-012-9171-0

Dutton, D. G., Nicholls, T. L., & Spidel, A. (2005). Female perpetrators of intimate abuse. *Journal of Offender Rehabilitation, 41*(4), 1–31.

Duwe, G., & Rocque, M. (2018, February 23). *Actually, there is a clear link between mass shootings and mental illness*. Retrieved from https://www.latimes.com/opinion/op-ed/la-oe-duwe-rocque-mass-shootings-mental-illness-20180223-story.html

Eckberg, D. (2015). Trends in conflict: Uniform Crime Reports, the National Crime Victimization Surveys, and the lethality of violent crime. *Homicide Studies, 19*(1), 58–87.

Egley, A., Jr., Howell, J. C., & Harris, M. (2014). *Juvenile justice fact sheet: Highlights of the 2012 National Youth Gang Survey*. Retrieved from http://www.ojjdp.gov/pubs/248025.pdf

Egley, A., Jr., Logan, J., & McDaniel, D. (2012). Gang homicides—five U.S. cities, 2003–2008. *MMWR: Morbidity & Mortality Weekly Report, 61*, 46–51.

Ehrhard-Dietzel, S. (2012). The use of life and death as tools in plea bargaining. *Criminal Justice Review, 37*(1), 89–109.

Eke, A. W., Hilton, Z. N., Harris, G. T., Rice, M. E., & Houghton, R. E. (2011). Intimate partner homicide: Risk assessment and prospects for prediction. *Journal of Family Violence, 26*(3), 211–216.

Engel, R. S., Tillyer, M. S., & Corsaro, N. (2013). Reducing gang violence using focused deterrence: Evaluating the Cincinnati Initiative to Reduce Violence (CIRV). *Justice Quarterly, 30*(3), 403–439.

Englebrecht, C., Mason, D. T., & Adams, M. J. (2014). The experiences of homicide victims' families with the criminal justice system: An exploratory study. *Violence and Victims, 29*(3), 407–421.

Eriksson, L., & Mazerolle, P. (2013). A general strain theory of intimate partner homicide. *Aggression and Violent Behavior, 18*(5), 462–470.

Eriksson, L., & Mazerolle, P. (2015). A cycle of violence? Examining family-of-origin violence, attitudes, and intimate partner violence perpetration. *Journal of Interpersonal Violence, 30*(6), 945–964.

Farr, K. (2018). Adolescent rampage school shootings: Responses to failing masculinity performances by already-troubled boys. *Gender Issues, 35*, 73–97.

Farrell, A. L., Keppel, R. D., & Titterington, V. B. (2011). Lethal ladies: Revisiting what we know about female serial murderers. *Homicide Studies, 15*(3), 228–252.

Farrell, N. (2014, December 19). "Angel of Death" who may be one of the world's worst serial killers. *Newsweek*. Retrieved from http://www.newsweek.com/2014/12/26/angel-death-one-worlds-most-prolific-serial-killers-292388.html

Farrington, D. P. (1989). Early predictors of adolescent aggression and adult violence. *Violence and Victims, 4*(2), 79–100.

Feder, G., Wathen, C. N., & MacMillan, H. (2013). An evidence-based response to intimate partner violence: WHO guidelines. *Journal of the American Medical Association, 310*(5), 479–480.

Federal Bureau of Investigation. (2003). *Crime in the United States, 2002*. Retrieved from https://www.fbi.gov/about-us/cjis/ucr/crime-in-the-u.s/2002

Federal Bureau of Investigation. (2008). *Serial murder: Multi-disciplinary perspective for investigators*. Retrieved from http://www.fbi.gov/stats-services/publications/serial-murder/serial-murder-july-2008-pdf

Federal Bureau of Investigation. (2013). *Expanded homicide data table 8*. Retrieved from https://www.fbi.gov/about-us/cjis/ucr/crime-in-the-u.s/2012/crime-in-the-u.s.-2012/offenses-known-to-law-enforcement/expanded-homicide/expanded_homicide_data_table_8_murder_victims_by_weapon_2008-2012.xls

Federal Bureau of Investigation (FBI). (2017). *Crime in the United States 2016*. Washington, DC: U.S. Government Printing Office.

Federal Bureau of Investigation. (2018). *Crime in the United States, 2017*. Retrieved from: https://ucr.fbi.gov/crime-in-the-u.s/2017/crime-in-the-u.s.-2017

Federal Bureau of Investigation. (n.d.). *Definitions of terrorism in the U.S. Code*. Retrieved from http://www.fbi.gov/about-us/investigate/terrorism/terrorism-definition

Fegadel, A. R., & Heide, K. M. (2015). Offspring-perpetrated familicide: Examining family homicides involving parents as victims [Epub ahead of print]. *International Journal of Offender Therapy and Comparative Criminology*.

Fegadel, A. R., & Heide, K. M. (2017). Offspring-perpetrated familicide: Examining family homicides involving parents as victims. *International Journal of Offender Therapy and Comparative Criminology*, 61(1), 6–24.

Ferguson, C. I. (Ed.). (2010). *Violent crime: Clinical and social implications*. Thousand Oaks, CA: Sage.

Ferrito, M., Needs, A., & Adshead, G. (2017). Unveiling the shadows of meaning: Meaning-making for perpetrators of homicide. *Aggression and Violent Behavior*, 34, 263–272.

Fiske, A. P., & Rai, T. S. (2015). *Virtuous violence*. Cambridge, UK: Cambridge University Press.

Flood, M. (2004, January 23). Booze, bravado and male honour make for a culture of violence. *The Sydney Morning Herald*. Retrieved from http://www.smh.com.au/articles/2004/01/22/1074732536608.html

Florida Department of Corrections. (n.d.). *Major prison gangs*. Retrieved from http://www.dc.state.fl.us/pub/gangs/prison.html

Flynn, E. A., & Silletti, L. C. (2018, October). *Violent crime reduction operations guide*. Columbia, MD: Bureau of Justice Assistance, US Department of Justice.

Foley, L. A., & Powell, R. S. (1982). The discretion of prosecutors, judges, and juries in capital cases. *Criminal Justice Review*, 7(2), 16–22.

Forte, S. (2006). Violence in the workplace: Awareness, prevention, and intervention. *Rivier Academic Journal*, 2(2), 1–11.

Fox, B. H., Jennings, W. G., & Farrington, D. P. (2015). Bringing psychopathy into developmental and life-course criminology theories and research. *Journal of Criminal Justice*, 43(4), 274–289.

Fox, C., & Harding, D. J. (2005). School shootings as organizational deviance. *Sociology of Education*, 78(1), 69–97.

Fox, J. A., & DeLateur, M. J. (2014). Mass shootings in America: Moving beyond Newtown. *Homicide Studies: An Interdisciplinary Journal*, 18(1), 125–145.

Fox, J. A., & Levin, J. (2015). *Extreme killing*. Thousand Oaks, CA: Sage.

Fox, J. A., Levin, J., & Fridel, E. E. (2018). *Extreme killing*. Thousand Oaks, CA: Sage.

Fox, J. A., Levin, J., & Quinet, K. (2012). *The will to kill: Making sense of senseless murder* (4th ed.). Upper Saddle River, NJ: Pearson.

Fox, J. A., & Swatt, M. L. (2009). Multiple imputation of the supplementary homicide reports, 1976–2005. *Journal of Quantitative Criminology*, 25(1), 51–77.

Fox, J. M., Brook, M., Stratton, J., & Hanlon, R. E. (2016). Neuropsychological profiles and descriptive classifications of mass murderers. *Aggression and Violent Behavior*, 30, 94–104.

Franzese, R. J., Covey, H. C., & Menard, S. W. (2016). *Youth gangs* (4th ed.). Springfield, IL: Charles C Thomas.

Frei, A., Vollm, B., Graf, M., & Dittman, V. (2006). Female serial killing: Review and case report. *Criminal Behaviour and Mental Health*, 16(3), 167–176.

Fridel, E. E., & Fox, J. A. (2018). Too few victims: Finding the optimal minimum victim threshold for defining serial murder. *Psychology of Violence*, 8(4), 505–514.

Fridel, E. E., & Fox, J. A. (2019). The quantitative study of serial murder: Regression is not transgression. *Aggression and Violent Behavior*, 44, 24–26.

Gabriel, M., Boland, C., & Holt, C. (2010). Beyond the cold hit: Measuring the impact of the national DNA data bank on public safety at the city and county level. *The Journal of Law, Medicine & Ethics*, 38(2), 396–411.

Gallagher, J. (2002). Homophobia for the defense. *Law Review*, 39(5), 34–37.

Garner, B. A. (Ed.). (1999). *Black's law dictionary* (7th ed.). St. Paul, MN: West Publishing.

Gartner, R. (1990). The victims of homicide: A temporal and cross-national comparison. *American Sociological Review, 55*(1), 92–106.

Geberth, V. J. (2008, May). Missteps at the homicide crime scene. *PI Magazine: Journal of Professional Investigators, 22*(3), 40–44.

Gebo, E. (2002). A contextual exploration of siblicide. *Violence and Victims, 17*(2), 157–168.

George, M. J. (1997). Into the eye of Medusa: Beyond testosterone, men, and violence. *The Journal of Men's Studies, 5*(4), 295–313.

Gibson, C. L., Swatt, M. L., Miller, J. M., Jennings, W. G., & Gover, A. R. (2012). The causal relationship between gang joining and violent victimization: A critical review and directions for future research. *Journal of Criminal Justice, 40*(6), 490–501.

Glasser, W. (1965). *Reality therapy: A new approach to psychiatry.* New York, NY: Harper & Row.

Glenn, A. L., Raine, A., Schug, R. A., Gao, Y., & Granger, D. A. (2011). Increased testosterone to cortisol ratio in psychopathy. *Journal of Abnormal Psychology, 120*(2), 389–399.

Glossip v. Gross, 576 U.S.— (2015).

Godwin, M. (1998). Victim target networks as solvability factors in serial murder. *Social Behavior and Personality, 26*(1), 75–84.

Goffman, E. (1967). *Interaction ritual: Essays on face-to-face behavior.* Garden City, NY: Doubleday.

Goldstein, H. (1977). *Policing a free society.* Cambridge, MA: Ballinger Publishing.

Gottfredson, M. R. (2018). General theory and global criminology: Childhood environments, problem behaviors, and a focus on prevention. *Asian Journal of Criminology, 13*(4), 347.

Grant, P., & Diehl, R. L. (2012). Participatory behavior at homicide scenes: Crowd formation or community continuity? *American Journal of Criminal Justice, 37*(3), 471–484.

Grawert, A., & Kimble, C. (2018, December 18). Crime in 2018: Updated analysis. *Brennan Center for Justice,* NYU School of Law. Retrieved from https://www.brennancenter.org/sites/default/files/publications/2018_09_CrimeUpdate_V2.pdf

Grawert, A. C., Onyekwere, A., & Kimble, K. (2018). *Crime and murder in 2018: A preliminary analysis.* Retrieved from https://www.brennancenter.org/analysis/crime-murder-2018

Green, B. A., & Zacharias, F. C. (2008). "The U.S. attorneys scandal" and the allocation of prosecutorial power. *Ohio State Law Journal, 69*(2), 187–254.

Grier, P. (2013, April 18). Boston Marathon bombing: Surveillance video catches potential suspects. *Alaska Dispatch News.* Retrieved from http://www.adn.com/article/20130418/boston-marathon-bombing-surveillance-video-catches-potential-suspects

Grubesic, T. H., & Pridemore, W. A. (2011). Alcohol outlets and clusters of violence. *International Journal of Health Geographics, 10*(1), 1–12. doi:10.1186/1476-072X-10-30

Guggisberg, M. (2012). An investigation into potentially lethal acts of male-perpetrated intimate partner violence. *Beijing Law Review, 3*(4), 198–205.

Haeney, O., Ash, D., & Galletly, C. (2018). School shootings – "It wouldn't happen here"? *Australian & New Zealand Journal of Psychiatry, 52*(5), 405–407.

Hansen, C. (2019, January 7). Florida schools will install facial recognition cameras. *USNews.com.* Retrieved from https://www.usnews.com/news/education-news/articles/2019-01-07/broward-county-schools-to-install-facial-recognition-cameras

Hare, R. D. (2003). *Hare psychopathy checklist—revised* (2nd ed.). Toronto, ON: Multi-Health Systems.

Harrell, E. (2011). *Workplace violence, 1993–2009.* Washington, DC: Bureau of Justice Statistics. Retrieved from http://www.bjs.gov/content/pub/pdf/wv09.pdf

Hart, J. L., & Helms, J. L. (2003). Factors of parricide: Allowance of the use of battered child syndrome as a defense. *Aggression and Violent Behavior, 8*(6), 671–683.

Hartley, R., Miller, H., & Spohn, C. (2010). Do you get what you pay for? Type of counsel and its effects on criminal court outcomes. *Journal of Criminal Justice, 38*(5), 1063–1070.

Hawk, S. R., & Dabney, D. (2019). Shifting the focus from variables to substantive domains when modeling homicide case outcomes. *Homicide Studies, 23*(2), 93–125.

Hayes, B., Mills, C. E., Freilich, J. D., & Chermak, S. M. (2018). Are honor killings unique? A comparison of honor killings, domestic violence homicides, and hate homicides by far-right extremists. *Homicide Studies, 22*(1), 70–93.

Hazelwood, R. R., & Burgess, A. W. (Eds.). (2009). *Practical aspects of rape investigation: A multidisciplinary approach* (4th ed.). Boca Raton, FL: CRC Press.

Heide, K. M. (1993). Parents who get killed and the children who kill them. *The Journal of Interpersonal Violence, 8*(4), 531–544.

Heide, K. M. (2013). *Understanding parricide: When sons and daughters kill parents*. New York, NY: Oxford University Press.

Heide, K. M. (2017). Parricide encapsulated. In F. Brookman, E. R. Maguire, & M. Maguire (Eds.), *The handbook of homicide* (pp. 197–212). Sussex, UK: John Wiley & Sons.

Heide, K. M., & McCurdy, J. (2010). Juvenile parricide offenders sentenced to death. *Victims & Offenders, 5*(1), 76–99.

Heide, K. M., & Petee, T. A. (2007). Parricide: An empirical analysis of 24 years of U.S. data. *The Journal of Interpersonal Violence, 22*(11), 1382–1399.

Heinrick, J. (2006). Everyone's an expert: The CSI effect's negative impact on juries. *The Triple Helix: The International Journal of Science, Society, and Law, 3*(1), 59–61.

Henson, J. R., & Olson, L. N. (2010). The monster within: How male serial killers discursively manage their stigmatized identities. *Communication Quarterly, 58*(3), 341–364.

Hewitt, A. N., Beauregard, E., Andresen, M. A., & Brantingham, P. L. (2018). Identifying the nature of risky places for sexual crime: The applicability of crime pattern and social disorganization theories in a Canadian context. *Journal of Criminal Justice, 57,* 35–46.

Hickey, E. W. (2006). *Serial murderers and their victims*. Belmont, CA: Thomson.

Hickey, E. W. (2013). *Serial murderers and their victims* (6th ed.). Belmont, CA: Wadsworth.

Hickey, E. (2015). *Serial murderers and their victims* (7th ed.). San Francisco, CA: Wadsworth.

Hodgkinson, S., Prins, H., & Stuart-Bennett, J. (2017). Monsters, madmen . . . and myths: A critical review of the serial killing literature. *Aggression and Violent Behavior, 34,* 282–289.

Hoffman, M. B., Rubin, P. H., & Shepherd, J. M. (2005). An empirical study of public defender effectiveness: Self-selection by the "marginally indigent." *Ohio State Journal of Criminal Law, 3,* 223–255.

Hogan, M., & Kleck, G. (1999). National case-control study of homicide offending and gun ownership. *Social Problems, 46*(2), 275–293. doi:10.2307/3097256

Holmes, R. M., & DeBurger, J. (1988). *Serial murder*. Newbury Park, CA: Sage.

Holmes, R. M., & Holmes, S. (2001). *Mass murder in the United States*. Upper Saddle River, NJ: Prentice Hall.

Holmes, R. M., & Holmes, S. T. (2010). *Serial murder*. Thousand Oaks, CA: Sage.

Homicide Research Working Group. (n.d.). *History of the Homicide Research Working Group*. Retrieved from http://www.homicideresearchworkinggroup.org/history.html

Hough, R. M., & McCorkle, K. D. (2015). *An examination of investigative practices of homicide units in Florida*. Published proceedings of the annual meeting of the Homicide Research Working Group.

Hough, R., & Tatum, K. M. (2014). Murder investigation and media: Mutual goals. *Law Enforcement Executive Forum, 14*(3), 71–85.

Huff-Corzine, L., McCutcheon, J. C., Corzine, J., Jarvis, J. P., Tetzlaff-Bemiller, M. J., Weller, M., & Landon, M. (2014). Shooting for accuracy: Comparing data sources on mass murder. *Homicide Studies, 18*(1), 105–124.

Hughes, L. A., & Short, J. F., Jr. (2005). Disputes involving youth street gang members: Micro-social contexts. *Criminology, 43*(1), 43–76.

Hunnicutt, G. (2007). Female status and infant and child homicide victimization in rural and urban counties in the U.S. *Gender Issues, 24*(3), 35–50. doi:10.1007/s12147-007-9046-0

Hunnicutt, G., & LaFree, G. (2008). Reassessing the structural covariates of cross-national infant homicide victimization. *Homicide Studies, 12*(1), 46–66.

Jaffe, P. G., Dawson, M., & Campbell, M. (2013). Developing a national collaborative approach to prevent domestic homicides: Domestic homicide review committees. *Canadian Journal of Criminology & Criminal Justice, 55*(1), 137–155.

James, N. (2018). Recent violent crime trends in the United States. *Congressional Research Service: Report,* 1–38.

Jansen, S., & Nugent-Borakove, M. E. (2007). *Expansions to the castle doctrine: Implications for policy and practice*. Alexandria, VA: National District Attorneys Association. Retrieved from http://www.ndaa.org/pdf/Castle%20Doctrine.pdf

Jenkins, J. P. (2014). Luis Garavito. *Encyclopedia Britannica*. Retrieved from http://www.britannica.com/EBchecked/topic/1245871/Luis-Garavito

Johnson, C. (2013, May 13). New Orleans shooting: Suspect caught on surveillance video of Mother's Day parade violence. *The Huffington Post*. Retrieved from http://www.huffingtonpost.com/2013/05/13/new-orleans-shooting-video-suspect_n_3265339.html

Kaplan, R. (2007). The clinicide phenomenon: An exploration of medical murder. *Australasian Psychiatry*, *15*(4), 299–304.

Karch, D. L., Logan, J., McDaniel, D., Parks, S., & Patel, N. (2012). Surveillance for violent deaths—National Violent Death Reporting System, 16 states, 2009. *MMWR Surveillance Summaries*, *61*(6), 1–43.

Katsavdakis, K. A., Meloy, J., & White, S. G. (2011). A female mass murder. *Journal of Forensic Sciences*, *56*(3), 813–818. doi:10.1111/j.1556-4029.2010.01692.x

Kaufman, D. B. (1932). Poisons and poisoning among the romans. *Classical Philology*, *27*(2), 156–167. Retrieved from http://penelope.uchicago.edu/Thayer/E/Journals/CP/27/2/Poisoning*.html

Keeney, B. T., & Heide, K. M. (1994). Gender differences in serial murderers: A preliminary analysis. *Journal of Interpersonal Violence*, *9*(3), 383–398.

Kelleher, M. D., & Kelleher, C. L. (1998). *Murder most rare: The female serial killer*. Westport, CT: Praeger.

Kelling, G. L., & Wilson, J. Q. (1982). Broken windows. *Atlantic Monthly*, *249*(3), 29–38.

Kennedy, M. (2019, January 2). *Florida commission approves report on Parkland, Fla., school shooting*. Retrieved from https://www.asumag.com/safety-security/florida-commission-approves-report-parkland-fla-school-shooting

Keppel, R., & Weis, J. (1994). Time and distance as solvability factors in murder cases. *Journal of Forensic Sciences*, *39*, 386–401.

KidsHealth. (2012). *Munchausen by proxy syndrome*. Retrieved from http://kidshealth.org/parent/general/sick/munchausen.html#

Kinnell, H. G. (2000). Serial homicide by doctors: Shipman in perspective. *British Medical Journal*, *321*(7276), 1594–1597.

Kirsch, L. (2006). Heating up cold cases. *The Forensic Examiner*, *15*(2), 34–35.

Knight, Z. G. (2006). Some thoughts on the psychological roots of the behavior of serial killers as narcissists: An object relations perspective. *Social Behavior & Personality: An International Journal*, *34*(10), 1189–1206.

Knight, Z. G. (2007). Sexually motivated serial killers and the psychology of aggression and "evil" within a contemporary psychoanalytical perspective. *Journal of Sexual Aggression*, *13*(1), 21–35.

Kremen, A. M. (2014). Suicide in the name of honor: Why and how U.S. asylum law should be modified to allow greater acceptance of honor-violence victims to prevent "honor suicides." *William & Mary Journal of Women & the Law*, *21*(1), 213–236.

Kruttschnitt, C., & Carbone-Lopez, K. (2006). Moving beyond the stereotypes: Women's subjective accounts of their violent crime. *Criminology*, *44*(2), 321–352. doi:10.1111/j.1745-9125.2006.00051.x

Kruttschnitt, C., Gartner, R., & Hussemann, J. (2008). Female violent offenders: Moral panics or more serious offenders? *Australian & New Zealand Journal of Criminology*, *41*(1), 9–35. doi:10.1375/acri.41.1.9

Labuschagne, G. N. (2006). The use of a linkage analysis as evidence in the conviction of the Newcastle serial murderer, South Africa. *Journal of Investigative Psychology & Offender Profiling*, *3*(3), 183–191.

Lake, C. R. (2014). Rampage murderers, part I: Psychotic versus non-psychotic and a role for psychiatry in prevention. *Psychiatric Annals*, *44*(5), 215–225.

Laqueur, W. (1999). *The new terrorism: Fanaticism and the arms of mass destruction*. New York, NY: Oxford University Press.

Laqueur, W. (2006). Terrorism: A brief history. *Foreign Policy Agenda*, *12*(5), 20–23.

Lauritsen, J. L., Heimer, K., & Lynch, J. P. (2009). Trends in the gender gap in violent offending: New evidence from the National Crime Victimization Survey. *Criminology*, *47*(2), 361–399. doi:10.1111/j.1745-9125.2009.00149.x

Law Center to Prevent Gun Violence. (2013, November 1). *Guns in schools policy summary* [Web log post]. Retrieved from http://smartgunlaws.org/guns-in-schools-policy- summary/

Leary, T., Southard, L., Hill, J., & Ashman, J. (2017). The Macdonald Triad revisited: An empirical assessment of relationships between triadic elements and parental abuse in serial killers. *North American Journal of Psychology*, *19*(3), 627–640.

Leistedt, S. J.-J., Linkowski, P., & Bongaerts, X. (2011). The myth of virginity: The case of a Franco Belgian serial killer. *Journal of Forensic Sciences*, *56*(4), 1064–1071.

Lennings, C. J. (2002). Children who kill family members: Three case studies from Australia. *Journal of Threat Assessment*, 2(2), 57–72.

Leshner, A. I., Altevogt, B. M., Lee, A. F., McCoy, M. A., & Kelley, P. W. (2013). *Priorities for research to reduce the threat of firearm-related violence*. Washington, DC: National Academies Press.

Lester, D. (2014). Murder-suicide in workplace violence. *Psychological Reports*, *115*(1), 28–31. doi:10.2466/16.17.PR0.115c14z4

Lester, D., & White, J. (2012). Which serial killers commit suicide? An exploratory study. *Forensic Science International*, *223*(1–3), 56–59.

Léveillée, S., Marleau, J., & Dubé, M. (2007). Filicide: A comparison by sex and presence or absence of self-destructive behavior. *Journal of Family Violence*, 22(5), 287–295.

Levenson, L. (1998). Working outside the rules: The undefined responsibilities of federal prosecutors. *Fordham Urban Law Journal*, 26(3), 551–572.

Levine, J. P. (2014). Deconstructing the politics of three-strikes sentencing reforms in California. *ACJS Today*, 39(2), 29–33.

Lieber, L. (2007). Workplace violence—What can employers do to prevent it? *Employment Relations Today*, *34*(3), 91–100.

Liem, M., & Koenraadt, F. (2008). Familicide: A comparison with spousal and child homicide by mentally disordered perpetrators. *Criminal Behaviour and Mental Health*, *18*(5), 306–318.

Liem, M., Levin, J., Holland, C., & Fox, J. (2013). The nature and prevalence of familicide in the United States, 2000–2009. *Journal of Family Violence*, 28(4), 351–358.

Liem, M., & Reichelmann, A. (2014). Patterns of multiple family homicide. *Homicide Studies*, 18(1), 44–58.

Litwin, K. J. (2004). A multilevel multivariate analysis of factors affecting homicide clearances. *Journal of Research in Crime and Delinquency*, 41(4), 327–351.

Liu, Y. Y., Yang, M., Ramsay, M., Li, X. S., & Coid, J. W. (2011). A comparison of logistic regression, classification and regression tree, and neural networks models in predicting violent re-offending. *Journal of Quantitative Criminology*, 27(4), 547–573.

Loeber, R. (1996). Developmental continuity, change, and pathways in male juvenile problem behaviors and delinquency. In J. D. Hawkins (Ed.), *Delinquency and crime: Current theories* (pp. 1–27). New York, NY: Cambridge University Press.

Loomis, D., Marshall, S. W., & Ta, M. L. (2005). Employer policies toward guns and the risk of homicide in the workplace. *American Journal of Public Health*, *95*(5), 830–832.

Lovgren, S. (2004, September 23). "'CSI' effect" is mixed blessing for real crime labs. *National Geographic News*. Retrieved from http://news.nationalgeographic.com/news/2004/09/0923_040923_csi.html

Lubaszka, C., & Shon, P. (2013). Reconceptualizing the notion of victim selection, risk, and offender behavior in healthcare serial murders. *Journal of Criminal Psychology*, 3(1), 65–78.

Luckenbill, D. F. (1977). Criminal homicide as situated transaction. *Social Problems*, 25(2), 176–186.

Lucke-Wold, B. P., Turner, R. C., Logsdon, A. F., Bailes, J. E., Huber, J. D., & Rosen, C. L. (2014). Linking traumatic brain injury to chronic traumatic encephalopathy: Identification of potential mechanisms leading to neurofibrillary tangle development. *Journal of Neurotrauma*, *31*(13), 1129–38.

Lund, L. E., & Smorodinsky, S. (2001). Violent death among intimate partners: A comparison of homicide and homicide followed by suicide in California. *Suicide & Life—Threatening Behavior*, 31(4), 451–459.

Maclin, T. (2006). Is obtaining an arrestee's DNA a valid special needs search under the Fourth Amendment? What should (and will) the Supreme Court do? *The Journal of Law, Medicine & Ethics*, 34, 165–187.

Madfis, E. (2017). In search of meaning: Are school rampage shootings random and senseless violence? *Journal of Psychology*, *151*(1), 21–35.

Mann, M. D. (2006). The "CSI effect": Better jurors through television and science? *Buffalo Public Interest Law Journal*, 24(1), 157–183.

Markowitz, S. (2001). Alcohol and violence. *National Bureau of Economic Research Reporter*. Retrieved from http://www.nber.org/reporter/fall01/markowitz.html

Marleau, J. D., Auclair, N., & Millaud, F. (2006). Comparison of factors associated with parricide in adults and adolescents. *Journal of Family Violence*, 21(5), 321–325. doi:10.1007/s10896-006-9029-z

Matthew Shepard and James Byrd, Jr. Hate Crimes Prevention Act, 18 U.S.C. § 249 (2009).

Matza, D. (1964). *Delinquency and drift*. New York, NY: John Wiley & Sons.

McElrea, F. W. M., & Katounas, J. (2001). Restorative justice in prisons --a New Zealand experience. *ICPA News*. Retrieved from http://www.napierlibrary.co.nz/assets/mcelrea/restorative-justice-in-prisons.pdf

McGarrell, E. F., Chermak, S., Wilson, J. M., & Corsaro, N. (2006). Reducing homicide through a "lever-pulling" strategy. *JQ: Justice Quarterly, 23*(2), 214–231. doi:10.1080/07418820600688818

McMahon, S., & Armstrong, D. Y. (2012). Intimate partner violence during pregnancy: Best practices for social workers. *Health & Social Work, 37*(1), 9–17.

Meehan, D. C., & Kerig, P. K. (2010). Youth, school, and gang violence. In C. J. Ferguson (Ed.), *Violent crime: Clinical and social implications* (pp. 121–146). Thousand Oaks, CA: Sage.

Melton, J. G., & Bromley, D. G. (2002). Challenging misconceptions about the new religions–violence connection. In D. G. Bromley & J. G. Melton (Eds.), *Cults, religion, and violence* (pp. 42–56). Cambridge, UK: Cambridge University Press.

Mercier, B., Norris, A., & Shariff, A. F. (2018). Muslim mass shooters are perceived as less mentally ill and more motivated by religion. *Psychology of Violence, 8*(6), 772–781.

Messing, J. T., & Heeren, J. W. (2004). Another side of multiple murders: Women killers in domestic context. *Homicide Studies, 8*(2), 123–158.

Messner, S. F., & Rosenfeld, R. (2013). *Crime and the American dream* (5th ed.). Belmont, CA: Wadsworth.

Miethe, T. D., & Regoeczi, W. C. (2004). *Rethinking homicide: Exploring the structure and process underlying deadly situations*. Cambridge, UK: Cambridge University Press.

Miller, L. (2008a). Criminal profiling in serial homicide investigations. *Practical Police Psychology, 63*(9), 150–156.

Miller, L. (2008b). Workplace violence: Practical policies and strategies for prevention, response, and recovery. *International Journal of Emergency Mental Health, 9*(4), 259–279.

Mize, K. D., & Shackelford, T. K. (2008). Intimate partner homicide methods in heterosexual, gay, and lesbian relationships. *Violence and Victims, 23*(1), 98–114.

Moffitt, T. E. (1993). Adolescence limited and life course persistent antisocial behavior: A developmental taxonomy. *Psychological Review, 100*(4), 674–701.

Myers, W. C. (2004). Serial murder by children and adolescents. *Behavioral Science and the Law, 22*(3), 357–374.

Myers, W. C., Husted, D. S., Safarik, M. E., & O'Toole, M. (2006). The motivation behind serial sexual homicide: Is it sex, power, and control, or anger? *Journal of Forensic Sciences, 51*(4), 900–907.

National Center for Injury Prevention and Control, Division of Violence Prevention. (2017). *School-associated violent death study*. Retrieved from https://www.cdc.gov/violenceprevention/youthviolence/schoolviolence/SAVD.html

National Center for Injury Prevention and Control, Division of Violence Prevention. (2019). *National Violent Death Reporting System – An overview*. Retrieved from https://www.cdc.gov/violenceprevention/datasources/nvdrs/index.html

National Center for Statistics and Analysis. (2018, October). *2017 fatal motor vehicle crashes: Overview*. (Traffic Safety Facts Research Note. Report No. DOT HS 812 603). Washington, DC: National Highway Traffic Safety Administration.

National Gang Center. (2014). *National Youth Gang Survey analysis*. Retrieved from http://www.nationalgangcenter.gov/Survey-Analysis

National Gang Intelligence Center. (2016). *2015 National Gang Report*. Retrieved from https://www.hsdl.org/?abstract&did=792574

Neuilly, M., Zgoba, K. M., Tita, G. E., & Lee, S. S. (2011). Predicting recidivism in homicide offenders using classification tree analysis. *Homicide Studies, 15*(2), 154–176.

Neumayer, E., & Plümper, T. (2011). Foreign terror on Americans. *Journal of Peace Research, 48*(1), 3–17.

Newman, K. S., Fox, C., Harding, D. J., Mehta, J., & Roth, W. (2004). *Rampage: The social roots of school shootings*. New York, NY: Basic Books.

Newman, D. W. (1995). Jury decision making and the effect of victim impact statements in the penalty phase. *Criminal Justice Policy Review, 7*(3–4), 291–300.

Newton, P. J., Johnson, C. M., & Mulcahy, T. M. (2006). *Investigation and prosecution of homicide cases in the U.S.: The process for federal involvement*. Washington, DC: U.S. Department of Justice. Retrieved from https://www.ncjrs.gov/pdffiles1/nij/grants/214753.pdf

Nieuwbeerta, P., McCall, P., Elffers, H., & Witte-brood, K. (2008). Neighborhood characteristics and individual homicide risks: Effects of social cohesion, confidence in the police, and socioeconomic disadvantage. *Homicide Studies, 12*(1), 90–116.

NVDRS Overview Fact Sheet available at https://www.cdc.gov/violenceprevention/datasources/nvdrs/index.html Centers for Disease Control, National Violent Death Reporting System, accessed August, 16, 2019.

Nugent-Borakove, E., & Worrall, J. (2008). *The changing role of the American prosecutor*. Albany: State University of New York Press.

O'Leary, K. D., Smith-Slep, A. M., & O'Leary, S. G. (2007). Multivariate models of men's and women's partner aggression. *Journal of Consulting and Clinical Psychology, 75*(5), 752–764.

O'Neill, M. (2004). Understanding federal prosecutorial declinations. *The American Criminal Law Review, 41*(4), 1439–1498.

Occupational Safety and Health Administration. (n.d.). *Business case for safety and health—Costs*. Retrieved from https://www.osha.gov/dcsp/products/topics/business-case/costs.html

Office of Juvenile Justice and Delinquency Prevention. (2014). *A law enforcement official's guide to OJJDP comprehension gang model*. Retrieved from https://www.nationalgangcenter.gov/Content/Documents/LE-Officials-Guide-to-OJJDP-Comprehensive-Gang-Model.pdf

Office of the Surgeon General (US); National Center for Injury Prevention and Control (US); National Institute of Mental Health (US); Center for Mental Health Services (US). (2001). *Youth violence: A report of the Surgeon General*. Rockville, MD: Office of the Surgeon General (US). Retrieved from https://www.ncbi.nlm.nih.gov/books/NBK44294/

Office of the U.N. Special Adviser on the Prevention of Genocide. (2009). *OSAPG analysis framework*. Retrieved from http://www.un.org/en/prevent-genocide/adviser/pdf/osapg_analysis_framework.pdf

Office on Violence Against Women. (2019). *About the office*. Retrieved from http://www.justice.gov/ovw/about-office

Ortman, J. M., Velkoff, V. A., & Hogan, H. (2014). *An aging nation: The older population in the United States*. Washington, DC: U.S. Census Bureau.

Pampel, F. C., & Williams, K. R. (2000). Intimacy and homicide: Compensating for missing data in the SHR. *Criminology, 38*(2), 661–680.

Papachristos, A. (2009). Murder by structure: Dominance relations and the social structure of gang homicide. *The American Journal of Sociology, 115*(1), 74–128.

Parkin, W. S., & Gruenewald, J. (2017). Open-source data and the study of homicide. *The Journal of Interpersonal Violence, 32*(18), 2693–2723.

Peck, J. H., & Heide, K. M. (2012). Juvenile involvement in fratricide and sororicide: An empirical analysis of 32 years of U.S. arrest data. *Journal of Family Violence, 27*(8), 749–760.

Perri, F. S., & Lichtenwald, T. G. (2007). A proposed addition to the FBI criminal classification manual. *The Forensic Examiner, 16*(4), 18–30.

Perri, F. S., Lichtenwald, T. G., & McKenzie, P. (2008). The lull before the storm: Adult children who kill their parents. *The Forensic Examiner, 17*(3), 40–54.

Petrosky, E., Blair, J. M., Betz, C. J., Fowler, K. A., Jack, S. P., Lyons, B. H. (2017). Racial and ethnic differences in homicides of adult women and the role of intimate partner violence — United States, 2003–2014. *MMWR Morb Mortal Wkly Rep 2017, 66*(28), 741–746. doi: http://dx.doi.org/10.15585/mmwr.mm6628a1

Phipps, C. (1999). Responding to child homicide: A statutory proposal. *The Journal of Criminal Law and Criminology, 89*(2), 536–614.

Pinker, S. (2011). *The better angels of our nature: Why violence has declined*. New York, NY: Viking Press.

Pizarro, J. (2017). Gang homicide in the United States: What we know and future research directions. In F. Brookman, E. R. Maguire, & M. Maguire (Eds.), *The Handbook of Homicide* (pp. 197–212). Sussex, UK: John Wiley & Sons.

Platania, J., & Berman, G. L. (2006). The moderating effect of judge's instructions on victim impact testimony in capital cases. *Applied Psychology in Criminal Justice, 2*(2), 84–101.

Poland, J. M. (2011). *Understanding terrorism: Groups, strategies, and responses* (3rd ed.). Upper Saddle River, NJ: Prentice Hall.

Polk, K. E. (1994). *When men kill: Scenarios of masculine violence*. Cambridge, UK: Cambridge University Press.

Polk, K. E. (1997). A reexamination of the concept of victim-precipitated homicide. *Homicide Studies, 1*(2), 141–168.

Pope, P. B. (2011). Prosecutorial investigation standards. *Criminal Justice, 26*(1), 4–11.

Pornari, C. D., Dixon, L., & Humphreys, G. W. (2013). Systematically identifying implicit theories in male and female intimate partner violence perpetrators. *Aggression and Violent Behavior, 18*(5), 496–505.

Porter, S., & Woodworth, M. (2007). "I'm sorry I did it . . . but he started it": A comparison of the official and self-reported homicide descriptions of psychopaths and non-psychopaths. *Law and Human Behavior, 31*(1), 91–107. doi:10.1007/s10979-006-9033-0

Poston, B., & Rubin, J. (2014, August 9). LAPD misclassified nearly 1,200 violent crimes as minor offenses. *Los Angeles Times*. Retrieved from http://www.latimes.com/local/la-me-crimestats-lapd-20140810-story.html#page=1

Potter, R. H., & Rosky, J. W. (2013). The iron fist in the latex glove: The intersection of public health and criminal justice. *American Journal of Criminal Justice, 38*(2), 276–288.

Pridemore, W. A. (2002). What we know about social structure and homicide: A review of the theoretical and empirical literature. *Violence & Victims, 17*(2), 127–156.

Pridemore, W. A. (2008). A methodological addition to the cross-national empirical literature on social structure and homicide: A first test of the poverty-homicide thesis. *Criminology, 46*(1), 133–154.

Pridemore, W. A. (2011). Poverty matters: A reassessment of the inequality–homicide relationship in cross-national studies. *British Journal of Criminology, 51*(5), 739–772.

Prieur, A. (2018). Towards a criminology of structurally conditioned emotions: Combining Bourdieu's field theory and cultural criminology. *European Journal of Criminology, 15*(3), 344–363.

Putrill, M. (2011). Everybody's got a price: Why Orange County's practice of taking DNA samples from misdemeanor arrestees is an excessive fine. *The Journal of Criminal Law & Criminology, 101*(1), 309–334.

Pyrooz, D. C., Wolfe, S. E., & Spohn, C. (2011). Gang-related homicide charging decisions: The implementation of a specialized prosecution unit in Los Angeles. *Criminal Justice Policy Review, 22*(1), 3–26.

Raine, A. (2013). *The anatomy of violence: The biological roots of crime*. New York, NY: Random House.

Ramsay, S. (2001). Audit further exposes UK's worst serial killer. *Lancet, 357*(9250), 123–124.

Ramsey, C. B. (2010). Provoking change: Comparative insights on feminist homicide law reform. *Journal of Criminal Law and Criminology, 100*(1), 33–108.

Ramsland, K. (2007). When women kill together. *The Forensic Examiner, 16*(1), 64–66.

Rasmusen, E., Raghav, M., & Ramseyer, M. (2008). Convictions versus conviction rates: The prosecutor's choice. *American Law and Economics Review, 11*(1), 47–78.

Reid, J. A., & Sullivan, C. J. (2012). Unraveling victim–offender overlap: Exploring profiles and constellations of risk. *Victims & Offenders, 7*(3), 327–360. doi:10.1080/15564886.2012.685216

Reid, S. (2017). Developmental pathways to serial homicide: A critical review of the biological literature. *Aggression and Violent Behavior, 35*, 52–61.

Ressler, R. K., Burgess, A. W., & Douglas, J. E. (1988). *Sexual homicide: Patterns and motives*. Lexington, MA: Lexington Books.

Retief, F. P., & Cilliers, L. (2004). Poisons, poisoning, and poisoners in ancient Rome. *Medicina Antiqua*. Retrieved from http://www.ucl.ac.uk/~ucgajpd/medicina%20antiqua/sa_poisons.html

Reynolds, V., & Carlson, M. S. (2018). Atlanta Area DA: We Need to Do Something about Gangs. *Prosecutor, Journal of the National District Attorneys Association, 51*(1), 10–12.

Rhee, S. H., & Waldman, I. D. (2002). Genetic and environmental influences on antisocial behavior: A meta-analysis of twin and adoption studies. *Psychological Bulletin, 128*(3), 490–529.

Rhee, S. H., & Waldman, I. D. (2011). Genetic and environmental influences on aggression. In P. R. Shaver & M. Mikulincer (Eds.), *Human aggression and violence: Causes, manifestations, and consequences* (pp. 143–163). Washington, DC: American Psychological Association. doi:10.1037/12346-008

Richinick, M. (2014, June 4). *Nearly 30 people have been killed at school since Newtown*. Retrieved from http://www.msnbc.com/morning-joe/nearly-30-more-students-killed-newtown

Riedel, M., & Regoeczi, W. C. (2004). Missing data in homicide research. *Homicide Studies, 8*(3), 163–192.

Riedel, M., & Welsh, W. (2011). *Criminal violence: Patterns, causes, and prevention* (3rd ed.). New York, NY: Oxford University Press.

Roane, K. R. (2005, April). The CSI effect. *U.S. News & World Report, 138*(15), 48–54.

Roberts, A. (2007). Predictors of homicide clearance by arrest: An event history analysis of NIBRS incidents. *Homicide Studies, 11*(2), 82–93.

Roberts, A. (2011). Hispanic victims and homicide clearance by arrest. *Homicide Studies, 15*(1), 48–73.

Roberts, A. (2015). Adjusting rates of homicide clearance by arrest for investigation difficulty: Modeling incident- and jurisdiction-level obstacles. *Homicide Studies, 19*(3), 273–300.

Roberts, J. (2013). Effective plea bargaining counsel. *The Yale Law Journal, 122*(8), 2650–2673.

Roberts, L. D., & Indermaur, D. W. (2008). The "homogamy" of road rage revisited. *Violence & Victims, 23*(6), 758–772.

Rodgers, G. (2014, November 8). Teen found not guilty by reason of insanity. *The Des Moines Register*. Retrieved from http://www.desmoinesregister.com/story/news/crime-and-courts/2014/11/07/cody-metzker-madsen-first-degree-murder-not-guilty-insanity/18645809/

Rose, M., Nadler, J., & Clark, J. (2006). Appropriately upset? Emotion norms and perception of crime victims. *Criminal Law Review, 30*(2), 203–219.

Ruderman, W. (2012, June 28). Crime report manipulation is common among New York police, study finds. *New York Times*. Retrieved from http://www.nytimes.com/2012/06/29/nyregion/new-york-police-department-manipulates-crime- reports-study-finds.html?_r=1

Rugala, E. A., & Isaacs, A. R. (Eds.). (2002). *Workplace violence: Issues in response*. Quantico, VA: Federal Bureau of Investigation. Retrieved from https://www.fbi.gov/stats-services/publications/workplace-violence

Rydberg, J., & Pizarro, J. M. (2014). Victim lifestyle as a correlate of homicide clearance. *Homicide Studies, 18*(4), 342–362.

Sachmann, M., & Harris Johnson, C. M. (2014). The relevance of long-term antecedents in assessing the risk of familicide-suicide following separation. *Child Abuse Review, 23*(2), 130–141.

Sampson, R. J., & Groves, W. B. (1989). Community structure and crime: Testing social disorganization theory. *American Journal of Sociology, 94*(4), 774–802.

Sampson, R. J., & Laub, J. H. (1993). *Crime in the making: Pathways and turning points through life*. Cambridge, MA: Harvard University Press.

Sampson, R. J., & Raudenbush, S. W. (1999). Systematic social observation of public spaces: A new look at disorder in urban neighborhoods. *American Journal of Sociology, 105*(3), 603–651.

Sampson, R. J., Wilson, W. J., & Katz, H. (2018). Reassessing "toward a theory of race, crime, and urban inequality": Enduring and new challenges in 21st century America. *Du Bois Review: Social Science Research on Race, 15*(1), 13.

Schildkraut, J., & Hernandez, T. C. (2014). Laws that bit the bullet: A review of legislative responses to school shootings. *American Journal of Criminal Justice, 39*(2), 358–374.

Schroeder, D. (2007). DNA and homicide clearance: What's really going on? *Journal of the Institute of Justice and International Studies, 7*, 279–298.

Schwartz, J. (2010). Murder in a comparative context. In C. J. Ferguson (Ed.), *Violent crime: Clinical and social implications* (pp. 276–299). Thousand Oaks, CA: Sage.

Scott, H., & Fleming, K. (2014). The female family annihilator: An exploratory study. *Homicide Studies, 18*, 59–82.

Scovell, D. (2010, February). Crime scenes: To preserve and protect. *Police, 34*(2). Retrieved from http://www.policemag.com/channel/patrol/articles/2010/02/to-preserve-and-protect.aspx

Serran, G., & Firestone, P. (2004). Intimate partner homicide: A review of the male proprietariness and the self-defense theories. *Aggression and Violent Behavior, 9*(1), 1–15.

Shaw, C., & McKay, H. (1942). *Juvenile delinquency in urban areas*. Chicago, IL: University of Chicago Press.

Shelley, M. (n.d.). *What's a cult?* Retrieved from http://www.christianitytoday.com/iyf/advice/faithqa/what-is-cult.html

Siegel, R. (Host). (2017, November 28). *All things considered: Libyan involved in Benghazi attack convicted of terrorism charges, but acquitted of murder* [Audio Podcast]. Retrieved from https://www.npr.org/2017/11/28/567065558/libyan-involved-in-benghazi-attack-convicted-of-terrorism-charges-but-acquitted

Sillito, C. L., & Salari, S. (2011). Child outcomes and risk factors in U.S. homicide-suicide cases 1999–2004. *Journal of Family Violence, 26*(4), 285–297.

Simmons, C. A., Duckworth, M., & Tyler, E. (2014). Getting by after a loved one's death by homicide: The relationship between case status, trauma symptoms, life satisfaction, and coping. *Violence and Victims, 29*(3), 506–522.

Simons, E. (2006). Faith, fanaticism, and fear: Aum Shinrikyo—The birth and death of a terrorist organization. *Forensic Examiner*, *15*(1), 37–45.

Singer, J., Miller, M. K., & Adya, M. (2007). The impact of DNA and other technology on the criminal justice system: Improvements and complications. *Albany Law Journal of Science & Technology*, *17*, 87–125.

Skeem, J. L., Polaschek, D. L. L., Patrick, C. J., & Lilienfeld, S. O. (2011). Psychopathic personality: Bridging the gap between scientific evidence and public policy. *Psychological Science in the Public Interest*, *12*(3), 95–162.

Smart, R., Asbridge, M., Mann, R., & Adlaf, E. (2003). Psychiatric distress among road rage victims and perpetrators. *The Canadian Journal of Psychiatry*, *48*, 681–688. Retrieved from https://ww1.cpa-apc.org/Publications/Archives/CJP/2003/november/smart.asp

Smith, D. J., & Ecob, R. (2007). An investigation into causal links between victimization and offending in adolescents. *The British Journal of Sociology*, *58*(4), 633–659. doi:10.1111/j.1468-4446.2007.00169.x

Smith, S. G., Fowler, K. A., & Niolon, P. H. (2014). Intimate partner homicide and corollary victims in 16 states: National violent death reporting system, 2003–2009. *The American Journal of Public Health*, *104*(3), 461–466.

Smith, S. M., Patry, M. W., & Stinson, V. (2007). The CSI effect: Reflections from police and forensic investigators. *The Canadian Journal of Police & Security Services*, *5*(3), 125–133.

Soothill, K., & Wilson, D. (2007). Theorizing the puzzle that is Harold Shipman. *The Journal of Forensic Psychiatry and Psychology*, *16*(4), 685–698.

Spinelli, M. G. (2005). Infanticide: Contrasting views. *Archives of Women's Mental Health*, *8*(1), 15–24.

Stamatel, J. P. (2009). Correlates of national-level homicide variation in post-Communist East-Central Europe. *Social Forces*, *87*(3), 1423–1448.

Stauffer, A. R., Smith, M. D., Cochran, J. K., Fogel, S. J., & Bjerregaard, B. (2006). The interaction between victim race and gender on sentencing outcomes in capital murder trials. *Homicide Studies*, *10*(2), 98–117.

Stewart, E. A., & Simons, R. L. (2010). Race, code of the street, and violent delinquency: A multilevel investigation of neighborhood street culture and individual norms of violence. *Criminology*, *48*(2), 569–605. doi:10.1111/j.1745-9125.2010.00196.x

Stöckl, H., Devries, K., Rotstein, A., Abrahams, N., Campbell, J., Watts, C., & Moreno, C. G. (2013). The global prevalence of intimate partner homicide: A systematic review. *The Lancet*, *382*(9895), 859–865.

Stout, D. (2008, March 25). John E. List, 82, killer of 5 family members, dies. *The New York Times*. Retrieved from http://www.nytimes.com/2008/03/25/nyregion/25list1.html?_r=0

Stretesky, P., Schuck, A., & Hogan, M. (2004). Space matters: An analysis of poverty, poverty clustering, and violent crime. *JQ: Justice Quarterly*, *21*(4), 817–841.

Stroud, J., & Pritchard, C. (2001). Child homicide, psychiatric disorders and dangerousness: A review and empirical approach. *British Journal of Social Work*, *31*(2), 249–269.

Stuart, H. (2003). Violence and mental illness: An overview. *World Psychiatry*, *2*(20), 121–124.

Sutherland, E. (1947). *Principles of criminology*. Philadelphia, PA: J. P. Lippincott.

Szubin, A., Jensen, C. J., & Gregg, R. (2000). Interacting with "cults": A policing model. *FBI Law Enforcement Bulletin*, *69*(9), 16–24.

Taylor, R., & Jasinski, J. L. (2011). Femicide and the feminist perspective. *Homicide Studies*, *15*(4), 341–362.

Taylor, S., Lambeth, D., Green, G., Bone, R., & Cahillane, M. A. (2012). Cluster analysis examination of serial killer profiling categories: A bottom-up approach. *Journal of Investigative Psychology & Offender Profiling*, *9*(1), 30–51.

Terman, R. L. (2010). To specify or single out: Should we use the term "honor killing"? *Muslim World Journal of Human Rights*, *7*(1), 1–39.

Tiesman, H. M., Gurka, K. K., Konda, S., & Amandus, H. E. (2012). Workplace homicides among U.S. women: The role of intimate partner violence. *Annals of Epidemiology*, *22*(4), 277–284.

Toch, H. (1969). *Violent men: An inquiry into the psychology of violence*. Chicago, IL: Aldine.

Torry, Z. D., & Billick, S. B. (2010). Overlapping universe: Understanding legal insanity and psychosis. *Psychiatric Quarterly*, *81*(3), 253–262.

Toryanski, K. (2007). No ordinary party: Prosecutorial ethics and errors in death penalty cases. *Federal Lawyer*, *54*(1), 45–52.

Turunen, T., & Punamäki, R. (2014). Psychosocial support for trauma-affected students after school shootings in Finland. *Violence and Victims*, *29*(3), 476–491.

Twiss, R. (2007). A view from the bench: Keys to a successful direct. *The Army Lawyer*, *3*(2), 28–41.

United Nations Office on Drugs and Crime (UNODC). (2014). *Global study on homicide 2013*. Vienna, Austria: Author. Retrieved from https://www.unodc.org/documents/gsh/pdfs/2014_GLOBAL_HOMICIDE_BOOK_web.pdf

Ulmer, J. T., & Johnson, B. (2004). Sentencing in context: A multilevel analysis. *Criminology*, *42*(1), 137–177.

United Nations Office on Drugs and Crime. (2014, April 10). *Some 437,000 people murdered worldwide in 2012, according to new UNODC study*. Retrieved from https://www.unodc.org/documents/gsh/pdfs/GSH_Press_release_-_EN.pdf

United Nations Office on Drugs and Crime. (2018). *Global study on homicide 2018*. Vienna, Austria: Author. Retrieved from https://www.unodc.org/documents/gsh/ pdfs/2014_GLOBAL_HOMICIDE_BOOK_web.pdf

United States Department of Justice, Federal Bureau of Investigation. (2017). *Uniform crime reporting statistics, 2017*. Retrieved from https://ucr.fbi.gov/crime-in-the-u.s/2017/crime-in-the-u.s.-2017

United States Department of Justice. (2017, December 14). Office of Justice Programs. Bureau of Justice Statistics. *National Crime Victimization Survey, 2016*. Ann Arbor, MI: Inter-university Consortium for Political and Social Research [distributor]. Retrieved from https://doi.org/10.3886/ICPSR36828.v1

United States Department of Labor. (n.d.). *Workplace violence program*. Retrieved from https://www.dol.gov/oasam/hrc/policies/dol-workplace-violence-program.htm

United States Department of Labor, Bureau of Labor Statistics. (2018). *National census of fatal occupational injuries in 2017* [News release USDL-18-1978]. Retrieved from https://www.bls.gov/news.release/pdf/cfoi.pdf

United Nations National Library of Medicine. (n.d.). *Munchausen disorder by proxy*. Retrieved from https://www.nlm.nih.gov/medlineplus/ency/article/001555.htm

Van Patten, J. (2010). Suing the prosecutor. *South Dakota Law Review*, *55*(2), 214–252.

Vecchi, G. (2009). Principles and approaches to criminal investigation, part 1. *Forensic Examiner*, *18*(2), 8–13.

Verma, A. (2007). Anatomy of riots: A situational crime prevention approach. *Crime Prevention & Community Safety*, *9*(3), 201–221.

Viñas-Racionero, R., Schlesinger, L. B., Scalora, M. J., & Jarvis, J. P. (2017). Youthful familicidal offenders: Targeted victims, planned attacks. *Journal of Family Violence*, *32*(5), 535–542.

Vossekuil, B., Fein, R., Reddy, M., Borum, R., & Modzeleski, W. (2002). *The final report and findings of the Safe School Initiative: Implications for the prevention of school attacks in the United States*. Washington, DC: U.S. Department of Education and U.S. Secret Service.

Wadsworth, T., & Roberts, J. M. (2008). When missing data are not missing: A new approach to evaluating supplemental homicide report imputation strategies. *Criminology*, *46*(4), 841–870.

Walker, L. E. (1977). Battered women and learned helplessness. *Victimology*, *2*(3/4), 525–534.

Walker, L. E. (1979). *The battered woman*. New York, NY: Harper & Row.

Walsh, J. A., & Krienert, J. L. (2009). A decade of child-initiated family violence: Comparative analysis of child–parent violence and parricide examining offender, victim, and event characteristics in a national sample of reported incidents, 1995–2005. *The Journal of Interpersonal Violence*, *24*(9), 1450–1477.

Warf, B., & Waddell, C. (2002). Heinous spaces, perfidious places: The sinister landscapes of serial killers. *Social & Cultural Geography*, *3*(3), 323–345.

Washington Post Investigative Team (2019, January 7). Murder with impunity. *The Washington Post*. Retrieved from https://www.washingtonpost.com/graphics/2018/investigations/unsolved-homicide-database/?noredirect=on&utm_term=.a0baa894e0b2

Watkins, A. M., & Melde, C. (2018). Gangs, gender, and involvement in crime, victimization, and exposure to violence. *Journal of Criminal Justice*, *57*(C), 11–25.

Websdale, N. (1998). *Rural women battering and the justice system*. Thousand Oaks, CA: Sage.

Weiss, S. J. (2005). *Missouri v. Seibert*: Two-stepping towards the apocalypse. *Journal of Criminal Law & Criminology*, *95*(3), 945–984.

Weizmann-Henelius, G., Grönroos, L., Putkonen, H., Eronen, M., Lindberg, N., & Häkkänen-Nyholm, H. (2012). Gender-specific risk factors for intimate partner homicide: A nationwide register-based study. *Journal of Interpersonal Violence*, *27*(8), 1519–1539.

Wellford, C., & Cronin, J. (2000, April). Clearing up homicide clearance rates. *National Institute of Justice Journal*, 2–7. Retrieved from http://www.ncjrs.gov/App/Publications/abstract.aspx? ID=181728

Wemmers, J. (2009). Where do they belong? Giving victims a place in the criminal justice process. *Criminal Law Forum, 20*(4), 395–416.

Wheatcroft, J. M., & Ellison, L. E. (2012). Evidence in court: Witness preparation and cross examination style effects on adult witness accuracy. *Behavioral Sciences & the Law, 30*(6), 821–840.

White, J. H., Lester, D., Gentile, M., & Rosenbleeth, J. (2011). The utilization of forensic science and criminal profiling for capturing serial killers. *Forensic Science International, 209*(1), 160–165.

Whitman, T. A., & Akutagawa, D. (2004). Riddles in serial murder: A synthesis. *Aggression & Violent Behavior, 9*(6), 693–703.

Wickens, C. M., Mann, R. E., Stoduto, G., Ialomiteanu, A., & Smart, R. G. (2011). Age group differences in self-reported aggressive driving perpetration and victimization. *Transportation Research Part F: Psychology and Behaviour, 14*, 400–412.

Widyanto, M. R., Soedarsono, N., Katayama, N., & Nakao, M. (2010). Various defuzzification methods on DNA similarity matching using fuzzy inference system. *Journal of Advanced Computational Intelligence and Intelligent Informatics, 14*(3), 247–255.

Willmott, D., Boduszek, D., & Robinson, R., (2018). A psychodynamic-behaviorist investigation of Russian sexual serial killer Andrei Chikatilo. *The Journal of Forensic Psychiatry and Psychology.* doi: 10.1080/14789949.2017.1416658

Wilson, J. S., & Websdale, N. (2006). Domestic violence fatality review teams: An interprofessional model to reduce deaths. *Journal of Interprofessional Care, 20*(5), 535–544.

Wilson, M., Daly, M., & Daniele, A. (1995). Familicide: The killing of spouse and children. *Aggressive Behavior, 21*(4), 275–291.

Wolfgang, M. E. (1958). *Patterns in criminal homicide.* Philadelphia: University of Pennsylvania Press.

Wolfgang, M. E., & Ferracuti, F. (1967). *The subculture of violence: Towards an integrated theory in criminology.* London, UK: Tavistock.

Wombacher, K., Herovic, E., Sellnow, T., & Seeger, M.W. (2018). The complexities of place in crisis renewal discourse: A case study of the Sandy Hook Elementary School shooting. *Journal of Contingencies and Crisis Management, 26*(1), 164–172.

Yardley, E., & Wilson, D. (2016). In Search of the "Angels of Death": Conceptualising the Contemporary Nurse Healthcare Serial Killer. *Journal of Investigative Psychology and Offender Profiling,* (1), 39–55.

Young, J. (2003). Merton with energy, Katz with structure: The sociology of vindictiveness and the criminology of transgression. *Theoretical Criminology, 7*(3), 389–414.

Zavala, E., & Spohn, R. (2013). The role of vicarious and anticipated strain on the overlap of violent perpetration and victimization: A test of general strain theory. *American Journal of Criminal Justice, 38*(1), 119–140. doi:10.1007/s12103-012-9163-5

Zehr, H. (2001). *Transcending: Reflections of crime victims.* Intercourse, PA: Good Books.

Zehr, H., & Mika, H. (1998). Fundamental concepts of restorative justice. *Contemporary Justice Review, 1*(1), 47.

Zeoli, A. M., & Webster, D. W. (2010). Effects of domestic violence policies, alcohol taxes and police staffing levels on intimate partner homicide in large US cities. *Injury Prevention, 16*(2), 90–95.

INDEX

Political influences. *See* Societal influences;
    Sociopolitical crime
Polk, Kenneth, 70, 72, 75
Pope, P. B., 236
Porco, Christopher, 110–111
Positivism
    biological factors, 57–60
    overview, 56
    psychological factors, 60–61
Post-traumatic stress disorder (PTSD), 101, 255
Pound, Ezra, 155
Powell, Susan Cox, 105 (box)
Power/control killers, 195
Prado, Lorenzo, 117
Premeditation, 234
Presumptive tests, 220
Prevalence of Mental Illness (U.S. CRS), 123
Prevention and reduction, crime
    community, role of, 263, 265–266
    conflict resolution training, 71
    legislation, role of, 259–261
    public health perspective, 257–259, 259 (figure)
    research on, 48, 262–263
    terrorism and, 186
The Price of Honor (film), 112 (box)
Pridemore, W. A., 66, 77
Prison gangs, 156, 159
"Promoting Effective Homicide Investigations"
    (Carter), 206
Property crime, 19, 42
Prosecutorial investigation standards, 236
Prosecutors, role of, 219, 221, 230, 235,
    236–237
Psychological theories, 60–61
Psychopathy, 60–61, 196
Psychopathy checklist (PCL-R), 61
Public defender, 239
Public health perspective of violence and homicide,
    257–259, 259 (figure), 266 (figure)
Public health services, 257–259, 259 (figure)
Public policy. *See* Policy implications
Pulse nightclub shooting, 185, 185 (box)
Punishment as retribution, 260–261
Pyrooz, D. C., 237

Qualitative comparison analysis, 25
Qualitative research methods, 24–25
Quinet, K., 63 (box)

Race and ethnicity
    of offenders, 34 (table), 35
    serial killings and, 191
    social disorganization theory and, 65
    of victims, 34 (table), 35

Racketeering Influenced and Corrupt Organizations
    (RICO) Act, 158
Rader, Dennis, 191 (box), 202
Rage, 124
Rai, T. S., 90
Raine, Adrian, 58, 260 (box)
Ramos, Jarrod, 145 (box)
Rampage (Newman), 121–122
Rampage killings. *See* Mass murders
Ramsey, C. B., 95
Ramsey, JonBenét, 216 (box)
Rape
    forcible, 16 (table)
    legacy, 16 (table)
    revised definition of, 16 (table)
Rational choice theory, 56
Raudenbush, S. W., 67
Red flag laws, 134, 267 (box)
Red-collar crime, 111
Regoeczi, W. C., 3, 25, 76
Reichelmann, A., 102, 103, 110
Religious institutions, 152
Research methods, 24–25, 51
Responding to Domestic Violence (Buzawa, Buzawa, &
    Stark), 86
Ressler, R. K., 79
Restorative justice, 255–256, 256 (box)
Retribution and punishment, 260–261
Revolutionary Armed Task Force, 181
Revolutionary suicide, 166
Richinick, Michele, 120
RICO Act, 158
Ridgway, Gary Leon, 194 (box), 196
Riedel, M., 8
Right-wing terrorist groups, 181
Riots, 76
Risk assessment, 92, 93 (exhibit), 147–149,
    148 (exhibit)
Road rage, 74–75
Robbery, 17 (table)
Roberts, A., 35
Roberts, J. M., 19, 244
Roberts, L. D., 75
Rocque, Michael, 138
Rohrer, Glenn, 247 (box)
Roof, Dylann, 185 (box)
Rosenfeld, R., 66
Rousseau, Jean-Jacques, 155
Route 91 Harvest Music Festival shootings,
    43, 138
Routine activities theory, 33, 66–67, 74,
    100, 201
Rowe, Raymond, 225 (box)
Rubin, P. H., 239